WOMEN'S ISSUES

CRIMES AGAINST WOMEN

WOMEN'S ISSUES

Additional books in this series can be found on Nova's website under the Series tab.

Additional E-books in this series can be found on Nova's website under the E-books tab.

WOMEN'S ISSUES

CRIMES AGAINST WOMEN

DAVID WINGEATE PIKE
EDITOR

A Project of the
American Graduate School of International Relations and Diplomacy

AGS American Graduate School in Paris

Nova Science Publishers, Inc.
New York

For permission to use material from this book please contact us:
Telephone 631-231-7269; Fax 631-231-8175
Web Site: http://www.novapublishers.com

Additional color graphics may be available in the e-book version of this book.

LIBRARY OF CONGRESS CATALOGING-IN-PUBLICATION DATA
Servidio, Eileen.
Crimes against women / Eileen Servidio and David Wingeate Pike.
p. cm.
Includes bibliographical references and index. ISBN 978-1-61470-813-1 (softcover)
1. Women--Crimes against. I. Pike, David Wingeate. II. Title.
HV6250.4.W65S486 2010
362.88082--dc22
2010012153

Published by Nova Science Publishers, Inc. † New York

Dedication

To all women who suffer from the cruelty of mankind.

Today, far too many women are subjected to violence and made to feel shame. The real shame belongs to a world that often blames women for the crimes committed against them, and allows such widespread violence to continue.

Thoraya Ahmed Obaid, Executive Director, UNFPA, 2006

Enlighten the people, generally, and tyranny and oppressions of body and mind will vanish like spirits at the dawn of day.

Thomas Jefferson

CONTENTS

PREFACE

The idea for this collective work originated in early 2006, at the time that the American Graduate School of International Relations and Diplomacy (AGSIRD) founded its Research Center. It was decided to select a theme from within feminism, using the term feminism in its widest context.

Look around the world and nine-tenths of all the world's suffering is borne by women. A large part of the male half of the world is perfectly happy to see it remain so, and to keep in place the laws that leave half the world barely inside the human race, so that women find themselves not merely abused but at the mercy of customs and laws in whose formation they had no hand, and over which they have no influence.

The project at hand, once announced, quickly caught on. It required an absolute minimum of advertising. A single announcement was enough to attract the forty contributors who responded. Among the dozen whom we lost by the wayside was Fadela Amara, founder of the French movement Ni Putes ni Soumises; her reason for withdrawing was her appointment by President Nicholas Sarkozy in 2007 to the Ministry of Urban Affairs. Ideally, in our presentation of the essays, we would have liked to strike a perfect geographical balance, with every continent equally represented, and every country with the worst abuses included. We are conscious of the lacunae to be found here. We have in no sense covered the world, and we know it. But no work of this length could claim to be comprehensive, and a project such as this has to compromise or it never sees the light of day.

In my sixth Circular Letter to Contributors, I urged them not only to uncover crimes and evoke pity for the victims but to do whatever possible to stir the human conscience (or more precisely, the male conscience) to stand up against the abuses that mock our claims to the irresistible march of progress. This project will have achieved its real purpose only when a future work dedicated to the suffering of women is written, unlike this one, by a large majority of men.

It has not been possible to publish all the essays that we received, reviewed and edited. We nevertheless hope to produce a second volume of *Crimes against Women* in which these essays can find their place.

The book owes much to the assistance of five AGSIRD students who joined the project in the closing year: Anthoula Parianos, who helped in the often nerve-wracking work of correspondence; Irina Massovets, who helped Anthoula in trimming the Abstracts and the CVs, who brought order to the Endnotes, and who helped in researching the Introduction; Nicolette Bundy, who gave general assistance; and to Tammy Lee Fortier and Yasmeen R. Hussain, who gave the work a final tweaking. To all assistants I offer my thanks, but especially to Anthoula Parianos.

David Wingeate Pike
Director of Research, AGSIRD

Paris, 9 July 2009

FOREWORD

Taslima Nasrin

Winner of the 2004 UNESCO-Madanjeet Singh Prize
for the Promotion of Tolerance and Non-Violence

Women—whether they are rich or poor, beautiful or ugly, black or brown or white or yellow, married or unmarried, illiterate or literate—all suffer oppression because of religion, tradition, culture and customs devised by men.

I come from a country where, for a married couple, the worst thing is to give birth to a female baby. It is not uncommon for such a wife to be divorced, or to spend the rest of her life in disgrace.

In my country it its the destiny of a woman to be ruled by her father in childhood, by her husband while in youth and middle-age, and by her son when she is old.

Far too many women are the victims of slavery, human trafficking, and all kinds of discrimination. Men throw acid on their bodies, burn their faces, smash their noses, gouge their eyes, and walk away happy. Women are beaten, flogged, stoned to death. If they are raped, they are accused of having allowed the rape, and the rapists are set free.

Violence against women is not considered a crime in my country. Let me give you the example of fifteen-year-old Yasmin. Employed as a maid, she was raped by her master. She fled from the master's home and was observed by the police as she walked toward her parents' house. The police told her it was not safe for a girl to be walking on the road at night. They offered her a ride home in their van, and then what happened? Six policemen raped her, killed her, and threw her body into the bushes. When news of Yasmin's murder broke, villagers demonstrated against the police. The police shot at them, killing seven. The government then issued a statement that Yasmin was a girl of bad character, a prostitute, and that the police had every right to treat her as they did. Such a tragic event is not a rarity in Bangladesh, and I know that it happens in other countries as well.

Crimes Against Women, in my opinion, is one of the most important books on the question of the oppression of women. Its essays, written by activists and academics, cover all forms of violence occurring worldwide. It is surprising that many countries that proudly call themselves democracies have still not ratified several clauses of the United Nations "Convention on the Elimination of All Forms of Discrimination Against Women." And many countries that have ratified the clauses of the Convention do not implement it and remain reluctant to take action against the perpetrators of crime against women.

So long as women are considered inferior human beings, crimes against women will not be considered as crimes against humanity. The problem cannot be solved simply by women's achieving economic freedom and education. The problem can be solved only by exposing, and then changing, cultural traditions, customs and religious practices that harm humanity by debasing women.

When men are tortured, it is considered a crime. When women are tortured, it is dismissed as a custom, a part of the tradition. Millions of people literally believe in the propriety of throwing live women onto their husband's funeral pyre, or mutilating female genitals, since it is accepted as tradition and has formed part of the culture. This sick mentality of the past must end. We now live in the 21st century. Men as well as women that believe that women's rights are human rights must continue to fight without compromise against all such inequalities and injustices.

There are laws against crimes committed against women, but they must be implemented. Children must be taught in school about equality between men and women, which is difficult for children to understand when they see adults around them treating women as slaves, sexual objects, and child-bearing machines. It will be difficult to achieve justice without a true revolution of ideas.

I congratulate David Pike for editing a book that truly raises our consciousness concerning the many problems that exist and the need to resolve these problems as quickly as possible.

Taslima Nasrin
Winner of the 2004 Unesco Prize

INTRODUCTION: CRIME WITHOUT PUNISHMENT

David Wingeate Pike

> 'There is no blanket approach to fighting violence against women. What works in one country may not lead to desired results in another. Each nation must devise its own strategy. But there is one universal truth, applicable to all countries, cultures and communities: violence against women is never acceptable, never excusable, never tolerable....
>
> We must unite. Violence against women cannot be tolerated, in any form, in any context, in any circumstance, by any political leader or by any government.
>
> The time to change is now. Only by standing together and speaking out can we make a difference.'[1]
>
> UN Secretary-General Ban Ki-moon, 2009

Crimes committed by men, under laws written by men to protect men, leading at times to trials, trials conducted by men, with juries composed of men, responding to male judges who hand down verdicts that favour men. Everywhere the oppressor's wrong, the law's delay, the insolence of office, ...

Can any particular factor be singled out as most responsible for the wrongs inflicted on women? Ingrid Betancourt, the Franco-Colombian woman held captive for six years by Colombia's insurgent movement FARC, would never consider herself the worst abused woman of our time, but in an interview on French television after her liberation in July 2008 she summed up what might be called the basic problem. After describing the abysmal conditions of living as a prisoner of the FARC, being chained perennially to a post, exposed to the insects, deprived of vegetables and fruit, refused all medical treatment, she summed it all up: 'The worst was the wickedness of men' [*Le pire, c'était la méchancheté des hommes.*][2]

'*La méchanceté des hommes.*' Can it be that one gender is preternaturally more disposed to cruelty than the other? If so, is it a psychological condition that can be cured?

---

[1] See UN Secretary-General's campaign on End Violence against Women: http://endviolence.un.org/ and UN Secretary-General Ban Ki-moon's remarks on International Women's Day in New York, 5 March 2009: http://www.un.org/News/Press/docs/2009/sgsm12127.doc.htm.

[2] Ingrid Betancourt, interviewed on French television (TF1) by Claire Chazal, 4 July 2008.

The legal battle in defence of women was first joined in 18th century England, before male feminists such as Goethe or George Bernard Shaw threw their hat into the ring. In London in the 1750s, three fashionable hostesses took stock of the male-chauvinist society in which they lived and saw in it a repressive attitude that condemned even the brightest women to positions of inferiority. The circle that they formed, and which took its name from the blue worsted stockings that they favoured, was far from focused, for they had little idea where they were headed. What gave the movement its impetus was the French Revolution, on which its most famous member, Mary Wollstonecraft, quickly pounced, launching a pamphlet in 1790 entitled *A Vindication of the Rights of Men,* and another in 1792 under the title *A Vindication of the Rights of Woman*, which made her famous overnight.

The next century came and went with no perceptible change anywhere in the status of women. Even the proclamation of 8 March as Women's Day was uneven in its adoption, though the date commemorated two early events in the women's struggle: the strike in 1857 by textile workers in New York which was brutally suppressed by the police, and the fire in 1909, again in New York, when 140 women, most of them young, were burnt to death in a factory. It was not until 1975, when the United Nations proclaimed it so, that 8 March became International Women's Day. The UN followed up on 1979 with a Convention on the Elimination of all Forms of Discrimination against Women (CEDAW). The treaty was duly signed in 1980 by US President Jimmy Carter, but it has languished in the US Senate ever since. A series of World Conferences on Women organized by the UN was notable in 1995 for the attendance in Beijing of 40,000 women.[3] The culmination of international efforts to bring women's rights to the foreground of collective action came on 17 December 1999, when the UN General Assembly, in its resolution 54/134, designated 25 November as International Day for the Elimination of Violence against Women. The date chosen commemorates the brutal assassination in 1960 of the three Mirabal sisters, political activists in the Dominican Republic, on orders of Dominican dictator Rafael Trujillo (1930–1961).[4] The date coincides with the opening of an annual campaign, launched in 1991 and known as Sixteen Days of Activism against Gender Violence, whose closing day (10 December) marks the day already designated in 1950 as International Human Rights Day.

Another milestone came with the creation in 1969 of the UN Population Fund (originally known as the UN Fund for Population Activities, or UNFPA), an organization that does for women what Unicef does for children. It advocates for their health and protection. Its present director Thoraya Obaid rails against the widespread impunity of crimes 'that not only encourages further abuses and suffering but also sends the signal that male violence against women is acceptable or normal.'[5] In November 2006 the UN Population Fund (UNPF) issued a report documenting horrific gender violence in countries around the planet, sometimes perpetrated under the protective rubric of 'traditional cultural practices' or religious customs.

[3] The rights of women in China received an unexpected exposure in the middle of the 2008 Olympiad held in Beijing. The Chinese government had announced that the Chinese people had the right to demonstrate, provided only that they apply to the authorities for permission. Two Chinese women in their late 70s wanted to protest the inadequate compensation they felt they had received when the government, years earlier, had seized their homes for urban development. When they responded to the invitation, they were promptly arrested and sentenced to 're-education through labour.'

[4] 'International Day for the Elimination of Violence against Women,' the United Nations: http://www.un.org/depts/dhl/violence/index.html The Mirabal sisters, born into an upper-class family who had lost most of their fortune, had formed an opposition to the Trujillo regime known as the Movement of the Fourteenth of June.

[5] 'Violence against women,' unsigned editorial, *The Boston Globe*, 8 December 2006.

The problems are widespread, multifaceted and deeply rooted, and the list provided by the UNPF is not inclusive of all the forms of crimes committed:

- the systematic disappearance and murder of women;
- rape as a routine weapon of war;
- traumatic fistula: (a debilitating side effect of violent rape or unsafe childbirth);
- mutilation of women, including breast-ironing, a form of mutilation performed in parts of Africa by mothers on their own daughters in a desperate attempt to make them unattractive to violent, predatory men;
- forced marriage or bride-kidnapping: 80 millions girls are forcibly married before their 18th birthday, many before they are 12, despite the fact that pregnancy is the leading cause of teenage death; bride-kidnapping, described as a 'tradition' in Kyrgyzstan and other central Asian countries, amounts to little more than rape and enslavement.[6]

In January 2008, the Office of the United Nations High Commissioner for Refugees (UNHCR) published a *Handbook on the Protection of Women and Girls* which pointed up another danger facing women in war-torn areas. 'Upon return and reintegration, women and girls are frequently excluded from the peace processes… [and] often suffer continued violence and discrimination in reconstruction and rehabilitation activities. In the absence of male relatives, especially following conflict, women and girls may assume non-traditional roles and face discrimination and prejudice as a result.'

In February of that year 2008, UN Secretary-General Ban Ki-Moon launched his campaign "UNite to End Violence against Women," calling for immediate change. Violence against women, he made clear, poses a serious threat to the achievement of internationally agreed development goals, including the Millennium Development Goals. Stretching from 2008 to 2015, the campaign calls on all governments, civil society, women's organizations, young people, the private sector, the media and the entire UN system to join forces in addressing the global pandemic of violence against women and girls.[7] In furtherance of this, on 14 November of the same year, Ban designated the South African-born actress Charlize Theron as a UN Messenger of Peace, with a focus on ending violence against women. Theron, the tenth celebrity to be named to the position,[8] was already a women's rights activist and animal rights activist. In 2006, in partnership with the Entertainment Industry Foundation, she had founded the Charlize Theron Africa Outreach Project to work to improve the life of South Africa's impoverished, especially those suffering from HIV/AIDS. Theron also filmed a series of public service announcements in support of the Cape Town Rape Crisis Centre, urging no tolerance for rape or domestic violence.

Amid so many crimes, so many fields of crime, to give pride of place (or shame of place) to any particular field is open to argument, but Women Missing and the Slave Trade are logical places to start.

---

[6] Ibid.

[7] See UN Secretary-General's campaign on End Violence against Women: http://endviolence.un.org/.

[8] See United Nations Messengers of Peace: http://www.un.org/sg/mop/.

1. Women Missing

The number of women around the world who are demographically "missing" was recently estimated by the United Nations at between 113 million and 200 million. Every year, said its report, from 1.5 million to 3 million women and girls lose their lives as a result of gender-based violence or neglect. Ayaan Hirsi Ali, a Somali-born Dutch legislator who was living in Amsterdam under 24-hour protection because of death threats against her by Islamic radicals,[9] was undismayed by the danger she faced and called for a tribunal such as the Court of Justice in The Hague to investigate the disappearance of these 100-200 million women. 'The victims scream their suffering,' she wrote. 'It is not so much that the world does not hear them; it is that fellow human beings choose not to pay attention.' Focusing on a particular group whom she considers largely responsible for women's suffering, she added: 'Islamists are engaged in reviving and spreading a brutal and retrograde body of laws. Wherever the Islamists implement Shariah, or Islamic law, women are hounded from the public arena, denied education and forced into a life of domestic slavery. Cultural and moral relativists sap our sense of moral outrage by claiming that human rights are a Western invention.'[10]

Shariah law, nevertheless, is not monolithic. Much of Muslim law was codified many centuries after the prophet died, by male jurists who came up with laws that met the needs of their time, resulting in a variety of Sunni and Shiite schools of thought, but leaving no such thing as a consensus that could provide a single version of Shariah.[11]

2. The Slave Trade, Renamed Human Trafficking

One of the distinctions of Islam is that it shares with Christianity the ignominy of running the African slave trade, albeit thriving long before the arrival of any non-African. While the Christian churches have for long called slavery the greatest single blight on Western

[9] Ayaan Hirsi Ali, a former member of the Dutch Parliament, wrote the screenplay of the film Submission, with scenes of abused women with Koranic texts written on their flesh. In 2004, Hirsi Ali collaborated with Theo van Gogh on the film Submission, and subsequently published her book Infidel (New York: Free Press, 2007). In autumn of that year, Van Gogh was murdered in Amsterdam by Mohamed Bouyeri (Dutch-born of Moroccan parents) who slit his throat as he would an animal, leaving a five-page death threat against Hirsi Ali pinned to his body with a knife.

[10] Ayaan Hirsi Ali, 'Women go "missing" by the millions,' 31 March 2006; Stephen Castle, 'Target of threats, writer asks EU to pay for security,' *International Herald Tribune* (Paris), 15 February 2008.

[11] For this reason, Muslims are not unanimous on the question of enforcing the wearing of the headscarf. Australia's senior Muslim cleric, Sheikh Taj el-Din al-Hilali, described women who do not wear head scarves as 'uncovered meat' who invite rape ('Muslim cleric's remarks denounced by [Australian Prime Minister John] Howard'), Associated Press, *International Herald Tribune*, 27 April 2006). Aqsa Pervez was a 16-year-old Pakistani-Canadian in Ontario who removed her headscarf, at which point her father strangled her and then called the police to confess. Those who sympathized with the father called her death an 'honour killing,' suggesting that every Muslim father was entitled to murder his daughter for taking off a headscarf. Others insisted that it was just a case of domestic violence, as though religion and culture had nothing to do with the murder. A case in Berlin in January 2008 received wider coverage. A 23-year-old Turkish girl named Hatun Sürücü became the sixth Muslim woman in as many months to be murdered by a relative in that city for being 'too Western' (Mona Eltahawy, 'Caught in the clash of civilizations' *International Herald Tribune*, 19 January 2008). Sürücü, according to another source, was 'living like a German,' a crime, in her family's opinion, that only her death could expiate. The killing was entrusted to her youngest brother, who shot her several times, point blank, at a Berlin bus stop. Only the killer was charged, and because he was underage, he received a reduced sentence. The family left the courtroom in high spirits, and the father rewarded the convicted boy with a watch ('German justice failures,' *Spiegel Online*, 29 March 2007).

civilisation, Islam has been less outright in its self-denunciations. 'The Koran,' writes Alice Whealey, an eminent American scholar of the era, 'most certainly condones treating women and slaves (of any race) as social and political inferiors, and it positively enjoins treating non-Muslims as enemies to be fought militarily and either killed (as polytheists) or treated as inferiors (non-Muslim monotheists); cf. Koran 9:29).'[12] More commonly, non-Muslims are dismissed as non-believers (in Arabic, *takfir*).

What has certainly not disappeared from the world is enslavement. The slave trade was abolished in the British Empire by the British Parliament's Slave Trade Act of 1807, and in the United States in 1865 by the 13th amendment to the Constitution. In recent times, international laws have been introduced to put an end to slavery's modern forms. Among these laws is the UN Protocol Against Trafficking in Persons, making trafficking an international crime. The protocol was ratified in 2003 and has been signed by 117 countries, but that leaves two-fifths of the UN membership uncommitted. What is missing is political will, of the kind that two centuries ago inspired men like Granville Sharp and William Wilberforce to devote their whole lives to the cause of anti-slavery.

In March 2007, Antonio Maria Costa, executive director of the UN Office on Drugs and Crime, described contemporary slavery as 'a booming international trade that involves several million people a year being trafficked in bondage,' and launched a global initiative to end the traffic. The International Labour Organization estimated in the same month that there are 12.3 million people across the globe in forced work, unpaid and under threat of violence. The U.S. government reported in 2008 that every year between 600,000 and 800,000 people are being shipped like commodities across international borders to serve as slave labour. Of these, 80 per cent are female and 50 percent are children, with the majority of them forced into the commercial sex trade. Traffickers lure women with promises of jobs as nannies or restaurant workers in countries supposedly offering them a better life. Often the women, in a desperate attempt to escape extreme poverty or dangerous living conditions, pay significant sums of money for their passage.

In Europe the most common destination of the traffic, according to a UN report, is Germany, Italy, Belgium and Greece. In the United States, the best estimates indicate that 40,000 to 50,000 people are held in slavery at any given time, with about 17,000 people brought into the country every year and forced to work for nothing. New York being one of the top cities for trafficking, the city's chapter of the National Organization of Women (NOW), under its president Sonia Ossorio, opened an aggressive campaign called 'Ending the Business of Trafficking.' Its purpose was to introduce a state law that would recognize trafficking as a crime, and by June 2007 they had succeeded.[13]

---

[12] Alice Whealey, 'Religion: Islamic colonization and Christian missionaries,' World Association of International Scholars (WAIS), Stanford, 20 June 2007.

[13] Elizabeth Rosenthal, 'UN fund set to combat human trafficking,' *International Herald Tribune*, 27 March 2007; Melody Drnach, Acting Vice President, National Organization for Women, 'Stop the sale of women: combat trafficking in the U.S.,' *International Herald Tribune*, 19 September 2007; Richard Bernstein, 'Good intentions: putting antislavery fight at risk,' *International Herald Tribune*, 10 April 2008. Bernstein refers to the recent work of E. Benjamin Skinner, *A Crime so Monstrous: Face to Face with Modern-Day Slavery* (New York: Free Press, 2008). Cf. the published memoir of the young Cambodian crusader Somaly Mam, *Le Silence de l' innocence* (Paris: Anne Carrière, 2005).

3. Rape in War, and Programmed Rape

'Throughout history,' wrote Irene Kahn, secretary general of Amnesty International, 'women's bodies have been considered the legitimate booty of victorious armies. Custom, culture and religion built an image of women as bearing the "honour" of their communities, so that destroying a woman's physical integrity became a means by which to terrorize, demean and defeat entire populations, as well as to punish, intimidate and humiliate women.'[14] Although prohibited under international law, rape and other gender-based violence in the course of armed conflict are rarely prosecuted because of the difficulty of establishing any system of justice. What gave impetus to the cry for greater accountability was the new variety of motives behind the act of rape in time of war.

Rape in the context of war has been legendary since the rape of the Sabine Women (which was in fact merely abduction), but programmed rape is a modern phenomenon. It could be said that the rape of 2 million German women by the Red Army in 1945 fitted this mould, because the orders given out by political commissars were 'to break the pride of the German women.'[15] What followed in the Balkan Wars brought added refinement, as armies set out to demoralize their adversaries either by degrading their women or by impregnating them with the seed of their enemies, and hence repopulating entire areas.

'Rape in war has been going on since time immemorial,' remarked Stephen Lewis, a former Canadian ambassador now in Africa as UN envoy for AIDS, to Nicholas Kristof of the *New York Times*, 'but it has taken a new twist as commanders have used it as a strategy of war.' The world woke up to this phenomenon in 1993, after discovering that Serbian forces had set up a network of 'rape camps' in which women and girls, some as young as 12, were held as slaves. Since then, similar patterns of systematic rape have been seen in many countries, and it has become clear that mass rape is not just a by-product of war but also sometimes a deliberate weapon. Kristof writes:

> There are two reasons for this. First, mass rape is very effective militarily. From the viewpoint of a militia, getting into a fire-fight is risky, so it is preferable to terrorize civilians sympathetic to a rival group and drive them away, depriving the rivals of support. Secondly, mass rape attracts less international scrutiny than piles of bodies, because the issue is indelicate and the victims are usually too ashamed to speak up. In Sudan, the government has turned Darfur into a rape camp. The first person to alert me to this was Zahra Abdelkarim, who had been kidnapped, gang-raped, mutilated—slashed with a sword on her leg–and then left naked and bleeding to wander back to her Zaghawa tribe. In effect, she had become a message to her people: Flee, or else. Since then, this practice of 'marking' the Darfur rape victims has become widespread: typically, the women are scarred or branded, or occasionally

---

14 Irene Khan, secretary general of Amnesty International, 'Justice for the unacknowledged casualties of war', *International Herald Tribune*, 18 December 2004.

15 Cf. Manfred Wille, 'Eastern Germany under the Soviets,' in: David Wingeate Pike, ed. *The Closing of the Second World War: Twilight of a Totalitarianism* (New York and Frankfurt am Main: 2001). The American sociologist J. Robert Lilly examined a quite different dimension, the rape of French and German women by US Army troops in the Allied advance from Normandy to the Elbe. His book *Taken by Force: Rape and American GIs in Europe during WWII* (New York: Palgrave Macmillan, 2007) became a widely distributed film documentary in which some of the released violators as well as their victims were interviewed. A number of the violators had been hanged.

> have their ears cut off. This is often done by police officers or soldiers, in uniform, as part of a coordinated government policy.[16]

While rape is always humiliating, it was the humiliation itself that had become the centrepiece in the crime. Speaking out often requires great courage. In 1996, at an international conference that I co-organized at Stanford University under the title 'War Crimes and War Criminals,' the participants included the French psychiatrist Catherine Bonnet who spoke of the problems of disclosure ('Particularitiés du dévoilement des viols'). The keynote speaker was the South African jurist Richard Goldstone, Chief Prosecutor at the International Criminal Court, who displayed a new brand of toughness. Two years later the ICC introduced its Rome Statute, which defined a broad spectrum of sexualized violence as crimes against humanity and war crimes that included, apart from rape and sexual slavery, such violations as forced pregnancy and sterilization. In the case of Iraq, writes Diane King, rape is frequently used as a weapon of sectarian conflict:

> When a Shiite militiaman rapes a Sunni woman, for example, he is seen as potentially implanting a Shiite into her womb. He is causing her to suffer dual humiliations: she is sexually violated, with all of the personal implications that that would carry in any culture. But the rape further serves like a Trojan horse: thereafter an offspring bearing the rapist's identity may well be hidden inside her body, an enemy who will emerge in nine months. Cross-sectarian rape as a weapon of political conflict can thus force a woman to nurture her own enemy. But in actual practice, this rarely happens. Rather, the tragedy of rape is compounded when a member of that woman's group eliminates her and any enemy offspring through an 'honour killing' or an 'honour suicide'.[17]

The mass rape of Muslim women in Bosnia resulted ultimately in the UN Security Council, on 20 June 2008, unanimously approving a resolution classifying rape as a weapon of war. Already on 22 February 2001, Florence Mumbal, a judge from Zambia sitting on the International Criminal Tribunal, gave her verdict in the case of three Serbs who, in the Bosnian city of Foca in 1992, had imprisoned young Muslim girls whom they raped, tortured and enslaved. The three men were the first in European legal history to be sentenced for crimes against humanity, but the argument was lost on the accused who did not understand why they were standing trial. 'I could have killed them, but I saved their lives. Rape? What kind of a crime is that compared with killing people?'[18]

A new danger confronting women emerged with the increased dispatch of American women soldiers to war zones. Women currently make up some 15 percent of the U.S. active-duty forces, and 11 percent of the soldiers in Iraq and Afghanistan. More than 191,500 women who have served in the Middle East since 2001 have returned home, and in 2008 the newly established U.S. Department of Veterans Affairs was facing a pressing crisis: women traumatized not only by combat but also by sexual assault and harassment from their fellow service members. Nearly a third of female veterans say they were sexually assaulted or raped while in the military, and 71 percent to 90 percent say they were sexually harassed by men

---

[16] Nicholas D. Kristof, 'The weapon of rape,' *International Herald Tribune*, 17 June 2008.

[17] Diane King, 'Using rape as a weapon,' *International Herald Tribune*, 9 June 2007.

[18] Slavenka Drakulic, 'Rape as a weapon of war,' *International Herald Tribune*, 27 June 2008. Drakulic, a Croatian journalist, is a contributing editor for the New York weekly *The Nation*.

with whom they served. The report mentioned that rape can lead to other medical crises, including diabetes, asthma, chronic pelvic pain, eating disorders, miscarriages and hypertension.[19]

4. Female Genital Mutilation

Female genital mutilation, a traditional initiation ceremony involving partial or total removal of the external female genitalia for cultural or religious reasons, is practised, according to the World Health Organization, in 28 African countries, many of them in West Africa.[20] Jessica Neuwirth, president of the international women's rights organization Equality Now, has said: 'Everyone who's been cut knows someone who died from cutting. They die from bleeding, or later from infection, or sometime later in life they suffer from enormous health problems.'[21] In Darfur, where many girls, as part of female circumcision rites, have their vaginas sewn shut with a wild thorn, the effects of rape are tragically enhanced.[22]

The first full-scale medical study of female genital mutilation, conducted in 2006, revealed what health workers had long known. 'Female genital mutilation,' declared Adrienne German, president of the International Women's Health Coalition based in New York, 'is a health issue, a killer of women and children, as well as a human rights issue.' More than 100 million women worldwide have undergone genital mutilation, most of them in childhood, often without anaesthesia or sterile technique. The procedure varies in severity, from a full excision of the clitoris and labia to a lesser procedure in which only the former is removed. Pain, bleeding and infection are immediate consequences. The procedure's mortal dangers, it was also found, extend to childbirth, rising by more than 50 percent the likelihood that the woman or her baby would not survive. Doctors suspect that the procedure is also linked to a later risk of urinary infections. In the country-by-country study, rates of genital mutilation ranged from a high of 83 percent in Sudan to a low of about 40 percent in Ghana. One country involved in the study, Senegal, had outlawed the more extensive form of the procedure in 1998. Elsewhere, the procedure throve on the myth, in a number of African cultures, that genital mutilation is part of a coming-of-age ceremony, and defenders of the custom continue to contend that it is a cultural practice, no different from male circumcision in the Jewish religion, with few, if any, proven long-term health consequences.[23]

---

[19] Helen Benedict, 'America's women warriors,' *International Herald Tribune,* 27 May 2008. Benedict, a professor of journalism at Columbia University, is the author of the novel *The Opposite of Love; Half Black, Half White in a Black-and-White World* (New York: Penguin, Viking 2007) and the forthcoming *The Lonely Soldier: The Private War of Women Serving in Iraq*.

[20] 'West Africans fight female genital mutilation in France,' IRIN, Paris, 23 June 2008.

[21] Bob Herbert, 'Punished for being female,' *International Herald Tribune*, 3 November 2006.

[22] Nicolas D. Kristof, 'Ministry of Rape', *International Herald Tribune*, 23 November 2005.

[23] Elisabeth Rosenthal, 'Genital cutting's deadly legacy,' *International Herald Tribune*, 2 June 2006.

5. Enforced Chastity and Its Corollary

A growing number of young women in France and elsewhere seek help from plastic surgeons for hymenoplasties, an operation in which the hymen is recreated from already torn tissue. There are no reliable statistics, but Caroline Fourest, who researched the subject for a television documentary, said the number of women undergoing the operation has risen to about 100 a year. 'In my culture, not to be a virgin is to be dirt,' said a French student of Moroccan descent, perched on a hospital bed in Paris while she awaited surgery. 'Right now, virginity is more important for me than life.'[24] Hymen repair had become in 2008 a subject both of comedy[25] and (in France) of legal wrangling resulting from the case of a North African man claiming annulment after discovering on his wedding night that his bride was not a virgin.[26] Fadela Amara, the French Minister of Urban Affairs, and herself of Muslim origin, called the ruling 'a fatwa against the emancipation of women.' The French Secretary of State for Social Affairs Valérie Létard said the decision represented 'a regression in the status of women,' and scores of feminists and lawyers warned that it could create a precedent, increasing the pressure on young Muslim women in Europe to remain chaste or to undergo an increasingly popular surgery to reconstitute their hymens before getting married.[27]

6. Child Marriage

Child marriage can have many detrimental affects on a young girl's life. Once wed, these girls are pressured to have children rapidly, often before their bodies are prepared to handle childbirth. Girls younger than 15 are five times more likely to die in childbirth than women in their 20s. The National Action Center, based in Washington and attached to the National Organization of Women (NOW), has issued a stern report. The proportion of females wedded before the age of 15 in the Indian states of Rajasthan and Uttar Pradesh is 36 percent, in Bangladesh 37 percent, in North Nigeria 48 percent, and in the Amhara region of Ethiopia 50 percent.[28]

7. Domestic Abuse

In the words of Amnesty International, domestic violence is the biggest human rights scandal of our times.[29] 'The most common form of serious abuse against women and girls

[24] Elaine Sciolino and Souad Mekhennet, 'A medical path back to virginity,' *International Herald Tribune*, 11 June 2008.

[25] Davide Sordella's 2007 film comedy *Corazones de Mujer* (*Women's Hearts* in its English translation) is the story of a Moroccan-born woman living in Italy who takes a road trip to Casablanca for the operation.

[26] Elaine Sciolino and Souad Mekhennet, 'A medical path back to virginity,' *International Herald Tribune*, 11 June 2008.

[27] Katrin Bennhold, 'Religion and law clash in France,' *International Herald Tribune*, 3 June 2008.

[28] National Action Center, National Organization for Women (NOW), 12 June 2008.

[29] Claire Bigg, 'Russia: domestic violence continues to take heavy toll,' Radio Free Europe/Radio Liberty (15 December 2005): http://209.85.229.132/search?q=cache:ZmqVr__vSKIJ:www.rferl.org/content/Article/1063891.html+amnesty+international+domestic+violence+the+biggest+human+scandal+of+our+times&cd=1&hl=fr&ct=clnk&gl=fr.

around the globe,' wrote Bob Herbert in the *New York Times*, 'is violence by intimate partners.' An international study conducted in 2006 by the World Health Foundation agreed that violence against women by their live-in spouses or partners was widespread. While it conceded that most partner abuse was hidden, and only a tiny fraction was reported to the authorities, it stated that rates of partner violence ranged from 15 percent in Yokohama, Japan, to 71 percent in rural Ethiopia. 'In all but one setting,' it concluded, 'women were at far greater risk of physical or sexual violence by a partner than from violence by other people.'[30]

Another report showed that a huge percentage of female murder victims, even in such developed countries as Australia, Canada, Israel and the United States, are killed by current or former husbands or boyfriends. A study of young female murder victims in the United States found that homicide was the second leading cause of death for girls aged 15 to 18, and that 78 percent of all the homicide victims in the study had been killed by an acquaintance or intimate partner.[31]

The situation in the United States was the subject of a wide investigation of all races and classes by the National Organization for Women. Its report in 2006 showed that every year some 1.2 million women are forcibly raped by their current or former male partners, some more than once. As for battering, although an annual average of only 572,000 assaults by intimates are reported to federal officials, the most conservative estimates show that from 2 to 4 million women are battered each year, while every day four women die from these assaults. As for the impact on children, those who have witnessed violence at home are five times more likely to commit violence when they become adults. It was as a result of NOW's efforts that in 1994 the United States Congress finally adopted the Violence against Women Act.[32]

In its 2008 report on Russia, Amnesty International stated: 'Violence against women in the family was widespread. Government support for crisis centres and hotlines was totally inadequate. No measures under Russian law addressed violence against women in the family.'[33] The World Organization against Torture (OMCT) expressed similar concern in its report 'Violence against women in Russia,' which spoke of women suffering at the hands not only of private individuals but also state officials.[34] Domestically, the Internal Affairs Ministry reported in 1996 that 80 percent of all murders were committed within families. Currently, around 14,000 women die every year at the hands of their husbands, intimate partners or relatives, figures that might be compared with those in the United States, where with more than twice the population only 1,200 such deaths were reported in 2001.[35] In Russia, 30 percent of married women are regularly subjected to physical violence, while in 2005, according to Amnesty International, nearly 60 percent of women had experienced

---

[30] Elizabeth Rosenthal, 'Study exposes extent of abuse of women,' *International Herald Tribune*, 6 October 2006.

[31] Bob Herbert, 'Punished for being female,' *International Herald Tribune*, 3 November 2006.

[32] 'Violence against women in the United States,' NOW, 25 October 2006.

[33] Amnesty International report 2008 on Russia: http://archive.amnesty.org/report2008/eng/regions/europe-and-central-asia/russian-federation .

[34] 'Russia: Widespread Violence Against Women,' report of the UN Committee on Economic, Social and Cultural Rights, World Organization against torture (Geneva, 17 November 2003): http://209.85.229.132/search?q=cache:5d5sJ3heUcsJ:www.omct.org/index.php%3Fid%3DEQL%26lang%3Deng%26articleSet%3DPress%26articleId%3D3805+A+beating+man+is+a+loving+man+russian+proverb&cd=6&hl=fr&ct=clnk&gl=fr.

[35] Mariya Rasner, 'Russian Women Struggle to Survive Domestic Violence,' Women's ENews (03/10/05): http://www.womensenews.org/article.cfm?aid=2215 .

aggression from a current or former husband, lover or significant other.[36] A full 90 percent had ether witnessed domestic violence between their parents or had experienced it first hand in their current relationship.[37]

The root of the problem lies in the absence in Russian law of a legal term for domestic violence, and as a result it is not recognized as a distinct crime. Nor is marital rape specifically criminalized. Law enforcement officials and society in general tend to view domestic violence not as a crime but as a private matter between the spouses.[38] Indeed, in a recent survey 43 percent of respondents reported that domestic violence is a private matter, and women are frequently blamed for having provoked the violence.[39]

The plight of Russian women spans all socio-economic classes, and the root cause, going beyond alcoholism, drug abuse and poverty, is to be found in traditional attitudes.[40] Many women shrink from divorce for fear that people will look down upon them for failing to build a family. An observer reports: 'Divorce is not stigmatized in Russia, but being alone is. There is a general pressure to get married as soon as possible, and as a result many women marry men they hardly know.'[41] Despite the fact that many women are more educated than their male companions, many blame themselves and find reasons not to report the crime, whether out of fear of public scorn, fear of revenge, or fear of becoming homeless. While there are forty-five NGOs listed as members of the Russian Association of Crisis Centres 'Stop Violence', they cannot provide psychological or legal assistance to more than a small number of battered women, and almost all of these centres are located in the European part of Russia.[42]

In Western Europe meanwhile, there was growing outrage, especially in Germany, at the increasing laxity of the courts in cases of domestic violence based on cultural difference. In a celebrated case in May 2006, a 26-year old German citizen who was the mother of two complained to the police of being beaten by her husband. The woman's name was never disclosed, but she had been born in Germany into a Moroccan family and in 2001 had married, in Morocco, a Moroccan citizen. They then settled in Germany. In May 2006 she obtained a separation, but she continued to be beaten and threatened with death by her husband. She filed for fast-track divorce. In January 2007, the German judge in Frankfurt, Christa Datz-Winter, saw no cause for alarm and rejected the plea, writing that 'both partners come from a Moroccan culture in which it is not uncommon for a man to exert a right of corporal punishment over his wife,' precisely because, 'in their religion, the woman is the property of the husband.' In the Koran, she wrote, 'the honour of the man, simply put, is tied to the chastity of the woman. For a man with an Islamic upbringing, the fact that a woman is

---

36 'Domestic Violence in Russia: Ending the Silence,' United Nations Population Fund (UNFPA): http://www.unfpa.org/gender/docs/fact_sheets/domestic_violence_russia.doc.

37 'Domestic Violence in Russia: Ending the Silence,' United Nations Population Fund (UNFPA): http://www.unfpa.org/gender/docs/fact_sheets/domestic_violence_russia.doc.

38 'Violence against women in the Russian Federation,' Amnesty International: http://www.amnesty.org/russia/womens_day.html.

39 'Domestic Violence in Russia: Ending the Silence,' United Nations Population Fund (UNFPA): http://www.unfpa.org/gender/docs/fact_sheets/domestic_violence_russia.doc.

40 'Domestic Violence in Russia: Ending the Silence,' United Nations Population Fund (UNFPA): http://www.unfpa.org/gender/docs/fact_sheets/domestic_violence_russia.doc.

41 Mariya Rasner, 'Russian Women Struggle to Survive Domestic Violence,' Women's ENews (03/10/05): http://www.womensenews.org/article.cfm?aid=2215.

42 'Violence against women in the Russian Federation,' Amnesty International: http://www.amnesty.org/russia/womens_day.html.

living according to Western cultural rules is by itself considered a violation of his honour.' She then added, in quoting Sura 4, verse 34: 'The Koran contains both the husband's right to use corporal punishment against a disobedient wife and the establishment of the husband's superiority over the wife. Men are in charge of women. A man's honour is injured when a wife behaves in an unchaste manner.' While such an interpretation of the Koran is no longer standard among moderate Muslims, some of whom quickly pointed out that not all Muslims use violence against their wives, it was nevertheless understood that for a woman married to a Muslim to follow Western styles of behaviour could be considered 'unchaste'—and punishable. In the case before her, Judge Datz-Winter argued, 'there is no evidence of "an unreasonable hardship" to justify an immediate divorce. The woman should have expected that her husband, who had grown up in Morocco, would exercise the right to use corporal punishment granted to him by his religion.' Her conclusion ran: 'The exercise of the right to castigate does not fulfil the hardship criteria as defined by Paragraph 1565 in German federal law. It must be taken into account that both man and wife have Moroccan backgrounds.'[43]

The judge's ruling at once turned the case into a *cause célèbre*. Put plainly, ran one response, the judge was arguing that a woman who marries a Muslim should know what she's getting into. Michaela Sulaika Kaiser, of the Network for Muslim Women, remarked: 'For Muslim men, this is like putting oil on a fire, that a German judge thinks it is perfectly all right for them to hit their wives. ... In my work educating sexist and short-sighted Muslim men, do I now have to convince German courts that women are also people on the same level with men and that they, like any other humans, have the right to be protected from physical and psychological violence?'[44] Roland Pofalla, general secretary of the conservative Christian Democratic Union (CDU), told the mass-daily *Bild* : 'When the Koran is put above the German constitution, I can only say: "Goodnight, Germany".'[45]

The German constitution won the argument. Datz-Winter's ruling was denounced in March 2007 by Justice Minister Brigitte Zypries, who replied that 'sharia has no place in Germany' and removed the judge from the trial, but not before the press, inside and outside Germany, had found much to deplore. Armin Laschet, of the CDU, saw the Frankfurt ruling as 'the latest link in a chain of horrific rulings handed down by German courts,' rulings in which so-called honour killings have been treated as manslaughter and not murder.' Seyran Ates, a Berlin women's rights activist, railed against the German judiciary's 'unspoken policy of appeasement' toward aggressive Muslims : 'Out of a sense of misguided tolerance, judges treat the values of Muslim subcultures as a mitigating circumstance and, in doing so, are helping to pave the way for a gradual encroachment of a fundamentalist Islam into Germany's parallel Muslim world.' Indeed, in summer 2004, the German Federal Ministry for Social Affairs had ruled that 'polygamous marriages must be recognized in Germany if they are legal under the laws of the native country of the individuals in question.' This meant that immigrants from countries where polygamy is legal—notably Morocco, Algeria and Saudi Arabia—could add a second wife to their government health insurance policies without having to pay an additional premium.

---

43 'German judge quotes Koran to beaten wife,' *Home Page*, 21 March 2007, quoting the daily *Frankfurter Rundschau.*

44 Veit Medick and Anna Reimann, 'A German judge cites Koran in divorce case,' *Spiegel Online International*, 21 March 2007; Mark Landler, 'German judge cites Koran, stirring up cultural storm,' *The New York Times*, 23 March 2007.

45 Mark Landler, 'Germany cites Koran in rejecting divorce,' *The New York Times*, 22 March 2007.

After the Moroccans it was the Turks who drew the most attention in Germany. The Frankfurt District Court ruled in 2003 (before the ruling was reversed in 2004 by the Federal Constitutional Court) that a Turkish-born man who had stabbed to death his German-born wife was guilty of no more than manslaughter, because his wife had disobeyed him and was even insolent enough to demand a divorce. 'He had acted,' said the court, 'out of an excessive rage and sense of outrage against his wife, based on his Anatolian socio-cultural moral concepts. Divorce would have violated his family and male honour derived from these moral concepts.' These concepts, moreover, could be inculcated into youth in Germany as well as into youth in Turkey. Judith-Gerling Tamer, an educator at the Elisi Evi Support Center for women and girls in the Kreuzberg district of Berlin, reported what Turkish girls from conservative families told her about their fathers and brothers: 'They have the right to beat us.'

Elsewhere, in Algeria, the imam Abdelkader Bouziane, whose property includes two women, recommends handing out beatings in such a way that 'the results are not apparent to infidels.' In Spain, Mohammed Kamal Mustafa, imam of Fuengirola, offers more specific advice, recommending in his book *Women in Islam* (published in 2001) how women should be beaten. 'The rod should be thin and light. If you beat their hands and feet with rods that are too thick, he warns, you risk leaving scars.' For inciting violence against women the imam was sentenced to 15 months in prison, but he was released after 22 days and told to spend six months studying Articles 10, 14, and 15 of the Spanish constitution. The first two Articles treat of the dignity of the person; the third, of equality before the law and the prohibition of cruel treatment.[46]

In Saudi Arabia—where children can still be sentenced to death, usually by beheading, even if no such execution has been carried out since 1996—women cannot vote, cannot drive, cannot attend university without their father's permission, cannot freely marry or divorce, and cannot be treated in a hospital or travel without the written permission of a husband or other male guardian. In 2002, 15 schoolgirls died when officers of the morality police would not let them out of their burning school building—and barred fire-fighters from saving them—because the girls were not wearing the headscarf and black cloak that all women must wear in public. Then, in 2007, among so many crimes that squeeze the heart, the story of the girl from al-Qatif carried a special poignancy.

Early in 2007, a 19-year-old girl belonging to Saudi Arabia's Shiite minority was about to be married and asked a former boyfriend to return a photograph she had given to him. They were sitting in a car when they were kidnapped at knife-point by seven men who released the man and gang-raped the girl. Since the girl, referred to only as 'the girl from al-Qatif', was sitting in a car with a man unrelated to her, she was charged with *khilwa*, or 'illegal mingling', which under Wahhabi Islamic law amounted to a grave crime. The fact that she was the victim of rape did not enter the case, and she was sentenced to 90 lashes. The sentence was appealed by her lawyer, the well known human rights activist Abdul-Rahman al-Lahem. Farida Deif, of Human Rights Watch, interviewed the girl and her lawyer and learned from them that one of the rapists had filmed the assault with his phone. The judges refused to allow the evidence, and in November 2007 they suspended his licence and

[46] *Washington Times*, 29 September 2005; Matthias Bartsch, Andreas Brandt, Simone Kaiser, Gunther Latsch, Cordula Meyer and Caroline Schmidt, 'German Justice Failures: Paving the way for a Muslim parallel society,' *Spiegel Online*, 29 March 2007.

commuted her sentence to 200 lashes and six months' imprisonment. In mid-December King Abdullah granted a pardon to the woman, but by then the case had become global news. Ayaan Hirsi Ali, now a resident scholar at the American Enterprise Institute, summoned all Muslims who define themselves as 'moderate' to find the courage to stand up against such abuses. Citing a passage in the Koran 24:2 where believers are enjoined not to be moved by compassion ('Let no compassion move you'), she responded: 'It is this order to choose Allah above his sense of conscience and compassion that imprisons the Muslim in a mindset that is archaic and extreme.'[47]

* * * * * * *

Several of the countries included in this book are among the worst offenders against womankind. Their governments may be trying hard or not trying very hard at all to address the wrongs inflicted. A heavy duty is thus relegated to the media, where no one does more to expose the sufferings of women than Nicholas D. Kristof of the *New York Times.* 'I firmly believe,' he writes, 'that the central moral challenge of this century, equivalent to the struggles against slavery in the 19th century or against totalitarianism in the 20th, will be to address sex inequality in the Third World.'[48]

The act of robbing a woman of her dignity, as woman and as human being, should make any male of any age or group recoil in disgust. Look at the list of authors of this book and you will find mainly women. A change in the fortunes of women, and an end to the everyday ugliness in gender relations, will become clear only when another book similar to this will be made up of essays written primarily by men.

---

[47] Ayaan Hirsi Ali, 'Islam's silent moderates,' *The New York Times*, 7 December 2007.

[48] Nicolas D. Kristof, 'Sentenced to rape,' *International Herald Tribune*, 30 September 2004.

PART I: CRIMES AGAINST WOMEN IN CONCEPT AND LAW

In: Crimes Against Women
Editor: David Wingeate Pike

ISBN 978-1-61470-813-1

Chapter 1

THE LAWS GOVERNING CRIMES AGAINST WOMEN CONSTITUTING *OBLIGATIO ERGA OMNES*

***Farhad Malekian*•**

INTRODUCTION

The immoral and criminal acts committed against women throughout the 20th century, especially the grave violations of human rights and international humanitarian law of armed conflict, have continued into the 21st, especially in the former Yugoslavia, Rwanda, Darfur, Sierra Leone and Iraq, where such violations have spurred the system of international law and international criminal justice to struggle against this criminal behaviour. Despite such efforts, both national and international, they have not succeeded in stemming the increase in such crimes whether in peace or wartime. It is necessary to examine how these crimes, committed either by individuals, groups or by the authorized acts of state officials themselves, have somehow escaped prosecution and punishment whether on the national or the international level.

The purpose of this study is therefore twofold. Firstly, to examine the precepts of international criminal law that recognizes crimes against women as international crimes. Secondly, to examine whether certain crimes are an integral part of *jus cogens* and *obligatio erga omnes* and consequently binding on all states without regard to whether they signed or ratified certain international conventions. As a matter of fact and of law, since the major international movements concerning crimes against women are of recent vintage, it would be impossible to reach the heart of the matter without knowing the origin of the sources and the scope of the application of the law. Various researches have been conducted into violence and rape in international criminal law, but few are the studies about the origins of the law. For these fundamental reasons, this chapter examines various parts of the law. These include the

• Distinguished Professor, director of the Institute of International Criminal Law, Uppsala, Sweden, A non-profit institute dedicated to international human rights, justice, peace and the full application of the principle of equality.

sources of the law that apply to crimes against women, the subjects of the law, and various acts whose commission may be recognized in international law as crimes against women.

[1] Of particular importance is the question whether the prohibition of crimes against women constitutes an integral part of the international criminal justice system? This study therefore deals with different areas of the law and ends with the central question concerning the nature and essence of the law and its impact on contemporary international relations. Finally, the chapter examines the reasons why the provisions concerning the prohibition of crimes against women have repeatedly failed in international relations. The key terms in the study thus consist of women, crime, justice and *jus cogens*.

DEFINING CRIMES AGAINST WOMEN

Although the term 'crimes against women' is a recent innovation, unlawful and criminal acts against women have repeatedly been committed throughout human history.[2] Crimes against women refer to any action or omission which may, by one means or another, severely violate the equality, liberty, dignity, integrity and security of women in time of war or peace.

---

[1] For international criminal law see Ludwig von Bar, *Das Internationale Private- und Strafrecht*, 523 (1862); Alfred Hegler, *Prinzipiendes Internationalen Strafrechts* (1906); Friedrich Meili, *Lehrbuch des Internationalen Strafrechts und Strafprozessrechts* (1910); Josef Kohler, *Internationales Strafrecht* (Stuttgart, 1917); Maurice Travers, *Le Droit Pénal International et sa mise en oeuvre en Temps de Paix et en Temps de* Guerre (5 vols. 1920-1922); H. Donnedieu de Vabres, Introduction à *L'Étude du Droit Pénal International* (1922); H. Donnedieu de Vabres, *Les Principes modernes du Droit Pénal International* (1928); Vespasian V. Pella, 'Plan for World Criminal Code', 17 *Revue Internationale de Droit Penal* (1946); Vespasian V. Pella, 'Fonctions pacificatrices du Droit Pénal supranational et fin du système traditionnel des Traités de Paix,' *Le Droit International Public* 1 (1947); Nino Levi, *Diritto Penale Internationale* (1949); Georg Schwarzenberger, 'The Problem of an International Criminal Law,' 3 *Current Legal Problems* 263 (1950); Hans-Heinrich Jescheck, *Die Verantwortlichkeit der Staatsorgane nach Völkerstrafrecht* (1952); Vespasian V. Pella, 'La codification du droit pénal international,' 56 *Revue Génerale de Droit International Public* 337 (1952); K. Siegert, *Grundlinien des Völkerstrafprozessrechts* (1953); Stefan Glaser, Introduction à *L'Étude du Droit International Pénal* (1954); Antonio Quintano-Ripolles, *Tratado de Derecho Penal Internacional e Internacional Penal* (2 vols. 1955-1957); Stefan Glaser, *Infraction internationale* (1957); Georg Schwarzenberger, The *Frontiers of International Law* 181-209 (1962); *International Criminal Law* (G.O.W Mueller and E.M. Wise eds. 2 vols., 1965); Stefan Glaser, Droit *International Pénal: son origine, son état actuel et son développement, L'indice pénal* (1968); Stefan Glaser, *Droit International Pénal Conventionnel* (2 vols, 1970); Edward M. Wise, 'Prolegomenon to the Principles of International Criminal Law,' 16 *New York University Law Review* 562 (1970); Claude Lombois, *Droit Pénal International* (1971); Stanislaw Plawski, *Étude des principes fondamentaux du Droit International Pénal* (1972); *A Treatise on International Criminal Law: Crimes and Punishment* (M. Cherif Bassiouni and Ved P. Nanda, eds. 2 vols. 1973); *La Belgique et le Droit International Pénal* (Bart de Schutter ed., 1975); Quincy Wright, 'The scope of International Criminal Law: A conceptual framework,' 15 *Virginia Journal of International Law* 562 (1975); L.C. Green, 'An International Criminal Code - Now?,' 3 *Dalhousie Law Journal* 560 (1976); M. Cherif Bassiouni, *A Draft International Criminal Code and Draft Statute for an International Criminal Tribunal*; Farhad Malekian, *International Criminal Law: The Legal and Critical Analysis of International Crimes* (2 vols. 1991); Farhad Malekian, *The Concept of Islamic International Criminal Law, A Comparative Study* (1994); Farhad Malekian, *The Monopolization of International Criminal Law in the United Nations: A Jurisprudential Approach* (2nd ed, 1995); M. Cherif Bassiouni, *International Criminal Law*, 3 vols., 1999); Farhad Malekian, '*International Criminal Responsibility' in International Criminal Law* 153; M. Cherif Bassiouni, *Introduction to International Criminal Law* (2003).

[2] Kelly Dawn Askin, *Crimes Against Women: Prosecution in International War Crimes Tribunals* (1997); Marian Meyers, *New Coverage of Violence Against Women* (1997). See also 'Prevalence of war-related sexual violence and other human rights abuses among internally displaced persons in Sierra Leone,' 287 *The Journal of the American Medical Association*, 513-21 (2002); Catharine A. MacKinnon, *Are Women Human? and other International Dialogues* (2006).

This includes legislative, cultural, political and religious attitudes, freedom of action, and discrimination in the application of social, educational, procedural and customary norms. Included in particular is the method of extracting information by acts of violence, sexual interference (whether physical or psychological), the denial of international regulations during criminal proceedings or procedures, illegal punishments, penalties, and implementation of various methods of capital punishment.[3]

In using the term 'crimes against women' we also mean the standard of recognition which is internationally given to certain acts in order to recognize and identify them as international crimes under the system of international criminal law. This recognizes the existence of certain facts such as conventions, customs, resolutions, national or international judicial decisions and general principles of law, from which a large number of rules for the recognition of crimes against women are deducted and presented. A considerable number of international conventions, directly or indirectly dealing with these questions, do indeed exist. The purpose of all these conventions is to point out which acts constitute crimes against women.[4] Accordingly, there are a number of acts which may be classified as crimes against women. These crimes, from the perspective of historical evolution of the norms of international criminal law, are *inter alia*:

- War crimes
- Crimes against humanity
- Genocide
- Enslavement
- Torture

[3] Unfortunately, some countries follow very harsh rules in imposing capital punishment, ignoring the fact that capital punishment itself already abolished in international criminal law. Others derive the rules for the punishment of women from theological provisions, arguing that it is permitted because it cleanses society of devilish behaviour. A clear example of this is the violation by the Islamic Republic of Iran of the human rights of women. Cf. www.iran-e-azad.org/stoning/women.html - 15k (last visited 21 October 2006), www.wfafi.org/ - 70k (last visited 21 October 2006); www.amitiesquebec-israel.org/texts/stoning.htm - 4k (last visited 21 October 2006); ipsnews.net/news.asp?idnews=34939 - 40k (last visited 21 October 2006). In particular see resolution of the General Assembly on the condemnation of Iran for violations of human rights and of women's dignity and integrity. The United Nations condemns the public executions, floggings, arbitrary sentences, torture and discrimination against women. See Res. 59/205 of 20 December 2004. In particular, the resolution condemns '(f) The failure to comply fully with international standards in the administration of justice, the absence of due process of law, the refusal to provide fair and public hearings and right to counsel, the use of national security laws to deny the rights of the individual and the lack of respect for internationally recognized legal safeguards, inter alia, with respect to persons belonging to religious minorities, officially recognized or otherwise; (g) The systemic discrimination against women and girls in law and in practice, despite some minor legislative improvements, and the refusal of the Guardian Council to take steps to address this systematic discrimination, noting in this context its rejection, in August 2003, of the proposal of the elected parliament to accede to the Convention on the Elimination of All Forms of Discrimination against Women; (h) The continuing discrimination against persons belonging to minorities, including Christians, Jews and Sunnis, and the increased discrimination against the Bahá'ís, including cases of arbitrary arrest and detention, the denial of free worship or of publicly carrying out communal affairs, the disregard of property rights, the destruction of sites of religious importance, the suspension of social, educational and community-related activities and the denial of access to higher education, employment, pensions and other benefits; (i) The continuing persecution, including through the systematic and arbitrary use of prolonged solitary confinement, and arbitrary sentencing to prison of human rights defenders, political opponents, religious dissenters and reformists.'

[4] See Jonathan I. Charney, 'Progress in International Criminal Law,' 93 AJIL 452-456 (1999); see also Malekian, 1 *International Criminal Law*, supra, note 1, 226-7.

- Trafficking
- Sexual exploitation
- Rape
- Discrimination on the basic of sex

This study concentrates on the concept of crimes against women under the principles of international criminal law and does not engage in the description of various concepts of crimes against women under domestic systems. Furthermore, some of the crimes listed above may, because of their nature, character, definition and the source of the application of the law, overlap one another and therefore share the basis for the identification of the crime.[5] In order for any one of the above actions to be treated under the jurisdiction of the International Criminal Court (ICC),[6] they must also come under the Statutes of the Court. However, this does not restrict the Court in resorting to other relevant sources of international criminal law. Similarly, national courts dealing with crimes against women may apply the provisions of national and international criminal law, depending on the circumstances of each case and the gravity of the crime.

One cannot deny that the concept of crimes against women under national legal systems may, in many instances, overlap with the concept of crimes against women in international criminal law.[7] In other words, national legal systems are obliged to respect certain definite rules of international criminal law concerning the prevention of certain acts against women. It is in fact, an international legal duty of states to fulfil their given international obligations in accordance with the sources of international criminal law.[8]

---

[5] For instance, rape may be identified as torture, crimes against humanity, war crimes and genocide. For some of these crimes see *Nikolic Rule 61 Decision* para 33, in which the Chamber considered 'sexual assaults inflicted on women in circumstances such as those described by the witnesses, may fall within the definition of torture as submitted by the Prosecutor.'

[6] The ICC is the first permanent international criminal court to be developed under the auspices of the United Nations Organization. The Statute of the ICC was adopted in Rome on 17 July 1998 by the United Nations Diplomatic Conference of Plenipotentiaries on the Establishment of an International Criminal Court. It came into force on 1 July 2002 based on the deposit of 60 instruments of ratifications. The Assembly of States Parties is the heart of the ICC, consisting of the representative of all states parties. The Assembly is in fact the legislative body of the Court. After the adoption of the Rome Statute, a Preparatory Commission for the International Criminal Court was convened by the United Nations. The Commission after examination of many rules and provisions achieved consensus on the Rules of Procedure and Evidence and the Elements of Crimes which were later adopted by the Assembly of States Parties. This achievement together with the Rome Statute and the Regulations of the Court which was adopted by the judges, constitute the framework of the Court regulating its basic texts for its structure, scope of jurisdiction and limitation of its functions. According to Article 4 of the Statute, the ICC has international legal personality and capable of entering into international treaties with different states parties. The ICC has authority over natural persons (Article 1). It may bring them under its jurisdiction for the serious crimes of international concern. These are genocide, crimes against humanity, war crimes, and (if it is permitted by the Security Council of the United Nations) over crimes of aggression. The ICC cannot act concerning a case as long as it is under investigation by a national criminal jurisdiction. If the national jurisdiction is not able to investigate the case or shields the accused from criminal liability, the ICC may have jurisdiction over the case due to the principle of complementarity.

[7] See Measuring Violence against Women: A Review of the Literature and Statistics, www.aph.gov.au/library/INTGuide/SP/ViolenceAgainstWomen.htm - 92k – (last visited 26 October 2006).

[8] This is known as *pacta sunt servanda*.

ELEMENTS OF CRIMES AGAINST WOMEN

Recognition of international crimes is generally based on the existence of certain elements which are fundamentally essential for the identification of certain acts as crimes under the provisions of international criminal law. For instance, the classification of crimes against humanity,[9] war crimes,[10] genocide,[11] torture,[12] trafficking and enslavement has been legislated with due regard to the proof of certain elements that are, according to the legislators, necessary for the indication of the crimes and criminality. There is, however, no special international convention which presents solely crimes against women and the elements necessary for their identification. Therefore, these elements may be examined with due regard to the provisions of different international documents applicable to crimes against women.

i) One of the most essential conditions for the recognition or non-recognition of an act constituting a crime against women is its identification as a crime under international criminal law.[13] This means that there must be certain provisions or rules which have, implicitly or explicitly, recognized the existence of certain acts as crimes against women.[14] This is the principle of *de lege lata.*[15] The principle implies the legality of attributing criminal responsibility to those who have, by one means or another, committed crimes against women. Thus, a crime against women means a violation of one of the sources of international criminal law such as custom, convention, general principle of law, or a consolidated resolution of the General Assembly concerning the prohibition of crimes against women. Since such crimes constitute an integral part of the international law of *jus cogens*, these norms are obligatory.[16]

ii) In order for an act to be identified as a crime against women, it has to be directed against the dignity or integrity of the woman, as in the case of rape.[17] Thus, any act of rape or forceful prostitution against a man may not come within the framework of the provisions prohibiting and recognizing crimes against women. The law may, however, be useful.[18]

iii) The concept of crimes against women arises whenever a crime is committed against a woman. Thus, the relevant provisions of international criminal law apply without any especial need to have more than one victim. There is therefore no special requirement, as in the case of crimes against humanity or genocide, in order to show

[9] See Article 7 of the Statute of the ICC.

[10] Ibid, Article 8.

[11] Ibid, Article 6.

[12] Convention against Torture and Other Cruel, Inhuman or Degrading Treatment or Punishment, G.A.Res. 39/46 (10 December 1984).

[13] See Article 7(g), ICC; Article 5(g), ICTY; Article 3(g) ICCR and Article 2(g), Special Court for Sierra Leone.

[14] Ibid.

[15] Ibid.

[16] See David S. Mitchell, 'The prohibition of rape in international humanitarian law as a norm of jus cogens: clarifying doctrine,' 15 *Duke Journal of Comparative and International Law*, 219-258 (2005).

[17] Ibid. 234-5.

[18] However, in certain situations, a court may, in collecting evidence, refer to the existing law applicable to crimes against women such as the definition of rape.

that the crime was committed on a widespread or massive scale.[19] This means that a single act of violence against a woman, such as rape, is by itself sufficient for the proof of guilt.[20] One of the reasons for this is to prevent the criminal from escaping prosecution and punishments.[21] Another reason is to avoid tying the elements of crimes against women to other principles of international criminal law or their juridical statutes such as the principle of massive commission.[22]

iv) Crimes against women are not limited to war or peacetime. They may be committed at any time. These crimes are not restricted either by the element of the systematic, as in the case of genocide or crimes against humanity. However, in certain situations, knowledge of committing a crime, based on the identification of certain acts as crimes within the provisions of criminal legislation, may be the essential factor for the law governing a crime against women to be appropriately implemented. The principle of knowledge is limited to certain crimes such as involvement in the slave trade of women or their subsequent exploitation. This is because the term "knowledge" concerns the *mens rea*, which means the intent to commit an action or omission constituting a crime against women. The *mens rea* comprises also the intent to commit the underlying reasons for violence with broad knowledge that a crime is being committed.

The term 'knowledge' is also, from various points of views, subject to debate and may not easily be proved. That is the reason why certain obvious violations or crimes against women should not necessarily be tied up with the principle of knowledge. The reason is to prevent various methods of avoiding prosecution. For instance, the use of torture for extracting information, or an act of rape by a person, does not need to invoke the principle of knowledge. The illegal nature of the action is sufficient for the proof of knowledge. Even in the case of slave-trading, the accused must present solid proof to the contrary. That requires proving that he or she was not in any way or form engaged in the act of slavery. In any case, the plea of superior order or the claim of lacking sufficient information concerning the criminality of the action may not be any ground to escape the consequences of the crime.

Sources of the Law

The philosophy behind the protection of women in international law should be studied from the perspective of various sources of law that recognize certain actions or omissions as crimes against women.[23] Basically, the sources of international criminal law derive from the

---

19 We should, however, not forget that sexual violence against women also constitutes genocide. Anne-Marie L.M. De Brouwer, *Supranational Criminal Prosecution of Sexual Violence: The ICC and the Practice of the ICTY*, 75 (2005).

20 See *Akayesu Tril judgment*, 598.

21 Ibid.

22 Ibid. 677-688.

23 For study on sources of international law consult Malekian, *The System of International Law: Formation, Treaties, Responsibility*, 21-51 (1987).

content of Article 38 of the International Court of Justice.[24] Accordingly, these are international conventions, customs, general principles of law, judicial decisions and the doctrines of the most highly qualified publicists. Each one of these sources has own interpretation and scope in defining violations against women. Certain resolutions of the General Assembly or the Security Council of the United Nations, however, may also be considered as an important source for the recognition of an act or omission constituting a serious violation against women. Most importantly, conventional, customary and general principles of law may provide varying definitions and applications of the law and present them as an integral part of their own systems.

As a result, all sources of the law may serve to complement one another or serve in isolation, without any particular need for proof of its provisions. Simultaneously, a judicial decision rely on all these sources without due regard to their classifications as the primary or the secondary sources of the system of international law. For the recognition of acts or omissions against women, a court may apply customary international criminal law even if the conventional provisions of the law may be silent. In other words, the rules of customary and conventional international criminal law are equally considered an integral part of *de lege lata* and, in certain important aspects, as an absolute part of *jus cogens* norms.[25]

CONVENTIONS

Conventional international criminal law constitutes one of the permanent sources governing the prohibition of crimes against women.[26] The reason for this is that international conventions are that part of the law that have been signed and ratified by a considerable number of states and are consequently considered as a positive part of international law applicable to crimes against women.[27] This means that the contracting parties to an international convention which deals, directly or indirectly, with the subject of crimes against women should, at all times, respect the provisions of the relevant convention.[28]

The difference between a convention as a source of crimes against women and other sources applicable to crimes against women is that the relevant law is fixed and consolidated in the written international law and may not juridically be avoided or ignored in the practice

---

[24] See Ian Brownlie, *Principles of Public International Law*, 3-29 (2003).

[25] See infra.

[26] This is because most of the arguments on the prohibition of crimes against humanity are based on conventional international law. For instance see *Protocol to Prevent, Suppress and Punish Trafficking in Persons Especially Women and Children, Supplementing the United Nations Convention against Transnational Organized Crime.* Adopted and opened for signature, ratification and accession by General Assembly resolution 55/25 of 15 November 2000. See also *Optional Protocol to the Convention on the Rights of the Child on the Sale of Children, Child prostitution and Child Pornography;* adopted and opened for signature, ratification and accession by General Assembly resolution A/RES/54/263 of 25 May 2000.

[27] Ibid.

[28] For instance, according to Article 8 of the Optional Protocol to the Convention on the Rights of the Child on the Sale of Children, Child Prostitution and Child Pornography, 'States Parties shall adopt appropriate measures to protect the rights and interests of child victims of the practices prohibited under the present Protocol at all stages of the criminal justice process…' These provisions are also strengthened by the provisions of Article 9. It reads that 'States Parties shall adopt or strengthen, implement and disseminate laws, administrative measures, social policies and programs to prevent the offences referred to in the present Protocol. Particular attention shall be given to protect children who are especially vulnerable to such practices…'

of states, organizations, groups or individuals.[29] While the content of conventional international law governing the prohibition of crimes against women may, from various point of views, be disputed, its legal characterizations, purposes and aims are unchangeable and may not be altered by any other element of interpretation.[30] For example, the prohibition governing white-slave traffic is fundamentally clear, but many international conventions on this matter have been ratified and many different interpretations have been expressed.[31]

The value of conventional international law is therefore based on the definitions of the elements of the crimes and the borderline of their applicability to those who have, implicitly or explicitly, violated its provisions.[32] Thus conventional international law governing crimes against women has its own framework of accountability, as does the application of the concept of international criminal responsibility to those who have committed crimes against women.[33] Moreover, due to the spirit of the 1973 Vienna Convention on the Law of Treaties, the duties of the parties to international conventions are fixed and should therefore be carried out by the parties.[34] This is known as *pacta sunt servanda*. The obligations of conventional international law applicable to crimes against women, like other sources of the law, should be respected not only in time of peace but also in time of war. Some of the prohibitions of crimes against women in conventional international criminal law include the white-slave traffic,[35] trafficking in females, sexual use of children, the sale of women, torture, discrimination and rape,[36] or, in the case of the Republic of South Africa, prostitutes living under *apartheid*.[37]

CUSTOMS

Custom is another source of international law.[38] The second source of the law governing the prohibition of crimes against women can be understood from the norms of customary

---

[29] For instance, the examination of the Protocol in the above illustrates that states have certain international duties and obligations to fulfil their conventional obligations. This is *pacta sunt servanda*. Ibid.

[30] This should be compared with customary international law. See the relevant section below.

[31] For example, see the International Convention for the Suppression of White Slave Traffic, signed in Paris in May 1910, and other subsequent instruments.

[32] For instance, consult the provisions of Article 7 of the ICC concerning crimes against humanity.

[33] See Article 25 of the ICC on individual criminal responsibility.

[34] The Vienna Convention was formulated in 1969 and went into effect in 1980. The Convention has been since 1949 the heavy task of the International Law Commission which elaborates the provisions of already customary international law into the framework of the Vienna Convention. The Convention has a large number of provisions and articles concerning the drafting, formulation, interpretation and coming into force of international treaties. It clarifies in what circumstances the provisions of a treaty are valid or invalid. The Convention also provides a basic approach to the peremptory norms of international law or *jus cogens*. It is in fact an important source for the recognition of treaties preventing crimes against women. On the interpretation of the Vienna Convention, consult Clive Parry, 'The Law of Treaties', in *Manual of Public International Law* 75 (Max Sørensen, 1978).

[35] For a study on apartheid see Farhad Malekian, 1 *International Criminal Law*, supra note 1, at 324-75; L.Rubin, Apartheid in Practice (1971); J.K. Feimpong and S. Azadon Tiewel, 'Can Apartheid successfully defy the international legal system?' 5 L.J. Black, 287 (1977); Garry Seltzer, 'The rule of the South Africa Criminal Code in implementing Apartheid,' 8 *Georgia Journal of International Law and Comparative Law*, 176 (1978).

[36] For some of these crimes consult M. Cherif Bassiouni., *Introduction to International Criminal Law* (2003).

[37] See note 35.

[38] According to the International Court of Justice, custom may constitute another source of international law. For this reason certain acts must be settled in the practice of states and such acts must be regarded as obligatory.

international law which prohibit certain acts or omissions against women and recognize them as serious violations of their rights.[39] Customary norms governing the prohibition of crimes against women pertain to those norms that have achieved a higher level of international recognition in the actual practice of states and within the opinion of highly qualified publicists and therefore have an obligatory character. Such norms govern slavery, rape and trafficking.

The problem of customary norms of international law relating to the prohibition of crimes against women is that the relevant norms may be very weak, and different reasons and interpretations may be given for their violations. For example, in many wars in the past, women have been raped despite the provisions of customary international law.[40] Furthermore, not only have women in wartime been employed by the home state for sexual purposes[41] but they have also been subjected to slavery or to institutions similar to slavery.[42]

More obviously, the elements of customary norms pertaining to the prohibition of crimes against women such as duration, the generality of the relevant practice, consistency or uniformity and even the use of the term 'general practice accepted as law' (employed in the Statute of the International Court of Justice) are very controversial indeed.[43] This is because States may give different political and juridical reasons concerning uniformity, duration or general practice. This was one of the reasons why customary international criminal law concerning the prohibition of rape against women was seriously violated by the conflicting parties during the conflicts in Yugoslavia where thousands of women, including young girls and children, were raped because of the non-existence of an appropriate definition of rape as an international crime. We should nevertheless emphasize that violation of customary or conventional rules cannot in any way reduce their juridical values.

JUDICIAL DECISIONS

The decisions delivered by national or international courts may also be regarded as one of the important sources for the recognition of crimes against women. The problem of judicial

See *North Sea Continental Shelf*, I.C.J. 42, 44 (1969). See also 'Case Concerning the Continental Shelf,' I.C.J. 29 (1985), 27.

39 'Sexual violence affects a nexus of rights under international protection. The right to life, to physical and psychological integrity, to security, to personal liberty, and to dignity and honour form part of the essential principles of human rights or the so-called core rights, which should be respected by states. These rights are part of the conventional law of human rights and form part of customary international law.' Statement by the Commission for the Historical Clarification of Human Rights Violations and Acts of Violence concerning the Suffering of the Population of Guatemala.. *Report from the United Nations Commission of the Secretary-General* (1994). http://shr.aaas.org/guatemala/ceh/mds/spanish/toc.html (Spanish), cited and quoted in Ana Elena Obado, *The International Criminal Court: An Opportunity for Women* (2004). www.whrnet.org/docs/issue-international_court.html - 69k (last visited 27 October 2006).

40 In fact rape has been a common policy during armed conflicts. It has been applied by military forces as an instrument of ethnic cleansing in enemy territories. Clear examples are the raping of women in military conflicts in Peru, Myanmar, Haiti, Kashmir, Somalia, Bosnia-Herzegovina, Rwanda and Sierra Leone. James R. McHenry III, 'The prosecution of rape under international law: Justice that is long overdue,' *Vanderbilt Journal of Transnational Law*, vol. 35, 1269-1311 (2002), 1310.

41 *Farhad Malekian*, 'Prohibition governing child soldiers constituting an integral part of jus cogens and obligatio Erga Omnes,' XVII World Congress of the International Association of Youth and Family Judges and Magistrates (2006).

42 For instance, in Darfur sexual violence was used as a weapon of war. amnesty.org/library/index/engafr540762004 - 146k (last visited 26 October 2006).

43 See Michel Virally, '*The Sources of International Law*,' in *Manual of Public International Law*, supra, note 28.

decisions is that they are not formal or direct sources of international law and have been looked upon as authoritative evidence of how the relevant law may be interpreted in certain given cases. There have been long discussions, therefore, about the legal validity of judicial decisions. The common idea is based on the wording of Article 59 of the Statute of the ICJ which clearly states that 'The decision of the Court has no binding force except as between the parties and in respect of that particular case.' Article 59 has thus been variously interpreted, and it is the general conclusion that most judicial decisions are applied only for the given case. There are, however, some reservations regarding the provisions of Article 59 where certain judicial decisions have attained the level of law making force. These are when:

a) the decision of an international criminal court relates to the high level of internationalization of certain provisions which have important effects on the consolidation of international human rights protecting women,[44]
b) the decision of an international criminal court refers to the full application of the provisions of humanitarian law of armed conflicts which have been differently interpreted by the conflicting parties or the accused concerning the prevention of crimes against women,[45]
c) a judicial decision of an international criminal court may, because of protection of certain customary norms, concerning prohibition of crimes against women such as rape, prove the absolute binding effect of the norms on relations between states,[46]
d) a judicial decision reached unanimously by the judges may play a decisive role in developing the principles of general international law concerning the protection of women,[47]
e) judicial decisions of international criminal courts established under the United Nations authority may, because of their important role in eliminating certain acts or conducts, create *law-making norms*, such as the decisions concerning rape of the International Criminal Tribunal for the former Yugoslavia (ICTY), the International Criminal Tribunal for Rwanda (ICTR) and the Court for Sierra Leone which provide analogies and evidence for similar cases by other international courts.[48]

---

[44] These are such as the judgments of the ICTY, ICTR and Special Court for Sierra Leone governing the prohibition of rape in armed conflicts. See Judgment, *Akayesu* (ICTR 96–4-T), Trial Chamber I, 2 September 1998; see also Michelle Jarvis, 'An Emerging Gender Perspective on International Crimes' in *International Criminal Law Development in the Case Law of the ICTY*, 157-192 (eds. Gideon Boas and William Schabas, 2003), 186.

[45] Ibid.

[46] Julie Mertus, "Judgment of Trial Chamber II in the Kunarac, Kovac and Vukovic Case," March 2001: www.asil.org/insights/insigh65.htm - 35k - (last visited Oct.23, 2006).

[47] Ibid.

[48] For instance, the provisions of the Nuremberg Tribunal that have been variously debated in the writings of international lawyers have obviously had decisive effects on the development of international law. This is also the case concerning its judgments. The general conclusion is that they have protected the provisions of natural law governing the protection of human beings including women. They have therefore had an effect in the creation of the Universal Declaration of Human Rights.

General Principles of Law

The term 'general principles of law' is another source for the recognition of crimes against women in international criminal law. The term refers to the general norms of law that are similar to one another under most domestic systems and, because of their common interest in protecting subjects of the law, hold important functions in identifying the common rules of law practised or legislated in the domestic systems of most States. These rules concern consent, good faith, the right to damages, and the prohibition of certain violations against women such as rape, enslavement, or sexual interference through various acts of force.[49]

In international criminal law, general principles of law refer to the equality of all nations before international criminal courts, equality in the application of international criminal norms, the legal validity of international criminal conventions, the rejection of the principle of impunity, the protection of women from unlawful and immoral acts of governments, the protection of family unity and the prohibition of rape and enslavement both in war and peace. The term 'general principles of international criminal law' may sometimes refer, in its broader interpretation, to the framework of the international law of *jus cogens*.[50]

Resolutions of the United Nations

Certain resolutions of the United Nations which refer to the rights of women and provide them with certain protections also contribute to the recognition and prevention of crimes against women.[51] Resolutions of the General Assembly may have fully legal or semi-legal effect in recognizing certain acts or omissions as constituting crimes against women.[52] A resolution of the General Assembly along these lines that has been adopted unanimously or by an overwhelming majority vote creates norms for the future conduct of States. States and individuals who stand accused of committing crimes against women are not entitled to reject the juridical value of such resolutions.[53] For this reason, the relevant resolutions must fulfil certain necessary conditions in order to be identified as law-making force.[54] An example of law-making force is provided by the provisions of the 1993 Declaration on the Elimination of Violence against Women. A declaration such as this establishes the obligations and duties of all States not to engage in activities that may go against the principles of the declaration.[55] The entire framework of the 1993 Declaration is indeed based on several international

---

49 This is because slavery or living under slave conditions is one of the most serious problems for a number of nations. It was on this basis that the United Nations made 2004 the Year of Anti-Slavery. This was in order to bring serious attention to the rapid development of trafficking, slavery and other institutions similar to slavery. See www.antislavery.org/homepage/news/UNslaveryyear090104.htm - 12k - (last visited 1Nov. 2006).

50 See the relevant section infra.

51 See Res.58/185 (22 December 2003); A/RES/48/104 (23 February 1994); A/RES/57/179 (30 January 2003).

52 Ibid.

53 There are several ways to evaluate the juridical value of a resolution of the General Assembly. See Farhad Malekian, Monopolization of International Criminal Law in the United Nations: A Jurisprudential Approach, supra, note 1, 78-9.

54 Ibid.

55 Proclaimed by General Assembly Resolution 48/104 of 20 December 1993.

instruments, the values of which have already been consolidated in the system of international law.[56]

PUBLICISTS

Another source governing the protection of women and the prevention of crimes against women is the writing or the teaching of the most highly qualified publicists as 'subsidiary means for the determination of rules of law.'[57] Although this source may influence juridical and critical analysis of certain norms of international criminal law, its application as legal evidence is very narrow and may create long and immeasurable controversies between different States. Publicists in one part of the world may refuse to recognize certain acts or omissions as crimes against women, while in another part publicists may have quite different opinions.

It is nevertheless undeniable that the views of publicists are broadly invoked in the settlement of certain issues.[58] More importantly, the views of publicists may sometimes refer to the published works, drafts, proposals and reports of prestigious establishments such as the Harvard Research Institute.[59]

In general, one has to be cautious concerning the opinions of publicists when they are used to show proof of crimes against women and to apply criminality.[60] Such references may have the effect of increasing or decreasing the recognition of crimes against women.[61]

JUS COGENS

In the recent conflicts in Europe, Asia, South America and Africa, massive abuses of the principles of international criminal law and severe violations of the dignity and integrity of women have created, under the principles of *jus cogens*, a normative character for the rights of women that cannot be denied by any national or international legislation. The consequence is that these violations, because of their similarity to other international crimes such as crimes

---

[56] The Declaration lists a number of instruments which denote the rights of women and principles concerning the protection of women from unlawful suffering. These include the Universal Declaration of Human Rights (1948), the International Covenant on Civil and Political Rights (1966), the International Covenant on Economic, Social and Cultural Rights (1966), the Convention on the Elimination of All Forms of Discrimination against Women (1979), and the Convention against Torture and Other Cruel, Inhuman or Degrading Treatment or Punishment (1984). See also Farhad Malekian, *Documents on the Principles of International Human Rights* (2007).

[57] Article 38 of the Statute of the ICJ.

[58] In the North Sea Continental Shelf Case, *opinio juris* was regarded as important evidence for the settlement of customary international law. North Sea Continental Shelf (1969), ICJ 42, 44.

[59] One of the clear examples of jurists' opinions may be found in the reports of the International Law Commission of the United Nations concerning certain important matters of interest.

[60] It is also difficult and problematic to distinguish between qualified and non-qualified jurists. This is because there may be many good international lawyers who are highly qualified in their own countries but whose writings are in languages that are not in common use in other countries.

[61] See generally Kelly Dawn Askin, *Crimes against Women: Prosecution in International War Crimes Tribunals* (1997); Marian Meyers, *New Coverage of Violence Against Women* (1997).

against humanity, genocide, slavery, torture and apartheid-type discrimination may be categorized under the international law of *jus cogens*.

Jus cogens norms are that part of international criminal law which are binding on all States without regard to their signature or ratification of any particular international convention.[62] They constitute the peremptory norms of international criminal law, the derogation of which may pertain to the violations of the consolidated principles of international legal order.[63] The functions of *jus cogens* norms are not only to limit the conventional freedom of States, but also to restrict the traditional international legal personality of States regarding certain acts that have an important function for the maintenance of international peace, equality, justice and the fundamental rights of man. In other words, *jus cogens* norms imply a high degree of internationalization of certain norms that carry a substantive message promoting the natural and positive laws of man that have continuous validity for mankind. Based on the fact that the fundamental rights of man must be respected and are an integral part of the Declaration of Human Rights,[64] any act of brutality against women may therefore constitute an integral part of *jus cogens*.

Consequently, the prevention of crimes against women, in the cause of maintaining international peace, equality, and the fundamental principles of human rights and justice, are an integral part of the legal responsibilities of all States. They should struggle continuously against violations of those rights of women that are integrated into *jus cogens* norms. The claim that the law governing crimes against women constitutes *jus cogens* and *obligatio erga omnes* is based on several important principles of international law:

a) the Declaration of Human Rights constitutes an integral part of *jus cogens*;[65]
b) numerous international conventions before the outbreak of the Second World War prohibited sexual violence against women;
c) numerous conventions concerning the protection of the fundamental rights of women imply the prohibition of crimes against women;
d) legislation covering crimes against humanity, war crimes and torture also infers the prohibition of crimes against women;[66]
e) the international humanitarian law of armed conflict explicitly and implicitly recognizes severe acts of violence against women as war crimes;[67]
f) the spirit of conventions on slavery strictly prohibits violations of their rules including those governing sexual slavery;[68]

---

[62] Barcelona Traction, Light and Power Company Ltd., Judgment, 1972. ICJ Rep., 34.

[63] According to Article 53 of the 1969 Vienna Convention, 'A treaty is void if, at the time of its conclusion, it conflicts with a peremptory norm of general international law. For the purposes of the present Convention, a peremptory norm of general international law is a norm accepted and recognized by the international community of states as a whole as a norm from which no derogation is permitted and which can be modified only by a subsequent norm of general international law having the same character.'

[64] Resolution 217 A (III).

[65] See Ian Brownlie, *Principles of Public International Law,* 514-15 (3rd ed. 1979).

[66] See Convention on the Non-Applicability of Statutory Limitations to War Crimes and Crimes Against Humanity (New York, 26 November 1968).

[67] For instance, see the 1948 Geneva Conventions and their 1977 Protocols; Declaration on the Protection of Women and Children in Emergency and Armed Conflict, proclaimed by General Assembly Res. 3318 (XXIX) of 14 December 1974.

g) all types of trafficking are absolutely prohibited;[69]
h) contemporary general international law demands the prohibition of violence against women;[70]
i) customary international law has under no circumstances permitted the use of violence against women either in wartime or in peacetime;[71]
j) resolutions of the General Assembly call for the prohibition of the use of violence toward women during armed conflict;[72]
k) resolutions of the General Assembly strengthen the existing international conventions to prevent any crimes against women;[73]
l) national legislations are continuously promoting the rights of women and prohibiting crimes against them;[74]
m) national courts are bringing strong suits against those accused of committing crimes against women;[75]
n) the Statutes of *ad hoc* international tribunals recognise many types of sexual violence constituting crimes against women;[76]
o) the judgment of the above courts also state the important function of international legislation governing the prohibition of crimes against women;[77]
p) the Statute of the ICC rejects any claim supportive of a crime against women in armed conflicts;[78]
q) the present proceedings of the ICC emphatically outlaw crimes against women;
r) the Convention on the Rights of the Child and its Protocol demand that all States prohibit all sexual violence against women;[79]
s) the Convention of the Labour Organization also recognises sexual exploitation as a crime against women.[80]

What is needed here is not to list all the other reasons to prove that the prohibition of crimes against women constitutes an integral part of *jus cogens*, but rather to emphasize that all these prohibitions are enforceable on all States regardless of their juridical, military,

---

[68] See the 1919 Convention of Saint-Germain-en-Laye; the 1926 Convention of Slavery; Amendment of the 1926 Convention by 1953 Protocol; the 1956 Supplementary Convention on the Abolition of Slavery, the Slave Trade, and Institutions and Practices Similar to Slavery.

[69] See the 1904 International Agreement for the Suppression of White Slave Traffic; the 1910 International Convention for the Suppression of White Slave Traffic; the 1921 International Convention for the Suppression of the Traffic in Women and Children; the 1933 International Convention for the Suppression of the Traffic in Women of Full Age.

[70] www.whrnet.org/docs/issue-international-court.html - 69k (last visited 27 October 2006).

[71] Ibid.

[72] See Res.58/185 (22 December 2003); A/RES/48/104 (23 February 1994); A/RES/57/179 (30 January 2003).

[73] Ibid.

[74] For some analysis of the German legislations concerning violence against women consult www.ipu.org/wmn-e/subjects.htm - 10k (last visited 26 October 2006).

[75] Ibid.

[76] See David S. Mitchell, 'The prohibition of rape in international humanitarian law as a norm of jus cogens: clarifying doctrine,' 15 *Duke Journal of Comparative and International Law*, 219-258 (2005).

[77] Ibid.

[78] Articles 6, 7 and 8 of the Statute.

[79] See, for example, the 1989 Convention on the Rights of the Child; the 1995 Amendment to Article 43 (2) of the Convention on the Rights of the Child; the 2000 Optional Protocol to the Convention on the Rights of the Child on the Involvement of Children in Armed Conflict.

[80] See the International Labour Organization, Worst Forms of Child Labour Convention 182 (1992).

economic or political interests. In another sense, the prohibition of crimes against women are *obligatio erga omnes*, which means that States have international legal duties and responsibilities to implement certain rules of conducts that have been recognized as *jus cogens* norms. The term *obligatio erga omnes* denotes the juridical essence or juridical indication of a norm of *jus cogens* that has to be legislated, applied and implemented by States without due regard to other principles. The reason for this is that *obligatio erga omnes* is the concept of practical implementation of *jus cogens* norms, and this should not be denied by any other act to the contrary.[81] Since rape, sexual abuse, sexual slavery, trafficking, exploitation of women and many other similar acts of violence against women are widely acknowledged international crimes, there can be no doubt that crimes against women constitute an integral part of *jus cogens*.

SUBJECTS OF CRIMES AGAINST WOMEN

A subject of crimes against women is a person capable of possessing rights and duties within the system of national or international legislation including human rights and having capacity to demand her rights by bringing a claim by a legal representative before national or international criminal courts with due regard to the procedural rules.[82] The body of international criminal law deals exclusively with individuals. They are subjects of that legal discipline by virtue of their positions as victim, witness, accused or guilty of having committed international crimes.[83] Therefore, individuals may have different positions or functions for the enforcement of the procedures of the law within the jurisdiction of an international criminal court.[84] The basic reason for this is that the purpose of international criminal law is to protect the international human community from unlawful and immoral acts of individuals, groups, organizations, governments and states.[85]

Subjects of the law governing crimes against women who are protected by the relevant law are generally all women without regard to their age, nationality or religion, or their cultural, political, social and economic attitudes and so forth.[86] In a word, subjects of protection under the law governing crimes against women are *females*.[87] The law thus protects all womankind, and specifically:

- female children of all ages[88]
- female youth of all ages[89]

[81] See generally Christian J. Tams, *Enforcing Obligations Erga Omnes in International Law* (2005).

[82] For instance, states are the most recognized subjects of international law, or individuals are the subjects of international human rights.

[83] See for a discussion on the subjects of law see Malekian, 1 *International Criminal Law*, supra, note 1, 30-53.

[84] Ibid.

[85] Ibid.

[86] These are some of the fundamental principles of international human rights. See the Declaration of Human Rights which is an integral part of customary and *jus cogens* international criminal law.

[87] See generally Kelly Dawn Askin, *Crimes Against Women: Prosecution in International War Crimes Tribunals, supra, note 2.*

[88] See generally Convention on the Right of the Child. Adopted and opened for signature, ratification and accession by General Assembly resolution 44/25 of 20 November 1989, entry into force 2 September 1990. www.unhchr.ch/html/menu3/b/k2crc.htm - 63k (last visited 23 October 2006).

- women of all ages[90]
- female children, female youth and women who are stateless[91]
- vulnerable women such as those belonging to minority groups, indigenous women, women living in rural or remote communities, destitute women, migrant women, refugee women, women in institutions or in detention, elderly women, women with disabilities and women in situations of armed conflict.[92]

THE PERPETRATORS OF CRIMES AGAINST WOMEN

Crimes against women are committed by a broad range of subjects of international criminal law. They include individuals, groups, organizations and States. There may not be any difference among these subjects, since all are complementary to one another and present the same issue. In certain cases, a single individual may engage in the commission of a crime

---

[89] Ibid.

[90] There are a number of international conventions which protect women, by one means or anther, from unlawful and immoral acts. For instance, see the International Agreement for the Suppression of White Slave Traffic (1904); International Convention for the Suppression of the White Slave Traffic (1910); International Convention for the Suppression of the Traffic in Women and Children (1921); Convention of Slavery (1926); International Convention for the Suppression of the Traffic in Women of Full Age (1933); Universal Declaration of Human Rights (1948); Convention on the Political Rights of Women (1952); Amendment of the 1926 Convention by 1953 Protocol; Supplementary Convention on the Abolition of Slavery, the Slave trade, and Institutions and Practices Similar to Slavery (1957); International Convention on the Elimination of All Forms of Racial Discrimination (1966); International Covenant on Economic, Social and Cultural Rights (1976); International Covenant on Civil and Political Rights (1966); Optional Protocol to the International Covenant on Civil and Political Rights (1966); Declaration on the Elimination of Discrimination against Women (1967); Declaration on the Protection of Women and Children in Emergency and Armed Conflict (1974); Convention on the Elimination of All Forms of Discrimination Against Women (1979); Convention against Torture and Other Cruel, Inhuman or Degrading Treatment or Punishment (1987); Convention on the Rights of the Child (1989); Amendment to article 8 of the International Convention on the Elimination of All Forms of Racial Discrimination (1992); International Labour Organization, Worst Forms of Child Labour Convention 182 (1992); Declaration on the Elimination of Violence Against Women (1993); Amendment to article 43 (2) of the Convention on the Rights of the Child (1995); Amendment to article 20, paragraph 1 of the Convention on the Elimination of All Forms of Discrimination against Women (1995); Statute of the International Criminal Court (1998); Optional Protocol to the Convention on the Elimination of All Forms of Discrimination Against Women (1999); Protocol to Prevent, Suppress and Punish Trafficking in Persons Especially Women and Children, Supplementing the United Nations Convention against Transnational Organized Crime (2000); Optional Protocol to the Convention on the Rights of the Child on the Sale of Children, Child Prostitution and Child Pornography (2000); Optional Protocol to the Convention on the Rights of the Child on the Involvement of Children in Armed Conflict (2000).

[91] The question of stateless women is indeed a serious problem of international relations. These groups of women are less protected and have suffered more from inhuman and immoral acts of governments, and especially the legislations of most states do not give any attention to the protection of this category who may, for one reason or another, have come under the statute of stateless persons. Therefore, it must be stated that in the application of the law concerning crimes against women, no specific distinction may be made between women or girls who are protected under their own national legislations and those who are considered stateless in accordance to Refugee Laws. It is also rightly asserted that governments, United Nations agencies and any other international human rights organizations should not only prevent crimes against wome, but also "grant citizenship rights and property rights to stateless women, so that they can avail themselves of a broad range of government services and assure the future of their families." www.refugeesinternational.org/content/article/detail/6527 - 20k; www.womeninblack.net/stats/wib2000. html - 5k (last visited 21 October 2006).

[92] See Declaration on the Elimination of Violence against Women, General Assembly Resolution 48/104 of 20 December 1993.

against women, and in other cases, the perpetrator may engage, collectively or in groups, in actions which are controlled by a criminal organization.

Among the most frequent forms of crimes against women is that practised by State or governmental organizations which, implicitly or explicitly, engage in the commission of the crime. This is seen especially in time of armed conflict, in the form of rape. Similar engagement may also be committed in peacetime, such as trafficking in young women. Crimes against women committed under the state legal personality are therefore considered to be one of the most dangerous forms of violating the law governing the protection of women.[93]

CRIMES AGAINST HUMANITY

The philosophy underlying the prevention of crimes against humanity is very broad indeed. It implies many inhuman actions which are customarily and conventionally recognized as crimes against humanity. Conventionally, the terminology can be traced back to the Armenian genocide perpetrated by the Ottoman Turkish government,[94] and was later expanded under the Nuremberg Charter, the ICTY, ICTR, the Criminal Court for Sierra Leone, and especially in the Statute of the ICC.[95] In accordance with conventional and customary law, crimes against humanity constitute an integral part of *jus cogens* in contemporary international criminal law.[96]

The Nuremberg Tribunal did not identify crimes against women as crimes against humanity.[97] In fact, under the proceedings of the Tribunal,[98] rape was completely ignored.

---

[93] For example, acts of rape, crimes against humanity, war crimes and genocide in the former territory of Yugoslavia constituted, without doubt, acts of state policy.

[94] M. Cherif Bassiouni, *Crimes Against Humanity in International Criminal Law* 168 (1992).

[95] The abbreviations are in order for the International Criminal Tribunal for the Former Yugoslavia, the International Criminal Tribunal for Rwanda, and the permanent International Criminal Court.

[96] However, there are some differences between these three concepts and therefore one has to be very cautious with reference to these three categories of international criminal law sources. See the relevant sections.

[97] Article II (c) of the Control Council No. 10 refers to the term "rape". It reads: " (c) Crimes against Humanity: Atrocities and offences, including but not limited to murder, extermination, enslavement, deportation, imprisonment, torture, rape, or other inhumane acts committed against any civilian population, or persecutions on political, racial or religious grounds, whether or not in violation of the domestic laws of the country where perpetrated," emphasis added. If the same proposition concerning rape had been entered into Article 6 (c) of the Nuremberg Charter, the situation may have been different in international criminal law. But, Article 6 (c) of the Charter refers instead to the term 'other inhuman acts,' which is very broad and may be interpreted differently. This shortcoming of the Charter made clear that conventional international justice did not openly endorse the criminalization of rape under armed conflicts.

[98] For consideration of the Nuremberg Tribunal, see generally Sheldon Glueck, 'By what tribunal shall war offenders be tried?' 56 *Harvard Law Review* 1059 (1942-3); Sheldon Glueck, *The Nuremberg Trial and Aggressive War* (New York, 1946); *The Judgment of the International Military Tribunal for the Trial of German Major War Criminals, Nuremberg 1946,* H.M. Stationery Office Cmd. 6964; Robert H Jackson, Foreword. 'The Nuremberg Trial Becomes a Historical Precedent,' 20 *Temple Law Quarterly* (1946-7); Stimson, Henry L., 'The Nuremberg, Trial, Landmark in Law,' 25 *Foreign Affairs* 179 (1946-7); Trials of War Criminals Before the Nuremberg Military Tribunals under Control Council Law No. 10 (Nuremberg, 1946-1949; George Augustus Finch, 'The Nuremberg Trial and International Law,' 41 *American Journal of International Law* 20 (1947); Hans Kelsen, 'Will the Judgement of the Nuremberg Trial Constitute a Precedent in International Law?' 1 *International Law Quarterly* 153 (1947); Arthur K Kuhn, 'International Criminal Jurisdiction,' 41 A.J.I.L. 430 (1947); F.B. Schick, 'The Nuremberg Trial and the International Law of the Future,' 41 A.J.I.L. 770 (1947); Wright, Quincy, 'The Law of the Nuremberg Trial,' 41 A.J.I.L. 38

Subsequent tribunals, however, have indeed classified rape as a crime against humanity which, in its own term, constitutes a crime against women.[99] The tribunals for the former Yugoslavia, Rwanda and Sierra Leone have made clear that they have the power to prosecute persons responsible for crimes such as rape when committed in armed conflict.[100] This means that acts of rape directed against any civilian population are regarded as crimes against humanity.[101]

Consequently, certain relevant provisions of crimes against humanity concerning rape are also an integral part of crimes against women. In other words, perpetrators of crimes against humanity are simultaneously violating the relevant law concerning the protection of females. However, a clear distinction should be made between rape and other crimes against women that constitute crimes against humanity in the statutes of international criminal tribunals and the ICC, and those crimes which do not fall under the rubric of crimes against women. None of the recognized crimes against humanity in the statutes of *ad hoc* tribunals is enforceable in peacetime. Nevertheless, certain crimes against women committed in peacetime that are recognized under the provisions of *ad hoc* tribunals and the ICC may qualify as crimes against humanity without the need to refer to an attack on a civilian population. Such crimes include rape, sexual slavery, enforced prostitution, forced pregnancy and any other form of sexual violence, including acts of violence committed by government officials or entities while the victims are, for one reason or another, in prison.[102]

(1947); International Military Tribunal, Trial of the Major War Criminals Before the International Military Tribunal in Nuremberg (1947); Hans Ehard, 'The Nuremberg Trial against the major war criminals and international law,' 33 A.J.I.L. 223 (1949); Trials of War Criminals Before the Nuremberg Military Tribunals under Control Council (1951); Farhad Malekian, *International Criminal Responsibility of States: A Study on the Evolution of International Responsibility of States with Particular Emphasis on the Concept of Crime and Criminal Responsibility* (1985).

99 See Art. 5(g) of the Statute of the International Tribunal for the Prosecution of Persons Responsible for Serious Violations of International Humanitarian Law Committed in the Territory of the Former Yugoslavia Since 1991, U.N. Doc. S/25704 at 36, annex (1993) and S/25704/Add.1 (1993), adopted by Security Council on 25 May 1993, U.N. Doc. S/RES/827 (1993) hereinafter ICTY; Art. 3(g) of the Statute of the International Criminal Tribunal for the Prosecution of Persons Responsible for Genocide and Other Serious Violations of International Humanitarian Law Committed in the Territory of Rwanda and Rwandan Citizens Responsible for Genocide and Other Such Violations Committed in the Territory of Neighbouring States, between 1 January 1994 and 31 December 1994. S.C. Res. 955, U.N. SCOR, 3453d mtg., U.N. Doc. S/RES/955 (1994), hereinafter ICTR; Art. 2(g), Art.3 (e), Art.15 (4) of the Statute of the Special Court for Sierra Leone, having been established by an Agreement between the U.N. and the Government of Sierra Leone pursuant to Security Council Res. 1315 (2000) of 14 August 2000, hereinafter the Special Court.

100 This is regardless of the national or international character of armed conflict.

101 It must also be borne in mind that acts of rape are traditionally considered to be committed against women. The relevant articles of the tribunals, however, seem to apply their definition to any civilian which has been the victim of rape. For example, the ICTR "shall have the power to prosecute persons responsible for the following crimes when committed as part of a widespread or systematic attack against any civilian population on national, political, ethnic, racial or religious grounds…." Article 3.

102 One of the problems of the use of the terminology "crimes against humanity," is that it is employed in connection with armed conflicts and is rarely used during times of peace. Obviously, because of the gravity of the offences against females, it should also be employed in international law to cover peacetime. In particular, criminalization of the acts has not succeeded, either in war or peace. The provisions of the Convention on Apartheid clearly state that apartheid constitutes crimes against humanity. This means that apartheid directed against women also constitutes crimes against humanity. See the introduction to the 1973 International Convention on the Suppression and Punishment of the Crime of Apartheid (General Assembly Resolution 3068), XXVIII.

CONCLUSION

The philosophy of justice, human rights, peace and practice should normally be identical.[103] This is what is expected by the creation of international legal systems. The international protection of women is surely an integral part of international human rights law that cannot be denied by any realistic international lawyer. It is also an integral part of international criminal law, humanitarian law and labour law.

By virtue of the long existence of customary and conventional international law, the protection of women also constitutes an integral part of *jus cogens* norms. In other words, the law governing the prohibition of crimes against women is a consolidated part of international criminal law. This confers international legal duties and responsibilities on all States in order to implement the principle of *obligatio erga omens*. One may list a considerable number of actions or omissions which come undoubtedly under the relevant law. Simultaneously, crimes against women such as rape and trafficking may be classified under slavery, crimes against humanity, war crimes, genocide, torture and apartheid-type discrimination. This means that crimes against women in a wider aspect have a deep connection with other international crimes that have already been recognized in international criminal law.

Despite these definitions, crimes against women will surely continue to increase. Such crimes include not only the trafficking of women, rape, sexual slavery, exploitation and torture, but also the smuggling of very young girls. The rationale behind crimes against women is not solely the existence of multinational corporations but also the prevalence of strong sexual feelings and antagonisms within men that induce them to ignore criminal law wherever it might seem necessary for the fulfilment of a particular personal or governmental purpose. What is needed in contemporary international relations, therefore, is not the implementation of conventions preventing crimes against women but rather the full application of the principle of *equality* in the Charter of the United Nations Organization. In order to reach the heart of the problem, *equal norms* and *equal justice* must be imposed on all States, without regard to their military and political strength. The assessment of criminal justice does not rest primarily on the intent of the criminal but on the action itself, since it derives from unequal conditions. Sexual equality will create a balance in the philosophy of justice and the application of human rights, together with a reciprocal and equal understanding of international problems such as rape, slavery and trafficking. This will be of great service in preventing conflict and the sexual sufferings that accompany conflict. It will do much to prevent war, including rape and other sexual sufferings during armed conflict. Thus, laws to prevent crimes against women will no longer fail, as they do today, because a constitutional balance will be attained in the application of juridical, political, economic and moral justice in international relations.

The essence of international criminal justice is not so much the prosecution of criminals as it is respect for the scale of norms that derive from sympathetic understanding. International criminal justice should not therefore be classified as the norm of prevention and punishment but as a norm of establishing common equality among all human beings and nations.

---

[103] The reality is indeed different. Cf. Farhad Malekian, *Condemning the Use of Force in the Gulf Crisis* (1994); Michael Mandel, *How America Gets Away With Murder, Illegal Wars, Collateral Damage and Crimes Against Humanity* (2004).

Justice is not something that should be decreed by conventions or governments, but by the international spirit of respect for self-governing norms that prohibit crimes against women. This is what we may call the humanization of human rights.

In: Crimes Against Women
Editor: David Wingeate Pike

ISBN 978-1-61470-813-1

Chapter 2

THE HUMAN RIGHTS DESIGN: A CRITIQUE OF 'UNIVERSALITY' IN A PATRIARCHAL WORLD

Ruchi Anand

> Violence against women and girls continues unabated in every continent, country and culture. It takes a devastating toll on women's lives, on their families, and on society as a whole. Most societies prohibit such violence — yet the reality is that too often, it is covered up or tacitly condoned.
>
> UN Secretary-General Ban Ki-Moon, 8 March 2007[1]

INTRODUCTION

The international human rights design can be traced to the embodiment of human rights provisions in the United Nations Charter and the Universal Declaration of Human Rights sixty years ago. The 60th anniversary of the Universal Declaration of Human Rights is an opportunity to remind ourselves that the task of securing universal human rights is not ended; it has merely begun. Human rights cannot be universal without human rights for women. Since human rights of women are still in jeopardy, we need to continue our efforts to move the human rights discourse for women from rhetoric to reality.

Women, the world over, still suffer disproportionately from stark violations of their human rights. Although the Universal Declaration of Human Rights (1948) enshrines principles of equality, justice, and fairness irrespective of distinction of any kind including sex, these are yet to be fully translated into reality. Several developments ever since 1948 mark the progress in the field of women's human rights. Among the international milestones[2]

---

[1] 'Violence against women : facts and figures,' United Nations Development Fund for Women (UNIFEM), 2007 : http://www.unifem.org/attachments/genderissues/violence_against_women/facts_figures_violence_against_women_2007.pdf.

[2] '30 years of change,' United Nations Development Fund for Women (UNIFEM), 2006 : http://www.unifem.org/campaigns/30th_anniversary/through_the_years.php.

are; the International Conference on Human Rights, Teheran (1968),[3] the First UN World Conference on Women, Mexico City (1975),[4] the United Nations International Decade for Women (1976-1985),[5] the Convention on the Elimination of All Forms of Discrimination Against Women (CEDAW, 1979),[6] the Second World Conference on Women, Copenhagen (1980),[7] the Third World Conference on Women, Nairobi (1985), the Safe Motherhood Conference, Nairobi (1987), the UN International Conference on Human Rights, Vienna (1993),[8] the United Nations Fourth World Conference on Women, Beijing (1995),[9] the Millennium Declaration and Millennium Development Goals (MDGs), New York (2000), [10] and the Commission on the Status of Women 10-Year Review and Appraisal, New York (2005).[11] At the 2005 meeting, it was established that although some improvements had been made towards protecting the human rights of women, the overall condition of women's human rights abuses are still deplorable.

Millions of women all over the world continue to live in conditions of abject deprivation of their fundamental human rights for no other reason than that they are women. The pandemic proportions of violence against women are shocking. Examples of these types of crimes against women are innumerable. Rape as a weapon of war is used by combatants in conflicts (e.g. Afghanistan, Democratic Republic of Congo, Iraq, Kosovo, Rwanda, Sierra Leone), women are physically beaten in their homes at astounding rates (e.g. Pakistan, Peru, Russia, South Africa, Uzbekistan), women are bought and sold, trafficked and forced into prostitution (e.g. Burma, Dominican Republic, Moldova, Nigeria, Thailand, Ukraine), women face government-sponsored discrimination that renders them unequal before law (e.g. Jordan, Kuwait, Morocco, Saudi Arabia), women and girls are forced to marry, women in prisons face sexual assault by their jailers, women's sexual freedoms are curtailed by strict familial and cultural sanctions including beating, stoning, acid attacks, death (e.g. N. Africa, W. Asia, S. Asia), women's access to their own bodies in terms of reproductive choices have been

[3] Affirmed that couples 'have a basic human right to determine freely and responsibly the number and spacing of their children.' State of world population, Introduction: Birth of a New Global Consensus, United Nations Population Fund (UNFPA), 2004: http://www.unfpa.org/swp/2004/english/ch1/page5.htm .

[4] The goals that marked this conference were gender equality, elimination of gender discrimination; full participation of women in development, contribution by women to world peace. Delegates to this conference called for an international covenant to protect women's rights.

[5] This was a result of the 1975 conference. UNIFEM was established as a result, as was the UN Development Fund for Women. The majority of UN member states agreed to incorporate a national 'plan' for women.

[6] The International Bill of Rights for Women is currently ratified by 90 percent of UN members. The Convention on the Elimination of All Forms of Discrimination against Women (CEDAW) has received 185 ratifications: http://www.un.org/womenwatch/daw/cedaw/states.htm.

[7] It emphasized three goals: equal access to education, employment opportunities, and health care.

[8] It declared boldly that women's rights are human rights, and condemned violence against women as human rights abuse. World Conference on Human Rights, Vienna, Austria, 14-25 June 1993: http://www.unhchr.ch/html/menu5/wchr.htm.

[9] The Platform for Action 12: critical areas of concern for achieving equality, development and peace by setting targets to be met. Fourth World Conference on Women, The Platform for Action, DPI Brochure, Beijing, China, 4-15 September 1995: www.un.org/womenwatch/daw/beijing/dpibrochure.html.

[10] Eight broad development goals to be achieved by 2015 were set: 1) Eradicate extreme poverty and hunger; 2) Achieve universal primary education; 3) Promote gender equality and empower women; 4) Reduce child mortality; 5) Improve maternal health; 6) Combat HIV/AIDS, malaria and other diseases; 7) Ensure environmental sustainability; and 8) Develop a global partnership for development: www.un.org/millenniumgoals.

[11] 'Review and Appraisal of the implementation of the Beijing Declaration and Platform for Action and the outcome of the twenty-third special session of the General Assembly,' 28 February–11 March 2005: www.un.org/womenwatch/daw/Review/english/49sess.htm.

constrained, millions of girls are declared "missing" owing to sex-selective abortions or infanticide.[12] These are merely the tip of the iceberg.

This global epidemic against women's human rights makes us question where international law fits within women's experience, and whom the system serves and protects. Apparently, women and girls suffer disproportionately from violence, be it in peace or war, at the hands of the state, the community and the family. The invisibility of the costs of gender-based violence coupled with the cultural acceptances of violence against women makes it pervasive and even systemic in nature. Section 2 highlights some feminist critiques of international law based on a historical, theoretical assessment of women's human rights up until the Universal Declaration of Human Rights. Section 3 emphasizes aspects of the CEDAW that seek to remedy some of the loopholes of the Universal Declaration of Human Rights, and the Concluding Section will re-ignite the debate surrounding the violations of women's human rights today, sixty years after the Universal Declaration of Human Rights was instated. It will question whether the international legal mechanism, without stringent enforcement capabilities, presents solutions to the violations against women's human rights. What alternatives exist other than trying to fight a losing battle against the institution of patriarchy?

THE UNIVERSAL DECLARATION OF HUMAN RIGHTS: A FEMINIST CRITIQUE

Over time, there has been a moral recognition of the need for the international codification and monitoring of women's human rights.[13] Women have been active participants in the struggle for human rights, i.e. in wartime resistance, anti-colonial struggles, anti-authoritarian struggles. However, since the concept and language of rights has its origins in the liberal political tradition that focuses primarily on the public activities of male citizens, women's issues had received limited recognition in major legal documents. These historic legal documents include the Virginia Declaration of Rights, which was the precursor to the American Declaration of Independence of 1776, the French Declaration (Déclaration des Droits de l'homme et du citoyen) of 1789, the American Declaration's Bill of Rights of 1789, and the Universal Declaration of Human Rights of 1948, all defining human rights claims.[14]

These and other such documents draw from John Locke's natural rights theory, which characterized individual prerogatives as 'political and civil freedom to be guaranteed, by the state.'[15] These declaratory documents impose some non-binding obligations on states to work towards safeguarding these claims. The problem with the Lockean natural rights theory is that it assumes that each individual is an autonomous being, disregarding the significance of social, political and economic contexts of each individual as also his or her race, class and

[12] Human Rights Watch: http://www.hrw.org/women/ ; 'Stop violence against women,' Amnesty International's campaign: http://www.amnesty.org/en/campaigns/stop-violence-against-women.

[13] Tim Dunne and Nicholas J. Wheeler, 'Introduction: Human rights and the fifty years' crisis,' in Tim Dunne and Nicholas J. Wheeler, eds., *Human Rights in Global Politics* (Cambridge: Cambridge University Press, 1999), pp. 1-28.

[14] Marguerite Guzman Bouvard, *Women Reshaping Human Rights: How Extraordinary Activists Are Changing the World* (SR Books, 1996).

[15] Ibid., p. ix.

gender. Another problem is that it 'locates all power within the state, which must either be constrained from interfering in individual lives or create legislation to ensure individual freedom.'[16] Although this theory provides the basis of contemporary law on rights, it does not recognize that each individual's relationship with his/her family, culture, religion, ethnicity, etc. may be a source of oppression too, jeopardizing the individual freedom guaranteed by the state.

By ignoring the possibility of violation of rights in the context of family and culture and religion, the Lockean theory establishes a dangerous dichotomy between the 'public' and 'private' spheres that defenders of human rights for women have treated sceptically.[17] Often, the perspective of the human rights of women (just like those of particular races, classes or ethnic groups) is constrained by the over-disciplined constructions[18] of these oppressed groups' states and cultures.[19]

A growing segment of the international women's rights movement argued for the need to make human rights abuses against women, especially the gender-specific ones that occur primarily in the private sphere, more visible.[20] Their main contention was that redress of the injustice, grievance and deprivation experienced by women solely because of their gender has not been adequately accomplished by the international law of human rights.

Human rights theorists attempted to analyse the reasons for the ineffective universal design of human rights in addressing specific violations of women's rights. Ken Booth, for example, argued that three tyrannies, namely the tyranny of the present tense, cultural essentialism and scientific objectivity, 'imprison human rights potentialities in a static, particularistic and regressive discourse, reproducing prevailing patterns of power rather than the reinvention of the politics of human possibility.'[21] For change towards a progressive human rights design that addresses specific women and minority rights, there is a need for the elimination of these three tyrannies.

The tyrannies of the present tense are the generalizations that arise out of a particular historical moment leading to constrained political imagination. This kind of tyranny is communitarian in nature and focuses on the dominant ideology of the time – patriarchy for instance.

> Patriarchy defined by Gerda Lerner, is as follows:
>
> Patriarchy in its wider definition means the manifestation and institutionalization of male dominance over women and children in the family and the extension of male dominance over women in society in general. It implies that men hold power in all-important institutions of

---

[16] Ibid., p. x.

[17] The public-private dichotomy is discussed in greater detail in another section of this chapter.

[18] For a detailed account on the social construction of the 'other,' see: Evelyn Hammonds, 'Race, Sex and Aids: The Construction of "Other"' in: Margaret L. Andersen, ed., *Race, Class, and Gender: An Anthology* (Belmont, CA: Wadsworth, 1995). See also: Lack Donnelly, 'The Social Construction of International Human Rights' in: Tim Dunne and Nicholas J. Wheeler, eds., *Human Rights in Global Politics* (Cambridge University Press, 1999).

[19] K. Booth, 'Three tyrannies', in Tim Dunne and Nicholas J. Wheeler, eds., *Human Rights in Global Politics* (Cambridge: Cambridge University Press, 1999), p. 61.

[20] For a detailed account on the difference between gender and sexism, see: Johnnetts B. Cole, 'Commonalities and Differences,' in: Margaret L. Andersen, ed., *Race, Class, and Gender: An* Anthology (Belmont, CA: Wadsworth, 1995).

[21] K. Booth, 'Three tyrannies,' in: Tim Dunne and Nicholas J. Wheeler, eds., *Human Rights in Global Politics* (Cambridge: Cambridge University Press, 1999), p. 32.

society and that women are deprived of access to such power. It does not imply that women are either totally powerless or totally deprived of rights, influence and resources.[22]

Patriarchy is an institutionalised system of male dominance that gradually creates a structuralized network through which women are the major victims. One of the controlling devices of patriarchy is the public-private dichotomy.

The distinction between public/private lives in international law is one of the principal theoretical barriers to adequately addressing women's human rights.[23] The public-private dichotomy at the level of the state (women: private; men: public) and international law (domestic law: private; international law: public) distinction leaves women's lives outside the scope of legal redress.[24] This makes women's lives stand outside the scope of international law, and also outside the scope of national law. As a result, 'women's lives are treated as being within a doubly private sphere, far from the concerns of the international legal order.'[25]

There are, therefore, two levels of the public-private dichotomy, which helps us to explain why we argue that women are marginalized from mainstream international legal discourse. The one level of the public-private dichotomy is based on gender. This dichotomy can, to a large extent, explain the dynamics behind male dominance in the areas of power and authority, i.e. the public arena. The domain of law, economics, politics, the workplace, and intellectual life are regarded as the 'public' realm and as the natural province of men. The home and children are stereotypically viewed as the domain of women. What is problematic is the asymmetrical value that is given to the public (male domain) as compared to the private (female domain). The naturalness of this dichotomy is based on some deeply embedded beliefs about gender and gender roles in society the world over. The public-private dichotomy confers primacy on the male world and undermines the role of women in spheres traditionally constructed as 'public.' Celina Romany contends, 'the public/private distinction continues to be a manifestation of legal privilege that dispenses licenses along gender lines.'[26]

Donna Sullivan expressed it thus:

> These three factors – the state centred nature of international law, the dominance of civil and political rights discourse, and deference to the institution of the family – account for much of the emphasis placed on direct violations of civil and political rights by the state and corresponding neglect of gender-specific abuses in private life. The challenge is not to shift the focus away from gross violations of civil and political rights by the state but, first, to broaden the normative framework to include the abuses suffered by women that do not fit this paradigm because they occur at the hands of 'private' individuals; and then to develop

[22] Gerda Lerner, *The Creation of Patriarchy* (New York: Oxford University Press, 1986), p. 239.

[23] Donna Sullivan, 'The Public/Private Distinction in International Human Rights Law,' in: Julie Peters and Andrea Wolper, eds., *Women's Rights Human Rights: International Feminist Perspective* (London: Routledge, 1995), p. 128.

[24] The public-private dichotomy is not merely a gendered issue but is closely inter-twined with issues of race and class, racial and ethnic groups and between urban and rural environments. According to Sullivan, 'the shared feature of the public/private distinction in different contexts is the attribution of lesser economic, social or political value to the activities of women within what is defined as the private sphere.' Donna Sullivan, 'The Public/Private Distinction in International Human Rights Law,' in: Julie Peters and Andrea Wolper, eds., *Women's Rights Human Rights: International Feminist Perspective* (London: Routledge, 1995), p. 128.

[25] Hilary Charlesworth and Christine Chinkin, 'The Gender of *Jus Cogens,' Human Rights Quarterly*, Vol. 15, February 1993, p. 74.

[26] Celina Romany in: Rebecca J. Cook, ed., *Human Rights of Women: National and International Perspectives* (Philadelphia: University of Pennsylvania Press, 1994), p. 90.

effective international monitoring and implementation mechanisms in this area. The distinction in international law is one of the principal theoretical barriers to this effort.[27]

Rights for women must be situated in 'the experiences of women rather than men,' challenging the patriarchal structures that ignore many social practices which fall in the domain of the 'private,' i.e. sexuality, reproduction, sex-based violence, etc.[28]

The purpose of the state's laws and practices must serve feminist goals in order to achieve human rights for women. By this standard, those states would be called feminist that, through their laws, empower women to resist sex-based dominance and to exert their claims against male power in all spheres, both public and private.[29]

The tyrannies of cultural essentialism come from perpetuated values, structures and traditions that propagate the conservative power interests emerging from religion or culture or tradition, marginalizing many people and interests at the global and local levels. For instance, traditionalist practices for the most part are based on masculine values, often hostile to women. Yoko Ono refers to women as 'the niggers of the world,' owing to the marginalization they have faced irrespective of their race, class, sexual orientation, culture and nationality.[30] Napoleon's law, probably due to the history of patriarchal subordination, actually classified women as 'lifelong, irresponsible minors.'[31] Women were perceived as, and still are in many parts of the world, the property of their husbands (and before marriage, of their fathers and brothers). Men, particularly husbands, thus considered themselves in charge of the legal and social responsibilities of their wife's actions. As such, women were required to obey their husbands (and other men in the family), even to the extent of self-deprivation and denial. Their place was considered to be at home and not in the 'public.'[32] These trends are still visible in many cultures.

The tyrannies of scientific objectivity, as the third impediment to progressive politics, imply that science, under the garb of being value-free, objective and apolitical, is a means to perpetuate the status quo. Booth argues that any idea that attempts at universality, i.e. science, has the potential of being not only totalitarian and dangerous but also utopian. Universality, be it of human rights or any other issue, is a flawed assumption because there are no universal values.[33]

For example, the Universal Declaration of Human Rights (1948) states that: 'No one shall be subject to torture or to cruel, inhuman or degrading treatment or punishment.' One can assume that this covers violence against women, i.e. rape, sexual terrorism and domestic violence, but the gender-neutral vocabulary puts the onus on the women victims of gender-

---

27 Donna Sullivan, 'The Public/Private Distinction in International Human Rights Law,' in: Julie Peters and Andrea Wolper, eds., *Women's Rights Human Rights: International Feminist Perspective* (London: Routledge, 1995), p. 128.

28 Dorothy McBride Stetson, 'Human Rights for Women: International Compliance with a Feminist Standard,' *Women and Politics,* Vol. 15, No. 3, 1995, pp. 71-95.

29 Ibid., p. 73.

30 K. Booth, 'Three tyrannies,' in: Tim Dunne and Nicholas J. Wheeler, eds., *Human Rights in Global Politics* (Cambridge: Cambridge University Press, 1999), p. 39.

31 Celina Romany, in: Rebecca J. Cook, ed., *Human Rights of Women: National and International Perspectives* (Philadelphia: University of Pennsylvania Press, 1994), p. 95.

32 Ibid.

33 K. Booth, 'Three tyrannies,' in: Tim Dunne and Nicholas J. Wheeler, eds., *Human Rights in Global Politics* (Cambridge: Cambridge University Press, 1999), pp. 31-70.

based inhumane treatment to 'fit' into the description. The egalitarian premise of the Universal Declaration can in fact be detrimental to the protection of women's human rights. The human rights of women may not be 'universal' after all, since women's human rights often have culture-specific definitions of what constitutes human rights of women vis-à-vis their status in society. Commonalities across the globe are striking, since the universal law is that of patriarchy, but the culture-specific social standing of women may differ widely across the world.

Katrina Tomasevski contends that gender-neutrality in law-making can have discriminatory effects on women because the equal treatment of people in unequal situations 'perpetuates rather than challenges discrimination.' Therefore, the eradication of gender discrimination necessitates 'a recognition of the discriminatory heritage and action to remedy its effects and to establish safeguards against its perpetuation.'[34] Rebecca Cook reiterates Tomasevski's argument by asserting:

> The model (for the protection of human rights) uses a male standard of equality and renders women copies of their male counterparts. Thus women are forced to argue either that they are the same as men and should be treated the same, that they are different but should be treated as they were the same, or that they are different and should be accorded special treatment. The model does not allow for questioning the ways in which laws, cultures, or religious traditions have constructed and maintained the disadvantage of women, or to the extent to which the institutions are male-defined and built on male conceptions of challenges and harms.[35]

The 'sameness of treatment' approach puts women at a disadvantage and reduces their claims of specific gender-related crimes to 'invisibility' when the urgent need is 'visibility.' According to Kathleen Mahoney, 'By structuring equality around the male comparator, the assumption is made that equality exists and that from time to time, individuals will be discriminated against. The persistent disadvantage women suffer across the board because of societal biases is obscured.'[36] The question then becomes 'how can international human rights law support and deliver substantive equality?'

Hilary Charlesworth, for her part, contends that 'the search for universal, abstract, hierarchical standards is often associated with masculine modes of thinking. Women are relegated to the periphery of communal values.'[37]

Language is another issue that lends to gender evaluation of the Universal Declaration of Human Rights since it is not always objective nor value free. Edward Broadbent has pointed out:

> The language of human rights is powerful. It carries great moral authority, and is having an increasing impact on the peoples and the states of the world. If it is, however, to aspire to

---

[34] Katrina Tomasavski, *Women and Human Rights* (London: Atlantic Highlands; NJ: Zed Books, Women and World Development Series, 1993), p. xiii.

[35] Rebecca J. Cook, 'Women's International Human Rights Law: The Way Forward,' *Human Rights Quarterly*, Vol. 15, May 1993, p. 239.

[36] Kathleen E. Mahoney in: Rebecca J. Cook, ed., *Human Rights of Women: National and International Perspectives* (Philadelphia: University of Pennsylvania Press, 1994), p. 239.

[37] Hilary Charlesworth and Christine Chinkin, 'The Gender of Jus Cogens,' *Human Rights Quarterly*, Vol. 15, February 1993, p. 67.

> true universality, it must deal not only with different expectations and realities of North and South, East and West, but also different experiences of women and men. We must make the language of human rights relevant to women's lives.[38]

The language of universal human rights that is used is specifically geared towards 'men' and is not 'universal.' Although the documentation of human rights, as it exists today, does spell out various civil and political rights, it does not specifically address the social and economic rights of women. These rights need protection in a patriarchal world that renders women subject to certain kinds of restrictions solely as a consequence of their gender.

The Universal Declaration of Human Rights, for instance, lays down certain fundamental human rights, subject only to restrictions set forth by certain fundamental duties.[39] Some of the rights that the Declaration enlists are freedom, equality, dignity, life, liberty, property, marriage, movement, asylum, free choice of employment, peaceful assembly, equal pay, rest and leisure, adequate standard of living, protection from servitude, slavery, torture, cruelty, and arbitrary arrest. Article 1 of the Human Rights Declaration reads, 'All human beings are born free and equal in dignity and rights. They are endowed with reason and conscience and should act towards one another in a spirit of brotherhood.'[40] The use of the term 'brotherhood' in Article 1 is not very surprising, considering that it is followed by a Preamble which speaks of the 'conscience of mankind' being outraged by human rights violations. It reads, 'It is essential, if man is not to be compelled to have recourse, as a last resort, to rebellion against tyranny and oppression, that human rights should be protected by the rule of law.'[41]

At the level of the State, each country has some norms governing the protection or violations of human rights. For example, the United States of America has the American Declaration of the Rights and Duties of Man.[42] Ironically, this document is applicable to both men and women of the United States of America. The preamble of this document reads:

> All men are born free and equal, in dignity and in rights, and being endowed by nature with reason and conscience, they should conduct themselves as brothers one to another... Rights and duties are interrelated in every social and political activity of man... And since moral conduct constitutes the noblest flowering of culture, it is the duty of every man to hold it in high respect.[43]

Such male-centred language in legal documentation of the Universal Declaration of Human Rights is not a mere folly of documentation and gender-neutrality but an instrument of sex-discrimination, which has its roots in the male-dominated legal structures at the national and international levels. Women have not had the opportunity to enjoy the rights and liberties on the same footing as men, as they are entitled to, supposedly, by virtue of their being 'human.' In the field of human rights, which is simply a reflection of the patriarchal

---

[38] Edward Broadbent, 'Getting Rid of Male Bias,' in: Joanna Kerr, ed., *Ours by Right: Women's Rights as Human Rights* (London; Ottawa; Atlantic Island, New Jersey: North-South Institute Zed Books, 1993): p. 12.

[39] Burns H. Weston, Richard A. Falk, Anthony A. D'Amato, *Basic Documents in International Law and World Order* (Salt Lake City: West, 2nd ed., 1990), p. 298.

[40] Ibid.

[41] Ibid.

[42] Ibid., p. 293.

[43] Ibid.

traditions that govern states, societies and families, being 'human and man' is not quite the same as being 'human and woman.' This is apparent in the differential recognition, treatment, and recourse that men and women get in response to their claims of violations of their rights. According to Charlotte Bunch, 'the narrow definition of human rights, recognized by many in the West as solely a matter of state violation of civil and political liberties, impedes consideration of 'women's rights.'[44] Corrective language, as opposed to gender-neutral language, allows for woman-centred solutions, without reference to male action.[45]

STEPS IN THE RIGHT DIRECTION: CEDAW

The Convention on the Elimination of All Forms of Discrimination against Women (CEDAW) departs from the general human rights instruments that address 'sex-based discrimination' in neutral terms, by naming women as the group disadvantaged from sex-based discrimination. Instead it foregrounds the social and cultural underpinnings of such discrimination, thereby extending the application of human rights to the private sphere for women, and more importantly, highlighting the connection of the public sphere with the private sphere. The inequality of women within the family, the workplace and in public life derives its ideological basis from the social construction of women's capabilities and roles. The journey from the neutral to the specific and from the public to the private was not easy, but a slow and strongly contested struggle.[46]

The CEDAW attempted to remedy the shortcomings of the human rights design of its predecessors. Gender equality is clearly articulated as a goal in the context of sex-based discrimination. The State obligations imposed by the CEDAW are those that attempt to eliminate the many different forms of gender-based discrimination that women face.

The CEDAW adopts the 'substantive equality' or 'equality of results' model implying that the CEDAW goes beyond appraising equality in formal and legalistic terms and examines their impact on the rights and lives of women. Under the CEDAW, the State must demonstrate that its policies allow women to experience equality instead of simply demonstrating that there are no laws that discriminate against women. Under the CEDAW, States are not only responsible to show that they are fostering gender equality but are also responsible for discrimination perpetrated by individuals and organizations. The CEDAW clearly appreciates that efforts to achieve gender equality have to address changes at the 'private' sphere of politics—in culture, the family, and interpersonal relations.[47]

The CEDAW articles define specific forms of discrimination, explain the nature and scope of States' obligations, and make recommendations to State parties for implementing their obligations under the treaty. The CEDAW discusses issues such as trafficking and prostitution, public and political life, international affairs, nationality, education, employment,

---

[44] Charlotte Bunch, 'Women's Rights as Human Rights: Toward a Re-Vision of Human Rights,' *Human Rights Quarterly*, 12(4), 1990, p. 488.

[45] Gender bias is not the only problem associated with a universally drawn out Human Rights convention. Similar problematics arise for people situated in different races, classes, cultures and ethnicities.

[46] 'CEDAW: Restoring Rights to Women,' UNIFEM, South Asia Regional Office (New Delhi: Partners for Law in Development, 2004), p. 17. http://www.unifem.org.in/cedaw.html.

[47] Lee Waldorf, Christine Arab and Menaka Guruswamy, 'CEDAW and the Human Rights Based Approach to Programming: a UNIFEM Guide' (May 2007): www.unifem.org/attachments/products/CEDAW_HRBA_guide_pt1_eng.pdf.

health care, economic and social life, rural women, equality before the law, and equality in marriage and family life.[48]

The CEDAW is controlled by a treaty body composed of 23 gender-equality specialists elected by State-parties. However, once its members are elected, they operate independently of their countries. Regionally representative, the Committee Members at present are from Algeria, Bangladesh, Brazil, China, Croatia, Cuba, Egypt, France, Germany, Ghana, Israel, Italy, Jamaica, Japan, the Republic of Korea, Malaysia, Mauritius, the Netherlands, Portugal, Singapore, Slovenia, the Republic of South Africa, and Thailand. [49]

Quite simply the CEDAW acknowledges that gender equality is a human right. Once gender equality is understood as a human right it needs no additional justification, and the legitimacy of work to advance gender equality does not depend on proving its usefulness for other purposes, such as those of development, or economic growth.[50]

Other gender-related highlights of the CEDAW are:

- The principle of indivisibility on human rights, i.e. there is no hierarchy among human rights;
- The acceptance of the equal status of all human rights;
- The acknowledgement of the interdependent and interrelated nature of human rights;
- The acceptance that equality and non-discrimination are two sides of the same coin;
- The political empowerment of women through participation and inclusion;
- The integration of women's human rights into national constitutions.

The CEDAW explicitly states that the responsibilities to protect human rights of women extend to private life as well as public life. In this sense, it tries to overcome the public-private dichotomy that had distanced women's human rights violations (in the 'private' sphere) from visibility. [51]

CONCLUSION

The CEDAW (1979) represented only a small step towards the humongous goal of establishing and securing women's rights as human rights. The Vienna Declaration and the Programme for Action (1993) was the first of its kind to accept women's human rights as 'inalienable, integral and indivisible part of universal human rights' that 'should form an integral part of the United Nations human rights activities.'[52] Each step in the struggle for achieving the task of accepting and implementing women's rights as human rights has been difficult, cumbersome and full of obstacles. Why is it such a difficult task to establish women as human beings? Why is it so difficult for women to be treated as equal?

---

[48] Ibid., pp. 8-9.
[49] Ibid.
[50] Ibid., p. 13.
[51] Ibid., pp. 28-37.
[52] Vienna Declaration and Programme of Action, United Nations World Conference on Human Rights, (12 July 1993): http://www.unhchr.ch/huridocda/huridoca.nsf/(Symbol)/A.CONF.157.23.En?OpenDocument.

Why is it so difficult for women's concerns to be heard? A part of the answer may lie in concerns over implementing the standards already laid down by national and international laws. The more formidable task is to fight the battle against patriarchy, mindful of the wording of Audre Lorde: 'The master's tools will never dismantle the master's house.'[53]

[53] Audre Lorde, *Sister Outsider: Essays and Speeches* (Berkeley: The Crossing Press, 1984).

In: Crimes Against Women
Editor: David Wingeate Pike
ISBN 978-1-61470-813-1

Chapter 3

Ethical and Meta-Ethical Approaches to Violence Against Women

Angèle Kremer-Marietti

Meta-ethics or Philosophical Ethics

The central question of our time is ethics. Unlike morals, which carry an implicit reference to their eternity and to the supposed universal understanding of good and evil, while allowing for different and variable moralities, the question of ethics opens with a reflection on human behaviour. Ethics is a noetic discipline inseparable from a method and it implies a philosophy. In examining the current state of our philosophical, social, historical, psychoanalytical, and anthropological knowledge, we see that knowledge now argues across the broadest human field.

Meta-ethics, a philosophical discipline inaugurated by George Edward Moore (1873-1958),[1] relates to the theory and practice of morals and is inseparable from philosophical method and scientific knowledge, not only human and social but natural. Moore raised two initial questions: 'What kind of things deserve by themselves to exist?' and 'What kind of action do we have to pursue?' To these two questions of current morals, Moore added a third of some distance from the other two: 'To what extent can any ethical proposal be proven or refuted; corroborated or put in doubt?' This question is more difficult than the first two, because it relates to ultimate reason. Moore thus insists on the need for finding either the 'causal truths' or evidence sufficiently fundamental to support the first two questions. One can speak of meta-ethics, which is to be distinguished from normative ethics and applied ethics.

[1] G.E. Moore, *Principia Ethica* (Cambridge: Cambridge University Press, 1903). See also Françoise Armengaud, *G. E. Moore et la genèse de la philosophie analytique* (Paris: Méridiens Klincksieck, 1985).

NATIONAL AND INTERNATIONAL PENAL ETHICS AND THE QUESTION OF FEMALE GENDER[2]

Male and female genders cannot be thought of separately, one without the other; it is a system in two interdependent terms. Beliefs about psycho-sexual differences or ideals of femininity and masculinity, and attitudes towards sex roles in various institutional sectors have all had their influences on the question of female gender.[3]

Ruwen Ogien[4] denounces a kind of 'moral panic' ambience and affirms that the true rational debate can occur once incantations and stereotypes are denounced. Like Socrates we must rediscover the citizen and republican values which are ours. And the essential question appears to be: does ethical speech have a proper argumentation, a particular logic and methodology? These are questions which meta-ethics can answer and enable us to draw up a typology of our positions. In theory, penal ethics examines every aspect of criminal law, balancing the right to punish against the alternative of an imposed rehabilitation and constraint.

The matter is well illustrated in the case of Spain. Ever since 1978 the Spanish Constitution has affirmed, in its Article 15, the universal right to life: 'Every individual has the right to life and physical and mental well-being.'[5] Following the First World Congress against the Death Penalty, held in Strasbourg in January 2001, it can be said that international penal ethics has much evolved.

The struggle against the death penalty started in the 18th century under the impulse of visionary thinkers such as Olympe de Gouges (1748-1793),[6] who was one of the first to claim justice for women, and Cesare Beccaria (1738-1794), who can be regarded as the founder of penal ethics within a law-abiding State. Beccaria denounced the use of torture as a means of extracting evidence and proposed the abolition of capital punishment for crimes under common law. It was in memory of Beccaria that the French statesman Robert Badinter, who has republished his work,[7] introduced into the French Assembly in autumn 1981 the bill that abolished the death penalty whatever the crime. As Badinter remarked: 'As long as we continue to shoot, poison, behead, hang, torture or stone to death, there will be no respite in this world for all those who believe that life, for all humanity, is the supreme value, and that there cannot be such a thing as justice that kills.'

From the criminal in question, let us pass to the victim in question. The masculine/feminine relationship would be the counterpart of a more general relationship: that between persecutor and persecuted. This relationship presupposes a distinction, even a

---

[2] The concept of gender in France is of recent importation. It has an unquestionable advantage: it is dynamic, contrary to the French concept of 'sex': gender has a moving history, while sex refers to a functional static, with a biological base. Over a long period, a dissymmetrical system existed in which the 'male sex' was the single reference to the universal human.

[3] 'Consistency of Female Gender Attitudes: A Research Note by Mirra Komarovsky, Ellen R. Mayer,' in: *Social Forces*, Vol. 62, No. 4 (June 1984), pp. 1020-1025.

[4] Ruwen Ogien, *La Panique morale* (Paris: Grasset, 2004).

[5] Article 15 of the Spanish Constitution, accepted by referendum, on 6 December 1978.

[6] Sophie Mousse, *Olympe de Gouges et les droits de la femme* (Paris : Éditions du Félin, Les Marginaux, 2003). Mousse closes with a "Postambule": « *Femme, réveille-toi ; le tocsin de la raison se fait entendre dans tout l'univers, reconnais tes droits.* (...) *L'homme esclave a multiplié ses forces, a eu besoin de recourir aux tiennes pour briser ses fers. Devenu libre, il est devenu injuste envers sa compagne. Ô femmes ! Femmes, quand cesserez-vous d'être aveugles ?* »

division, between gender and 'conditions', or more precisely 'the feminine condition' of which feminists no longer want to speak. Genevieve Fraisse[7] writes: 'The term "female condition" was used to extol the eternal feminine. The eternal feminine anchored itself in the supposedly specific nature of women. The concept of the "female condition" was based upon the same model as that of 'social condition' and 'human condition'. On this question Hannah Arendt rightly commented that the expression 'human condition' is preferable to the term 'human nature'. 'Human nature' presupposes a fixity which the 'human condition' does not presuppose. If the concept of 'female condition' may be negative because of its fixity, indeed, the concept of 'human condition' is positive: it implies the possibility of occasional changes in the human person, directly related to human activity and, through this activity, the possibility of improvements in humanity.

If now we turn to Hume, in Book III ('Of Morals') of his *Treatise of Human Nature* (1739-40), he indicated very clearly that modesty and chastity were indeed womanly virtues: he made the precise point that these were the ineluctable virtues of the 'fair sex'. Hume thus extended a kind of moral chador on women, whatever their age. But would such presupposed opinions, concerning a 'nature' desired by men as proper to women, cover, directly or indirectly, ill-behaviour or ill-treatment? Scientists now think that some relationship exists between human intelligence and sexual antagonism,[8] because the rapid increase in our brain size was evolutionarily marked by the development of language. With a more sophisticated means of communication, doors were opened to a refined and precise system of various signals and responses. These systems can be super-stimulated through emotional or instinctual reactions, which can change the receptive nature in favour of the gene-set responsible for compensating for the over-stimulation. What was once thought overwhelming would become the norm.

Does this scientific exposition also explain the observations of the anthropologists? What, in the eyes of the anthropologists, is the nature of female gender? Thanks to Maurice Godelier,[9] we discover that the social difference and opposition between the two genders in every day life is very well traced. Godelier depicts the Baruyas in New Guinea as a classless patrilineal society, without a particular government and under strong male domination. Women in that society are kept away from weapons, money and religious power. Indeed, it is a very ancient society! But sadly what appears there to the ethnological eye can be tacitly found nowadays in the most recent biological research.

Such research into the difference between the two sexes became obsessed with the subject of 'how to make males?'[10] It was generally considered that the female sex was the sex by default and that to 'make males' one needed something in addition. It was further believed that sexual differentiation came from the male chromosome Y, in which case there was no need to seek the female entity since there was no such entity to seek. But recently, precisely

[7] Geneviève Fraisse, « En finir avec la condition féminine », Conférence de l'AFFDU (Association Française des Femmes Diplômées des Universités), 5 February 2005 : Masculin/Féminin : Mythes scientifiques et Idéologies.

[8] Gregory Campbell, 'Male vs. Female: Gender Conflict as an Evolutionary Force,' *Journal of Young Investigators*, 3 May 2003.

[9] « Mythe fondateur de la domination masculine dans la vie et les sciences : une perspective anthropologique », in *Féminin Masculin* sous la direction de Catherine Vidal, avec Geneviève Fraisse, Maurice Godelier, Pascal Picq, Joëlle Wiels, Évelyne Peyre, Catherine Marry, Gaïd Le Maner-Idrissi (Paris : Syndicat National de l'Édition, 2006).

[10] Joëlle Wiels et Evelyne Peyre, « Le sexe: un continuum ? », in *Féminin Masculin*, op. cit.

in 1994, by studying a certain kind of fetal malformation, Neil Brockdorff explained that there is a gene in the X chromosome which also determines the sex:[11] a cell can render inactive an entire chromosome, and reduce to silence the genetic information which it carries. Such is the function, in the human female and other female mammals, of one of two X chromosomes of each cell.

EXAMINING THE DESIRE TO IMPOSE VALUES

Meta-ethics of the masculine/feminine relation must be recognized as the basis of current penal ethics which punish the crime when the crime is proven. This meta-ethics demands an end not only to discrimination against women but also to discrimination against men whenever men depend upon the same implicit 'principle': for example, in crimes perpetrated against homosexuals. Whether it is a question of women or men, what is unfortunately found is a cultural basis resting on the idea that human generation consists of a defect of equality of statute and treatment between the two specific categories of gender.

A change of mentality, through the promulgation of anti-sexist laws, needs to be adopted and applied. Such laws should be the equivalent of anti-racist laws, laws that reinforce the punishment in accordance with additional crimes such as aggravated assault and rape. Laws should prohibit any form of sexual mutilation on minors such as excision or infibulation. It is a matter of enhancing penal ethics by taking into account the aggravating circumstances of sexist nature in any assault against a person, whether it be murder, violence, sequestration, or 'crimes of honour', for a supposed non respect of a moral, religious or social obligation, or for a limited right to sexuality (cases of 'loss of virginity', relation out of marriage, relation between people of different religious confession...).

There is also the question of recognizing the right of any woman to gynaecological examinations, even practised by men, as with abortion even for foreign women without regular papers. We must also introduce the concept of non-consent into the law defining rape of an adult, by removing the concept of penetration that seeks unjustifiably to establish a difference between rape and sexual crimes. Finally, we must rescind, in treating victims of rape, the 'investigation of morality' clause that denies a person whose morality is deemed 'doubtful' the right to be considered the victim of a crime, when in fact the assault falls under the rubric of non-consent. Equally deserving of prohibition are forced marriages, together with the effective punishment of those who organized such unions.

One might believe that the meta-ethics that inspires current penal ethics is formulated in extenso in the already promulgated laws which apply. However, this is not altogether true, since we also find, in those meta-ethics that are specific to criminal law, the product of ambient mentalities and inarticulate opinions concerning the feminine/masculine difference. Parts of the meta-ethics related to sexuality are indeed enshrined in legal doctrines, reflected

---

[11] Brockdorff N., « L'inactivation du chromosome X », in *Recherche*, 1994, n° 262, pp. 136-141, Société d'éditions scientifiques, Paris, 1970. Also Aersens J ; Chaffenet M. ; Baens M ; Matthijs G. ; Van Den Berghe H. ; Cassiman J.-J. ; Marynen P. ; "Regional assignment of seven Loci to 12p13.2-pter by PCR analysis of somatic cell hybrids containing the der (12) or the der (X) chromosome from a mesothelioma showing t(X;12)(q22;p13)" in *Genomics*, 1994, vol. 20, n° 1, pp. 119-121 (San Diego: Academic Press, 1987). Also: Jamel Chelly, « Retards mentaux liés au chromosome X », *Médecine sciences*, 2000, vol. 16, n° 3, pp. 363-372.

as they are in the entirety of legal statements proffered by judges, professors of law, lawyers and researchers, whether in statements in favour of the status quo or, on the other side, in statements directed towards a change.

With regard to the female person in particular, normative ethics and penal ethics generally depend upon an unconscious meta-ethics, compounded of ignorance, prejudice, and even criminal tradition. Whereas human and civil rights, which also concern women, are in political life a permanent reminder of our dignity as citizens, it is of interest to note in legal speech an illogical disconnect between the legal person and the human being. On the one hand, the concept of continuity of the legal person is supported and maintained. On the other hand, we note the absence in juridical argument of what binds the legal person to the living reality of a human being, titular of rights as well as duties, the right to remain alive and not to undergo aggression either of the body or the mind.

In: Crimes Against Women
Editor: David Wingeate Pike

ISBN 978-1-61470-813-1

Chapter 4

THE ROME STATUTE OF THE INTERNATIONAL CRIMINAL COURT (2002): THE IMPACT OF THE COALITION OF WOMEN'S GROUPS

Cenap Çakmak

INTRODUCTION

The International Criminal Court (ICC) created under the Rome Statute[1] is now up and running. Cited as a small revolution,[2] the creation of the ICC will probably have a notable impact on the fate of international law as well as the conduct of world affairs.[3] Most scholars recognize the unprecedented role that global civil society actors played during the adoption of the Rome Statute establishing the Court.[4]

In an attempt to assure the best outcome out of the process, civil society actors organized themselves in the form of a coalition. On 10 February 1995, the NGO Coalition for an International Criminal Court (CICC) was founded as a 'broad-based network of NGOs and international law experts.' It was constructed loosely, without any formal decision-making structure. In addition, at the beginning, the founders decided not to formulate a common position except to 'advocate for the creation of an effective, just and independent International Criminal Court.'[5] Acting in accordance with this mandate, the Coalition

---

1 Rome Statute of the International Criminal Court, U.N. Doc. A/CONF.183/9. (Rome Statute).

2 Marlies Glasius, 'Expertise in the Cause of Justice: Global Civil Society Influence on the Statute for an International Court,' in Marlies Glasius, Mary Kaldor ve Helmut Anheier (eds.), *Global Civil Society 2002* (Oxford: Oxford University Press, 2002), p. 137.

3 For the ICC's role in world politics, see, Cenap Çakmak, 'The International Criminal Court in World Politics,' *International Journal on World Peace,* Vol. 23, Issue 1, 2006, pp. 3-40.

4 For instance, international lawyer Steven R. Ratner notes, 'a lot of progress has been due to very, very effective work by both transnational and domestic NGOs.' 'The International Criminal Court and the Limits of Global Judicialization,' *Texas International Law Journal,* Vol. 38, Issue 3, 2003, p. 447.

5 Marlies Glasius, "Expertise in the Cause of Justice: Global Civil Society Influence on the Statute for an International Court," p. 146.

overwhelmingly affected the course of negotiations at the Rome Conference and contributed a great deal to the adoption of a progressive final text.[6]

A complex entity with hundreds of NGO members, the CICC represented the least common denominator: the promotion of a fair, independent and strong ICC. For this reason, its agenda did not adequately address gender issues; this observation led the women's groups to create a separate coalition (the Women's Caucus for Gender Justice, now Women's Initiative for Gender Justice)[7] to ensure the adoption of a women-friendly text at the conference. However, all Women's Coalition members remained also as members in the CICC.

WOMEN'S CAUCUS AT THE ROME CONFERENCE

Arguably, the most visible and indisputable imprint of global civil society upon the ICC is reflected in the gender-friendly provisions as outlined in the final Statute. The contribution of women's groups to the whole process through which the ICC was created was so substantial and decisive that it would be fair to say that, without this contribution, the Court would have looked far different from the one now standing.

In recognition of the large-scale crimes committed against women especially during wartime, women's rights advocates insisted throughout the conference on the inclusion of a gender language in the final statute.[8] Another primary motive behind the extensive involvement of women's groups in the ICC process was the observation that women issues in general have been largely ignored in the creation of international law. During the early stages of the ICC process, the overall tendency was to create a court to be framed in accordance with existing international laws, which had little reference to women issues.[9] Women's groups that have long been dedicated to the promotion of women's rights saw the revived idea of a permanent Court as an opportunity to achieve their goals.[10]

To this end, they first decided to unite individual organizations and form an umbrella entity.[11] In February 1997, leading women's groups formed the Women's Caucus for Gender Justice to improve the original 1994 International Law Commission (ILC) draft,[12] which paid

---

6 For detailed analyses of the Coalition's contributions at the Conference see, amongst others, the following: Marlies Glasius, *The International Criminal Court: A Global Civil Society Achievement* (London and New York: Routledge, 2006); William R. Pace and Mark Thieroff, "Participation of Non-Governmental Organizations," in Roy S. Lee (ed.), *The International Criminal Court: The Making of the Rome Statute, Issues, Negotiations, Results* (The Hague: Kluwer Law International, 1999), pp. 391-398; William R. Pace and Jennifer Schense, "The NGO Coalition's Contribution to the Making of the Elements of Crime and Rules of Procedure," in Roy S. Lee (ed.), *The International Criminal Court: Elements of Crimes and Rules of Procedure and Evidence* (Ardsley, NY: Transnational Publishers, 2001), pp. 705-734.

7 For more information, see, http://www.iccwomen.com.

8 Rhonda Copelon, 'Gender Crimes as War Crimes: Integrating Crimes against Women into International Criminal Law,' *McGill Law Journal*, Vol. 46, Issue 1, 2000, p. 234.

9 Rana Lehr-Lehnardt, 'One Small Step for Women: Female-Friendly Provisions in the Rome Statute of the International Criminal Court,' *Brigham Young University Journal of Public Law*, Vol. 16, Issue 2, 2002, p. 339.

10 Ibid., p. 319.

11 Ibid., p. 319.

12 Draft Statute for an International Criminal Court, Report of the International Law Commission, U.N. GAOR, 49th Sess., Supp. No. 10, at 43, U.N. Doc. A/49/10 (1994) (The 1994 ILC Draft Statute).

almost no attention to gender issues.[13] Because they observed that gender concerns were not adequately promoted by members of the existing Coalition, the groups advocating women's rights decided to create this separate coalition.[14] However, it should be noted that the Caucus was at the same time a member in the Steering Committee of the CICC. Within a very short time, the number of the member organizations represented in the Caucus dramatically increased, making this 'sub-coalition' a significant actor in the negotiations. Initially, its established goals were mostly focused on 'the definition of gender, a reference to gender in a general non-discrimination clause, a gender dimension to the definition of slavery, the inclusion of persecution on the basis of gender as a component of crimes against humanity, and protection for and gender-sensitive treatment of victims and witnesses.'[15]

With the inauguration of the Rome Conference, the Caucus started its strong lobbying activities. During the first day, the women's groups submitted documents in which they complained about the general ignorance of the international community towards gender-related issues. It also called for the appointment of a Gender Legal Advisor in the Office of the Prosecutor.[16] Furthermore, a member NGO in the Caucus urged that the final Statute should include crimes against women as prosecutable crimes before the Court, and must 'reflect the special needs of women in cases of sexual violence.'[17] On the second day of the conference, the Italian Women's Caucus stated that 'an ICC must incorporate gender in all aspects of its jurisdiction and operations if it is to be an effective instrument of universal justice,' and urged the inclusion in the Court's jurisdiction of sexual violence, sexual slavery, prostitution, forced pregnancy and sterilization.[18] A similar call was made the following day by the Asian Centre for Women's Human Rights (ASCENT).[19]

The work of the Women's Caucus throughout the conference was in many respects different from that of the CICC. For instance, it worked closely with the United States for the inclusion of gender-friendly provisions in the language of the statute.[20] Moreover, it had to struggle with religious groups represented in the CICC.

The most important challenge for the Women's Caucus was raised by the Arab League countries and by the Holy See. Arab delegations made attempts to exclude some elements of

---

[13] Marlies Glasius, 'How Activists Shaped the Court,' *The Magazine, Crimes of War Project*, 2003, http://www.crimesofwar.org/icc_magazine/icc-glasius.html.

[14] Marlies Glasius, 'Who is the Real Civil Society? Women's Groups versus Pro-Family Groups at the International Criminal Court Negotiations,' In Jude Howell and Diane Mulligan (eds.), *Gender and Civil Society* (London and New York: Routledge, 2004), p. 5.

[15] Glasius, 'How Activists Shaped the Court,' *The Magazine, Crimes of War Project*, 2003, http://www.crimesofwar.org/icc_magazine/icc-glasius.html.

[16] 'Court Must Fill Gender Gap in International Law, Insists Women's Caucus,' *On the Record ICC*, Vol. 1, Issue 2, June 16, 1998.

[17] 'OXFAM and the International Criminal Court,' OXFAM Statement at the Rome Conference, 15 June 1998, available via the official ICC website: http://www.icc-cpi.int/legaltools/.

[18] Alison Dickens, 'Women-Friendly Tribunal Sought,' *The International Criminal Court Monitor*, Special Issue 3, 17 June 1998, p. 5.

[19] It urged 'the words rape, sexual slavery, enforced prostitution, enforced pregnancy, mass rape and other forms of sexual violence be used and specifically listed as war crimes, crimes against humanity and grave breaches of the human rights of women' in the final statute. 'Asian Centre for Women's Human Rights (ASCENT): Statement to the United Nations Conference of Plenipotentiaries on the International Criminal Court,' 18 June 1998, Rome.

[20] Lehr-Lehnardt, 'One Small Step for Women: Female-Friendly Provisions in the Rome Statute of the International Criminal Court,' p. 319.

crimes relevant to gender crimes, including forced pregnancy,[21] which had been practiced as a method of ethnic cleansing during the internal war in Bosnia, and involved 'raping a woman and then keeping her confined so she is forced to carry the baby to full term.'[22] The primary fear of the Arab states, and thus the basis of their objection to the inclusion of forced pregnancy into the language of the final text, was that in this case they would be compelled to adopt national legislation legalizing abortion.[23]

However, in addition to Arab states and the Vatican, some pro-family groups in the CICC, especially REAL (Realistic, Equal, Active, For Life), stated the same opposition. Women of Canada was very active in opposing the inclusion of forced pregnancy as a war crime, on the grounds that it might lead to the legalization of abortion.[24] Rhonda Copelon, Professor of Law at City University of New York who attended the conference as a member of the Women's Caucus, notes that, in addition to the Vatican and the Islamist Arab League countries, a number of North American right-wing NGOs constituted the biggest challenge to the women's coalition. Those groups included the International Human Life Committee, the David M. Kennedy Center, and Canada's JMJ [Jesus, Mary and Joseph] Children's Fund and REAL Women.[25] She also asserted that there were a number of states other than those falling into the above category which did not have any interest at all in the Caucus' agenda. In other words, they were simply not concerned about the inclusion of gender issues on the negotiation table.[26]

Despite the above difficulties and challenges involved, the women's groups effectively secured the adoption of a final text that contained provisions favourable to them. To achieve this success, they used a wide range of tactics and strategies. Their members were always vibrant and hard-working. To this end, Glasius notes that 'the Women's Caucus was highly visible in Rome,' with 12 to 15 people at the conference venue all the time.[27] Wisely, most of them chose to approach female state delegates. This tactic worked very well; within a very short time, the Caucus gained the support of a number of states, among them Australia, Bosnia, Canada, Costa Rica, Mexico, the Netherlands, Sweden, and ten sub-Saharan countries including the Republic of South Africa. The support of these particular countries was vital. Two of them (the Netherlands and Canada) consecutively chaired the conference. Two others (Sweden and the Republic of South Africa) chaired working groups focusing on different parts of the Statute, and Australia chaired the negotiations on gender issues.[28]

The support of Bosnia was arguably the most important and crucial for at least two reasons. First, it was victimized by the war crimes largely committed against women during

---

[21] Steven C. Roach, 'Arab States and the Role of Islam in the International Criminal Court,' *Political Studies*, Vol. 53, Issue 1, 2005, p. 143.

[22] Marlies Glasius, 'How Activists Shaped the Court,' *The Magazine, Crimes of War Project*, 2003, http://www.crimesofwar.org/icc_magazine/icc-glasius.html.

[23] Roach, 'Arab States and the Role of Islam in the International Criminal Court,' p. 148.

[24] Marlies Glasius, 'How Activists Shaped the Court,' *The Magazine, Crimes of War Project*, 2003, http://www.crimesofwar.org/icc_magazine/icc-glasius.html.

[25] Rhonda Copelon, 'Gender Crimes as War Crimes: Integrating Crimes against Women into International Criminal Law,' p. 234.

[26] Ibid., p. 234.

[27] Marlies Glasius, 'Who is the Real Civil Society? Women's Groups versus Pro-Family Groups at the International Criminal Court Negotiations,' p. 5.

[28] Ibid., p. 5. It should also be noted that some members of the Women's Caucus directly took part in the negotiations under the delegations of states. In other words, they officially represented their countries, and negotiated on behalf of their governments. For instance, one member joined the Canadian delegation while another joined the Costa Rican delegation. See, Ibid., p. 6.

the internal war in the early 1990s. They had first-hand experience and recognized the need to address gender-related crimes. To this end, their insights and contributions had indeed a dramatic impact on changing the delegates' views. Second, as a predominantly Muslim country in Europe, Bosnia had the potential to convince the Arab League states whose perspective was quite contrary to that of the Women's Caucus.

To this end, the Bosnian delegation reportedly lobbied for the support of the Muslim countries to include gender-related crimes in the final text.[29] Most of the time, the Bosnian call was supported by all the conference delegations. It submitted concrete proposals to all the delegates. For instance, at the beginning of the conference, the Bosnian delegation circulated a discussion paper which made a call for the inclusion of forced pregnancy as a war crime. In the paper, Bosnia argued that the real issue at the conference was 'providing victims with proper legal status by explicit recognition of this crime.'[30]

The Women's Caucus was also able to receive considerable support from African states for almost the same reason. The need to address situations such as the extensive perpetration of international crimes against women during the killing campaign in Rwanda brought the African countries to the side of the women's groups.[31] In general, the activities of the Women's Caucus included briefings, the preparing and distributing of legal position papers, and statements shaming those governments not in favour of a gender-friendly court.[32]

Another factor in their success was their mobility within the conference: they attended the plenary sessions and most of the working group meetings, as well as meeting the delegates in their free time in cafeterias, NGO receptions and other informal occasions.[33] At the plenary sessions, member organizations as well as individuals affiliated with the Women's Caucus made a number of statements regarding the issues they deemed important. For instance, in an attempt to convince the delegates, women's groups issued a press statement whereby they insisted that listing forced pregnancy as a war crime and a crime against humanity in the Statute would 'not affect national abortion laws, or the omission to provide abortion.'[34]

On another occasion, three leading women's groups declared that the gender issues on which they had focused needed to be addressed at the conference, as over 70 percent of the victims of war crimes were women.[35] Drawing attention to the worldwide commission concerning the trafficking in women and children, the women's rights groups also tried to

---

[29] 'National Abortion Laws will not be Undermined by Inclusion of Forced Pregnancy as a Crime Against Humanity, Pledges Women's Caucus: Bosnian government agrees, lobbies with Muslim countries,' *On the Record ICC*, Vol. 1, Issue 9, June 29, 1998, available at: http://www.advocacynet.org/news_view/news_82.html.

[30] 'Enforced Pregnancy Issue Turns into Abortion Debate,' *The International Criminal Court Monitor*, Special Issue 9, 25 June 1998, p. 7.

[31] See for instance 'Africa Pushing Gender Concerns,' *Terra Viva*, Issue 12, 30 June 1998, p. 4.

[32] Lehr-Lehnardt, 'One Small Step for Women: Female-Friendly Provisions in the Rome Statute of the International Criminal Court,' p. 319.

[33] Ibid., p. 320.

[34] 'National Abortion Laws will not be Undermined by Inclusion of Forced Pregnancy as a Crime Against Humanity, Pledges Women's Caucus,' *On the Record ICC*, Vol. 1, Issue 9.

[35] Anna Bliss, 'Perspective on Gender: Over 70% of Victims of War are Women and Children, Say Campaigners,' *On the Record ICC*, Vol. 1, Issue 10, 30 June 1998, available at: http://www.advocacynet.org/news_view/news_118.html.

save a proposal that would make 'the trafficking in women and children a clearly recognized crime against humanity.'[36]

To a large extent, the efforts of the women's groups at the conference received global support. They convinced the delegates that 'existing international laws were inadequate and thus should not be incorporated into the ICC,' and asserted that 'customary international law had progressed to such a point that it could fill in the gaps that existing treaties and conventions could not.'[37] Their proposals were thus generally welcomed, and the final statute had the imprints of the substantial part of the recommendations contained in those proposals.[38]

More importantly, many state delegates openly acknowledged their contribution and influence throughout the negotiations. For instance, David Stoelting, Vice-Chair of the Working Group on the ICC Rules of Evidence and Procedure, notes:

> The Women's Caucus for Gender Justice deserves praise for effectively advocating positions on the definitions of crimes and the qualifications of ICC personnel designed to ensure appropriate recognition of sexual violence and gender issues. The Women's Caucus achieved significant results, as many delegations worked with it in crafting appropriate treaty language.[39]

The women's groups' success can be measured by the gender-friendly language and provisions of the final statute. Almost all of the concerns the Women's Caucus had at the beginning were addressed by the delegates.[40] Even the most contentious issue, that of 'forced pregnancy,' was resolved in the way the Caucus had favoured. As was noted by Rhonda Copelon, the Caucus had two goals in relation to the future court's substantive jurisdiction over crimes. One was to secure into the statute the insertion of certain crimes of sexual violence as crimes always prosecutable by the court without any prior authorization or notification. The second was to ensure the recognition of sexual violence as no less egregious as other forms of violence, including torture, enslavement, genocide, and inhumane treatment.[41]

The final statute openly states that the crimes of 'Rape, sexual slavery, enforced prostitution, forced pregnancy, enforced sterilization, or any other form of sexual violence of comparable gravity' are crimes against humanity,[42] prosecutable and punishable by the court without any prior authorization from a third party. Moreover, 'persecution against any identifiable group or collectivity on political, racial, national, ethnic, cultural, religious, or

---

[36] 'Trafficking of women and children must be a crime against humanity, says Women's Caucus,' *On the Record ICC*, Vol. 1, Issue 14, July 7, 1998, available at: http://www.advocacynet.org/news_view/news_87.html.

[37] Lehr-Lehnardt, 'One Small Step for Women: Female-Friendly Provisions in the Rome Statute of the International Criminal Court,' p. 340.

[38] Ibid., p. 340.

[39] David Stoelting, 'Non-Governmental Organizations and the International Criminal Court,' *World Order under Law Reporter*, published by the International Law Section of the American Bar Association, 1999, available at: http://www.morganlewis.com/.

[40] Marlies Glasius, 'How Activists Shaped the Court,' *The Magazine, Crimes of War Project*, 2003, http://www.crimesofwar.org/icc_magazine/icc-glasius.html.

[41] Rhonda Copelon, 'Gender Crimes as War Crimes: Integrating Crimes against Women into International Criminal Law,' p. 235.

[42] Rome Statute of the International Criminal Court, U.N. Doc. A/CONF.183/9, Article 7(1)(g).

gender grounds'[43] is a crime against humanity punishable under the Rome Statute. Van der Vyver notes that inclusion of 'gender-specific crimes as a distinct category' in the final text 'represented a major achievement of the Women's Caucus.'[44] Similarly, Rhonda Copelon contends that 'the Rome Statute contains an impressive list of sexual and gender crimes and represents an important breakthrough.'[45]

Another major success of the Women's Caucus at the Rome Conference was the references made by the Statute to the fair representation in and gender-friendly structure and organization of the Court it created. At the conference, the Caucus considered the issue of the Court's composition and administration from the perspective of 'a dual standard, one based on gender expertise and one on biology.'[46] That is to say, the panels of judges should include gender experts (male and female), and men and women should be fairly represented in the Court's judicial, administrative, and prosecutorial posts. At the end, despite the strong opposition from some conservative groups, the delegates adopted the provision, calling on the States to 'take into account the need for a fair representation of female and male judges'[47] as well as 'the need to include judges with legal expertise on specific issues, including, but not limited to, violence against women or children.'[48] Commenting on the above provisions, van der Vyver further asserts that these gender-related considerations also have to be taken into account when the Prosecutor and Registrar appoint staff to their respective offices, and the Prosecutor is furthermore instructed to appoint advisors with legal expertise in gender and sexual violence and violence against children.[49]

However, it should be noted that, despite the breakthroughs secured through the adoption of the Rome Statute in terms of gender friendliness, the Women's Caucus described the final text as 'a "limited" achievement for gender justice, echoing the concern of other activists that it contained a number of large loopholes that would make it difficult for perpetrators of core crimes to be brought to justice.[50] The opt-out clause, that allows the States seven years of immunity from the Court's jurisdiction over war crimes was a particular disappointment for the women's groups.

CONCLUSION

Despite their dissatisfaction with some of the provisions of the Rome Statute, women's groups at the conference achieved most of their prescribed goals. Given that the final text was a reflection of a broad-base compromise between the NGOs and the State delegates, it was only natural that the Statute would contain some loopholes as seen from the civil society perspective. But the insertion of female-friendly provisions in the language of the Rome

---

[43] Ibid., Article 7(1) (h).

[44] Johan D. Van der Vyver, 'Civil Society and the International Criminal Court,' *Journal of Human Rights,* Vol. 2, Issue 3, 2003, p. 432.

[45] Rhonda Copelon, 'Gender Crimes as War Crimes: Integrating Crimes against Women into International Criminal Law,' p. 238.

[46] Ibid., p. 240.

[47] Rome Statute, Article 8(a) (iii).

[48] Ibid., Article 8(b).

[49] Johan D.Van der Vyver, 'Civil Society and the International Criminal Court,' p. 433.

[50] Alison Dickens, 'Women Withhold Final Verdict,' *Terra Viva,* Issue 26, 18 July 1998.

Statute was a great breakthrough, considering especially the overwhelming opposition staged by conservative and religious NGOs as well as delegates from some Islamic countries and the Holy See.

REFERENCES

Primary Sources

'Asian Centre for Women's Human Rights (ASCENT): Statement to the United Nations Conference of Plenipotentiaries on the International Criminal Court,' 18 June 1998, Rome.

Draft Statute for an International Criminal Court, Report of the International Law Commission, U.N. GAOR, 49th Sess., Supp. No. 10, at 43, U.N. Doc. A/49/10 (1994).

'OXFAM and the International Criminal Court,' OXFAM Statement at the Rome Conference, 15 June 1998, available via the official ICC website: http://www.icc-cpi.int/legaltools/

Rome Statute of the International Criminal Court, U.N. Doc. A/CONF.183/9.

Periodicals, NGO Publications

Africa Pushing Gender Concerns, *Terra Viva*, Issue 12, 30 June 1998, p. 4.

Bliss, Anna, 'Perspective on Gender: Over 70% of Victims of War are Women and Children, Say Campaigners,' *On the Record ICC,* Vol. 1, Issue 10, 30 June 1998, available at: http://www.advocacynet.org/news_view/news_118.html

'Court Must Fill Gender Gap in International Law, Insists Women's Caucus,' *On the Record ICC,* Vol. 1, Issue 2, 16 June 1998.

Dickens, Alison, 'Women-Friendly Tribunal Sought,' *The International Criminal Court Monitor*, Special Issue 3, 17 June 1998, p. 5.

Dickens, Alison, 'Women Withhold Final Verdict,' *Terra Viva,* Issue 26, 18 July 1998.

'Enforced Pregnancy Issue Turns into Abortion Debate,' *The International Criminal Court Monitor,* Special Issue 9, 25 June 1998, p. 7.

'National Abortion Laws will not be Undermined by Inclusion of Forced Pregnancy as a Crime Against Humanity, Pledges Women's Caucus: Bosnian government agrees, lobbies with Muslim countries,' *On the Record ICC,* Vol. 1, Issue 9, 29 June 1998, available at: http://www.advocacynet.org/news_view/news_82.html

Stoelting, David, 'Non-Governmental Organizations and the International Criminal Court,' *World Order under Law Reporter,* published by the International Law Section of the American Bar Association, 1999, available at: http://www.morganlewis.com

'Trafficking of women and children must be a crime against humanity, says Women's Caucus,' *On the Record ICC,* Vol. 1, Issue 14, 7 July 1998, available at: http://www.advocacynet.org/news_view/news_87.html

Secondary Sources (Scholarly Articles, Opinions)

Çakmak, Cenap, 'The International Criminal Court in World Politics,' *International Journal on World Peace,* Vol. 23, Issue 1, 2006, pp. 3-40.

Copelon, Rhonda, 'Gender Crimes as War Crimes: Integrating Crimes against Women into International Criminal Law,' *McGill Law Journal*, Vol. 46, Issue 1, 2000.

Glasius, Marlies, *The International Criminal Court: A Global Civil Society Achievement* (London and New York: Routledge, 2006).

Glasius, Marlies, 'Who is the Real Civil Society? Women's Groups versus Pro-Family Groups at the International Criminal Court Negotiations,' In Jude Howell and Diane Mulligan (eds.), *Gender and Civil Society* (London and New York: Routledge, 2004).

Glasius, Marlies, 'How Activists Shaped the Court,' *The Magazine, Crimes of War Project,* 2003, http://www.crimesofwar.org/icc_magazine/icc-glasius.html

Glasius, Marlies, 'Expertise in the Cause of Justice: Global Civil Society Influence on the Statute for an International Court,' in Marlies Glasius, Mary Kaldor ve Helmut Anheier (eds.), *Global Civil Society 2002* (Oxford: Oxford University Press, 2002).

Lehr-Lehnardt, Rana, 'One Small Step for Women: Female-Friendly Provisions in the Rome Statute of the International Criminal Court,' *Brigham Young University Journal of Public Law,* Vol. 16, Issue 2, 2002.

Pace, William R. and Jennifer Schense, 'The NGO Coalition's Contribution to the Making of the Elements of Crime and Rules of Procedure,' in Roy S. Lee (ed.), *The International Criminal Court: Elements of Crimes and Rules of Procedure and Evidence* (Ardsley, NY: Transnational Publishers, 2001), pp. 705-734.

Pace, William R. and Mark Thieroff, 'Participation of Non-Governmental Organizations,' in Roy S. Lee (ed.), *The International Criminal Court: The Making of the Rome Statute, Issues, Negotiations, Results* (The Hague: Kluwer Law International, 1999), pp. 391-398.

Ratner, Steven R., 'The International Criminal Court and the Limits of Global Judicialization,' *Texas International Law Journal,* Vol. 38, Issue 3, 2003.

Roach, Steven C., 'Arab States and the Role of Islam in the International Criminal Court,' *Political Studies,* Vol. 53, Issue 1, 2005.

Van der Vyver, Johan D., 'Civil Society and the International Criminal Court,' *Journal of Human Rights,* Vol. 2, Issue 3, 2003.

PART II: CRIMES AGAINST WOMEN IN TIMES OF CONFLICT

In: Crimes Against Women
Editor: David Wingeate Pike

ISBN 978-1-61470-813-1

Chapter 5

Rape and other Sexual Violence against Women and Girls in Armed Conflict: A Legal Look at the Issues

Eileen Servidio

Although historical statistics on the number of victims of rape and other sexual violence during armed conflict can neither be gathered nor relied upon, one may feel safe in saying the number of these types of crimes did not diminish in the 20th century. Nor has the 21st century begun in a manner that gives much hope for a rapid reduction. Sexual violence in armed conflicts has even been said to increase, in spite of the different international conventions signed to eliminate it and in spite of the creation of international courts that have handed down decisions, equating these acts with the worst of international crimes.

Rape and sexual violence were perpetrated by combatants in both World Wars, and in conflicts such as those in Sudan, Angola, ex-Yugoslavia, Sierra Leone, Rwanda, the Democratic Republic of Congo and Darfur.[1] During the Rwanda genocide alone, it has been estimated that 250,000 to 500,000 women and girls were raped by combatants.[2] The camps in former Yugoslavia, where women were kept and repeatedly raped and otherwise abused, became notorious. In most of the recent conflicts, the numbers cited of mass rape have certainly been greatly underestimated.

Resolution 1325 of the Security Council of the United Nations on Women, Peace and Security[3] proclaims that: 'civilians, particularly women and children, account for the vast majority of those adversely affected by armed conflict.' This study will focus on women and girls as victims of rape and other sexual violence during armed conflict.[4] It will briefly review a part of the existing international humanitarian law under which such acts may be provided

[1] These conflicts are unfortunately just a few of those that could be cited.

[2] Statistics of Amnesty International (anmesty.org/actforwomen/rwa-0704) cited by Joshua H. Joseph, 'Rethinking Yamashita: Holding Military Leaders Accountable for Wartime Rape,' in The State University of New Jersey, *Women's Rights Law Reporter,* Spring/Summer, 2007.

[3] Passed unanimously, 31 October 2000 (S/RES/1325).

[4] The author realizes that women and girls are not the only victims of these crimes in times of conflict, but they are the principal victims.

for. It will then present an overview of the work of the international courts that have applied these legal instruments in the area of rape and other sexual violence and have dramatically changed the legal perception of these crimes by recognizing them not only as genocide but as crimes against humanity, *inter alia*. The study will next consider why combatants are able to commit such crimes, and it will propose that a variety of elements needs to be addressed to find solutions to the problem. One of the elements that increase the possibility of sexual violence against women and girls during armed conflict may be the attitude taken toward women and girls during peacetime. It will conclude by suggesting that the creation of law condemning such acts in armed conflicts is necessary, but it is not a sufficient solution. The purpose of this study is thus to seek solutions that help to eliminate discrimination against women and girls during peacetime, and to argue that these solutions may very well play an essential role in reducing this form of violence in times of conflict.

Sexual violence has long been considered a crime under international customary law. However, rape and other sexual violence during armed conflict were usually punished, on those rare occasions when they were punished, under provisions of other international crimes. They were not necessarily international crimes in themselves. That is changing.

I. Existing International Law

The principal laws used by the different international criminal courts are the following: [5]

A. The four Geneva Conventions and their two Protocols:[6] The basis of international humanitarian law in times of conflict remains the Geneva Conventions and their two Protocols. Nevertheless, few provisions within them address directly the question of violence against women. By way of example: Convention I[7] provides that 'Women shall be treated with all consideration due to their sex' (Art. 12). And again in Convention III,[8] 'Women shall be treated with all the regard due to their sex and shall in all cases benefit by treatment as favourable as that granted to men' (Art. 14).

Although women are more and more often combatants, violence against them is primarily covered in Convention IV relative to the Protection of Civilian Persons in Time of War. This Convention provides a general protection of all civilians 'to alleviate the sufferings caused by war' (Art. 13). However, women are mentioned expressly and 'shall be especially protected against any attack on their honour, in particular against rape, enforced prostitution, or any form of indecent assault' (Art. 27).

Protocol I,[9] that reinforces *inter alia* the basic protections of civilians during conflicts, addresses directly the question of women in Article 76-1: 'Women shall be the object of

---

[5] This study cannot analyse all international law concerning rape or other violent sexual crimes during times of armed conflict. It will attempt to present some of the major instruments.

[6] All four Conventions date from 12 August 1949; the Protocols date from 12 December 1977. There is a Protocol III: 'Protocol additional to the Geneva Conventions of 12 August 1949, and relating to the Adoption of an Additional Distinctive Emblem' (8 December 2005) which concerns the recognition of an additional emblem which does not interest this study.

[7] For the Amelioration of the Condition of the Wounded and Sick in Armed Forces in the Field.

[8] Relative to the Treatment of Prisoners of War.

[9] Relative to the Protection of Victims of International Armed Conflicts.

special respect and shall be protected in particular against rape, forced prostitution and any other form of indecent assault.'[10]

The Conventions treat principally international conflict waged between at least two distinct States. However, Article 3, common to all four Conventions, sets forth some minimum standards to be followed in the case of armed conflict not of an international character that occurs in the territory of one of the Parties. Paragraph 1 of that Article is relative to the treatment of 'Persons taking no active part in the hostilities, including members of armed forces who have laid down their arms and those placed *hors de combat* by sickness, wounds, detention, or any other cause.' Those 'shall in all circumstances be treated humanely, without any adverse distinction founded on race, colour, religion or faith, sex, birth or wealth, or any other similar criteria.' The acts prohibited include murder of all kinds, mutilation, cruel treatment, torture, hostage taking, outrages upon personal dignity including humiliating and degrading treatment. Rape and sexual violence against women can be considered torture in some cases, and certainly outrages upon personal dignity in all cases.

Protocol II also addresses the question of protecting the victims of non-international armed conflicts by developing and supplementing Common Article 3. One finds several of the general prohibitions of violence that are already stated in the Conventions against all who have not taken part of or who have ceased to take part of the hostilities, such as outrages upon personal dignity, 'particularly humiliating and degrading treatment, rape, enforced prostitution and any form of indecent assault' and slavery and slave trade in all their forms (Art. 4).

The commentaries of the International Committee of the Red Cross (ICRC) on the different articles of the Conventions and the Protocols highlight the original purpose of the provisions. For example, the commentary in Article 27 concerning the treatment of women, Convention IV:

> Paragraph 2 denounces certain practices which occurred, for example, during the Second World War, when innumerable women of all ages, and even children, were subjected to outrages of the worst kind: rape committed in occupied territories, brutal treatment of every sort, mutilations etc. In areas where troops were stationed, or through which they passed, thousands of women were made to enter brothels against their will or were contaminated with venereal diseases, the incidence of which often increased on an alarming scale.
>
> These facts outrage the conscience of all mankind and recall the worst memories of the great barbarian invasions. They underline the necessity of proclaiming that women must be treated with special consideration. That is the object of this paragraph, which is based on a provision introduced into the Prisoners of War Convention in 1929, and on a proposal submitted to the International Committee by the International Women's Congress and the International Federation of Abolitionists. The provision is founded on the principles set forth in paragraph 1 on the notion of 'respect for the person', 'honour' and 'family rights.'
>
> A woman should have an acknowledged right to special protection, the special regard owed to women being, of course, in addition to the safeguards laid down in paragraph 1, which they enjoy equally with men.

[10] Paragraphs 2 and 3 of this article provide heightened protection for pregnant women and mothers with dependent children.

The Conference listed as examples certain acts constituting an attack on women's honour, and expressly mentioned rape, enforced prostitution, i.e. the forcing of a woman into immorality by violence or threats, and any form of indecent assault. These acts are and remain prohibited in all places and in all circumstances, and women, whatever their nationality, race, religious beliefs, age, marital status or social condition have an absolute right to respect for their honour and their modesty, in short, for their dignity as women.

The Conventions and their Protocols are often considered to protect women insufficiently in times of conflict either because the provisions are often too general or because they are simply not implemented. In addition, some contemporary feminists are critical of the provisions, because they give a much too traditional role to women. They underline the ICRC commentaries, such as the one just cited, that base the protection of women on notions such as honour. If these provisions are based on the honour of the female sex, it raises the question whether women who are raped are any longer honourable. Accordingly, these protections should be based not on such antiquated notions as honour but rather on the notions of human rights that are inalienable to all, regardless of sex, but with the recognition that it is women and girls that are overwhelmingly the victims of those acts.

B. The two Statutes of international ad hoc tribunals and the Statute of the International Criminal Court:[11]

The Statute of the International Criminal Tribunal for the former Yugoslavia (ICTY): The Statute was adopted on 25 May 1993 under Resolution 827 of the Security Council. That Resolution expressed great alarm for the continuing 'widespread and flagrant' violation of international humanitarian law occurring in the former Yugoslavia, particularly in Bosnia and Herzegovina. The International Tribunal for the former Yugoslavia has competence to prosecute any person responsible for serious violations of international humanitarian law committed in the territory of the former Yugoslavia since 1991. There have indeed been reports in this region of mass killings, massive, organized and systematic detention and rape of women, and the continuance of the practice of 'ethnic cleansing'.

More specifically, the Court has jurisdiction for grave breaches of the Geneva Conventions of 1949 such as torture or inhuman treatment, wilfully causing great suffering or serious injury to body or health, unlawful deportation or transfer or unlawful confinement of a civilian and even taking civilians as hostages, if these hostages are tortured or receive inhuman treatment.

The Statute grants the Court competence for violations of the laws or customs of war, and although the acts that are enumerated fall outside the domain of this study, the list is not exhaustive and it is evident that rape and violence during armed conflicts could be considered violations of the laws or customs of war.

Both genocide and crimes against humanity also lie within the jurisdiction of the Court. Genocide is defined as a certain number of acts committed 'with intent to destroy, in whole or in part, a national, ethnical, racial or religious group'. These acts include causing serious bodily or mental harm to members of the group, deliberately inflicting on the group conditions of life calculated to bring about its physical destruction in whole or in part and

---

[11] There are other *ad hoc* international criminal courts that are dealing with these crimes. See for example the Special Court for Sierra Leone where persons (particularly Charles Taylor the former president of Liberia) are accused of serious violations of international humanitarian law, war crimes and crimes against humanity including rape and sexual slavery. However, this study will concentrate on the two *ad hoc* tribunals that have most influenced this subject.

imposing measures intended to prevent births within the group. Those conspiring to commit genocide, those directly and publicly inciting such crimes, and those attempting to commit them as those in complicity, could all be considered guilty of this crime.

Concerning crimes against humanity, the Court has competence only insofar as these crimes are committed in armed conflict, whether this conflict is international or internal in character. However, the crime must be directed against the civil population. Even though this category lists directly the crime of rape, other acts on the list could cover sexual violence such as enslavement and torture and certainly these acts would be included in the catch-all phrase of 'other inhumane acts' by which the list ends.

The Statute of the International Criminal Tribunal for Rwanda (ICTR):[12] The ICTR has the power to prosecute persons responsible for serious violations of international humanitarian law committed in the territory of Rwanda and Rwandan citizens responsible for such violations committed in the territory of neighbouring States between 1 January 1994 and 31 December 1994. The competence *ratione materiae*[13] of the Court is extremely close to that of the ICTY. The differences are due to the difference in the circumstances of the two conflicts.

It is not surprising that the first international crime listed is that of genocide. Again we find the same prerequisite concerning the acts listed: that they are committed with the intent to destroy, in whole or in part, a national, ethnical, racial or religious group. The list of acts that follows in which sexual violence could be included are: causing serious bodily or mental harm to members of the group, deliberately inflicting on the group conditions of life calculated to bring about its physical destruction in whole or in part, imposing measures intended to prevent births within the group. As with the ICTY, it is not only the perpetrators of these acts that are punishable but also those who conspire, incite or attempt to commit such acts.

Concerning crimes against humanity, the Court has competence only where these acts are committed as 'part of a widespread or systematic attack against any civilian population on national, political, ethnic, racial or religious grounds.' We find the same acts that are listed in the Statutes of the ICTY.

The ICTR also has competence to prosecute persons having committed or having ordered the commission of serious violations of Article 3 common to the Geneva Conventions and the Additional Protocol II. These violations or the threat of them include *inter alia* violence to the life, health and physical or mental well-being of persons, and in particular murder as well as cruel treatment such as torture, mutilation or any form of corporal punishment, collective punishments, taking of hostages, outrages upon personal dignity, in particular humiliating and degrading treatment and finally rape, enforced prostitution and any form of indecent assault.

The Statute of the International Criminal Court (ICC): The formation of this permanent criminal court greatly benefited from the already existing two *ad hoc* courts, not only by their written Statutes, but also by the decisions that the two Tribunals have handed down. The subject of violence against women was one that the two *ad hoc* Courts viewed with great sensitivity, and the drafters of the Statutes of the ICC took into account not only some of the errors committed by the *ad hoc* Courts but also the experience acquired in prosecuting those accused of sexual violence during armed conflicts.

---

12 The Tribunal was created by Security Council Resolution 955, 8 November 1994.

13 That is to say, the different crimes that the Court has jurisdiction over.

According to the Rome Statute, the ICC has jurisdiction for the crime of genocide, crimes against humanity and war crimes.[14] Among the forms of crimes against humanity enumerated in the Statute, are enslavement, torture and rape, sexual slavery, enforced prostitution, forced pregnancy, enforced sterilization, or any form of comparable sexual violence or persecution of any identifiable group or collectivity on grounds such as gender. These acts will be considered by the ICC as crimes against humanity only if they are 'committed as part of a widespread or systematic attack directed against any civilian population…' Regarding war crimes, the Court has jurisdiction particularly where these acts have been committed 'as part of a plan or policy or as part of a large-scale commission of such crimes.' Included in these acts are grave breaches of the Geneva Conventions amongst which are torture, inhuman treatment, wilfully causing great suffering or serious injury to body or health or other serious violations of the laws and customs applicable in international armed conflict, including committing outrages upon personal dignity, in particular humiliating and degrading treatment, or committing rape, sexual slavery, enforced prostitution, forced pregnancy, enforced sterilization, or any form of sexual violence also constituting a grave breach of the Geneva Conventions. More or less the same acts fall under the jurisdiction of the Court when committed during an armed conflict that is not of an international character. However, the Court does not have jurisdiction in 'situations of internal disturbances and tensions, such as riots, isolated and sporadic acts of violence or other acts of a similar nature.'

The importance of these three instruments in prosecuting and punishing rape and other forms of sexual violence during armed crisis cannot be emphasized enough. However, no matter how important the provisions of the three Statutes are, it is what the courts do with these provisions; how they are interpreted—restrictively or extensively—and how they are implemented—again, restrictively or extensively—that one can truly gauge the consequences of these in the fight to end violence against women.

II. Cases before the International Courts

Rape and other sexual violence are not recent phenomena and have long been condemned. As early as 1474 at Breisach in Germany, in one of the first 'international courts,' Peter von Hagenbach was judged and convicted by twenty-seven judges from the Holy Roman Empire of violations of the 'Laws of God and of Man' for allowing his men to rape and kill innocent civilians and steal their goods. Nevertheless, although isolated judgments such as this one can be found, it is essentially through the ICTY and the ICTR that the concept of sexual violence in times of conflict has been developed.[15]

The case law of these two courts has greatly added to the acceptance that rape and other sexual violence be considered crimes against international humanitarian law in their own right. A look at some of the major decisions of these courts is in order before turning to the ICC.

---

[14] The ICC will also have jurisdiction in the case of crimes of aggression once a definition for that crime is determined by the members of the Court..

[15] Cases of sexual violence were noted before the two ad hoc courts following the Second World War, particularly before the International Military Court for the Far East. However, as already mentioned, these crimes were not crimes in themselves.

A. Examples of Cases before the ICTY[16]

The ICTY was created to resolve the conflict in ex-Yugoslavia and also to punish crimes committed during the conflict, particularly the crime of ethnic cleansing. Rape and other sexual violence against women and girls was in fact a premeditated strategy of terrorism, a method of systematic humiliation, intimidation and terror with the goal of ethnic cleansing.[17]

Prosecutor against Gagovic, Jankovic, Janjic, Kovac, Vukovic, Zelenovic, Kunarac and Stankovic [18]: A 1996 indictment by prosecutors at the ICTY legally treated, for the first time, sexual assaults such as torture and enslavement as a crime against humanity. The importance of this indictment cannot be stressed enough.

According to the indictment: Foca, a city and municipality located south-east of Sarajevo (Republic of Bosnia-Herzegovina) comprised a population of 40,513 persons of which 51.6% Muslim, 45.3% Serbian and 3.1% others.[19] The political and military take-over of the city, by regular military units from the Bosnian Serb army and irregular military units from Serbia and Montenegro, was completed by mid-April 1992. Muslim and Croat residents were arrested, men and women were separated and unlawfully confined, many civilians were killed, beaten or subjected to sexual assault. The Foca police were closely allied to the Serb forces. Many Muslim women were detained in such places as the Partizan Sports Hall or in houses and apartments used as brothels, operated by groups of soldiers, mostly paramilitary. The accused were members of the Foca police, military police or paramilitary leaders.

Among the general allegations of the indictment, it was stated that there existed at the time of the alleged crimes a 'state of international armed conflict, and partial occupation existed in the Republic of Bosnia-Herzegovina in the territory of the former Yugoslavia.' The acts were 'grave breaches' of the 1949 Geneva Conventions, and the victims were persons protected by these Conventions. The charges involving torture were allegedly 'committed by, or at the instigation of, or with the consent or acquiescence of, an official or person acting in an official capacity.' Those concerning crimes against humanity 'were part of a widespread or large-scale or systematic attack against a civilian population.' In this case, it was the Muslim population of Foca. The indictment considered that the acts of forcible sexual penetration 'can constitute an element of a crime against humanity, (enslavement under Article 5 (c), torture under Article 5 (f), rape under Article 5 (g)), violations of the laws and customs of war, (torture under Article 3 and Article 3(1) (a) of the Geneva Conventions) and a grave breach of the Geneva Conventions, (torture under Article 2(b)).' The acts of penetration are defined by the indictment as including 'penetration, however slight, of the vagina, anus or oral cavity, by the penis' and '(s)exual penetration of the vulva or anus is not limited to the penis.'

It was alleged that, on 3 July 1992, some of the accused had arrested Muslims. The women, who were first separated from the children, were asked to tell their interrogators where Muslim men and weapons were hidden. These women, if they were to lie, were

[16] As always, in such a short study, only certain cases can be cited. This study will provide only those indictments or judgments that best fit the issues discussed. It must be remembered that those indicted or condemned in the decisions cited may have been acquitted in a subsequent decision.

[17] For example, Muslim women were impregnated by Serbian men in order to purify their blood.

[18] IT-96-23 (1996).

[19] Census taken in 1991.

threatened with murder and rape. Two of the accused, and other soldiers under the command of a third suspect, gang-raped several of the women whom they accused of lying. One witness cited in the indictment claimed that a woman was raped by ten soldiers (vaginal penetration and fellatio) until she lost consciousness. The episode was said to have lasted one to two hours.

A second group of accusations concerned the fate of certain female detainees held in the Foca High School. Every evening, it was alleged, groups of Serb soldiers would choose some of the younger women who were then sexually assaulted, sometimes gang-raped. The women were threatened with death, either for themselves or their children, if they did not submit. Those who resisted were said to have been beaten. The indictment mentioned the deterioration of the physical and psychological health of these women due to these repeated assaults. As with the first group of charges, individual examples of these accusations were then given in the indictment.

The third group of accusations involved the persecution of female detainees in the Partizan Sports Hall by Dragon Gagovic, chief of police in Foca at the time and in charge of the detention of the female Muslim population. The detainees in Partizan were said to have suffered 'inhumane treatment, unhygienic facilities, overcrowding, starvation, physical and psychological torture, including sexual assaults.' Gagovic was accused not only in his capacity as the person in charge of the detention but also as the perpetrator of a brutal sexual assault against one woman who had formerly complained to him about other sexual assaults. After the assault, he allegedly said that if the woman told anyone of the rape 'he would find her in five different countries.'

The final charges consisted of accusations of torture, rape and enslavement either in the Partizan Sports Hall or in Karaman's House. The detention in Karaman's House was different from that in the Partizan Sports Hall in that the female detainees, numbering nine in all, were properly fed and had a key to lock out soldiers from entering. These women, in some cases only twelve or fourteen years old, were reserved for a special group of elite fighters commanded by Pero Elez, a Serb paramilitary. The detainees were allegedly subjected to 'repeated rapes and sexual assaults at night.' These women were also forced to work for the soldiers. Any woman not obeying orders was said to be beaten. They were also told that they would be killed 'after the soldiers had finished with them, because they knew too much.' During this period at least one of these women felt suicidal.[20]

Prosecutor v. Tadic:[21] The ICTY found Dusko Tadic, a Bosnian Serb, guilty of crimes against humanity. And although rape was listed in the amended indictment, these charges were later withdrawn. However, this case remains important for the prosecution of sexual violence. The Trial Chamber found that physical and sexual violence were violations of the laws and customs of war.[22] One of the accusations in the indictment was a particularly horrific one:

---

[20] The number of different charges in this indictment is indicative of the type of indictments handed down by the Prosecution. Often many charges were made against the accused. This has often been criticized. It is perhaps the idea that if enough charges are made, at least one of them can be proven.

[21] Case No. IT-94-1-T (7 May 1997).

[22] Although the violence in this case was directed against male prisoners, the principles of this decision are important for all cases of sexual violence.

> During the period between 1 June and 31 July 1992, a group of Serbs, including Dusko TADIC, severely beat numerous prisoners, including Emir KARABASIC, Jasmin HRNIC, Enver ALIC, Fikret HARAMBASIC and Emir BEGANOVIC, in the large garage building or hangar of Omarska camp. The group forced two other prisoners, 'G' and 'H', to commit oral sexual acts on HARAMBASIC and forced 'G' to sexually mutilate him. KARABASIC, HRNIC, ALIC, and HARAMBASIC died as a result of the assaults ....
>
> From that body of evidence before the Trial Chamber, it can be concluded that the beatings of the five named prisoners and of Senad Muslimovic did take place in the hangar, that G and Witness H were compelled to and did take part in the sexual assault on Fikret Harambasic, as alleged, and that G was compelled sexually to mutilate him by biting off one of his testicles. It can also be concluded from the evidence of Armin Kenjar, who wrote the date of the occurrence on the wall of his room, that all these events occurred on 18 June 1992. These eight victims were all Muslims.[23]

More generally, Tadic was accused of subjecting Muslims and Croats, inside and outside the different camps that had been set up, to a campaign of terror that included killings, torture, sexual assaults, and other physical and psychological abuse. The Trial Chamber concluded *inter alia* that cruel treatment may include "inhumane acts that cause injury to a human being in terms of physical or mental health or human dignity".

The Trial Chamber also discussed the interesting question: could a single act by a perpetrator constitute a crime against humanity? And although it was not an issue before it, the Trial Chamber did in fact seem to conclude that 'as long as there is a link with the widespread or systematic attack against a civilian population, a single act could qualify as a crime against humanity.'

The Trial Chamber added that certain acts not enumerated elsewhere in the Statute 'may also encompass other acts if they seek to subject individuals or groups of individuals to a kind of life in which enjoyment of some of their basic rights is repeatedly or constantly denied.' This is referred by the Court as persecution. It was noted that persecution could take many forms, including rape.[24]

Prosecutor v. Delalic, Mucic, Delic, Landzo (referred to as the *Celebici Case*)[25]: The *Celebici Case* is particularly complicated. Three of the defendants were Bosnian Muslims; the fourth, a Bosnian Croat. Some of the accusations against them concerned sexual assaults on detainees at the Celebici camp, a prison camp in Bosnia. Hazim Delic, a Bosnian Muslim deputy camp commander, was found guilty of a grave breach both of the Geneva Conventions and of the war crime definition of rape. Zdravko Mucic, the Bosnian Croat camp commandant, was found responsible for crimes committed at the camp, including sexual violence. Mucic's guilt was based on his command responsibility over the guards at the camp. It was considered that the crimes were committed so frequently and notoriously that the commandant could not have been ignorant of them. The importance of this case is that the ICTY recognized the rape of Bosnian Serb women prisoners at the Celebici prison camp as acts of torture. The act of rape was considered to inflict the grave physical and psychological pain that is the characteristic of torture. The Trial Chamber esteemed that sexual violence strikes at the very core of human dignity and physical integrity.'

---

23 The above details serve to demonstrate the type of sexual violence committed. In this case it was against men.

24 See also the decision of the Appeals Chamber Case No. IT-94-1-A (15 July 1999).

25 IT-96-21-T (16 November 1998).

Prosecutor v. Anto Furundzija:[26] The Trial Chamber, referring to the Appeal Chamber in the *Tadic Juridiction Decision*,[27] found that Article 3 of the Statute of the Court constitutes an 'umbrella rule' that 'covers any serious violation of a rule of customary international humanitarian law entailing, under international customary or conventional law, the individual criminal responsibility of the person breaching the rule'. Thus, the Chamber held that the offences of torture and outrages upon personal dignity, including rape, are covered by this article. Furundzija, a local Bosnian Croat military commander, was sentenced to 10 years of imprisonment for the following acts: while he was interrogating a Muslim woman who was nude, he allowed a subordinate soldier to threaten the woman by rubbing his knife on her inner thighs while saying he would put his knife inside her vagina if she did not tell the truth; the woman and a second victim, a Croatian soldier, were interrogated and beaten on their feet with a baton, the woman was repeatedly raped before a group of soldiers while Furundzija did nothing to stop these acts. It was considered that Furundzija's role was as grave as the persons actually inflicting the pain. This decision underlines the responsibility of the person in charge who is not necessarily the person performing the condemned acts.

Prosecutor v. Kunarac, Kovac and Vukovic :[28] The Trial Chamber condemned Kunarac, Kovac and Vukovic of various charges, including rape as a violation of the laws and customs of war, rape as a crime against humanity, outrages upon personal dignity as a violation of the law and customs of war, and enslavement as a crime against humanity. This case makes it extremely clear that rape constitutes both a war crime and a crime against humanity. The Court also found that the rapes in Foca constituted war crimes at once under international humanitarian law found in the Statues of the Court and, as an outrage upon personal dignity, under the provisions of the Geneva Conventions. On appeal concerning Kunarac, the Appeals Chamber held that rape may constitute torture.

Prosecutor v. Zelenovic:[29] The Trial Chamber sentenced Dragan Zelenovic, former Bosnian Serb soldier and military policeman, to 15 years imprisonment[30] for torture and rape of Bosnian Muslim women detained in the Foca municipality. He was in fact found personally responsible for nine of the rapes, eight of which were considered both rape and torture. As we have seen, women in eastern Bosnia and Herzegovina were repeatedly subjected to sexual assaults of rape and torture. The Trial Chamber remarked that "[t]he scars left by the sexual assaults were deep and will perhaps never heal. This, perhaps more than anything, speaks about the gravity of the crimes in this case".

---

[26] Case No. IT-95-17/1-T (10 December 1998).

[27] Case No. IT-94-1-AR72.

[28] IT-96-23-T/IT-96-23/1-T (22 February 2001).

[29] IT-96-23/2-S (4 April 2007).

[30] The seemingly 'light' sentence was explained by the Trial Chamber by the fact that Zelenovic pleaded guilty—a guilty plea could have a positive effect on establishing the truth and contributing to reconciliation in the region; by the fact that the victims were thus not obliged to relive the incidents by being forced to give evidence in Court; and of course by the time and effort saved by a guilty plea.The Chamber also gave weight to the fact that Zelenovic would cooperate fully with the Prosecution. And finally, the remorse shown by the accused was a factor in the sentencing.

B. A Case before the ICTR: Prosecutor v. Akayesu

The ICTR was created mainly to prosecute those responsible for the genocide perpetrated by the Hutu against the Tutsi that took place in Rwanda in 1994. The concept of genocide has been largely developed by the Court. The most important decision concerning sexual violence taken by this Tribunal has been the *Akayesu* case.

Prosecutor v. Akayesu:[31] The Trial Chamber of the ICTR found Jean Paul Akayesu guilty of nine of the fifteen counts proffered against him. The accusation included genocide, direct and public incitement to commit genocide and crimes against humanity.[32] Akayesu, a Hutu communal leader, was found guilty of a crime against humanity since he had witnessed and encouraged the rape of Tutsi women. Rape, when used for purposes such as intimidation, degradation, humiliation, discrimination, punishment, control or destruction, was held to be a violation of personal dignity and, as such, is torture when it is inflicted by, or at the instigation of, or with the consent or acquiescence of, a public official or other person acting in an official capacity.

Perhaps even more importantly, rape, which was committed on a massive scale in Rwanda during the conflict, was also recognized as genocide. We have seen that the international crime of genocide must be committed with the intent to destroy, in whole or in part, a national, ethnic, racial or religious group. This was recognized in the case of Akayesu since his acts—witnessing and encouraging rapes and the sexual mutilation of women—were committed in the course of a campaign of genocide against the Tutsi population. The Chamber esteemed that rape and other sexual violence was 'one of the worst ways of inflict [sic] harm on the victim' since the victim suffers both 'bodily and mental harm.' The sexual violence that took place was perpetrated with the intent to destroy the Tutsi group, by a 'destruction of the spirit, of the will to live, and of life itself.'[33]

C. Possible Definitions of Rape by the Two *ad hoc* Tribunals:

The international crime of rape is not defined by the Statutes of the two *ad hoc* Courts or by international humanitarian law. According to the Trial Chamber in *Akeyesu*, rape was the 'physical invasion of a sexual nature, committed on a person under circumstances which are coercive.' This definition is again used in *Prosecutor v. Delalic*. However, the definition was then narrowed down in *Furundija* to the notion of sexual penetration. After a review of definitions of rape in national legislations, the Trial Chamber found that the *actus reus*[34] of the crime of rape is:

---

[31] ICTR 96-4-T (2 September 1998).

[32] This judgment is particularly interesting since it is the first time an international court interpreted and applied the 1948 Convention of the Prevention and Punishment of the Crime of Genocide.

[33] The original indictment in this case had not included sexual violence. However, several women who testified during the trial spoke of rape. This led the Trial Chamber to ask the prosecutor to investigate in this area. An amended indictment was then filed charging Akayesu with three counts of rape as crimes against humanity. The genocide count also was added to include sexual violence.

[34] This, the act itself, is the material element of the crime, in opposition to the *mens rea* which is the mental element, that is to say, the intent of the perpetrator.

(i) sexual penetration, however slight:
  (a) of the vagina or anus of the victim by the penis of the perpetrator or any other object used by the perpetrator; or
  (b) of the mouth of the victim by the penis of the perpetrator;
(ii) by coercion or force or threat of force against the victim or a third person.

This definition is more restrictive. However, if the act cannot be considered rape according to this definition, there seems to be nothing that could prevent certain sexual violence from being esteemed inhumane, and thus a crime against humanity or a grave breach of the Geneva Conventions.

In *Kunarac*, the Trial Chamber considered that:

> [T]he Furundzija definition, although appropriate to the circumstances of that case, is in one respect more narrowly stated than is required by international law. In stating that the relevant act of sexual penetration will constitute rape only if accompanied by coercion or force or threat of force against the victim or a third person, the *Furundzija* definition does not refer to other factors which would render an act of sexual penetration non-consensual or non-voluntary on the part of the victim, which… is in the opinion of this Trial Chamber the accurate scope of this aspect of the definition in international law.

Therefore, the notion of consent should be understood in a wider framework. Thus the Court concluded that 'sexual autonomy is violated wherever the person subjected to the act has not freely agreed to it or is otherwise not a voluntary participant.' In this way, the *Kunarac* Trial Chamber agreed with the notion of penetration but was less restrictive with the concept of consent. 'Consent… must be consent given voluntarily, as a result of the victim's free will, assessed in the context of the surrounding circumstances.' The Chamber also considered that the *mens rea* of the perpetrator of the crime of rape was 'the intention to effect this sexual penetration, and the knowledge that it occurs without the consent of the victim'.

In *Prosecutor v. Gacumbitsi*,[35] the Appeal Chambers concluded that certain circumstances were so coercive in nature that any possibility of consent was impossible. Sylvestre Gacumbitsi was accused of instigating the rape of Tutsi women and girls. If they resisted, they were to be killed by the insertion of sticks into their genitals. Gacumbitsi was condemned of crimes against humanity by the Trial Chamber for instigating eight rapes. One of the victims died after being impaled by a stick. On appeal, the prosecutor argued that:

> non-consent of the victim and the perpetrator's knowledge thereof should not be considered elements of the offence that must be proved by the Prosecution; rather, consent should be considered an affirmative defence. It argues, *inter alia*, that when rape occurs in the context of genocide, armed conflict, or a widespread or systematic attack against a civilian population, genuine consent is impossible.

The Appeal Chamber asked two questions. First, what are the elements of rape and, second, how may these be proven? The Chamber held that the first question had already been answered by *Kunarac*; that is to say, rape consists of certain acts of sexual penetration

[35] ICTR-01-64 : Summary of Appeal.

occurring 'without the consent of the victim.' The 'non-consent' and the knowledge of this must then be proven by the prosecution, since they are elements of the crime. Concerning the second question of whether non-consent can be proven, the Chamber decided as follows:

> The Prosecution can prove non-consent beyond reasonable doubt by proving the existence of coercive circumstances under which meaningful consent is not possible. It is not necessary for the Prosecution to introduce evidence concerning the words or conduct of the victim or her relationship to the perpetrator. Nor need it introduce evidence of force. Rather, the Trial Chamber is free to infer non-consent as well as knowledge thereof from the background circumstances.

D. Cases before the International Criminal Court

The ICC has jurisdiction only for crimes committed since it entered into force on 1 July 2002.[36]

Darfur: In *Prosecutor v. Ahmad Muhammad Harun (Ahmad Harun) and Ali Muhammad Al Abd-Al-Rahman Ali Kushayb*[37] concerning the conflict in Darfur, the Pre-Trial Chamber of the ICC considered that there were reasonable grounds to issue warrants of arrest for both of these persons. Ahmed Harun served as Minister of State for the Interior of the Government of Sudan in charge of the management of the 'Darfur Security' and, as such, had coordinated the different bodies involved in the counter-insurgency, including the police, the armed forces, the National Security, the Intelligence Service and the Militia/Janjaweed. Ali Kushayb was considered one of the most senior leaders and commander of thousands of Militia/Janjaweed. It was alleged that the Sudanese Armed Forces and the Militia/Janjaweed had committed several criminal acts against civilians including murders, rapes and outrages upon the personal dignity of women and girls. Among the many charges were rape as constituting a crime against humanity and rape as constituting a war crime.

Northern Uganda: In 1994 the ICC opened investigations in Northern Uganda, focusing on crimes committed after 1 July 2002.[38] It had been estimated that at least 2,200 killings and 3,200 abductions recorded from July 2002 to June 2004 had taken place in over 850 attacks. Thousands of persons, especially children, were abducted. The boys were forced to be killers and the girls to be sexual slaves. In *Prosecutor v. Joseph Kony, Vincent Otti, Okot Odhiambo, Raska Lukwiya,*[39] *and Dominic Ongwen*, the two leaders of the LRA,[40] Kony and Otti, were charged *inter alia* with both rape and sexual enslavement.

Central African Republic: The Prosecutor for the ICC has also opened an investigation in the Central African Republic. The investigation will focus on the most serious of crimes committed during the armed conflict between 2002 and 2003, including allegations of rape

[36] These examples are used only to indicate the importance the new court appears to be putting on the crimes that interest this study. It must be stressed that by the time this article is published, the situation of these cases may have dramatically changed: charges could be dismissed, more accusations could be added. At the time of going to press, no cases have yet been decided by the Court.

[37] ICC-02/05-01/07.

[38] The date of the entry into force of the Rome Statute which created the ICC. The ICC can hear only cases concerning facts that took place since this date.

[39] All charges have been dropped against him due to the fact that he is now dead.

[40] Lord's Resistance Army.

and other forms of sexual violence against hundreds of victims. After a failed coup attempt, there were allegations of massive rape and other forms of sexual violence by armed individuals against civilians. According to the 'Background' information provided by the Office of the Prosecutor of the ICC,[41] '(s)exual violence appears to have been a central feature of the conflict.' The report claims that there were at least 600 victims of rape that occurred within a period of five months. It has been suggested that the numbers are higher. According to the report:

> Credible reports indicate that rape has been committed against civilians, including instances of rape of elderly women, young girls and men. There were often aggravating aspects of cruelty, such as rapes committed by multiple perpetrators, in front of third persons, sometimes with relatives forced to participate. The social impact appears devastating, with many victims stigmatized and in many cases infected with the HIV virus.

CONCLUSION

The jurisprudence of the two *ad hoc* Courts has made great strides in protecting women and girls against sexual violence during times of conflict. However, it is still too soon to predict the effects that these Courts will truly have on violence against women in future conflicts. The two *ad hoc* Courts were certainly limited by the fact that they concentrated on two particular conflicts, and their work is slowly coming to an end. The hope now is with the ICC.

Nevertheless, the ICC is under many restrictions concerning its jurisdiction, the least not being that it holds a 'complementary jurisdiction,' that is to say that the ICC can act only where a State does not act. Domestic courts' jurisdiction pre-empts the jurisdiction of the ICC.[42] If a case is being investigated or prosecuted or has been investigated by a national court having jurisdiction, the ICC will have no jurisdiction unless the State is 'unwilling or unable to genuinely carry out the investigation or prosecution.'[43] For example, in Central African Republic, the highest judicial body, the Cour de Cassation, announced that the national justice system was unable to carry out such complicated proceedings to properly investigate and prosecute the alleged crimes.[44] However, in the case of Sudan, Khartoum did not cooperate, and the ICC prosecutors had much difficulty in their investigations. The Sudanese government had tried to demonstrate that they were able to prosecute themselves.[45]

---

41 « Situation in the Central African Republic » The Hague, 22 May 2007 (ICC-OTP-BN-20070522-220-A_EN).

42 Statute of the ICC, art. 1. The complementary nature of the ICC is also mentioned in the Preamble of its Statute.

43 Statute of the ICC, art. 17-1 (a).

44 Africa News, UN News Service, 22 May 2007 'Central African Republic : International Court Probes Killings, Sexual Crimes.'

45 There are exceptions to this rule, one of which we have seen: the fact that the domestic jurisdiction will not or cannot carry out the investigation or the prosecution. Another exception is where the State having jurisdiction has investigated the case but has decided not to prosecute where this decision resulted from the 'unwillingness or inability' to prosecute. The concept of unwillingness is recognized if one or more of the following circumstances exist:

Article 17-2:

a. The proceedings were or are being undertaken or the national decision was made for the purpose of shielding the person concerned from criminal responsibility for crimes within the jurisdiction of the Court …;

International courts are effective only when they have recognition and cooperation from the international community so that one may wonder how often the Court will find that the national proceedings are not being conducted properly. Such a decision could anger the State Party, in question and since membership in the Court is not mandatory for members of the United Nations, the State might consider withdrawing recognition of the Court.

This brings us to another limitation of the ICC. Not only is the jurisdiction of the Court limited to crimes committed on the territory of State Parties to the Court[46] or by their citizens or those referred to the Court by the Security Council, its competence is limited to the 'most serious of crimes of concern to the international community as a whole.' [47] This in itself should not be a problem, since we have seen that the *ad hoc* tribunals have recognized sexual violence in certain situations as constituting torture, crimes against humanity and even genocide, and these crimes are listed in the ICC's Statute. Nevertheless, the Prosecutor of the Court has refused many cases based on the criterion of the gravity of the violence. The Prosecutor takes into consideration many elements, including the number of victims of these crimes.[48]

In spite of these limitations, these courts have certainly enforced whatever international humanitarian laws exist in the area of sexual violence, by finding that certain forms of sexual violence committed during armed conflicts may be covered under some of the gravest of international crimes, such as crimes against humanity or genocide. Nonetheless, it would seem that before a real solution can be formulated, the problem must be understood. And here is the crux of it—it is surely not completely understood. Why is there such violence against women during armed conflicts? The fact that the various efforts made have not yet had any real effect might suggest that there are other factors involved.

Several theories attempt to explain the phenomenon. For years it was believed that sexual violence, which often happens during or right after a conflict, was just part of the 'game.' The women, as the goods of those conquered, were part of the winnings of the victors. It was a 'by-product' of the conflict. In contemporary armed conflicts, this may still be true to a certain extent. However, we have seen in more recent conflicts that such violence was much more than a by-product, it was in itself a strategic policy against the enemy; one more type of weapon to be used. [49]

---

b. There has been an unjustified delay in the proceedings which in the circumstances is inconsistent with an intent to bring the person concerned to justice;

c. The proceedings were not or are not being conducted independently or impartially, and they were or are being conducted in a manner which, in the circumstances, is inconsistent with an intent to bring the person concerned to justice.

[46] Although the United States signed the Treaty on 31 December 2000, not only has it not ratified the Convention but it has sent notice to the Court that ' the United States does not intend to become a party to the treaty' and 'accordingly, has no legal obligations arising from its signature of December 31, 2000.'

[47] Statute of the ICC, art. 5.

[48] See Bilan des Communications Reçues par le Bureau du Procureur de la CPI, 10 February 2006. Website of the United Nations.

[49] In a *Newsday* article reporting the systematic rape by Serb forces in northern Bosnia, statements by the victims interviewed suggested that the sexual assaults were not a 'by-product of the war' but rather 'a principal tactic of the war.' One of the women interviewed said that the man who abducted her told her that he was 'ashamed to be a Serb' and that they were under orders to rape the girls. Dr. Melika Kreitmayor who led the gynecological team that examined some of the victims from Brezovo Polje was cited in the article as saying that the motivation behind the rapes was 'to humiliate Muslim women, to insult them, to destroy their persons and to cause shock.' She continued by saying that the victims were not raped 'because it was a male instinct. They were raped because it was the goal of the war.' To support this, she said that some of the victims were taken and although not raped, were asked to say they were. Roy Gutman, 23 August 1992.

Since international humanitarian law is today an integral part of almost every Nation and since violations of this law are forbidden, one can only be bewildered when participants in contemporary armed conflicts choose to use these 'weapons.' The overwhelming majority of Nations are Parties to humanitarian conventions. The people of these Nations are not ignorant of these laws and principles. They are the basis of the 'morality' of the international community. Thus, it is extremely probable that those who are committing these crimes are aware that they are illegal.

Daniel Muñoz-Rojas and Jean-Jacques Frésard, two authors in a larger study conducted by the International Red Cross,[50] underlined several theories that did not pertain directly to sexual violence but instead to violations of international humanitarian law in general.[51] Their study demonstrated that combatants 'are subject to group conformity phenomena such as depersonalization, loss of independence and a high degree of conformity.'[52] Studies have shown that fighting men 'are generally motivated more by group pressure than by hatred or even fear.'[53] The soldier's reputation, the esteem of the group, and helping the group to succeed, are factors which reduce the individual's autonomy. The relations that 'bind the combatants are often stronger than those that bind a married couple.'[54] The individual has a natural tendency to believe that his group is superior to other groups, which in turn 'generates prejudices, simplifications and discrimination.'[55] These factors, according to the study, lead men to follow orders rather than follow their own moral convictions, particularly in a combat situation, where the 'individual is rendered more docile by military training and collective preparation for confrontation with an enemy that is often demonized and dehumanized.'[56] One of the most important results of this submission to authority is the disappearance of personal responsibility.[57]

In addition, the study of Muñoz-Rojas and Frésard illustrates that those combatants who are subject to humiliation and trauma are themselves more likely to violate international humanitarian law.[58] This is due to the 'cycle of vengeance' and also the 'spiral of violence.' That is to say, the violent threats and treatment to which they have been subject by their own group subsequently leads to their reproducing this violence.[59] Furthermore, it affords proof that having the knowledge of the law does not always lead to following it in 'real-life' situations. This behaviour is justified in that the combatant often feels himself to be the victim, which in turn allows him to commit the violations. Those fighting 'for survival cannot afford the luxury of humanitarian considerations and rules which could weaken' them, and

---

[50] The study, 'The Roots of Behaviour in War,' was aimed at assisting the International Red Cross to identify the factors that may help formulate a policy to prevent violations of international humanitarian law by combatants in armed conflicts.

[51] Daniel Muñoz-Rojas and Jean-Jacques Frésard, 'The Roots of Behaviour in War : Understanding and preventing IHL violations,' in *International Review of the Red Cross*, March 2004, Vol. 86, No. 853.

[52] Ibid, p. 193.

[53] Ibid, p. 194.

[54] Ibid.

[55] Ibid.

[56] Ibid.

[57] Stanley Milgram, *Obedience to authority : An experimental view* (New York : Harper & Row, 1974), cited by ibid, p. 195.

[58] Ibid, p. 195.

[59] Ibid, p. 196.

hence the old adage of the end justifying the means.[60] Illegitimate behaviour thereby becomes justified if not 'legal.'

Like many previous studies, this study has found that the violator of international humanitarian law is not usually one who is sick, psychopathic or even irrational. For the most part, it is the 'normal' individual who is committing these atrocities. The different factors defined in the study gradually lead to a moral disengagement.[61]

Muñoz-Rojas and Frésard make two recommendations: that international humanitarian law be made political and legal more than just moral, and that combatants be properly instructed in appropriate conduct and sanctioned when there are violations.[62] This latter measure could eliminate at least some of the crimes, sexual or otherwise, during conflicts. Nevertheless, it is doubtful that it would in fact eradicate the problem. The first recommendation, that international humanitarian law be more of a political and legal matter than a moral one, again seems limited. Violence against women, as we have seen, is already a legal matter, and the effect of the conventions, customs and principles in this area are far from being conclusive. The authors themselves argue that, under certain circumstances, an illegal action can be considered a justified one.

Law is a necessary factor. One cannot stress enough the importance of manifestations such as the approval by the Third Committee (Social Humanitarian and Cultural) of the United Nations of a recent draft resolution entitled 'Eliminating rape and other forms of sexual violence in all their manifestations, including as instruments to achieve political objectives,'[63] which was scheduled to be presented to the full Assembly for a vote this year.[64]

However, if law is a necessary factor, it is not a sufficient one. The study conducted by Muñoz-Rojas and Frésard treated violations of international humanitarian law in general. What does it signify for sexual violence against women and girls in armed conflicts? One of the factors underlined in the study is that the combatant group often feels superior to other groups, and this feeling of superiority creates prejudices, simplifications and discriminations that may lead to violations of international humanitarian law. To this must be added, in the case of violence against women, the prejudices, simplifications and discrimination that exist already in peacetime against women and girls. Given the tendency of all combatants to feel that their enemy is inferior, it follows logically that the segment within it which is viewed everywhere as inferior—that is, women and girls—will be treated as even more inferior, hence the readiness to tolerate the subsequent violations of international humanitarian law.

One may then ask, why sexual violence and not just violence in general against this sub-group? The reasons for this, unfortunately, are plausibly more historic and more imbedded in the deeper problems of society; violence against women is in fact often sexual. And necessarily so, where there is a will to demoralize and humiliate the enemy group.

This brings one to wonder if rape and other sexual violence during armed conflict are not directly related to attitudes towards women and girls at all times. Perhaps, in changing at all times the treatment of women and attitudes towards women, one would witness a reduction of

---

[60] Ibid, p.198.

[61] See theory of Erwin Staub, *The Roots of Evil : The Origins of Genocide and Other Group Violence* (Cambridge : Cambridge University Press, 1992), cited by ibid., pp. 199-200.

[62] Muñoz-Rojas and Frésard, already cited, p. 206.

[63] 15 November 2007, General Assembly GA/SHC/3906. Document A/C.3/62/L.16/Rev .2.

[64] The reader should remember that General Assembly Resolutions are not in themselves binding on the members of the United Nations and are thus not strictly law. However, they often lead to binding law.

sexual crime against women during armed conflicts. The United Nations has made great efforts in this domain. The following provide examples.

The Fourth World Conference on Women:[65] The Beijing Declaration proclaimed its intention 'to advance the goals of equality, development and peace for all women everywhere, in the interest of all humanity' and this through, *inter alia*, the empowerment and advancement of women and their full participation in the decision-making processes and access to power, through equal rights, opportunities, resources, the sharing of family responsibilities, the eradication of poverty by promoting women's economic independence, the recognition and reaffirmation of the right of all women to control all aspects of their health, 'in particular their own fertility', and the necessity of designing, implementing and monitoring, 'with the full participation of women,' gender-sensitive programmes. The Declaration states very clearly that 'women's rights are human rights.'

The Beijing Platform for Action restated that its objective was the empowerment of all women, and that the 'full realization of all human rights and fundamental freedoms of all women is essential' for this empowerment. Again, therefore, the emphasis was on the direct relationship between empowerment and human rights. Each Nation has the responsibility to implement the Platform for Action through national legislation. The reality of 'absolute poverty,' and particularly the 'feminization of poverty' with the 'continued violence against women and the widespread exclusion of half of humanity from institutions of power and governance,' can be stopped only by a 'radical transformation of the relationship between women and men to one of full and equal partnership.' The Platform not only underlined the importance of efforts of the United Nations to promote equality between the sexes[66] but also the essential role played by non-governmental organizations and feminist groups, which the text considers 'a driving force for change.' The Platform underscored the fact that discrimination against women begins at the 'earliest stages' of a woman's life, so that the girl child must be given the same chances as the boy child. However, it is pointed out that the girl child has less access to nutrition, education and, in general, other rights than boys have. Furthermore, these girls are also subjected to various forms of sexual and economic exploitation, paedophilia and forced prostitution being only two examples cited.

One of the critical areas in which the Platform demonstrated concern is of course violence against women. However, this violence is not an isolated issue but one directly related to the discriminatory attitude in many areas against women and girls. The Platform calls for the proposal of strategic objectives to eliminate the different areas of concern. It upheld that violence against women exists in all societies; that women are subjected to 'physical, sexual and psychological abuse that cuts across the lines of income, class and culture.' It underlined particularly that the 'low social and economic status of women can be both a cause and a consequence of violence against women.'

The concept of 'violence against women' was actually defined by the Platform as any act of gender-based violence that results in, or is likely to result in, physical, sexual or

[65] Fourth Conference on Women, Beijing, P.R.C., Sept. 4-15, 1995, Beijing Declaration and Platform for Action.

[66] For example, 1975 was declared the International Women's Year by the General Assembly that first brought focus on women's issues, the Conventions on the Elimination of All Forms of Discrimination against Women (adopted by the General Assembly, 1979 and entered into force 1981), the World Conference to Review and Appraise the Achievements of the United Nations Decade for Women : Equality, Development and Peace, which adopted the Nairobi Forward-looking Strategies for the Advancement of Women and the Fourth Conference on Women.

psychological harm or suffering to women, including threats of such acts, coercion or arbitrary deprivation of liberty, whether occurring in public or private life.

A non-exhaustive list of examples then followed. A special mention was dedicated to the violation of the human rights of women in situations of armed conflict, underscoring particularly murder, systematic rape, sexual slavery and forced pregnancy. Nonetheless, the list included also family violence such as dowry-related violence, marital rape, female genital mutilation, general community violence against women including rape, sexual harassment and intimidation at work, and violence perpetrated or condoned by the State.

The Platform itself mentioned that violence against women 'derives essentially from cultural patterns, in particular the harmful effects of certain traditional or customary practices, and all acts of extremism linked to race, sex, language or religion that perpetrate the lower status accorded to women in the family, the workplace, the community and society.'

One could therefore conclude that violence against women in times of armed conflict can be fought effectively only if discrimination against women is eliminated at all times. It has been recommended to governments that they condemn any tradition, custom or religious practice that promotes violence, that they enact legislation to prevent as well as punish violence against women, and that they periodically revise such legislation. Governments should also help victims to obtain judicial aid, create and strengthen institutional mechanisms that help women to report violence, promote active and visible policies to increase knowledge and awareness of the causes and consequences of violence, and to ratify and implement international humanitarian norms in this area.[67]

A recent draft General Assembly Resolution[68] underlines again the importance of the Beijing Declaration and Platform for Action for 'the achievement of gender equality and the empowerment of women' and the necessity for the States to transform these into 'effective action'. The draft Resolution mentions the progress made but also stresses the need for much more. It also affirms that efforts must be made 'primarily at the national level,' to be supported by 'enhanced international cooperation.' The Draft also reaffirms the concept of gender mainstreaming as a globally accepted strategy to achieve the goals of Beijing.[69] The Draft Resolution admits that gender balance is far from being achieved. It once again emphasizes the importance for this balance that women play an important role 'in the prevention and resolution of conflicts and in peacekeeping.' Finally, it encourages all Parties, States, the United Nations system, international organisations and all sectors of civil society to intensify their action towards the goals set out.

Eliminating discrimination against women by empowering them in peacetime may be, among other important measures, an essential element in changing attitudes towards them during armed conflict. The effectiveness of the different declarations, platforms and resolutions will depend in part on their being converted into binding law.

---

[67] One such instrument is the Convention on the Elimination of All Forms of Discrimination against Women adopted by the General Assembly of the U.N., 18 December 1979. The Convention condemns all forms of discrimination against women and calls for a policy of eliminating such discrimination.

[68] A/C.3/62/L.89.

[69] According to the Office of the Special Advisor on Gender Issues and Advancement of Women, Department of Economic and Social Affairs, gender mainstreaming is a strategy but not a goal in itself. It involves 'ensuring that gender perspectives and attention to the goal of gender equality are central to all activities-policies development, research, advocacy/dialogue, legislation, resource allocation, and planning, implementation and monitoring of programmes and projects' (www.un.org/womenwatch/osagi).

No doubt a positive result will be achieved only when international courts begin to prosecute and condemn nations not only in wartime but in peacetime too, for their violations of the laws forbidding discrimination against women and girls.

In: Crimes Against Women
Editor: David Wingeate Pike

ISBN 978-1-61470-813-1

Chapter 6

DEFINING RAPE IN CONFLICT-AFFECTED AREAS

Robynn Collins

INTRODUCTION

In conflict-affected areas[1] around the world, individual rights and security, are particularly for women and girls threatened for a variety of social, economic and political reasons. Decreased stability and security leave women and girls at increased risk of being raped. This chapter is a short synopsis of a broad scan of journalistic, narrative, anecdotal and empirical accounts of the ways in which women and girls have been and continue to be raped in eight conflict-affected areas: Bangladesh, Bosnia-Herzegovina, Darfur, Democratic Republic of the Congo, East Timor, Liberia, Rwanda, and Uganda.[2] The study upon which this chapter is based both classifies the varieties of rape and examines the social, cultural and religious responses to the children born as a result of each type of rape. This chapter focuses solely on the four typologies of rape exposed.

This chapter sets out to show that 'rape' is a contested term, and to question its meaning when it is used to describe the many types of rape that women and girls experience. Rape has been explained in varying contexts by a range of diverse motives, with different meanings and consequences. In conflict-affected areas, rape is not solely violence against an individual. It also has (and these contexts, is meant to have) perpetual socio-political effects not only on the victim and the family of the victim but also on the collective consciousness of the entire community, as well as on the child born as a result of rape and forced pregnancy—the war-

---

[1] For the purposes of this study, conflict-affected areas are those that have been impacted by militarized violence, armed conflict, and war. Even in the aftermath of overt conflict, these regions may not yet be politically, socially, or economically stable and are often loosely referred to as 'post-conflict' areas, despite the structural and cultural violence that persists long after the conflict has 'cooled.' In areas affected by natural disaster, say, the Sri Lankan *tsunami* and Hurricane *Katrina* in New Orelans, women and girls are also at increased risk of the four types of rape.

[2] Robynn Collins, 'Towards Theorizing Rape in Armed Conflict: War-Born Children and the Perpetual Politics of a Genealogy,' unpublished MA Research/ Memoir, Conflict Studies Program, Saint Paul University, Ottawa, Canada, April 2005.

born child.[3] The consequences of rape can profoundly affect family structure and communal solidarity, as well as determine the future of these war-born children such as their right to security, citizenship and education.

The preliminary conclusions yielded by this larger study confirm that the motives and consequences of rape vary extensively according to circumstances, suggesting the need for equally diverse socio-cultural and legalistic responses. Rape in wartime is different from rape in peacetime. Variations in the definition and labeling of 'rape' call for enhanced reporting and monitoring mechanisms, which may not always work to their fullest capacity—thus leading to the ambiguity of the terminology used and/or the stigma attached to it.

Rape specific to conflict-affected areas can be broken into four classifications:[4] Strategic Rape, Tactical Rape, Collateral Rape, and Domesticated Rape. This typology of rape is far from definitive. However, the sooner a monitoring system can be constructed, the sooner a solution can be found to sanction the perpetrator and aid the victim/survivor in the appropriate ways which, as this chapter proposes, will vary widely depending on the type of rape and the context.

STRATEGIC RAPE

Rape has historically been understood as a natural by-product of war,[5] one that is unavoidable. In recent decades, however, there has arisen a greater awareness of the prevalence of rape in war. There is nothing natural or inevitable about wartime rape, as it is often premeditated, planned and carried out with a specific set of objectives in mind. Trailblazers on the topic of sexual violence in war have claimed that systematic rape, even strategic rape, is used as a *weapon* in dirty wars.[6] In June 2008, the United Nations Security Council adopted Resolution 1820 recognizing rape as a war tactic.

Strategic Rape can be characterized as a blueprint for a long-term plan. It is used to poison the roots of a community, by terrorizing and planting the genetic seeds in the wombs of women, which will change the ethnic composition of a society. Legalistically a crime against humanity,[7] Strategic Rape is the politically motivated desire to cleanse a community

[3] A war-born child (WBC) is a child that is conceived intentionally or unintentionally as a result of rape or forced pregnancy in a conflict-affected area. The prevalence of children being born in conflict-affected areas as a result of rape and forced pregnancy requires a word less context-specific and more general than what these children have been called (in various contexts by aid workers, scholars and community members) such as 'war babies,' 'enemy children,' 'children of shame,' 'monster babies,' 'enfants de mauvais souvenir,' and 'enfants non-désirés.'

[4] Robynn Collins, memoir cit.

[5] See Ruth Seifert, 'The Second Front: The Logic of Sexual Violence in Wars,' *Women's Studies International Quarterly* 19 (January 1996), pp. 35-43; and Sharon Fredrick (ed.). (2001) *Rape as Weapon of Terror* (New Jersey: Global Publishing, 2001).

[6] Anne Barstow, *War's Dirty Secret: Rape, Prostitution and Other Crimes Against Women* (Ohio: Pilgrim Press, 2000), p. 2.

[7] Crimes against Humanity refer to murder; enslavement; deportation or forcible transfer of a population; imprisonment or other severe deprivation of physical liberty in violation of fundamental rules of international law; torture; rape, sexual slavery, forced prostitution, forced pregnancy, forced sterilization, or any other form of sexual violence of comparable gravity; persecution against any identifiable group or collectivity for political, racial, gendered, ethnic, cultural, religious reasons, as defined in paragraph 3 of the Geneva Conventions of 1949; and any other inhumane acts of a similar character intentionally causing great suffering, or serious injury to body or to mental or physical health.

of its ethnic origins. This type of rape stems from xenophobia, the fear and hatred of an "other" ethnic or religious group. It is this hatred that drives perpetrators to destroy or at least reduce the possibility of the "other" being born. This is done by killing pregnant women, forcing sterilization, inducing abortion, killing the children of the enemy group.

Especially in situations of ethnic armed conflict, rape can be both a militaristic or nationalistic strategy. For example, the public and systematic raping of women or men by military forces has been used to force families to flee their homes. Another characteristic of this type of rape is the intentional neglect of women's reproductive wellbeing and/or the denial of options for women such as abortion clinics, which illustrates a wider systematic discrimination that is perpetuated by unwritten strategic political policies.

The long-term application of Strategic Rape occurs when one group forces another group to have its enemy's babies, thereby ensuring that the initial violence of the rape be perpetuated into the future. The underlying strategy is planned (by orders from high-ranking military commanders, police, or rebel groups) so as to ensure that babies will grow up to be just like their biological fathers and that there will always be one of 'us' among 'them.'

Women and young girls who become pregnant from this type of rape will often remain captive in enemy camps, and receive 'special treatment'[8] so as to ensure that they will give birth to babies of their enemy. Where pregnancies from Strategic Rape occur outside of captivity, there is the likelihood that the pregnancy is aborted or the baby killed at birth or sent to an orphanage.

Tactical Rape

Tactical Rape can be characterized by the need to fulfill short-term and immediate objectives such as establishing or maintaining control over a particular territory and its inhabitants. Military commanders and the leaders of armed groups may encourage the use of rape as a way to terrorize civilians. Perpetrators will be uniformed and armed. Tactical Rape is generally used to deliver a message to the population upon or within the body of the victim. This type of rape tends to be used to instill fear and explicitly communicate to people to stay out of a particular territory. It may barricade a community into a tight area, usually with no food or water nearby. The threat of this type of rape could be likened to a land mine; there is an element of chance and risk involved. If an individual leaves a safe area, such as the borders of a refugee camp, to fetch firewood, water or food, she or he run a higher risk of being raped; if they do not take this risk, however, they will be unable to feed themselves and their families and may starve to death. Tactical is not random rape, it is not 'sexual abuse' or 'exploitation'; there is indeed nothing sexual or exploitative about it.

The rape that continues to take place in the Democratic Republic of Congo suggests a definite pattern of sexual abuse against civilians.[9] Soldiers and rebel fighters engage in acts of rape by attacks on civilians, to scare the civilian population into submission. Combatants engage in opportunistic attacks, targeting individuals in their homes or while going about their daily business. In some contexts, cases of Tactical Rape become so frequent that women

[8] Special treatment as described by being transferred to makeshift infirmaries and being fed twice a day, because, as some of the Chetnik soldiers said, 'the women had to bear [our] healthy offspring' (*The New York Times*, 13 December 1992).

[9] Human Rights Watch : www.org/reports/2005/drc0305/4.htm.

and girls stop working in the fields or going to the market, take to hiding in the forest at night instead of walking home, and sometimes flee their homes altogether.[10] It is often while performing these basic tasks that this type of rape occurs.

COLLATERAL RAPE

Rape in conflict-affected areas where sex is considered exchangeable for money, security, food or weapons can be characterized as Collateral Rape. Since the rights and security of individuals, predominantly women and girls, are particularly threatened in these areas, they are especially vulnerable to rape. As the term implies, Collateral Rape is best understood as a type of transaction: 'If you let me do this to you, I will protect you, pay you, and offer you security.' Collateral Rape is highly prevalent in all stages of conflict where the scarcity of resources, economic desperation, and need for security are in evidence.

The prevalence of Collateral Rape is symptomatic of the commercialization of the body. This can take the form of what is erroneously called 'forced prostitution' (despite the context), being designed to sanitize the act of rape or implying permission to rape in exchange for money. It suggests that victims of this type of rape in some way have a choice.

The usual suspects of this type of rape are not only armed men but also include aid workers, peacekeepers, and police officers. Victims may be raped 'in exchange' for something, such as needing a male security escort to search after dusk for firewood or food. This tends to be a more private rape than the former two. It takes place in back alleys, hotel rooms, forests, first-aid tents. Although this type of rape is predominantly collateral in nature,[11] this is not to imply consent on the part of the survivor. Conversely, it is the threat of rape that might force the victim to enter into such 'transactions;' for at least in this way there remains the illusion of agency and free will, on the part of both the survivor and the perpetrator. A young woman may first be raped by militiamen in a Tactical Rape and later, driven by her need to survive, Collaterally Raped, neither action fitting into the parameter of 'forced prostitution.'[12] Another group that may be at heightened risk of Collateral Rape is abducted children who have been forced to become child soldiers; they often become trapped in a 'relationship' and might be raped day in and day out by their protectors/rebel husbands.

There are thousands of accounts that suggest differences in motives for rape from strategic to collateral, such as the case of a desperate young girl trading a UN peacekeeper two eggs for sexual favours. When asked about the rape the girl told a reporter: 'at least MONUC pay!'[13] The United Nations investigated 150 instances in which 50 peacekeeping troops in a Congo mission were suspected of having sexually abused or exploited women and

[10] Ibid.

[11] The term collateral is used loosely here. It is not meant to imply any inkling of free will or free choice on the part of the survivor, rather that the survivor is in a situation where he or she will be raped regardless of what is proposed to be 'traded'. One of the underlying components of collateral rape is that the perpetrator somehow creates the illusion that a trade can take place in 'exchange' for sex, using his position of power, money or protection as a weapon.

[12] Emily Wax, 'Congo's Desperate One-Dollar U.N. Girls, Shunned Teens, Many Raped by Militiamen, Sell Sex to Peacekeepers,' *Washington Post* Foreign Service, 21 March 2005.

[13] 'Sexual Assault Continues Unchecked in the Congo' www.feminist.com/newsvaw42.html. MONUC stands for UN peacekeepers in the Congo.

girls, some as young as twelve.[14] All the survivors were vulnerable, poverty-stricken young women and girls engaged in what the Congolese themselves called 'obligation' or 'survival' sex. These crimes, carried out by, but not limited to, United Nations Peacekeepers in Congo may be attributed to the unacceptable deficit in training and education available to peacekeepers and aid workers who work in conflict-affected areas.[15] While training and education in awareness and prevention of gender-based violence are offered by many organizations, most often they are offered only once in a career, amounting to a mere half-day training module.

Domesticated Rape

Rape that occurs after the militarized conflict has subsided or, more loosely speaking, in post-conflict, can be characterized as Domesticated Rape. This category derived from the reports and interviews of current and former humanitarian aid workers, some of whom stated that in this post-conflict the frequency of rape by armed men decreases while the incidence of rape by plain-clothed men, possibly including the victim's own neighbour or relative, escalates.[16] The rapists in this case might be amnestied soldiers, returnees from the conflict, former child soldiers, police officers, and the victim's own family members. Domesticated Rape can be attributed to an increase in displaced persons and to social, political and particularly economic stress, as well as a rise in domestic violence. These rapes can be more easily hidden from the family. Rape in post-conflict-affected areas becomes so normalized that women are more likely to remain silent about it.

In speaking with an informant (a former humanitarian aid worker) about the prevalence of domesticated rape, it was suggested that survivors of this type of rape are likely to find it easier to keep it hidden, and even if they don't, there is less of a stigma attached because rape has become so normalized and widespread- a part of the culture of violence. This type of violence is a symbolic driving force in the culture of impunity in which men and women find themselves. When asked about the term Domesticated Rape, another informant pointed out: 'This isn't the big bad rape we're hearing about now. The rapes we are hearing about now are the 'old' rapes, the ones that happened during conflict. What we are not hearing about is all the rapes that are taking place post-conflict.'[17]

Conclusion

This chapter has set out to examine the ways in which we use language to identify, investigate and respond to rape in conflict-affected areas. It is important to question the use of terms such as forced prostitution, sexual exploitation, and gender-laden forms of abuse. If the

---

[14] Ibid.

[15] Robynn Collins and Saskia Ivens, *Women, Peace and Security* : *The Canadian NGO Experience, The Canadian Peacebuilding Coordinating Commitee, Ottawa*, March 2007. (peacebuild.ca/upload/Final%20NGO%20Report%20EN.pdf).

[16] Personal interviews conducted by the author with current and former humanitarian aid workers and police investigators from conflict-affected regions, April 2005, Ottawa, Canada.

[17] Personal interview by the author, Ottawa, 4 April 2005.

language upon which we are building policies and theories that in turn determine practice are inherently faulty, misleading or not context-sensitive, it follows that the policies, theories and praxis are also flawed.

The gender-based language that has become unilaterally 'mainstreamed' and incorporated into the policy and practice of protecting human rights and offering aid (and responding to the crimes against civilians that happen somewhere in between), have inadvertently led to making broad conclusions about these crimes and the language that we use to respond to them. Identifying 'types' of rape would assist in defining responses as to why, when and how a family or community either ostracizes or integrates survivors of rape, as well as in offering support to survivors of these four types of violence.

Establishing an effective framework (better yet, *frameworks,* unbound by context-specific indicators) in policy and practice for responding to the various types of rape in conflict-affected areas, will be built upon and sensitive to cross-cultural theories of deep-rooted ethnic conflict, feminist theories of sexual violence, critical race theory, genetic myths, and theories of individual and group trauma. Another stride forward would be to require those organizations that have staff and partners in conflict-affected areas to provide mandatory training and codes of conduct on the prevention of sexual abuse and exploitation of women and girls[18] and protocols for reporting misconduct. These measures would serve to refute the attitude that has so far escaped critical questioning, that rape is a 'natural by-product' of war.

[18] The Inter-Agency Standing Committee (IASC) developed a set of commitments as a guide for organizations working in conflict-affected areas to use in creating codes of conduct for international development and humanitarian aid workers on the prevention of sexual abuse and exploitation. Guidelines for creating codes of conduct and responding to gender-based violence in conflict-affected areas can be found at: http://www.humanitarianinfo.org/iasc/content/products/docs/tfgender_GBVGuidelines2005.pdf.

Congo

'Sexual violence in Congo,' declared Sir John Holmes, the UN Under-Secretary General for Humanitarian Affairs and former British Ambassador to France, 'is the worst in the world. The sheer numbers, the wholesale brutality, the culture of impunity–it's appalling.'[1] The Guardian echoed the voice of Holmes, reporting that sexual violence in Congo was being used in the conflict as an instrument of war. Sexual violence was now so widespread that Médecins sans Frontières, the medical aid agency, reported that 75 percent of all the rape cases it dealt with worldwide were in eastern Congo, while Darfur in Sudan, despite its prominence in the media, figured only as a distant second.[2] Nicholas Kristof of the New York Times followed up, calling Congo's eastern part, where in some areas three-quarters of all women had been raped, 'the rape capital of the world.'[3]

The people of the now 'Democratic Republic of Congo' had suffered more than any other African colony after the 'humanitarian intervention' in 1885 of King Leopold III of the Belgians, who repudiated the Congo's native horrors simply to unleash his own. Europeans, ran the post-colonial refrain, were ill posited to comment on Africa's misfortunes, but this complaint had long lost its resonance. In December 2004, Kofi Annan, the former UN secretary general, stated that there was 'clear evidence that acts of gross misconduct have taken place' in the Congo mission of the UN, which had begun in early 2000 and was known by its French acronym MONUC (Mission des Nations Unies en République Démocratique du Congo). The 10,800 UN soldiers (classified as peace-keepers) and 1,000 civilian employees that made up the UN's Congo mission represented some fifty countries, and it was the peace-keepers from Morocco, Nepal, Pakistan, Tunisia and Uruguay who were now accused of sexual misconduct. The UN report gave details of the crimes committed against Congo women, and listed incidents in which some soldiers tried to obstruct the investigators.[4]

D.W.P.

---

[1] Jeffrey Gettleman, 'Epidemic of rape devastates Congo,' *International Herald Tribune*, 8 October 2007.

[2] 'Help reduce harmful child marriages worldwide,' National Action Center (NOW), 12 June 2008.

[3] Nicholas D. Kristof, 'The weapon of rape,' *International Herald Tribune*, 17 June 2008. Kristof nevertheless paid tribute to the doctors at Heal Africa Hospital and Panzi Hospital for their skill and humanity in working to repair the internal injuries of rape victims.

[4] Marc Lacey, 'In Congo, girls recall blue helmet–and rape,' *International Herald Tribune*, 20 December 2004. An HBO (Home Box Office) documentary film entitled *The Greatest Silence: Rape in the Congo* has been used by NGOs, internationally and locally, as a tool to expose the level of sexual violence against Congolese women and girls and to urge action on their behalf.

In: Crimes Against Women
Editor: David Wingeate Pike
ISBN 978-1-61470-813-1

Chapter 7

WARTIME RAPE IN THE CONGO

Stefan Kirchner

I. SYSTEMATIC SEXUAL VIOLENCE IN EASTERN CONGO

In the wars that in recent years have ravaged the Democratic Republic of Congo (D.R.C.),[1] the former Zaire, about four million people have been killed and hundreds of thousands of women have been raped.[2] Wartime rape is anything but new, and in Rwanda, Bosnia[3] and Darfur[4] it has been employed not only to terrorize the population but also to inflict genocide Recent news reports, however, from the Eastern provinces of North and South Kivu, concerning massive and systematic rape, were so shocking that even experienced professionals who have been working with rape victims for years could not believe what was happening.[5] In 2005, 42,000 rape victims were treated in South Kivu alone.[6] Taking into account how difficult it is for the victims to overcome shame and seek treatment, and then actually to travel to a hospital, many more women might never receive any treatment at all. In many cases the victims, ranging from infants to the elderly,[7] have been deliberately injured during or after the rape. Injuries were caused not only by gang rape but also by the deliberate

---

[1] For the purposes of this chapter, the term 'Congo' refers only to the Democratic Republic of Congo, also known as Congo-Kinshasa, as opposed to Congo-Brazzaville.

[2] Chris McGreal, 'Hundreds of thousands raped in Congo wars,' in: *The Guardian*, 14 November 2006, available online at http://www.guardian.co.uk/print/0,,329626772-110889,00.html..

[3] Cf. Pascale R. Bos, 'Feminists interpreting the politics of wartime rape: Berlin, 1945; Yugoslavia, 1992-1993,' in: 31 Signs: *Journal of Women in Culture and Society* (2006), pp. 995 et seq., at p. 1012.

[4] Cf. Amnesty international, *Sudan, Darfur – Rape as a weapon of war – Sexual violence and its consequences* (July 2004).

[5] Rob Nordland, 'Congo's wounds of war: more vicious than rape – The atrocity reports from eastern Congo were so hellish that Western medical experts refused to believe them – at first,' MSNBC, 13 November 2006, available online at
http://www.msnbc.msn.com/is/15704030/site/newsweek/page/3.

[6] McGreal, supra (fn. 2).

[7] The ages of the victims have been reported between 4 months and 84 years. Marion Pratt / Leah Werchick, 'Sexual Terrorism: Rape as a Weapon of War in Eastern Democratic Republic of Congo – An assessment of programmatic responses to sexual violence in North Kivu, South Kivu, Maniema and Orientale Provinces,' USAID / DCHA (2004), p. 7.

insertion of objects into the vagina, including gun barrels,[8] a practice already known from the war in Bosnia.[9] Often guns were fired into the victim's vagina at point blank range[10] in order to cause maximum damage, often with the intention to mark the victim for life, rather than kill her.[11] Perversely, different armed groups have developed trademark injuries to make their identity very clear to the civilian population.[12] These assaults include burning,[13] raping exclusively girls aged eleven to fourteen,[14] and tying the hands of the victims so tightly that later they have to be amputated.[15] Some victims actually had "their vaginas pulled out."[16] Thousands of victims suffer from fistulae, ruptures of the walls which separate the victim's vagina from her rectum.[17] Fistulae can render the patients incontinent.[18] The victims are then unable to control their bodily functions[19] and are thereby soaked in their own urine and feces,[20] which essentially ends their social lives.[21] Furthermore, many victims are kidnapped and held in sexual slavery for months.[22] Other victims are gang-raped in front of their husbands or children, often villages are raided and most men are killed, most women raped. In some villages, two out of three women are rape victims.[23]

According to UN staff and doctors in the region, all armed groups are involved in rapes[24] and, despite the 2002 Pretoria Accord which put an official end to the war, assaults and rapes continue to this very day. As a matter of fact, UN peacekeepers reported in early 2007 that the number of reported rapes is actually increasing.[25] The militias are now not so much attacking one another directly as attacking the villages that are thought to support other militias.[26] Civilians in Eastern Congo have become the prime target of the violence. What used to be a series of wars between many warring factions has turned into all-out terrorism by armed groups against unarmed civilians.

8 Emily Wax, 'A brutal legacy of Congo war – Extent of violence against women surfaces as fighting recedes,' in: *Washington Post*, 25 October 2003, p. A01; McGreal, supra (fn. 2).
9 The insertion of objects, including broken bottles and gun barrels, into the victim's vagina has already been described as a practice employed in Bosnia, cf. Bos, supra (fn. 3), at p. 1019, fn. 28.
10 Wax, supra (fn. 8); Nordland, supra (fn. 5).
11 Nordland, supra (fn. 5).
12 Ibid.
13 Ibid.
14 Ibid.
15 Andrea Böhm, 'Wenn Frieden Männersache ist: Gegen die Frauen im Kongo wird noch immer Krieg geführt,' in: *Die Zeit*, No. 50 (2006), available online at http://zeus.zeit.de/text/2006/50/kongo.
16 McGreal, supra (fn. 2).
17 Nordland, supra (fn. 5).
18 Ibid.
19 Wax, supra (fn. 8).
20 Nordland, supra (fn. 5).
21 Ibid.
22 Cf. Wax, supra (fn. 8).
23 Böhm, supra (fn. 15).
24 Nordland, supra (fn. 5).
25 UN News Service, 'DR Congo: army and police continue to violate civilians' human rights, says UN mission,' 21 February 2007, http://www.un.org/apps/news/printnewsAr.asp?nid=21635.
26 Nordland, supra (fn. 5).

II. SMALL STEPS TOWARD JUSTICE

Indeed, when it comes to offering the victims justice, there are sad parallels to the Rwanda genocide, notably in the impossibility of bringing all perpetrators to justice. Although thousands of women have been raped, and there are legal rules protecting the victims, by 2005 less than a dozen perpetrators had been prosecuted.[27] From the victim's perspective, however, there is an important change: whereas in the past it was the victims who were punished for having been raped, now it is the criminals who are on the defensive.[28] While the mind-set of many Congolese men does not change that easily, and rape victims continue to be shunned,[29] legislative changes are nevertheless a step in the right direction.

1. Congolese Criminal Law

Articles 167 to 171 of the Congolese Penal Code prohibit indecent, that is sexual, assault and rape, namely sexual assault involving penetration.[30] These crimes carry a sentence of from five to twenty years in prison.[31] The same punishment awaits kidnappers who physically torture their victims,[32] which covers cases in which girls and women are taken from their homes to be held as sex slaves.[33] Should torture or rape lead to the death of the victim, Congolese law demands life in prison or the application of the death penalty.[34] Of particular importance is the fact that a serious impairment to the health of the victim by the act of rape is considered to be an aggravating factor, resulting in a sentence of from one to ten years' imprisonment.[35] Examples include pregnancy caused by rape or leading to the contraction of a serious and painful disease.[36] The latter provision is more than necessary since it is estimated that two-thirds of the perpetrators are HIV positive[37] and up to 30 percent of all victims are thought to have been infected with HIV.[38] Fifty percent of victims are thought to have been infected with syphilis as well.[39]

Although the response of the Congolese government to the atrocities remains insufficient, some legislation has been introduced, namely Art. 169 no. 7 of the 2002 Military Penal Code[40] which replaced the 1972 Military Penal Code. To comply, at least formally, with

---

[27] Human Rights Watch, 'D. R. Congo: Tens of Thousands Raped, Few Prosecuted,' available online at http://www.hrw.org/english/docs/2005/03/07/congo/10258.html; for more in-depth information see Juliane Klippenberg, 'Seeking Justice: The Prosecution of Sexual Violence in the Congo War,' 17 *Human Rights Watch Reports* (March 2005), No. 1 (A).

[28] McGreal, supra (fn. 2).

[29] Tiare Rath, 'In war-riddled Congo, militias rape with impunity,' *Women's News*, 27 April 2003, http://www.womensenews.org/Article.cfm/dyn/aid/1307/context/cover.

[30] Juliane Klippenberg, 'The war within the war – Sexual violence against women and girls in eastern Congo,' Human Rights Watch (2002), p. 84.

[31] Ibid.; cf. Klippenberg, supra (fn. 27), pp. 28 et seq.

[32] Klippenberg, supra (fn. 30), p. 84.

[33] Ibid.

[34] Amnesty International, 'Democratic Republic of Congo – Mass rape: Time for remedies' (2004), p. 16.

[35] Ibid.

[36] Ibid.

[37] René Lefort , 'Congo: A hell on earth for women,' in: *Le Nouvel Observateur*, 11-18 September 2003.

[38] Ibid.

[39] Ibid.

[40] Cf. Klippenberg, supra (fn. 27), p. 28.

Congo's international obligations,[41] the Code now provides the death penalty in cases of sexual violence that amount to crimes against humanity, if committed in the context of a 'general or systematic attack'[42] on either the D.R.C. or the civilian population.[43] This includes sexual slavery, enforced prostitution, forced pregnancy, enforced sterilization and similarly grave crimes.[44] Yet the practical application of the D.R.C.'s domestic laws is found wanting, and the law lacks the deterrent effect required to prevent future atrocities. This is in part due to the enormity of the problem and to the government's inability to exert its rule over the affected parts of the country. But it must also be kept in mind that the traditional status of women in Congolese society is still reflected in the law, as shown in Art. 448 of the D.R.C.'s family code under which a married woman has to obtain her husband's permission to bring a case to court.[45] Given that many husbands respond to the rape of their wives by severing all contact with them[46] or by refusing to support them,[47] this already places a first legal obstacle on the victims' path to justice. This is, nevertheless, only the tip of the iceberg. In the D.R.C. women are second-class citizens and are often not aware of their rights. Rape victims often have to return to their parents' house, and the injuries described above, unless treated (and in many regions, only a fraction of victims will receive treatment), will make it impossible for them to participate in the everyday life of their society, let alone to seek justice in the courts. If they do so, it is usually only married women of good social standing who hold any chance of obtaining justice.[48]

2. International Law

A better, albeit still evolving, chance of obtaining justice is provided on the international level. While international human rights law lacks sufficient enforcement mechanisms vis-à-vis the militias, wartime rape is a violation of international humanitarian law,[49] the law governing the conduct of armed forces in times of conflict. Grave violations of the laws of war are punishable under international criminal law which dates back to the Nuremberg and

---

[41] The Code Pénal Militaire was changed by law No 024/2002 of 18 November 2002 in order to comply with the requirements of the Rome Statute establishing the International Criminal Court, an international treaty to which the D.R.C. is a party. Cf. also the Code Judiciaire Militaire, Loi No 023/2002 of 18 November 2002 and Pierre Akele Adau, 'Réforme de la justice militaire en RDC: le nouveau droit judiciaire et pénal militaire transitoire: un ´soft landing´ pour la Cour d´ordre militaire,' in: 42 *Congo-Afrique*: (2002), Issue No. 369/370, pp. 547 et seq.

[42] Art. 169 Code Pénal Militaire.

[43] Amnesty International, supra (fn. 34), p. 16.

[44] Ibid.

[45] Ibid., p. 10.

[46] Lefort, supra (fn. 37); Wax, supra (fn. 8), p. A01.

[47] Cf. Sarah Gieseke, 'Rape as a tool of war in the eastern Democratic Republic of Congo (2007),' p. 12.

[48] Ibid., p. 23.

[49] See also Theodor Meron, 'Rape as a crime under international humanitarian law,' in: 87 *American Journal of International Law* (1993), pp. 424 et seq.; Aiko Utsumi, 'How the violence against women was dealt with in war crimes trials,' in: Indai Lourdes Sajor (ed.), *Common Grounds* (1998), pp. 187 et seq.; Kelly Dawn Askin, 'Prosecuting wartime rape and other gender-related crimes under international law: Extraordinary advances, enduring obstacles,' in: 21 *Berkeley Journal of International Law* (2003), pp. 288 et seq.; Kelly Dawn Askin, *War Crimes against Women: Prosecution in International War Crimes Tribunals* (1997), pp. 262 et seq.; Christine Chinkin, 'Rape and sexual abuse of women in international law,' in: 5 *European Journal of International Law* (1994), pp. 1 et seq;. and Helen Durham, 'Women, armed conflict and international law,' in: 84 *International Review of the Red Cross* (2002), pp. 655 et seq.

Tokyo war crimes trials after the Second World War. Rape was already prohibited in Art. 44 of the 1863 Lieber Code[50] and the Hague Regulations respecting the Laws and Customs of War on Land, contained in annexes to the 1899 and 1907 Hague Conventions. Today, Art. 27 of the 4th Geneva Convention and Art. 4 (2) lit. e of the 2nd Additional Protocol to the Geneva Conventions prohibit rape, enforced prostitution and similar crimes.[51] The 1st Additional Protocol to the Geneva Conventions (AP I) extends the protection to everyone who is in the territory of a party to a conflict.[52] Art. 75 (2) AP I prohibits "outrages upon personal dignity, in particular humiliating and degrading treatment, enforced prostitution and any form of indecent assault" with regard to both sexes.[53] Art. 76 AP I demands that women are to be "the object of special respect and shall be protected in particular against rape, forced prostitution and any other forms of indecent assault." These rules contain not only an obligation not to harm women, but a positive obligation to protect them. Consistent with this protective approach, the UN demands that all acts of sexual violence be condemned and prosecuted.[54] Today rape is a war crime, and under Art. 8 (2) lit. b (XXII) and Art. 8 (2) lit. e (VI) ICC-Statute[55] it can be prosecuted by the International Criminal Court (ICC) in The Hague. Already the existing temporary International Criminal Tribunals have dealt with wartime rape cases.[56] In *Delalic*, the International Criminal Tribunal for the former Yugoslavia (ICTY) equated sexual violence with torture,[57] and in *Kunarac* sexual slavery, rape and violations of human dignity were considered to be war crimes and crimes against humanity,[58] to give only two examples. Art. 8 of the ICC Statute includes rape in the list of crimes over which it has jurisdiction, provided that the state in which the crimes was committed fails, for whatever reason, to take action. In the case of the D.R.C., the authorities are both unable to solve the problem and suspected of being unwilling to do so. A step in the right direction, however, was taken by the Congolese government in March 2004 when the criminal conduct of the country's regular armed forces was referred to the International Criminal Court.[59]

---

[50] Instruction for the Government of Armies of the United States in the Field, General Orders No. 100, 24 April 1863.

[51] Cf. Kofi Annan, 'Women, Peace and Security' – Study submitted by the Secretary-General pursuant to Security Council Resolution 1325 (2000), 1st ed., United Nations, New York (2002), p. 34.

[52] Ibid.

[53] Ibid.

[54] United Nations High Commissioner for Human Rights, Sub-Commission on the Promotion and Protection of Human Rights – Systematic rape, sexual slavery and slavery-like practices, Sub-Commission resolution 1999/16, 26 August 1999.

[55] Cf. Human Rights Watch, 'International Justice for Women: The ICC marks a New Era,' 1 July 2002, http://www.hrw.org/campaigns/icc/icc-women.htm; Valerie Oosterveld, 'Sexual slavery and the International Criminal Court: Advancing international law,' in: 23 *Michigan Journal of International Law* (2004), pp. 605 et seq.

[56] Cf. Kelly Dawn Askin, 'Sexual violence in decisions and indictments of the Yugoslav and Rwanda Tribunals: Current status,' in: 93 *American Journal of International Law* (1999), pp. 97 et seq.; Stephanie K. Wood, 'A woman scorned for "least condemned" war crime: precedent and problems with prosecuting rape as a serious war crime in the International Criminal Tribunal for Rwanda,' in: 13 *Columbia Journal of Gender and Law* (2004), pp. 274 et seq.; Catherine N. Niarchos, 'Women, war, and rape: challenges facing the International Tribunal for the Former Yugoslavia,' in: 17 *Human Rights Quarterly* (1995), pp. 649 et seq.; Kelly Dawn Askin, supra (fn. 49) and Richard Goldstone, 'The United Nations' War Crimes Tribunals: an assessment,' in: 12 *Connecticut Journal of International Law* (197), pp. 227 et seq.

[57] ICTY – Prosecutor v. Delalic, IT-96-21-T, Judgment, 16 November 1998.

[58] ICTY – Prosecutor v. Kunarac, IT-96-23-T, Judgment, 22 February 2001.

[59] ICC – Press Release: Prosecutor receives referral of the situation in the Democratic Republic of Congo, ICC-OTP-20040419-50-En, 19 April 2004.

The ICC's jurisdiction covers all crimes committed after 1 July 2002, when the Rome Statute, the international treaty which established the world's first permanent war crimes court, came into force. The first defendant, Thomas Lubanga Dyilo, the former leader of the Union of Congolese Patriots (UPC), one of the armed groups in the D.R.C. responsible for war crimes and crimes against humanity, was charged with recruiting child soldiers in Ituri,[60] a region north of the province of North Kivu. The decision by the ICC to prosecute Lubanga was important, because the recruitment of child soldiers, unlike rape, had not yet been dealt with by any international tribunal at the time that the ICC opened its proceedings.[61] To those recruiting child soldiers the ICC thus sent a warning, but the victims of rape in North and South Kivu are still waiting for the ICC to take action in their cases.

III. OUTLOOK

As stated initially, the wars in the D.R.C. have cost four million lives. In this context it is quite apparent that the International Criminal Court cannot be expected to step in for the D.R.C. government and bring justice to all victims. At present, the ICC's investigations do not focus on rape, thus allowing this abject practice to continue unpunished. In the long run, a lack of effective law enforcement could encourage potential perpetrators elsewhere, who have no reason yet to fear the consequences of raping women. This impression, sadly enough, is all too often true. Although the first steps have been taken to improve the women's situation, most of the credit is due to the women who summon up the courage to report their ordeals, thereby bringing the atrocities to light. Now it is up to the D.R.C. government as well as to the international community to take more effective action.

---

[60] Human Rights Watch. 'DR Congo: ICC Hearing Could Pave Way for Court's First Trial,' 8 November 2006, available online at http://hrw.org/snglish/docs/2006/11/08/congo14512_txt.htm.

[61] Meanwhile, on 20 June 2007, the Special Court for Sierra Leone convicted Alex Tamba Brima, Brima Bazzy Kamara and Santigie Borbor Kanu for terrorism, enslavement, rape, murder and recruiting child soldiers, Special Court for Sierra Leone, Case No. SCSL-04-16-T, Judgment of 20 June 2007; Clarence Roy-Macauley, 'Special Court convicts 3 of Sierra Leone war crimes,' in: *The Washington Post*, 21 June 2007, p. A16.

JAPAN

International interest in women's rights in Japan remain focused on the long-simmering dispute over the so-called 'comfort women' or sex slaves whom the Japanese authorities had pressed into service during the Second World War. The Japanese government, faced with the choice of expressing owabi, the ultimate term in Japanese apology, or of stone-walling, chose to continue its stonewall. On 30 July 2007, the US House of Representatives approved a resolution that once again urged Japan to formally apologize for forcing thousands of women to work as sex slaves for its military.[1] The next day Prime Minister Shinzo Abe described the resolution as 'regrettable' and strongly indicated that the Japanese government would not ever offer an official apology to the surviving victims.[2] The issue, fought over for a decade, has probably reached both its impasse and its terminal point.

D.W.P.

---

[1] 'U.S. House wants Japan apology for WWII sex crimes,' AP, *International Herald Tribune*, 31 July 2007.

[2] Tokyo, *International Herald Tribune*, 01 August 2007.

In: Crimes Against Women
Editor: David Wingeate Pike
ISBN 978-1-61470-813-1

Chapter 8

IMPERIAL JAPAN AND ITS "COMFORT WOMEN"

David Wingeate Pike

In the matter of bringing war criminals to trial, the experience of Japan in the postwar world was very different from that of Germany. The Tokyo War Crimes trials of 1946-1948 were forbearing in the number of those accused, and with the advent of the Cold War in 1948 the Japanese authorities were free to deal on a bilateral level with the countries they had overrun. Major crimes went uninvestigated. Only when on 20 December 1993 the United Nations gave the designation of war crime to wartime rape did the world begin to learn of a practice by the Japanese of kidnapping foreign women and forcing them to serve as prostitutes for the Japanese Army. What first caught the world's attention was the use by the Imperial authorities of the term *inanfu*, or 'comfort women', a term halfway between euphemism and cynicism. Other terms listed on the procurement roles, when these finally came to light, included references to the *inanfu* as 'items' or 'logs.' The words had a curious ring. They were an echo of the term *Stück* (piece, or item) used by the German SS as the official description of a prisoner in a concentration camp. 'Comfort woman' was equally reductive: the individual debased to mere instrumentality, or as the American journalist Ellen Goodman would later remark, the woman reduced to the sum of her services.[1] The *inanfu* was totally dispensable, and she did not need to know the meaning of her title to understand that she had been removed from the scroll of humanity.

For decades after its surrender in 1945, Japan succeeded more or less in its insistence that there was no proof that its military had enslaved foreign women in brothels. The truth about the brothels emerged when many of the surviving victims surmounted the wall of shame that had caused them to remain silent.

The secret of the brothels concerned the enslavement of some 200,000 women who were tricked or forced into prostitution for the benefit of Japanese soldiers in the Second World

---

[1] Ellen Goodman, *Boston Globe,* 17 March 2007.

War.[2] In hindsight, it was considered doubtful that the whole truth would ever have come to light had it not been for three factors: the work of a Japanese historian who discovered incriminating military records; the filing of a class-action lawsuit by a few of the surviving victims on the 50th anniversary of the attack on Pearl Harbor; and the long-sought visit to Korea of Kiichi Miyazawa, who had become Japan's Prime Minister on 5 November 1991.[3]

The historian was Yoshiaki Yoshimi, a professor at Chuo University in Tokyo who single-handedly debunked the government's invention that if a vast network of brothels did indeed exist for Japanese troops throughout the entire area, it was the work of private merchants and not the military. Combing through the archives of the Self-Defense Agency in the 1980s in his research on Japan's use of poison gas during the war, Yoshimi came across a military order to set up a brothel. One document carried the title 'Regarding the recruitment of women for military brothels,' and it ordered the speedy construction of 'facilities for sexual comfort.' The order bore the *hanko*, or personal stamps, of high-ranking commanders of the Japanese Army. Yoshimi passed the documents to a reporter of the Tokyo daily *Asahi Shimbun* on the eve of Miyazawa's visit to South Korea to meet President Roh Tae Woo. On 17 January 1992, Miyazawa addressed the National Assembly in Seoul and expressed his 'sincerest apology' over the affair.[4]

Most, perhaps 80%, of the *inanfu* were children and teenagers from Korea, a Japanese colony from 1910 to 1945. Since the comfort women were almost entirely *gaijin*, or foreigners, they were unlikely to disturb the conscience of the Japanese Government, which had also benefited from the ancient viewpoint that a raped woman is a defiled woman who would spend the rest of her life with her head buried in shame. The first woman to overcome all this and go public was a Korean, Kim Hak Soon, who testified in August 1991, no longer in shame but in anger. She announced her plan to take legal action against the Japanese Government, whereupon two other women stepped forward to join her. All three presented themselves at the Tokyo District Court on 7 December 1991 to file suit. One of the three was Jan Ruff, a Dutchwoman then living in the Netherlands East Indies and currently living in Australia. According to the records of the Netherlands war crimes trials, there were 34 other Dutch survivors in her category, and in December 1992 the United Nations arranged a public hearing in Tokyo at which Ruff gave a horrifying account. The hearing was relayed nationally on Japanese television, and Theo Van Boven, a Dutch law professor serving as Special Rapporteur of the U.N. Sub-commission on Human Rights, attended the meeting and submitted a report.[5]

Far from sympathizing with the women, Koichi Kato, the government's chief spokesman, reacted in defiance, denying that the Army had organized or administered the brothels and insisting at the same time that Japan considered the issue of reparations had been definitively settled by the 1951 San Francisco peace treaty. The word 'compensation' would remain

[2] Robin Bulman, *Washington Post* service, 13 August 1992 ; *International Herald Tribune*, compiled from dispatches, 3-4 September 1994 ; *International Herald Tribune* (Reuters), 6 June 1996 ; Andrew Pollack, *New York Times* service, 17 August 1996 ; *International Herald Trib*une (The Associated Press), 30 May 1997.

[3] *The Washington Post*, editorial, 20 January 1992 ; David E. Sanger, *New York Times* service, 29 January 1992.

[4] *The Washington Post*, editorial, 20 January 1992 ; David E. Sanger, *New York Times* service, 29 January 1992 ; Robin Bulman, *Washington Post* service, 13 August 1992.

[5] David E. Sanger, *New York Times* service, 29 January 1992 ; David E. Sanger, *New York Times* service, 10 August 1992 ; Leila Angara (Tokyo), *International Herald Tribune*, 3 September 1992 ; Georges Hicks, *International Herald Tribune*, 10 February 1993.

taboo, because the government feared that any payment made as compensation would unleash hundreds of thousands of demands from all those, from prisoners of war to forced laborers, who had suffered at the hands of the Japanese military during the war.[6]

The more Tokyo denied the evidence, the louder grew the denunciations. More and more women came forward to speak of their experiences, revealing that it was a highly developed and meticulously regulated system that dated back to 1938 and employed women also from the Philippines, Indonesia and China. When Tokyo claimed, in July 1992, that in Malaya there were no such stations, documents were unearthed in Tokyo showing that in Kuala Lumpur alone there were about 20, and Kuala Lumpur was only one of the 20 Japanese garrison towns in Malaya. On 6 July, Kato reversed himself, expressing 'sincere apology and remorse' on the part of the government, adding, 'My heart really aches.' Kato concluded by saying: 'We have no plan to extend this research into other issues,' leading *The New York Times* to call the apology 'neither spontaneous nor graceful.'[7]

The case began to widen. A conference of women's rights groups from six Asian countries (Hong Kong, Japan, the Philippines, South Korea, Taiwan and Thailand) established the Asian Network in Solidarity with Women Drafted for Sexual Slavery by Japan. Seventy of their delegates met in Seoul in August 1992, when Lee Yong Yeo of Korea spoke of being forced to have intercourse with 20 to 30 Japanese soldiers every day for five years. The Filipino delegation accused the government of former President Corazon C. Aquino of ignoring the evidence, and the conference ended with a condemnation of Japan for a 'brutal crime unprecedented in the whole history of mankind.'[8]

The Japanese Government continued to announce that it could find no documents to show that the women had been recruited by force, so that its embarrassment was the greater when, in the summer of 1992, Seiji Yoshida, a Japanese living in the Tokyo suburb of Abiko, appeared several times on television to confirm what he had written in a book in 1983, long before the issue became a major political dispute. Still retaining the pen name he had adopted to protect his family from reprisals, Yoshida confessed that he had been hired by the prefecture in Yamaguchi to lead a group of Korean police who raided Korean villages and selected the women. Japanese historians responded by attempting to discredit Yoshida, claiming there was no documentary evidence or other witness to back up his story. Among these was Professor Ikuhiko Hata of Takushoku University, who called it a fabrication: 'In Korea it was through official arrangements or it was voluntary.' The Japanese Government claimed that the women were either volunteers or were sold by their families to brokers, and it rejected proposals for public hearings on the issue, insisting that it would violate the privacy of the women.[9]

The women were certainly not concerned about their privacy. In the Philippines, the issue was so intense that the Foreign Secretary, Roberto Romulo, visited Tokyo in February 1993

---

[6] David E. Sanger, *New York Times* service, 29 January 1992 ; Robin Bulman, *Washington Post* service, 13 August 1992 ; Steven Brull, *International Herald Tribune*, 31 August 1994 ; James Sterngold, *New York Times* service, 1 September 1994 ; International Herald Tribune, compiled from dispatches, 3-4 September 1994 ; Barbara Rudolph, *Time*, 12 September 1994.

[7] David E. Sanger, *New York Times* service, 7 July 1992 ; *The New York Times*, 13 July 1992 ; *International Herald Tribune* (The Associated Press), 18 July 1994.

[8] Robin Bulman, *Washington Post* service, 13 August 1992.

[9] David E. Sanger, *New York Times* service, 10 August 1992 ; Robin Bulman, *Washington Post* service, 13 August 1992.

to discuss the question with his counterpart Michio Watanabe. On 2 April, 18 Filipina comfort women filed suit against the Japanese Government, each demanding $160,000 in compensation. A few days later, the first comfort woman resident in Japan, who was Korean, filed a suit demanding not monetary compensation but an official apology. An apology, with the implied admission of guilt, was still strongly resisted by the Japanese authorities, and to avoid it they began consideration of establishing a large fund for the benefit of surviving victims.[10]

For the Miyazawa government, 4 August 1993 was its last full day in office, and it marked the day by acknowledging, finally, that Japan had indeed recruited Asian and European women, 'often against their will,' into serving as prostitutes for Japanese soldiers. It admitted that the women had lived as captives of the military over a period of up to 13 years and had been paid nothing. Johei Kono, leader of the Liberal Democratic Party (LDP), spoke of Japan's 'firm determination never to repeat the mistake, by engraving such issues in our memories forever through the study and teaching of history.' But the government was not speaking for all the people. The director of the Bereaved Families Association, Sakae Suehiro, gave his response: 'Many of these women accepted the invitation of the businessmen who operated the comfort stations because they needed the money to help their families. I never heard before of forced recruitment or the involvement of the military.' The last was particularly disingenuous because the Army's attitude was well known: the comfort stations would help to prevent troops from raping local civilians, and the rape of civilians, if unchecked, would stiffen resistance to the Army as it swept across Asia.[11]

In 1994, the Netherlands Government entered the fray. On 24 January, it announced that it had evidence in its archives that between 200 and 300 Dutch or Dutch-Indonesian women had been forced into prostitution as comfort women for Japanese troops. A private Dutch foundation went to court in Tokyo the next day to demand compensation. Still determined to avoid compensation, the Japanese Government on 31 August offered 100 billion yen (about $1 billion) over five years beginning in 1995, not in compensation but in grants classified as 'gifts of atonement' which would fund such projects as 'centers for women's self reliance.' Since not a single yen would go to the women who survived the ordeal, the proposal was at once denounced by the women's groups, in a joint statement submitted to the Murayama government, as 'mere charity, inadequate and unacceptable.'[12] It was equally denounced by the International Commission of Jurists, a private advisory panel in Geneva, which on 22 November declared that Tokyo had a moral and legal duty to make financial restitution to the victims for the 'unimaginable violence and cruelty they had undergone,' and it urged the Japanese Government to pay at least $40,000 to each. Since fewer than 1,000 of the comfort women were still alive in 1995, the proposal was not expensive, but it fell on deaf ears. The government responded on 6 December with a refusal to change its plan.[13]

---

[10] Georges Hicks, *International Herald Tribune*, 10 February 1993.

[11] David E. Sanger, *New York Times* service, 29 January 1992 ; David E. Sanger, *New York Times* service, 7 July 1992 ; James Sterngold, *New York Times* service, 5 August 1993.

[12] *International Herald Tribune* (The Associated Press), 18 July 1994 ; *International Herald Tribune* (The Associated Press), 19 July 1994 ; Steven Brull, *International Herald Tribune,* 31 August 1994 ; James Sterngold, *New York Times* service, 1 September 1994 ; *International Herald Tribune,* compiled from dispatches, 3-4 September 1994 ; *International Herald Tribune* (The Associated Press), 23 November 1994 ; *International Herald Tribune* (Reuters), 7 December 1994.

[13] *International Herald Tribune* (Reuters), 7 December 1994 ; T. R. Reid, *Washington Post* service, 14 July 1995.

The women did not give up. A three-day conference opened in Seoul on 27 February 1995, attended by delegates from Japan, the Philippines, South Korea and Taiwan who were fully prepared to confront shame, anger and ridicule. Julia Partosa Porras of the Philippines recounted in tears how she had been abducted from her village at the age of 13, and she even named the Japanese officer who first raped her. The Japanese delegate Itsuko Ishikawa denounced her own country's women for not making every effort to reveal the facts to the Japanese people. The women continued to demand 'a clear and sincere apology in a resolution adopted by the Japanese Parliament.'[14]

Prime Minister Murayama was personally sympathetic to the appeal, but he faced an upper house that opposed any expression of remorse. The proposal of the private fund was as much as Murayama could offer, but he promised that each payment would be accompanied by a personal letter expressing 'humble apologies' and signed by him as Prime Minister.[15]

This did not end the matter. In the first major condemnation by the United Nations of acts of violence against women since the United Nations was created, the U.N. Special Investigator Radhike Coomaraswamy, a lawyer from Sri Lanka, submitted a 37-page report in which she cited meticulous records kept by the Japanese military on the comfort stations network, showing that army doctors examined the sex slaves to prevent the spread of venereal disease while 'little notice was taken of the frequent cigarette burns, bruises, bayonet stabs, and even broken bones inflicted on the women by the soldiers.' Coomaraswamy called upon the Japanese Government to accept full legal responsibility for 'the violence and savagery' that Japanese soldiers inflicted upon the comfort women, to make a public apology to the survivors, and to pay the compensation. The new government of Ryutaro Hashimoto at once refuted the charges and refused to pay.[16]

On 5 June 1996, the Japanese Government finally agreed to a price of 2 million yen (about $18,500) for each surviving comfort woman, whose numbers were now very much in question: 300 were identifiable, but many others could have kept their past a secret out of shame. Even now the payment was to come not from the Japanese Government but from the private fund it had created, known as the Asian Peace National Fund for Women.[17] Hashimoto's only concession was to pledge $6.3 million in medical and welfare services and to write to each 'a heartfelt letter with apology and remorse.' Although the letter said that Japan was 'painfully aware of its moral responsibility' in the affair, it could not dispel the feeling that the government remained grudging, and Yoshiaki Yoshimi, who had done more than anyone to reveal the truth about the brothels, pointed out that Hashimoto, who retained his nationalistic views regarding the Second World War, chose a less formal word for apology than others open to him.[18]

Only a handful of the women accepted Hashimoto's offer. The rest continued to refuse to accept the money as long as it came from a private fund, demanding direct payment and a real apology. It was just as well for the government that more of the comfort women did not

[14] *International Herald Tribune* (Agence France-Presse), 28 February 1995 ; *International Herald Tribune* (The Associated Press), 20 July 1995.

[15] Barbara Rudolph, *Time*, 12 September 1994 ; T. R. Reid, *Washington Post* service, 14 July 1995.

[16] *International Herald Tribune*, compiled from dispatches, 7 February 1996.

[17] *International Herald Tribune* (Reuters), 6 June 1996 ; *International Herald Tribune* (Agence France-Presse), 24 July 1996.

[18] *International Herald Tribune* (Reuters), 6 June 1996 ; Andrew Pollack, *New York Times* service, 17 August 1996 ; Kevin Sullivan, *Washington Post* service, 5 December 1996.

accept the offer, because the Fund, which was created to solicit private donations and had aimed at raising $10-20 million, had succeeded in raising only $4 million, which would not have been enough to cover even the first round of payments. On 12 January 1997, the Fund announced that seven South Korean women had been paid 5 million yen ($43,000), drawing a bitter reaction against Tokyo from the South Korean Government.[19] Once again, the issue reopened. Seiroku Kajiyama, Japan's chief government spokesman, suggested on 24 January 1997 that the comfort women were simply trying to make money and were no different from Japanese prostitutes who were operating legally. Hashimoto was due to meet South Korea's President Kim Young Sam the very next day. 'Some Japanese politicians say things that baffle the understanding of the Korean people,' Kim told the press, to which Hashimoto could only reply limply, 'I am sorry if this remark caused you displeasure.'[20]

The truth of the matter is that the remark represented a broad gauge of Japan's unrehabilitated public opinion. At a rally on 22 March 1997, at the Yasukuni Shrine, it was said again that the comfort women were willing prostitutes, and criticism was leveled especially at Yukio Hatoyama of the LDP, who remarked during a recent trip to South Korea that Japan should accept more responsibility for the comfort women. 'Hatoyama the disgusting traitor!' was the cry of the far right, and Hiroki Ooto, president of the ultra-nationalist Japan Alliance, declared that he favored the assassination of such traitors.

It seemed that the tergiversation would continue indefinitely. Every expression of a desire for a new start was almost immediately rescinded. Hashimoto's promise of August 1996 'to convey Japan's history accurately to future generations'[21] was at odds with the campaign in Japan to remove from Japanese textbooks any reference to the *inanfu*, resulting in another protest on 29 May 1997 by Filipina comfort women outside the Japanese Embassy in Manila. There was a widespread feeling in many Asian capitals that what the Japanese nationalists were saying publicly was what a great number of Japanese were thinking privately. Professor Lee Jung Hoon, Professor of Political Science at Yonsei University in Seoul, described it as Japan's basic 'unrepentance: they glorify and beautify their imperial heyday.'[22]

For three years it seemed that the women's cause had died at that point. Then suddenly, on 18 September 2000, it came back to life. Fifteen Asian women, from China, Korea, the Philippines and Taiwan, filed a class-action suit against Japan in a US federal court to seek compensation and an apology for being forced to work as sex slaves of the Japanese military in the 1930s and 1940s. The Japanese Government responded, on the following day, with an expression of 'remorse' together with a reminder that the government considered the issue closed. 'It is our position,' said a spokesman for the Japanese Foreign Ministry, 'that this has been solved legally by the San Francisco Peace Treaty and other related treaties and documents. We recognize that the honor and dignity of many women involved have been hurt by this issue, and we have been using various occasions to express our feelings of apology and remorse.'[23]

---

[19] *International Herald Tribune* (Agence France-Presse), 24 July 1996 ; Andrew Pollack, *New York Times* service, 17 August 1996 ; *International Herald Tribune* (Reuters), 13 January 1997.
[20] *International Herald Tribune* (The Associated Press), 27 January 1997.
[21] Andrew Pollack, *New York Times* service, 17 August 1996.
[22] *International Herald Tribune* (The Associated Press), 30 May 1997.
[23] *International Herald Tribune*, 20 September 2000.

This served only to incite a new interest in the details of the 1951 San Francisco Peace Treaty. Phyllis Hwang, a human rights lawyer from Taiwan, wrote: 'Japan's interpretation of the San Francisco Peace Treaty of 1951 is legally incorrect. The treaty addresses only claims for reparations brought by the Allied Powers, that is, government-to-government reparations, not claims brought by individuals.' Kwang referred back to the 1996 report on Japanese military sexual slavery written by Radhike Coomaraswamy, the UN special rapporteur on violence against women, which concluded that the San Francisco Treaty did not cover claims raised by former sexual slaves of the Japanese military and that the Japanese Government remained 'legally responsible.' Moreover, wrote Hwang, the San Francisco Treaty contained a provision on dispute settlement, granting the International Court of Justice jurisdiction over any dispute concerning the interpretation or execution of the treaty. In 1951, Japan had issued a declaration confirming that it would accept the jurisdiction of the ICJ for this purpose and that it would 'undertake to comply in good faith with the decisions of the Court.'[24]

In December of the same year 2000, in a Japanese court, 80 Filipino plaintiffs demanded 920 million yen ($9 million) in direct and official compensation, together with a direct and official apology to individuals. The court rejected the demand, and on 6 December the Tokyo High Court upheld the lower-court ruling, with the attorney Fumio Takemura arguing that under international law individuals were not allowed to sue a government for human rights abuses, and even if they were, the statute of limitations had expired. To this the plaintiff Carmecita Ramel, aged 74, responded: 'I will fight till I die. They are all criminals, the Japanese government.'[25]

The Japanese Government was given no rest. Two days later, on 8 December, a Women's International War Crimes Tribunal opened in Tokyo to put Japan on symbolic trial for the sexual enslavement of women in Asia. While the five-day mock trial carried no legal weight, its panel of four judges included Gabrielle McDonald, former president of the Yugoslavia War Crimes Tribunal, and Christine Chinkin, Professor of Law at the University of London. Those accused were the Emperor Hirohito and Japan's war leaders, both in the military and the government. Hirohito had died in 1989 without ever being charged with war crimes.

The mock-trial above all provided the plaintiffs with publicity, especially by holding the proceedings close to the Yasukuni Shrine. As the Japanese women's activist Yayori Matsui commented: 'Japan has not punished one single war criminal. Instead, they are enshrined at Yasukuni.' The eighty women who attended spoke of how girls as young as ten were sent to the brothels, where they serviced as many as 20 Japanese soldiers a day. Among the eighty was Moon Pil Gi, aged 74, who declared: 'I am here to be free of some of my anger. I want an apology from the emperor of this country.'

At the close of the trial, on 12 December, the tribunal found Hirohito guilty for his army's policy of systematically forcing Asian women into sexual slavery. 'The Emperor,' it declared, 'knew or should have known about the establishment of the system of comfort stations. Japan must act to redress the harm done to the women, by paying compensation.' The Japanese historian Hideaki Kase came at once to the defense of the accused: 'I don't believe the comfort women were forcibly abducted or forced into this profession. Most of

---

[24] Phyllis Hwang, Tokyo, *International Herald Tribune*, 13 December 2000.

[25] *International Herald Tribune*, 7 December 2000.

them were already prostitutes or young girls tricked into serving as prostitutes by Korean brokers and pimps.'[26]

Kase's comment incited the women to fury. On 26 March 2001, eight former South Korean sex slaves who were members of the Seoul-based Association of Pacific War Victims and Bereaved Families brought suit in a Tokyo district court, demanding 20 million yen ($162,000) each in compensation. The presiding judge, Shoichi Maruyama, rejected the demand and ordered the plaintiffs to pay the cost of the the lawsuits.[27] In the same week the High Court in Hiroshima reached a similar decision, overturning the only ruling by a Japanese court to have ordered compensation. Back in 1992, ten former sex slaves had sued for 380 million yen ($3.1 million) in compensation before the Shimonseki branch of the Yamaguchi District Court. The court had finally agreed, in 1998, that the Government had failed to enact laws to accommodate the payment of compensation to former sex slaves and ordered the Government to pay 900,000 yen ($7,260) to each of the ten women. The women and their supporters had hailed that ruling as a landmark decision, while at the same time three of the ten had appealed against the ruling on grounds that the payment was far below the amount they were seeking. The result now, on 29 March 2001, was that Toshiaki Kazanami, the presiding judge of the Hiroshima High Court, ruled against them, arguing that the abduction of the women to use them as sex slaves did not constitute a serious constitutional violation.[28]

The intransigeance of the Japanese Government was helped by the fact that the six nations to which the plaintiffs belonged were not fully united in their support of their citizens. None of the six could provide an accurate estimate of the number of their countrywomen who had been victims of the Japanese.[29] Not every country backed its countrywomen, least of all if it depended on Japan for trade and financial investment. Another factor was the refusal of many of the victims to come forward to present evidence, and a further factor, the refusal of many victims, even when offered compensation, to accept a monetary settlement in recompense for their ordeal.

Again, between 2001 and 2005, the matter seemed to have gone to rest. What brought it back to life was the fact that the unofficial fund (the Japanese Asian Women's Fund), set up by the Japanese Government in 1995 in lieu of an official acceptance of responsibility, was due to close down on 31 March 2007.

The Fund had been set up as a private fund, and it was made clear that the 'atonement' payments came from ordinary Japanese citizens, who contributed a total of about $4.8 million. Haruki Wada, executive director of the Fund and an historian at the University of Tokyo, did his best to present the program as Japan's first attempt since the end of the war to compensate its war victims individually. Critics saw it differently, as a new device of the Japanese Government to avoid its own responsibility. Even those who favored accepting the money said the Fund reflected an absence of moral clarity. Two Asian governments even offered their own money to discourage women from accepting Japan's, and only a tiny fraction of the former sex slaves accepted the Fund's money. Among the first to receive

---

[26] Doug Struck, Tokyo, *Washington Post*, 8 December 2000; The Associated Press, Reuters, 12, 13 December 2000.

[27] *International Herald Tribune* (The Associated Press, Agence France-Presse), Tokyo, 27 March 2001.

[28] *International Herald Tribune* (Reuters, The Associated Press, Tokyo), 30 March 2001.

[29] In the Netherlands, the estimate was between 200 and 300.

compensation were 78 Dutchwomen who, in The Hague on 13 July 2001, were each paid 50,000 guilders, or about $19,000.[30] Among the Asian survivors, 285 women in South Korea, Taiwan and the Philippines received almost $17,000 each, together with a letter of apology from the Japanese Prime Minister which did not inculpate the government. A total of $6.3 million was also provided by the Japanese Government in 'welfare services' to the 364 women.[31]

The women's cause was hindered by the lack of a common political will among the victim nations. In the Philippines, the government was too dependent on Japanese investment to criticize the Fund, and offered no assistance of its own. In the case of Indonesia, where there was hardly any record at all of the number of women forced into sex slavery, the issue of official war reparations was settled under a 1958 treaty which had remained undisturbed by the revelations regarding the comfort women. Tokyo had reduced Jakarta to a client state. In seeking direct compensation and an official apology on behalf of the Indonesian victims, Ines Thioren Situmorang, a young lawyer with the Indonesian Legal Aid Foundation, reported on what she had been taught in elementary school, where the textbooks show that comfort women were simply prostitutes. 'The current generation perceives comfort women as part of a system of voluntary prostitution. That is what our schools teach here.'[32]

In Taiwan, and especially South Korea, it was a very different matter. Faced with the official opposition of their governments to Tokyo's deal, some 40 women took the Japanese money secretly. Korean women probably constituted the largest group of the sex slaves. In South Korea, where distrust in the sincerity of Japan's apologies was coupled with fear of a revival of its militarism, the election of President Roh Moo Hyun in 2002 spelt an end to the country's policy of appeasing Japan. Under the 1965 Seoul-Tokyo treaty, Japan had offered no apology for colonial rule but provided $800 million in urgently needed economic aid. In return, the government of President Park Chung Hee, who not incidentally had served as a lieutenant in the Japanese Army, had renounced all claim to reparations. Demonstrations, curbed by martial law, had followed. Now, in April 2005, President Roh was reminding Japan that it had never won the trust and forgiveness granted to its former Axis allies in Europe. Yoon Mee Hyang, head of the Korean Council for the Women Drafted for Military Sexual Slavery by Japan, reminded Tokyo that it had made no legal reparation, meted out no punishment, offered no official apology. Accordingly, South Korean women were among the most defiant, and every Wednesday since 1992 a small group of fragile women had been rallying in Seoul in front of the Japanese Embassy, demanding an official apology and proper compensation.[33] Meanwhile, a North Korean group called the Measure Committee for Demanding Compensation to Comfort Women revealed (accurately) that Prime Minister Abe was the grandson of a Class A war criminal. 'Abe is obliged,' it stated, 'to reflect, more straightforwardly and sincerely, on the past crimes of Japan.'[34]

If most of the victims declined to come forward to describe their personal experiences, a few brave hearts responded to the call. The Korean Yun Soon Man told how she was raped

---

[30] *International Herald Tribune* (Agence France-Presse, The Hague), 14 July 2001.

[31] Norimitsu Onishi, Tokyo, *International Herald Tribune*, 25 April 2007.

[32] Donald Greenlees, Jakarta, *International Herald Tribune*, 15 August 2005.

[33] Choe Sang-Hun, Seoul, *International Herald Tribune*, 15 August 2005.

[34] Howard W. French, 'Letter from China', Shanghai, *International Herald Tribune*, 9 March 2007.

when only 14.[35] Another Korean, Moon Pil Gi, described how, at the age of 15, she had been whisked away from her rural village. Kil Won Ock, also Korean, was 13 when she was transported to a military brothel in Manchuria. 'After the war,' she said, 'I could never go to the public bathhouses because of shame that I was a woman raped by Japanese. I never had any of the pleasures that a Korean woman can expect: having a family, raising children, and obeying a husband and his parents. Who would take a woman like me as a wife?'[36] A Taiwanese, Wu Hsui-mei, then 23, was working in 1940 as a maid in a hotel when her Taiwanese boss handed her over to Japanese officers. Transported to Guangdong in South China, she was forced to have sex with 20 Japanese a day for almost year. Wu had abortions and became sterile.[37] Another witness was the Dutchwoman Jan Ruff-O'Herne. Ruff was in Java with her family when Japan invaded in 1942. She spent two years in a prison camp. One day in 1944, Japanese officers arrived, forced the girls to line up, and picked 10 of them, including Ruff, then 19: 'On the first night it was a high-ranking officer. After that a military doctor came to examine us for venereal diseases. Before examining me the doctor beat me and raped me. That's how well organized it was.'[38] Released from the comfort station, Ruff returned to prison camp in Java. Her parents swore her to silence. But it was in the camp, after Japan's defeat, that she met her future husband. Tom Ruff was one of the British soldiers who was assigned to guarding the camp. Before they were married, she told him her story, but after that he never wanted her to discuss it with him again, while she, for her part, could never bring herself again to have any sexual contact.[39]

It was Japan's persistent refusal, throughout the prime ministership of Junichiro Koizumi, to listen to outside voices, and especially those of its former victims, that invalidated all its pretensions of innocence at the top. 'Taking the victims' perspectives seriously,' wrote Martin Fackler, is the only way Japan can persuade the rest of Asia to trust it again.'[40]

Again there was a lull in activity until, in 2007, two movements came into play in opposite directions. The United States Government had strongly resisted being drawn into the disputes over history that continued to roil East Asia, and especially the dispute over the 'comfort women.' Its position was complicated by the fact that, during the postwar occupation, Japan's fear of rampaging American soldiers had led it to establish brothels with Japanese prostitutes serving these soldiers throughout Japan. What changed the situation was the victory of the Democrats in the 2006 US elections, giving an immediate impetus to a nonbinding resolution in the House of Representatives that called for Japan to 'formally acknowledge, apologize, and accept historical responsibility in a clear and unequivocal manner for its Imperial Armed Forces' coercion of young women into sexual slavery.' Spearheading the resolution was Mike Honda, a Californian Democrat who as a Japanese-American had spent childhood years in US internment camps. In February 2007 Honda arranged for three former sex slaves to testify in Congress. The South Korean Lee Yong Soo, aged 78, testified in the House that she had been kidnapped by Japanese soldiers at the age of 16 and raped repeatedly at an army brothel. 'I want Japan and the Japanese Prime Minister to

---

[35] Choe Sang-Hun, Seoul, *International Herald Tribune*, 15 August 2005.
[36] Choe Sang-Hun, Seoul, *International Herald Tribune*, 15 August 2005.
[37] Norimitsu Onishi, *International Herald Tribune*, 8 March 2007.
[38] Norimitsu Onishi, Sydney, *International Herald Tribune*, 8 March 2007; Ellen Goodman, *Boston Globe*, 17 March 2007.
[39] Martin Fackler, Tokyo, *International Herald Tribune*, 6 March 2007.
[40] Martin Fackler, Tokyo, *International Herald Tribune*, 15 August 2005.

apologize,' she said. 'As a victim who was forcibly taken, as someone who went through these events, I'm a living witness.'[41] The Dutch-Australian Jan Ruff O'Herne, told the Congress: 'An apology is the most important thing we want, an apology that comes from the government, not simply a personal one, because this would give us back our dignity.'[42]

Meanwhile, the Japanese declaration of 1993 had never satisfied the women because it came from Yohei Kono, the chief cabinet secretary at the time, and had not been adopted by the Parliament. Conversely, a group of conservatives in the governing Liberal Democratic Party was stepping up calls to rescind the non-ratified declaration. Shinzo Abe, who had become Prime Minister in the autumn of 2006, moved with the prevailing wind. Abe had spent his career trying to play down Japan's wartime past, and had been a leader in the efforts to revise Japan's wartime history. As Prime Minister, however, he began by softening his nationalistic tone, saying that he recognized the validity of the 1993 declaration, which offered an apology to the women. Predictably this angered his conservative base, and with his approval rates plummeting over a series of scandals, Abe was ready to reopen the entire case. On 1 March he refused to acknowledge that the Japanese military had set up brothels or forced, directly or indirectly, foreign women into sexual slavery. 'If Yoshiaki Yoshimi,' he now argued, 'had found documents in 1992 to show that the military had established the facilities, he had not found documents that proved that the military had forcibly recruited the women. There is no evidence to prove there was coercion, nothing to support it. So, in respect to this declaration, you have to keep in mind that things have changed greatly.' What had changed greatly was not the evidence but the temper of the new government. Nariaki Nakayama, the leader of the 120 LPD lawmakers intent on revising the declaration, issued a stunning announcement: 'Some say it is useful to compare the brothels to college cafeterias run by private companies, who recruit their own staff, procure foodstuffs and set prices.'[43] He later added: 'To say that women were forced into service by the Japanese military is off the mark. The issue must be reconsidered, based on truth, for the sake of Japanese honor.[44]

This ignited the women's cause as nothing else before it. In Seoul the *Joongang Daily* immediately responded: 'Germany, after repeated apologies and repentance over its Nazi history, gained international respect and trust. Japan must know that it has failed to gain such respect, despite its position as an economic superpower, because it has distorted history.'[45] This had the effect of forcing Abe, once again, to change his position. After denying that the women had been forced to work in the brothels, he declared on 5 March 2007 that he supported the 1993 declaration admitting that the military had had at least an indirect role in forcing the women into sexual slavery. 'In the broad sense,' he said, 'there was coercion.'[46]

No sooner had Abe admitted that there had been coercion than he again shifted his position. On that same 5 March the Prime Minister declared that while he would keep the 1993 statement he denied its central admission of the military's role, saying that there had been « no coercion, such as the authorities breaking into houses and kidnapping women. » It was private dealers, he insisted, that had coerced the women. Here Abe was admitting to more

41 Martin Fackler, Tokyo, *International Herald Tribune*, 6 March 2007.

42 Norimitsu Onishi, Sydney, *International Herald Tribune*, 8 March 2007.

43 Norimitsu Onishi, Tokyo, *International Herald Tribune*, 4 March 2007.

44 Howard W. French, editorial: 'Letter from China,' Shanghai, *International Herald Tribune*, 9 March 2007.

45 *International Herald Tribune*, 5 March 2007.

46 Martin Fackler, Tokyo, *International Herald Tribune, 6* March 2007.

than his closest allies in the LDP government were ready to admit, for these continued to dismiss the comfort women as prostitutes who volunteered for the work. No official Japanese documents, these allies affirmed, existed to prove the collaboration of the military in the recruitment of the women. With their support Abe went further, declaring that the US House resolution was « not based on objective facts » and that he would not change his position even if it were passed. If the US Congress were to demand an apology for his nation's use of foreign women as sex slaves, he said, Japan would refuse to comply: 'Testimony to the effect that there had been a hunt for comfort women is a complete fabrication.'[47] It was in vain that Japanese historians, using official documents and the diaries and testimonies of military officials, came forward to show that the Japanese military was involved, directly in this case and indirectly in that, in deceiving, luring, coercing and sometimes kidnapping outright the young women who served in the brothels.

Prime Minister Abe had turned himself into a national embarrassment. Minoru Morita, a political analyst running an independent think tank in Tokyo commented: 'It just looks bad for the Prime Minister to be getting involved in these sorts of historical details. His argument isn't going to sway world opinion anyway. Even if the military wasn't pointing guns at the women, they still could have been coerced.... In making such denials he is in effect dismissing as liars the aging women now coming forward with tearful testimony of their ordeals.'[48]

A lead editorial in the *International Herald Tribune* put a withering question to the Japanese Prime Minister : 'What part of "Japanese army sex slaves" does Shinzo Abe have so much trouble understanding and apologizing for ? ... These were not commercial brothels. Force, explicit and implicit, was used in recruiting these women. What went on in them was serial rape, not prostitution. The Japanese Army's involvement is documented in the government's own defense files. Last week Abe claimed that there was no evidence that the victims had been coerced. Abe seems less concerned with repairing Japan's sullied international reputation than with appealing to a large right-wing faction within the LDP that insists that the whole shameful episode was a case of healthy private enterprise. ... Japan is only dishonored by such efforts to contort the truth. ... It is time for Japan's politicians – starting with Abe – to recognize that the first step toward overcoming a shameful past is acknowledging it.'[49]

Therein lay the rub: admitting to shame. Japan's predicament was well understood in China, which also spoke of 'patriotic education' and enjoyed lecturing the Japanese about the need to respect 'correct history.' Abe's latest denial that Japanese soldiers had forced foreign women into sexual slavery came at the moment that China and Japan were celebrating the 35th anniversary of the resumption of diplomatic relations, to be marked by a visit to Tokyo in April of President Wen Jiabao, the first such visit in seven years. China's Foreign Minister Li Zhaoxing expressed his country's outrage at a news conference on 6 March during a meeting of the National People's Congress. Urging Japan to accept responsibility for its use of sex slavers, Li said: 'Japan should stand up to this part of history, take responsibility and

---

[47] Martin Fackler, Tokyo, *International Herald Tribune*, 6 March 2007. On 26 June 2007, the US House Foreign Affairs Committee nevertheless voted, 39 to 2, in favour of a resolution urging Japan to issue a formal apology for coercing thousands of women to work as sex slaves for its wartime military (The Associated Press, *International Herald Tribune*, 27 June 2007).

[48] Martin Fackler, Tokyo, *International Herald Tribune*, 6 March 2007.

[49] *International Herald Tribune*, 6 March 2007.

seriously view and properly handle this issue.'[50] Howard French commented drily from Shanghai: 'Young Chinese tend to know next to nothing about their country's own conquests, or even about atrocities committed in living memory by their own government.'[51]

If the Chinese Government did nothing to encourage their own women-victims to come forward, elsewhere in Asia the reaction was one of fury. « How can Abe lie to the world like that? », asked Wu Hsiu-mei, aged 90, in Taipei.[52] Abe's recalcitrance drew a rare rebuke from the US Government when John Negroponte, Deputy Secretary of State, during a visit to Tokyo, threw out a remark that was itself highly controversial: 'The forced mobilization of comfort women was the most deplorable act of the war.'[53]

The Japanese Government remained unmoved, no doubt betting on the hope that if it could survive the difficult month of March with its closing of the Private Fund it might be able to withstand all further challenges. This was infinitely preferable, it reasoned, to admitting to the nation's guilt, which could cost Japan the respect of the world. Abe accordingly went on television to express « sympathy for the injuries of the heart » but no more than that, inducing Andrew Horvat, an American professor in Japan to reply: 'If someone has to provide sexual services for 20 soldiers a day, she comes home with more than just "injuries of the heart." She comes home sterile, infected with a stubborn STD, and in a state of psychological trauma.'[54] Some voices inside the Japanese Parliament also challenged the Prime Minister. The opposition lawmakers Kiyomi Tsujimoto and Haruko Yoshikawa (Communist Party) asked Abe to explain his denial that the military had coerced the women. Abe responded on 16 March with a statement endorsed by the Cabinet, annoncing that a study begun in the early 1990s showed no evidence of the use of force by the Japanese military.[55] Ellen Goodman of the *Boston Globe* drew the only possible conclusion: 'Abe is saying in effect that the women are lying.' Mindy Kotler, of Asia Policy Point, expressed it more bluntly: 'Abe is calling these elderly survivors "lying whores".'[56]

Confident that if the Government could get through the month of March 2007 it would never have to admit to the truth, Nariaki Nakayama of the LPD again came forward, on 26 March, to deny that the women were coerced or that the Imperial Government was to blame: 'Where there's demand, business crops up.'[57] Again Abe refused to acknowledge that the State had been responsible for enslaving the women, to which the Korean Cho Yoon-Young responded: 'Japan will stubbornly keep denying the sex slavery until all the witnesses are gone, so they may strengthen their stances by saying that there is no evidence.'[58]

That prediction seemed to be borne out in July 2007 when once again the Japanese Government spurned a resolution approved by the US House of Representatives calling upon Japan to make its apology full and formal, unlike the nuanced or dismissive apologies that the Japanese Government had so often offered in the past. Representative Tom Lantos, the Democrat from California serving as chairman of the House Foreign Affairs Committee, denounced the 'nauseating efforts of those in Japan who would distort and deny history and

---

[50] Jim Yardley, Beijing, *International Herald Tribune*, 7 March 2007.
[51] Howard W. French, editorial : 'Letter from China,' *International Herald Tribune*, 9 March 2007.
[52] Norimitsu Onishi, *International Herald Tribune*, 8 March 2007.
[53] Howard W. French, editorial : ' Letter from China,' Shanghai, *International Herald Tribune,* 9 March 2007.
[54] Ellen Goodman, *Boston Globe*, 17 March 2007.
[55] *International Herald Tribune*, 17 March 2007.
[56] Ellen Goodman, *Boston Globe*, 17 March 2007.
[57] *International Herald Tribune*, 27 March 2007.
[58] Cho Yoon-Young, Seoul, letter, *International Herald Tribune*, 27 March 2007.

play a game of blame the victim. Inhumane deeds should be fully acknowledged. The world awaits a full reckoning of history from the Japanese Government.' What the resolution demanded was an apology no different from that which the US Government had given in 1988 to Japanese-Americans forced into internment camps during the war, an apology approved by Congress and signed into law by President Ronald Reagan. The reaction of Prime Minister Shinzo Abe was to dismiss the resolution as 'regrettable' and to indicate that the Japanese Government would not offer surviving victims an official apology.[59]

'If you have made mistakes in life,' commented the Dutch survivor Ellen van der Ploeg, who had refused to accept the monetary compensation, 'you must have the courage to say, "I'm sorry, please forgive me".'[60] Apparently it would be up to a future Japanese generation to see the matter in that light. Ellen Goodman in the *Boston Globe* made what might be the last appeal: 'The Japanese revisionists argue that history should make children proud of their country. Perhaps telling the truth would make them really proud.'[61]

[59] 'U.S. House wants Japan apology for WWII sex crimes,' The Associated Press, *International Herald Tribune*, 31 July 2007; Tokyo, *International Herald Tribune*, 01 August 2007.

[60] Ellen van der Ploeg, Houten, Netherlands, *International Herald Tribune*, 27 March 2007.

[61] Ellen Goodman, *Boston Globe*, 17 March 2007. The fight was not yet permanently abandoned. Yukio Hatoyama, while opposition leader in 2002, had told lawmakers that the Japanese government should 'offer compensation to the victims and restore their honour.' On 28 October 2009, when some dozens of survivors gathered in Tokyo to continue the protest, their spokeswoman, the South Korean Lee Yong-soo, proclaimed: 'Now Mr. Hatoyama is prime minister. It's time for him to settle the issue.' Hatoyama holds two master's degrees and a doctorate from Stanford. The new American ambassador to Tokyo, John Roos, was Hatoyama's contemporary at Stanford, where Roos received a JD. The comfort survivors could now look forward to hearing of new discussions of their plight between the Japanese Prime Minister and the American Ambassador.

GERMANY

Much has been written about 'ordinary Germans' who assisted in the work of Nazi Germany without sharing any deep commitment to its cause. Some of them were women, and some of them had positions which allowed them to see the system at its worst. These included SS secretaries and SS women-guards. Others, pressed into serving it as sex workers, experienced the system as its victims. With the end of the war, even those who had committed no crimes vanished into thin air, out of fear of reprisal. With the publication in 2007 of 118 photographs of the SS of Auschwitz in moments of play, Roger Cohen of the New York Times wrote in his column:

Historians are voyeurs; they like nothing more than reading other people's letters. They need to pry and put names to these faces of 'ordinary Germans' doing their jobs at Auschwitz. And what of the stories of Eva and Angela and Irmgard? Will any Germans step forward to claim these young women and give them real names rather than those invented here? With the years, Germany has gained confidence, prized open locked drawers, filled some of the absences. But these photos are an invitation to do more.[1]

D.W.P.

---

[1] Roger Cohen, 'Down time from murder,' *International Herald Tribune*, 24 September 2007.

In: Crimes Against Women
Editor: David Wingeate Pike
ISBN 978-1-61470-813-1

Chapter 9

WOMEN SS-GUARDS IN CONCENTRATION CAMPS IN NAZI GERMANY

Elissa Mailänder Koslov

To no one's surprise, the archives of the SS did not emerge intact from the Second World War. That they survived at all, after Reichsführer-SS Heinrich Himmler ordered their total destruction, is due to the bureaucratic nature of the system: camp administrators made copies galore. Among these surviving archives are the figures for the total number of the SS-guards in Nazi concentration camps in January 1945, at a time when only one of these (Majdanek) had been liberated. Accordingly, out of a total number of 37,674 SS camp guards, the female contingent (*SS-Aufseherinnen*) comprised 3,508, or roughly 10 percent.[1]

From 1933, women prisoners were interned in the prison of Moringen, and from 1937 also in the so-called Lichtenburg facility. From May 1939 until January 1941, the only concentration camp for women prisoners was Ravensbrück, situated 80 km from Berlin. With the ongoing war and the expansion of the concentration camp system, eleven other female camps were opened as annexes to male concentration camps.[2]

In all SS camps, whether concentrations camps or extermination camps, men and women prisoners were segregated. Ravensbrück, which remained the central concentration camp for women, had a small and separate male section, and in all the other camps with women

[1] Institut für Zeitgeschichte, München, Sammlung Schumacher 329, Fa-183.

[2]

Frauenkonzentrationslager	opening	closing/liberation
Ravensbrück	15.05.1939	30.04.1945
Stutthof	21.01.1941	25.04.1945
Auschwitz-Birkenau	26.03.1942	January 1945
Lublin-Majdanek	15.08.1942	July 1944
Riga Kaiserwald	15.03.1943	Summer 1944
Herzogenbusch	12.06.1943	05.09.1944
Kaunas	15.05.1943	Summer 1945
Vaivara	15.09.1943	29.06.1944
Mauthausen	05.10.1943	05.05.1945
Krakau-Plaszow	10.01.1944	Summer 1944
Bergen Belsen	07.08.1944	15.04.1945
Flossenbürg	14.03.1945	23.04.1945

inmates the areas for women were set up as special sections. In all these camps a small minority of female guards worked alongside a far larger number of male SS-guards. In Majdanek, for example, there were 28 German and Austrian female guards on the staff alongside 1,200 SS-men. This chapter focuses on the concentration camp experiences[3] of the women guards, analyzing the particular form of their working and social environment.

In Ravensbrück then, as elsewhere, women inmates were supervised by women guards. In recruiting the guards, the SS selected German and Austrian unmarried women aged from 21 to 45, preferably with no professional specialization. After a three-month training period in Ravensbrück, the new recruits became employees of the Reich. The weekly salary of an unmarried *SS-Aufseherin* was 185 Reichmark gross, or 105 RM net. In comparison, an unmarried female worker in the textile industry in 1944 earned 76 RM gross.[4]

Within the SS hierarchy, the *SS-Aufseherinnen* occupied an intermediate status. While they were hired as SS-guards, they did not hold actual membership in the SS as did the wives and daughters of the SS officers, non-commissioned officers and men; instead, they were classified as women auxiliaries of the Waffen-SS *(weibliches Gefolge der Waffen-SS).* The women guards wore uniforms and carried pistols while on duty, and once a week received regular arms training as well as ideological education. Furthermore, women SS guards were employed only in concentration camps, and not in extermination camps. If women guards happened to be present also at Majdanek and Auschwitz, that fact reflected the dual function of those camps. Women guards participated in the selection of prisoners for extermination, on the basis of physical fitness, but they were not involved in the killing process nor were they present at mass shootings or in servicing the gas chambers.

According to the camp regulation[5] established in Ravensbrück in 1939, based on the so-called 'Dachau model' elaborated by Theodor Eicke in 1933 and used as a model for all other camps for women, the primary function of the female (and male) SS-guards was to supervise the inmates and not to punish or kill them. Although these guidelines explicitly prohibited any maltreatment of the prisoners, the SS-personnel went about their functions in a brutal and bloody way so that physical violence gained large acceptance. As numerous camp inmates observed upon their arrival in Ravensbrück, the German and Austrian women guards who arrived as new recruits behaved bashfully, showing a certain inhibition. However, in the course of a three-month training period a change of behaviour in the women could be charted, and it took only a fortnight for the same shy women to become self-assured SS guards.

Many studies of concentration camp life show the brutality perpetrated in the Nazi camps as a 'logical' consequence of Nazi ideology and especially of its anti-Semitism. Even though the women guards were embedded in a strict paramilitary hierarchy, one should not consider them as robots in this institutional setting. Research has shown that the *SS-Aufseherinnen* did not simply obey orders but displayed a great deal of initiative.

To understand the commitment of the women guards, it is useful to look at their social background: the 28 women guards of Majdanek were born between 1901 and 1922, and included the unmarried, divorced and widowed. At the time of their training in Ravensbrück,

---

3 Michael Pollak, *L'Expérience concentrationnaire. Essai dur le maintien de l'identité sociale* (Paris : Metaillé, 2000).

4 Dörte Winkler, *Frauen im Dritten Reich* (Hamburg: Hoffmann und Campe, 1970), p. 202; Irmtraud Heike, 'Lagerverwaltung und Bewachungspersonal,' in: Claus Füllberg-Stolberg et al. (eds.), *Frauen in Konzentrationslagern. Bergen-Belsen, Ravensbrück* (Bremen: Edition Temmen, 1994), pp. 22, 221-240.

5 Archiv der Mahn- und Gedenkstätte Ravensbrück (ARa), II/3-1-15.

the youngest was 19 and the oldest 42, while their average age was 24. Most came from working or lower middle class families with many children. Without any professional qualifications they had previously found work only in factories or as domestic servants. The work they found in a concentration camp meant not only a steady job and a comfortable salary but also an improvement in their social status. It is therefore not particularly important whether the women were recruited or applied as volunteers. What is more useful is to examine their professional ambition and their identification with their work.

It was with their daily work that thousands of *SS-Aufseherinnen* supported and maintained the Nazi concentration camp system. It is important to perceive the concentration camps as a workplace where the employees wanted to do their job well. The post-war interrogations of former women guards showed that they had a particular understanding of their work: their ambition and their pride in having rendered good service remained with them in captivity. Their belief in dexterity and diligence as the pivot to achieving full Germanness alone explains how they could live and work over the course of several years in the climate of a concentration camp.[6]

It might appear inappropriate to speak of the 'everyday' in the context of an SS camp. The 'everyday' in this sense does not refer to formal routines. Rather it involves the living and working environment (*Lebenswelt*) in which people deal, on a daily basis, with a given reality and with one another. In examining this, not only the workaday experiences but also the private lives of the SS are of interest. Such an analysis enters the domains not only of work but of leisure, living conditions, nutrition and sexuality. Even though life in an SS camp was restricted, the women guards enjoyed a social life that included contacts with the civilian world outside the camp. To scrutinize the everyday life of the SS is not to banalize the camps but instead to historicize them. Furthermore, to raise questions about everyday realities serves to demonstrate that historical agents are not limited to people in commanding positions.

In the case of the 28 SS women guards at Majdanek who worked alongside 1,200 SS men, it would be wrong to assume that the women were entirely dominated by the men. The women guards used their margin of manoeuvre in the workplace to confront not only their male peers but even their male superiors. Some incidents reveal that they showed self-confidence in matters of work assignments and overtime work. At her trial in Vienna, the former camp guard Hermine Braunsteiner repeatedly claimed that, from the time she arrived at Ravensbrück in January 1944, she had held full command, with disciplinary authority, over 700 inmates and 23 female guards.[7] Braunsteiner's description of her functions as commandant of the auxiliary camp (*Nebenlager*) at Genthin, the last camp in which she played a role, reveals that she identified herself with her job and the power it conferred. In her testimony, she frequently mentioned a medal she had been awarded in recognition of her service in Ravensbrück. Although she stated that this honour was given without exception to all guards after three years of service, she could hardly hide a certain pride in the recognition that her work received, giving the lie to other assertions that the women guards were powerless to intervene.

---

[6] Alf Lüdtke, 'The Hand of Labour: Industrial Labour and the Power of Symbols in National-Socialism', in: *Nazism and the German Society, 1933-1945* (London: David F. Crew (ed.), 1994), pp. 67-109.

[7] Hermine Braunsteiner, 22.11.1949, Landesgericht Wien 7g Vr 5670/48, Dokumentationsarchiv des Österreichischen Widerstandes, p. 5.

As for the brutality perpetrated by the women guards, a dynamic which one might call 'gendered' is in evidence. Firstly, it seems that both the men and women guards intensified their cruelty against the prisoners whenever colleagues of the other sex were watching. Secondly, a significant distinction can be seen in the exercise of brutality: men and women guards both freely used their leather boots to mistreat prisoners, often causing their death. In practice, the *Aufseherinnen* very rarely made use of the firearm that was part of their equipment and which they were fully authorized to use. Instead, they resorted to whips and staves, and even more commonly, their hands and feet. By attributing to their female colleagues ineptitude in handling guns, the SS-men, irritated by the presence of uniformed and armed female guards, were recreating and protecting an exclusively 'male' space. The everyday work experience shows that the female guards resented the supercilious attitudes of their male colleagues.

Last but not least, the dominant gender-rule that perceives women as peace-loving caretakers also affected the perception and memory of the inmates. It is interesting that both female and male survivors remember the brutality perpetrated by the *Aufseherinnen* in more detail and with more precision than they remember the savage acts of SS-men. This might, to some extent, be due to the fact that, in the Nazi camps in general, the women guards were so few and thus conspicuous. What stunned the inmates most, however, was the sudden transformation of these guards from women into brutes. In their new role, they were defying the social and cultural norms that link womanhood to motherhood, compassion, and serenity. Most of the surviving prisoners argue that the women guards were more violent and cruel than their male colleagues. This is unlikely. More probably, the prisoners were shocked more than anything by the cruelty inflicted by the young SS-*Aufseherinnen*—some of whom were mothers themselves—on children and pregnant women. The violence of the male SS, on the other hand, was something they expected.[8]

[8] As Miranda Alison has stated, feminist theorists and activists address wartime violence to reify the male-perpetrator/female victim paradigm. Although women and girls are the predominant victims of violence, and men and boys the predominant agents, this perspective neglects the fact that women are sometimes perpetrators or instigators of wartime violence. She asserts that we have to theorize and analyze violence in regard to the presence of male victims and female agents. Miranda Alison, 'Wartime sexual violence: women's human rights and questions on masculinity,' in: *Review of International Studies* (2007), 33, pp. 75-90; cf. Laura Sjoberg, Caron E. Gentry, *Mothers, Monsters, Whores: Women's Violence in Global Politics* (New York: Zed Books, 2007).

In: Crimes Against Women
Editor: David Wingeate Pike
ISBN 978-1-61470-813-1

Chapter 10

WOMEN IN PRISONERS' BROTHELS IN NAZI GERMANY

Brigitte Halbmayr

Research on SS camp brothels started less than two decades ago, in 1994, with the study by Christa Paul entitled *Zwangsprostitution: Staatlich errichtete Bordelle im Nationalsozialismus*. It marked the first time an investigation had been undertaken into the existence of brothels for prisoners in Nazi concentration camps and the fate of the women who had worked there. The scientific community, in fact, has slowly gained interest in the subject, but only a few researchers, mainly women, have devoted themselves to it. In 2007, the exhibition 'Sex-Zwangsarbeit in NS-Konzentrationslagern,' was presented at the Ravensbrück memorial site.[1] In September of the same year, the annual European Summer School in Ravensbrück addressed the topic of forced prostitution during the wars of the 20th and early 21st centuries. The broad temporal and geographical frame that was chosen at this conference revealed that sexual exploitation was an essential component of war, albeit with certain variations.

To understand the specificity of camp brothels for prisoners, and the exploitation of the women committed there, one must first examine the reasons that led to their creation. A second question concerns the character of the prisoner-client and the daily routine–taking as an example of this the brothel in the concentration camp of Mauthausen. Thirdly, we need to examine the cases of the women who had to work there. Who were these women, how did they arrive there, what became of them, and how did others judge them, whether in the form of rumour, stigma, or defamation? Finally, we must consider the consequences of camp brothels in the general context of violence against women.[2]

---

[1] The exhibition was based on a smaller one created in 2005 by a student group in Vienna (Die Aussteller).

[2] My interest in this topic goes back to the late 1990s, when I prepared an oral history project with my colleague Helga Amesberger. At that time we interviewed 42 Austrian survivors of Ravensbrück, and some years later, we focused on the topic of sexual violence during NS-persecution (see: Helga Amesberger and Brigitte Halbmayr, 'Vom Leben und Überleben - Wege nach Ravensbrück.' *Das Frauenkonzentrationslager in der Erinnerung*, volume 1. *Dokumentation und Analyse*, volume 2: *Lebensgeschichten* (Vienna: Promedia, 2001); Helga Amesberger / Katrin Auer / Brigitte Halbmayr, *Sexualisierte Gewalt, Weibliche Erfahrungen in NS-*

CAMP BROTHELS: THEIR PURPOSE AND THEIR CLIENTELE

The first camp brothel for prisoners was opened in June 1942 in Austria in the concentration camp of Mauthausen (KL-M). This measure followed an order issued by Reichsführer-SS Heinrich Himmler after an inspection of the camp. A few months later, another brothel was opened in the nearby camp of Gusen, which formed a Nebenlager (branch camp) of Mauthausen. Another eight SS camps were provided with brothels for the use of prisoners. They consisted of–in chronological order of their installation– Auschwitz I (Gleiwitz), Auschwitz III (Monowitz), Buchenwald, Flossenbürg, Neuengamme, Dachau, Sachsenhausen, and Mittelbau-Dora.[3] In the SS jargon, the camp brothel was called 'Sonderbau' ('special building') and was later set up in less conspicuous places than was the case in Mauthausen, Gusen or Auschwitz.[4] The SS had begun to hush up the existence of such facilities whenever possible.

The main motivation behind the order of installing camp brothels was to stimulate arms production, extending to selected concentration camp prisoners the same privilege that had already been extended to male slave labourers employed in German factories; the sponsors were therefore the leaders of the SS economic system directing the arms industry (WVHA). Apart from the aspect of raising output and increasing profits for the companies, the brothel was intended by the SS to reduce the high level of homosexuality among the male inmates.[5] A special decree went into effect in 1943, one year after the first camp brothel was established in Mauthausen. Known as the Decree on Bonuses,[6] it established five types of prisoner benefits: 1. improved conditions of imprisonment; 2. extra rations; 3. cash bonuses; 4. purchase of tobacco. 5. visits to a brothel. The last bonus offered male prisoners, whose work was particularly important, an additional incentive for better work performance. The political prisoners, in fact, frowned upon the whole idea of a camp brothel, although some of

Konzentrationslagern (Vienna: Mandelbaum, 2004). Those research projects form the empirical basis of this chapter.

[3] Concerning the openings of the brothels: In Mauthausen the first ten women for the camp brothel arrived on 11 June 1942, coming from Ravensbrück. The brothel in Gusen opened some weeks later; see Andreas Baumgartner, *Die vergessenen Frauen von Mauthausen: Die weiblichen Häftlinge des Konzentrationslagers Mauthausen und ihre Geschichte* (Vienna: Verlag Österreich, 1997), 99, 215. In Auschwitz main camp, Block number 24, right next to the camp entrance, functioned as brothel from 30 June 1943. On almost the same day, forced sex work was introduced in Auschwitz-Monowitz; see Robert Sommer, 'Die Häftlingsbordelle im KZ-Komplex Auschwitz-Birkenau. Sexzwangsarbeit im Spannungsfeld der NS-Rassenpolitik' und der Bekämpfung von Geschlechtskrankheiten,' in: Akim Jah et al. (eds.), *Nationalsozialistische Lager. Neue Beiträge zur NS-Verfolgungs- und Vernichtungspolitik und zur Gedenkstättenpädagogik* (Münster: 2006), 91. In Buchenwald the brothel existed from July 1943; in Flossenbürg, from March 1944; in Neuengamme, from April 1944 (see Christa Paul, *Zwangprostitution*, 1994, 24, 26). In the concentration camp at Dachau, a brothel operated from April 1944; see Kerstin Engelhardt, 'Frauen im Konzentrationslager Dachau,' *Dachauer Hefte* 14 (1998), 224; and in Sachsenhausen, from August 1944 (see Christl Wickert, 'Tabu Lagerbordell,' 2002, 49). The prisoner brothel in Mittelbau-Dora dates from the beginning of 1945; see Robert Sommer, Der *Sonderbau. Die Errichtung von Bordellen in den nationalsozialistischen Konzentrationslagern* (Berlin: Magisterarbeit an der Humboldt-Universität zu Berlin, 2003), 54.

[4] In Mauthausen, for example, it was next to the main gate.

[5] Hermann Langbein, *Menschen in Auschwitz* (Vienna: Europa, 1987), 454. The brothel was also used in the form of punishment, as an experimental site for male prisoners who were convicted of homosexuality (paragraph 175 of the criminal code). In these 'renunciation tests' they had to prove their capacity as heterosexuals.

[6] In German, 'Prämienverordnung'; see 'Dienstvorschrift für die Gewährung von Vergünstigungen an Häftlinge,' 15 May 1943 (report by Oswald Pohl, head of the SS-Wirtschaftsverwaltungshauptamt), in: Bundesarchiv Berlin, NS 3/426.

them were among the 'clients.'[7] They saw in the decree an attempt by the SS to intensify the hierarchical order of the camp society, thereby weakening solidarity among the prisoners.[8] Neither the prisoners nor, of course, the SS gave much thought to the fate of the women forced into sexual labour.

Only a small group of men were ever meant to benefit from this specific camp institution: inmates who were consigned to do specific, highly important work for the armament industry or in the camp administration. In the beginning, almost the only inmates allowed into the brothel were German, but later on prisoners of other nationalities were admitted. In Mauthausen, according to Hans Maršálek, the camp's former Lagerschreiber II (second clerk) and later author, those who applied for a visit were primarily stonecutters. Jews and Russians were never admitted. In any event, the vast majority of the prisoners were not entitled to visit the brothel, besides which an equal number lacked the physical condition necessary for sexual relations.[9]

RECRUITMENT OF THE BROTHEL WORKERS

Without exception, the only women forced to work in camp brothels were female prisoners. Except for the brothels in Auschwitz-Gleiwitz and Auschwitz-Monowitz, to which women from the extermination camp of Auschwitz II (Birkenau) were sent, all the women came from Ravensbrück.[10] The recruitment of women was mainly performed in the hard conditions of the camp barracks, or the punishment block, where the conditions were even harder, but the SS also selected women immediately upon their arrival in the camp or during certain exercises: quarantine, musters in front of the barracks, roll calls, pseudo-medical examinations, and, towards the end of the war, in the supplementary tent-barracks.[11] A central place in the process of the selection for the brothel was the infirmary, the so-called *Revier*. Here the women were 'prepared' for their new duty: they were examined for sexually transmitted disease, the healthy ones getting disinfecting baths, sunray treatment, calcium, and better food. Some of the women were 'tested'– which often meant raped–by SS-men.[12]

---

[7] Christl Wickert, 'Tabu Lagerbordell. Vom Umgang mit der Zwangsprostitution nach 1945,' *Gedächtnis und Geschlecht. Deutungsmuster in Darstellungen des nationalsozialistischen Genozids*, eds. Insa Eschebach et al. (Frankfurt/New York: Campus, 2002), 92.

[8] Eugen Kogon, *Der SS-Staat. Das System der deutschen Konzentrationslager (*Munich: Wilhelm Heyne, 1998), 214; Hans Maršálek, *Die Geschichte des Konzentrationslagers Mauthausen:* Dokumentation (Vienna: Österreichische Lagergemeinschaft Mauthausen, 1995), 108, reports: 'As in Mauthausen, the existence of a brothel in Gusen was, on the one hand, an inexhaustible source of intrigue within the inmate-functionaries, and, on the other hand, a precious news centre for the SS camp leadership.'

[9] Hans Maršálek, Video-interview im Rahmen des Mauthausen Survivors Dokumentation Projekt (MSDP) 2003, AMM OH/ZP1/572_2, 14, 16.; concerning access to the camp brothel and its routine, see also David Wingeate Pike, *Spaniards in the Holocaust: Mauthausen, the Horror on the Danube* (London: Routledge 2000).

[10] Ravensbrück (in operation from May 1939 to the end of April 1945) housed some 130,000 women (and children) from all over Europe, together with 20,000 men in barracks separated from the women's but within the walls of the main camp. After Auschwitz-Birkenau, Ravensbrück was the biggest camp for female inmates. The main camp, situated approximately 80 kilometres north of Berlin, controlled more than 40 subsidiary camps (Nebenlager) spread over the entire territory of the Reich. Some 10,000 women died.

[11] In autumn 1944, when the camp became saturated by the continuing deportations, a big tent was erected between Blocks 24 and 26. The tent was used to accommodate up to 3,000 women and children, in conditions beyond imagining.

[12] Helga Amesberger et al. *Sexualisierte Gewalt*, 2004, 122 f.

Research on camp brothels shows that there were several ways in which a woman could find herself in the brothel commando. At first, the SS actually looked for women who had already worked as prostitutes before imprisonment, hoping that these women would guarantee a problem-free brothel routine. As a result of this procedure the rumour developed that the women had volunteered for this job.[13] In fact, even if they were former prostitutes, it does not necessarily follow that those women volunteered. Additionally, the SS sent many women to perform this work under false promises, namely, that after six months of brothel service they would be released from the concentration camp. However, there is evidence of only two women being released.[14] For all others, this promise was mere chicanery.

The recruitment of former prostitutes was an obvious attempt by the SS to maintain the fiction that the camp brothels were staffed only by those who, in the phrase of Reichsführer-SS Himmler, 'on account of their past life and attitude, needed to be reformed for a future upright life.... After the most stringent self-questioning, we should never have to reproach ourselves for having defiled a person who could have been rescued for the German Volk.'[15] In this manner, the range of women who fell into disgrace increased, and many new reasons were fabricated to persecute them. The inconsistency between the prosecution of prostitutes in the Third Reich, on the one hand, and their exploitation in brothels established by the state, on the other, is quite remarkable. Prostitution was punishable by incarceration in a concentration camp. Nevertheless, these same women were forced into sexual service – a shining example of the double standards inherent in SS regulations. According to official regulations, only 'Aryans' qualified to work in the brothels, but several examples prove the non-compliance with this rule[16]. A list of forced sex workers in the Dachau camp brothel shows that, from November 1944, the majority of the women wore the red triangle of political prisoner.[17] A document pertaining to the Mauthausen brothel refers to a Polish woman and a Roma woman from the Austrian province of Burgenland.[18] Claudia Schoppmann states that the SS were keen on sending lesbian women to the brothels for 're-orientation,' putting them back on the 'right path' of heterosexuality through sexual contact with men.[19] Reports such as these show to what extent the SS flouted their own regulations.

---

[13] See the discussion of this myth in Amesberger et al. *Sexualisierte Gewalt*, 2004, 107 ff; Brigitte Halbmayr, 'Sexzwangsarbeit in NS-Konzentrationslagern,' in: *Dokumentationsarchiv des Österreichischen Widerstandes* (ed.): Jahrbuch 2005, Schwerpunkt: Frauen in Widerstand und Verfolgung (Vienna:: Lit-Verlag 2005), 114 f.

[14] One of the women served in the camp brothel in Dachau (see Kerstin Engelhardt, *Frauen im Konzentrationslager Dachau*, 1998, 225) and one in Auschwitz (see Christa Paul, *Zwangsprostitution*, 1994, 41).

[15] Letter from SS-Obersturmbannführer R. Brandt, by order of Himmler to Pohl, 15 November 1945, quoted by Christa Paul, *Zwangsprostitution*, 1994, 31; author's translation.

[16] Concerning the danger faced by Jewish female inmates of sexual exploitation, see Na'ama Shik, 'Weibliche Erfahrungen in Auschwitz-Birkenau,' in *Genozid und Geschlecht, Jüdische Frauen im nationalsozialistischen Lagersystem*, ed. Gisela Bock (Frankfurt/New York: Campus, 2005), 110 ff; Myrna Goldenberg, 'Sex, Rape, and Survival: Jewish Women and the Holocaust,' in *Women and the Holocaust - A Cyberspace of Their Own*, http://www.theverylongview.com/WATH/ scholarly essays, n.d.

[17] Four out of 13 'Germans' (one of the 13 was Polish) belonged to the 'asocial' category and wore a black triangle. Eight were marked as 'political', and one as 'criminal' (Kestin Engelhardt, *Frauen im Konzentrationslager Dachau*, 1998, 225). Perhaps the large number of 'political' prisoners can be explained by the fact that women were arrested for having a relationship with a forced labourer ('forbidden contact'); they wore the red triangle of the 'political' class and were likely to be assigned to the camp brothels (Helga Amesberger et al. *Sexualisierte Gewalt*, 2004, 118).

[18] Archives of the Mauthausen Memorial K2; Grit Philipp, *Kalendarium der Ereignisse im Frauen-Konzentrationslager Ravensbrück* 1939-1945 (Berlin: Metropol, 1999), 145.

[19] Claudia Schoppmann, *Zeit der Maskierung. Lebensgeschichten lesbischer Frauen im Dritten Reich* (Frankfurt/Main; 1998), 22 f.

FORCED RECRUITMENT TO THE BROTHEL COMMANDO OR VOLUNTEERS?

It is evident that the SS, in selecting women, made equal use of force and deception. To say that the women volunteered for the work would be absurd. This rumour therefore has to be seen as an unfair stigmatisation of sex workers. Furthermore, one has to consider that, usually, prisoners did not know for what purpose they were transferred to another camp;[20] others saw in the brothel commando a last chance to survive. In the context of a concentration camp, choice and freewill are not proper terms; both have to be regarded under the aspect of terror, the permanent threat of death, and the ongoing fear of making a wrong decision. It is remarkable that no other group of concentration camp prisoners who were merely trying to increase their chances of survival was made the subject of such criticism. Indeed, any other woman who tried to change her outdoor job for an indoor job, to enter a Kommando where she had access to better food or clothing, or to leave a Kommando under a cruel Kapo for another with a more tolerant one—provided it was not at the expense of another inmate—would be praised for her 'strength of character, her 'resistance.' It would be termed a 'reasonable act.' Only in the case of those working in a camp brothel were the forcible aspects disregarded and the rumours allowed to run concerning their 'easy living,' and such inmates were understandably anxious after their liberation to dissociate themselves from the place, the people and the work they had done. The insinuations that they had volunteered, and even collaborated, with the Nazis worked to perpetuate the stigmatisation and criminalisation of the brothel workers. Such thinking throws further light on certain patriarchal norms, values and views regarding proper female behaviour. Neither the SS men nor the male clients–the latter seeking pleasure while complying with the system–were accused of exploiting or humiliating the women.

The expression 'forced sex work' instead of 'forced prostitution' is therefore preferable, in order to stress the fact that the women were mere subordinates in a work Kommando. The term 'prostitution', even under pressure ('forced prostitution'), properly pertains only to an exchange of sex for money. There is no proof that the women received anything at all. Furthermore, from the client's point of view, there was no selection. The sexual interaction usually was limited to a quarter of an hour, after which it was the turn of the next client.

[20] See the two testimonies in Christa Paul, *Zwangsprostitution*, 1994, of Ms. B. (45) and Ms. W. (53). Ms. B. who was selected for the brothel in Mittelbau-Dora: 'One day in spring 1945, during roll call several numbers were called, and mine was one of them. We were told that we were supposed to go to a—what was it called? They didn't say brothel, but a special commando. We were told to report to the orderly room. In the orderly room we were told: wait. We weren't told why we were supposed to go there' (author's translation). Ms. W. remembered her arrival in Buchenwald: 'There was an extra block, a barrack, just like barracks everywhere. The truck stopped. Doors opened, prisoners got out. The block was enclosed by a great wooden wall about 10 meters high all the way around. Between the block and the wooden wall was a distance of about two meters. That's where we were put. The two female guards then told us: We were now in a prisoner brothel, we would be well-cared for, we would be given proper food and drink, and as long as we submitted then nothing would happen to us. That's what was told to us' (author's translation).

Procedure for a Brothel Visit

The procedure for a visit to the brothel is well described by Hans Maršálek,[21] the former camp clerk whose duty it was to issue a pass authorizing the visit. This pass was a pre-printed form ("jump-card" in the camp vernacular) with which 'inmate [with his number] requests in full obedience to report and enter the brothel.'[22] Permission to visit the brothel was announced in public during the daily roll-calls. Between six and eight o'clock in the evening, the prisoner was escorted to the brothel situated in barrack 1, where he was registered, examined, and sometimes given an injection of a dubious substance, then sent to a tiny room to meet the woman. Both of them had to perform the coitus in a lying position; 'any other position was in violation of camp rules and was punished.'[23] The sexual interaction was checked by SS men through a peephole. Afterwards the woman had to wash herself with a disinfecting and contraceptive dilution. No other birth-control device was provided.[24] It seems that in Mauthausen the women had to accept ten men every evening, while reports from other camps refer to many more clients than ten.[25]

The Fate of the Women

What do we know about the lives of these women who were forced into sex work? Very little, in fact, because hardly any testimonies exist. For one reason, they were not asked, and for another, they were deeply ashamed of their experiences. They had already, during their imprisonment, been severely judged; they feared being humiliated and criminalized again. As a result, our only sources concerning these women are a few surviving SS documents and several testimonies from men. Apart from very few exceptions–some of them already quoted in the article–, our information sources are limited to a few SS documents and several testimonies from men.

We know from former male prisoners that the women forced into the brothel received better food and clothes, and had sufficient opportunity to wash themselves. In the case of Mauthausen, it is possible to deduce from a plan of Block 1 that they slept in the rear part, with two women to a room, and performed their work in the front part in small, single berths. There were always ten women bound to the brothel at a time. During the day they were strictly separated from the male prisoners. They were usually forbidden to leave the barrack, and were under constant surveillance by female SS guards. They were also strictly forbidden to form relationships with the 'clients.'

---

[21] Hans Maršálek, Videointerview, 2003.

[22] AMM (Archives of the Mauthausen Memorial) K2/2; author's translation.

[23] Hans Maršálek, *Die Geschichte,* 1995, 204 (authors's translation); see also Andreas Baumgartner, *Die vergessenen Frauen von Mauthausen*: *die weiblichen Häftlinge des Konzentrationslager Mauthausen und ihre Geschichte* (Vienna: Verlag Österreich, 1997), 100 and Hans Maršálek, video-interview, 2003, 17.

[24] Christl Wickert, 'Das große Schweigen, Zwangsprostitution im Dritten Reich,' *Werkstatt Geschichte* 13, 1996, 93 f. sees a further function of these viewers at the door: to prevent any conversation between the man and the woman. We can also presume a voyeurism on the part of the SS-men. There are also numerous rumours that the SS men, too, abused the women.

[25] In Sachsenhausen some women had to cater to 40 men per day (see Christl Wickert, 'Das große Schweigen,' 1996, 94).

How and what the women felt one can imagine by reading the report by W., who had served in the Buchenwald brothel: 'You become deadened. Life doesn't count anymore, because they ruined it completely.... You become indifferent, how should I say, you have no feeling, nothing can unsettle you. Without any will. They could have done with us anything they wanted to. We knew we were at their mercy, you couldn't resist them. We said to ourselves: the sooner the better. We had come to this. I was not the only one to say so.' [26]

Survivors of Ravensbrück have testified that many of the women returning from the camp brothel came back pregnant or with sexually transmitted diseases. Many of them were then subjected to abortions or to pseudo-medical experiments.[27] Former fellow-prisoners in Ravensbrück spoke of the emaciated, gaunt bodies and the dead gazes of the women who returned from the brothels.[28]

Regardless of the obvious distress of these women, former camp inmates, mainly red-triangle (political) prisoners, have nevertheless talked about them in a derogatory manner, categorizing them as 'asocial elements' and 'prostitutes' from whom one cannot expect high morals.[29] The men who visited the brothels were similarly stigmatised as 'anti-social' and 'criminal.'[30] This is testimony to the strong desire of ex-prisoners to distance themselves from this camp institution that has created such animosity.

Few are the sources available regarding the sexual assaults of SS-men against female inmates in general and against sex-workers in particular. The same is true for the brothels used exclusively by the SS camp guards.[31] What we do know is that women in the Ravensbrück camp were also selected to serve in the brothels of the SS. Reports by former camp inmates recount that the SS kept the first choice of women for themselves, the second choice for the brothels of the Wehrmacht, and the third for the prisoners. The SS-brothels were especially dreaded by the women. The rare testimonies–mostly passed on by a third person[32]–refer to unspeakable obscenity and perversion. The reports show that in SS-brothels the lack of a superior authority allowed uninhibited brutality over the women–quite in contrast to the camp brothels where contacts with the male prisoners were strictly regulated and controlled.

---

26 Ms W., quoted by Christa Paul 1994, *Zwangsprostituion*, 1994, 57 (author's translation).

27 Andreas Baumgartner, *Die vergessenen Frauen von Mauthausen*, 1997, 101; Bernhard Strebel, *Das KZ Ravensbrück. Geschichte eines Lagerkomplexes* (Paderborn: Schöning, 2003), 211; Hilde Boy-Brandt reports: 'Once a woman came back pregnant. An abortion was carried out immediately, without asking the woman' (MGR Archives of Ravensbrück Memorial: Doc. 15/17).

28 See Friederike Jandl in: Helga Amesberger and Brigitte Halbmayr, *Vom Leben und Überleben*, 2001, 114; and Irma Trksak in: Berger et al. *Ich geb dir einen Mantel, daß du ihn noch in Freiheit tragen kannst. Widerstehen im KZ - Österreichische Frauen erzählen* (Wien: Promedia, 1987), 124.

29 Christa Schikorra, 'Prostitution weiblicher KZ-Häftlinge als Zwangsarbeit. Zur Situation "asozialer" Häftlinge im Frauen-KZ Ravensbrück,' in: *Dachauer Hefte* 16 (2000), 120, 123 f.; Christa Paul, *Zwangprostitution*, 1994, 85 ff.; Amesberger et al, *Sexualisierte Gewalt* 2001, 105 ff.

30 Constanze Jaiser, 'Repräsentationen von Sexualität und Gewalt in Zeugnissen jüdischer und nichtjüdischer Überlebender,' in *Genozid und Geschlecht. Jüdische Frauen im nationalsozialistischen Lagersystem*, ed. Gisela Bock (Frankfurt/New York: Campus, 2005), 128.

31 See Robert Sommer, *Die Häftlingsbordelle im KZ-Komplex Auschwitz-Birkenau*, 2006, 97 ff.

32 See Anja Lundholm, *Das Höllentor. Bericht einer Überlebenden* (Hamburg: Langen-Müller, 1991), 125, reporting on a fellow prisoner.

Conclusion

The function of the camp brothels makes clear how women during National Socialism were sexually subjugated, humiliated and exploited. For many years, the experiences of women, particularly the forced sex-workers, in the SS camps remained unacknowledged. The long silence was based, for one thing, on the fear that referring to camp brothels as such would downplay the horror of a concentration camp and convey a false impression of living conditions there. For this reason, guided tours through memorial sites and ground plans of the camps avoided mention of the brothels. Both the male clients and the female sex-workers, anxious to protect themselves, have kept quiet, while historians of the SS camps, mainly male, have not paid much attention to this theme.[33] As a result, female researchers have taken the lead in bringing the subject to the public eye. Nevertheless, women who were labelled asocial and prostitutes were denied respect among the other groups of prisoners and have been subjected to discrimination until the present day. This is visible, for example, in the claims and entitlements for compensation payments in Austria. For the first time, with an amendment of the Opferfürsorgegesetz (Victims Welfare Act) of 2005, the Austrian government agreed to pay compensation to all who, under the Nazi regime, were persecuted on account of their sexual orientation or were victims of forced sterilization. This belated recognition, unfortunately, came too late for most of the victims. Nevertheless, exhibitions on camp memorial sites have now been adapted to commemorate the existence of the brothels, which are now included in the guided tours. Finally, the number of women who were subjected to sexual labour may not have been higher than 200, but the brothel Kommando in SS camps remains nonetheless a striking example of the sexual exploitation of women.

[33] Ibid.

PART III: CRIMES AGAINST WOMEN DERIVING FROM RELIGION, CUSTOM AND TRADITIONS

SOUTH AFRICA

Child rape, as opposed to forced marriage and child kidnapping, has been widely reported in South Africa. In a 12-month period ending in March 2005, the South African police estimated that there had been no fewer than 23,000 cases of child rape. According to a study of nine countries by the World Health Organization, the highest incidence of child sexual abuse was found in South Africa's neighbour Namibia.[1]

D.W.P.

---

[1] Sharon LaFraniere, 'Relentless scourge takes endless toll on the girls of Africa,' *International Herald Tribune*, 1 December 2006.

In: Crimes Against Women
Editor: David Wingeate Pike
ISBN 978-1-61470-813-1

Chapter 11

THE HIV-ANTIDOTE MYTH AND INFANT RAPE IN SOUTH AFRICA

Tomoyuki (Tom) Hashimoto

In November 2001, South African newspapers carried the cry of a nine-month-old baby whose SOS to the world triggered wide coverage in the international media. The baby had allegedly been raped by her six neighbours, including the baby's 66-year-old great-grandfather.[1] As for the motive, much of the media spotlighted a myth that sexual intercourse with virgins acted as an antidote for HIV and a cure for AIDS. This shocking news, known as the incident of 'Baby Tshepang', opened up wide discussion ranging from the mentality of baby rapists to the barbarity of rural South Africa.[2]

The claim that the rape was perpetrated as a healing ritual was duly dispelled by the authorities in January 2002. South African prosecutors revealed that the ex-boyfriend of the baby's mother–whose DNA was matched with the evidence–had been arrested for the rape of the baby and that the earlier arrest of the six neighbours had been a mistake.[3] The media further speculated that the real motive for the rape was revenge for the mother's decision to break off the relationship. It would seem that the assault on Baby Tshepang, one more among thousands of similar reports in South Africa, was eagerly embraced by a press that recognized its newsworthiness. As the South African playwright Lara Foot Newton observed, the international media stormed into South Africa expecting to find the barbaric myth at the heart of the crime.[4]

The widespread misreporting of this incident is indicative of three interrelated trends in South Africa. First, the virgin-cleansing myth indeed exists and is widely covered in the

---

[1] Adele Baleta, 'Alleged rape of 9-month-old baby shocks South Africa'. *The Lancet* 358 (17 November 2001): 1707. Other reports, however, say nothing about 'great-grandfather.' See 'Baby gang raped,' *Maclean's* 114.48 (26 November 2001): 12. Also: Michael Schmidt, 'Where the horror never ends', *Sunday Times* (Johannesburg), 24 March 2002.

[2] Jane Flangan, 'South African men rape babies as "cure" for AIDS', http://www.telegraph.co.uk, 11 November 2001.

[3] Michael Schmidt, 'Where the horror never ends'; also: Penny Wrenn, 'South Africa rape update,' *Essence* 33.7 (2002): 36.

[4] Rosalie Higson, 'Ugly aftermath of apartheid', *The Australian* (27 September 2005).

press. Second, alongside the sexual violence against women, babies are also frequent targets of abuse. Third, the confluence of these two trends created a situation in which the virgin-cleansing myth was used as a pretext for infant rape.

In its exposure of the virgin-cleansing myth, the press referred to and is widely communicated. the Teddy Bear Clinic in Johannesburg.[5] While the clinic reported that only one incident of child or infant assault has been associated with the virgin-cleansing myth, it added that the percentage of teenagers who believe in the link can be as high as 25 percent.[6] Another report from UNISA (University of South Africa) indicates that 18 percent of nearly 500 workers at a Daimler-Chrysler plant in East London believed in the myth, while the number went up to 32 percent of those participants interviewed in Gauteng–the country's economic hub.[7] No doubt many male HIV carriers, aware of their imminent death, fervently hope in the cleansing power of virgins. In short, they have nothing to lose. If the myth is true, they will be cured; if the myth is not true, they will live to serve only a fraction of their imprisonment.

Because HIV is invisible, but AIDS visible, traditional shamans and their faithful believers often demonize HIV. As HIV becomes a symbol of demonic figures, rural people start to believe that HIV carriers are bewitched and that AIDS is one of the symptoms of black magic. Sister Irene Bopela in Izingolweni, who has dealt with HIV carriers in a rural clinic, told a reporter that the majority of men that claimed to be bewitched had had affairs with people outside their own family and had brought HIV to their household. In her opinion, believing in magical causality is 'easier than facing up to guilt.'[8] The sense of powerlessness in the face of this 'demonic' HIV speeds the diffusion of the virgin-cleansing myth. The most grievous implication of this myth is the belief that the younger the virgin, the stronger are her curing powers.[9] Thus babies, who provide the greatest assurance of preserved virginity, become the ideal antidote to AIDS.

If the motive to rape virgins was solely the belief in their cleansing power, it would be recurrent not just in Africa but anywhere in the world. Examples of divine virgins are ubiquitous: the Christian Virgin Mary, Buddha in the form of the goddess of mercy Avalokitesvala (also known as Kuan Yin), the Greek Athena. The sociologist Lisa Vetton, interviewed by the BBC, commented that the recourse by those facing death to sexual intercourse with young girls was also a European phenomenon that acts as a stimulus to child prostitution.[10] It is nevertheless rare to hear on the major media about infant rape occurring outside of Africa.[11]

---

[5] Rachel Jewkes et al., 'The "virgin cleansing myth": Cases of child rape are not exotic,' *The Lancet* 359 (26 January 2002): 711.

[6] The Henry J. Kaiser Family Foundation, 'Daily HIV/AIDS Report', http://kaisernetwork.org, 13 February 2002.

[7] 'Focus on the Virgin Myth and HIV/AIDS,' UN Integrated Regional Information Network, 25 April 2002.

[8] R. W. Johnson, 'Analysis: infant rape captures AIDS crisis,' United Press International http://www.aegis.org/news/upi/2001/UP011106.html, 24 November 2001.

[9] Professor of Medical Anthropology Suzanne Leclerc-Madlala, at the University of KwaZulu-Natal, commented in *The Sunday Times* (1999) that HIV carriers often 'target girls under eight-years-old for sex in the belief that it will cure them of the dreaded disease'. Quoted in Christopher Stones and Mike Earl-Taylor, 'Letter from Grahamstown: HIV/AIDS, the so-called "virgin cure" and child rape in South Africa', Global Issues Gateway Online, http://www.gig.org, 13 December 2004.

[10] Barnaby Phillips, 'Baby rapes shock South Africa', BBC News Online, http://www.bbc.co.uk, 11 December 2001. Also: Christopher Stones and Mike Earl-Taylor, 'Letter From Grahamstown'.

[11] Some infant rape cases have been reported outside of Africa. See 'Probe ordered after teenager jailed for baby rape bid', Scottish Press Association, 21 October 2004; 'Victim's anguish that she could have prevented baby

The cynicism and egoism of the perpetrators require no comment. The defloration of the virgin is anything but an expression of worship, since the virginity is simply selfishly consumed, never to be restored. Furthermore, believers in the virgin-cleansing myth remain indifferent to the fate of the children after the intercourse. Physical injury, psychological trauma, and social discrimination are some of the consequences awaiting the victims of this 'healing' ritual whose horrors are described by the health educators, Graeme Pitcher and Douglas Bowley:

> To penetrate the vagina of a small infant, the perpetrators first need to create a common channel between the vagina and the anal canal by forced insertion of an implement. This action is analogous to the most severe form of female genital mutilation practiced in parts of Africa, introcision, in which the perineum is split with a finger, knife, or similar object, presumably to facilitate penetrative intercourse in girls as young as 5 years old sold into early marriage.[12]

As a result of this action, the baby bleeds while she is assaulted by HIV carriers. The risk of becoming infected by HIV is clearly high, and the pursuant AIDS often means death for an infant victim, who has a weaker immune system than an adult. Meanwhile, the believer in the virgin-cleansing myth will comfort himself while raping a baby with the tranquil vision of squeezing the deadly HIV out of his body and into hers.

Obviously, different cultures hold to different degrees of acceptance on the question of rape. In the United States and Europe, theoretically and legally speaking, men and women are equal. However, if men have unquestioned privileges over women, as has been common in African societies,[13] the acceptance rate of rape myths, expressed in terms such as 'only unethical women get raped' or 'women ask for it', is more likely to be higher than in egalitarian societies.[14] An article in *The Lancet*, a venerable London medical journal founded in 1823, describes Louisvale, the town of the Baby Tshepang incident, as 'a place of despair where men boast about their mistresses, sex with underage children is accepted, jobs are few, and alcohol and drug abuse are rife.'[15] As a result, according to Interpol, South Africa holds one of the highest rates of rape per capita,[16] while the BBC refers to South Africa as the 'rape capital of the world.'[17]

There are, of course, laws and law enforcement in South Africa against rape and sexual assault. 'Jack-rolling' (a South African term for 'recreational' gang rape) is labeled a crime or

rape', Press Association Newsfile (Canada), 3 May 2006; 'Hospital staff asked to give DNA after alleged baby rape', Australian Associated Press Newsfeed, 8 April 2006.

12 Graeme J. Pitcher and Douglas M. G. Bowley, 'Infant rape in South Africa,' *The Lancet* 359 (26 January 2002): 274-275. Furthermore, see Ndubuisi Eke, 'Female genital mutilation: What can be done?' *The Lancet Perspectives* 356 (December 2000): S57.

13 Throughout Africa, sexual violence against women and girls has been a 'weapon' to terrify civilians during conflicts. See: Graeme J. Pitcher and Douglas M. G. Bowley, art.cit.

14 Martha R. Burt, 'Cultural Myths and supports for rape', *The Journal of Personality and Social Psychology* 38, no. 2 (February 1980): 217-230. As many as three in ten South African men believe that women 'asked for it [sexual assault]'. Quoted in Eileen Meier, 'Child rape in South Africa', *Pediatric Nursing*. 6 December 2002.

15 Adele Baleta, art.cit.

16 Rachel L. Swarns, 'Grappling with South Africa's alarming increase in the rape of children', *The New York Times,* 29 January 2002.

17 'South Africa's rape shock', BBC News Online, http://bbc.co.uk, 19 January 1999 (BBC.co.uk); one figure shows 1.19538 rapes per 1,000 people. See: 'South Africa crime statistics', *Nation Master*, http://www.nationmaster. com/graph/cri_rap_percap-crime-rapes-per-capita, 29 January 2001.

'bad' among a majority of men, while it is considered 'good', 'just a game', or 'fun' among many teenage boys.[18] The roots of this difference have remained unanswered, and the teenage boys whose sisters are the victimes may answer differently from the majority. To borrow the words of the feminist historian Susan Brownmiller, rape is a declaration of 'male power' rather than of 'sexuality'.[19] Behind the high rate of rape in South Africa lies a long history of men's unquestioned sexual privileges.

Furthermore, because women in South Africa are more socially suppressed than women in Western countries, it is evident that the public treats rape and the victims of rape less seriously. Since Apartheid is still fresh in the public memory, the police and other authorities are not trusted: the transition of the police force from enforcers of social discrimination into protectors of the people cannot be achieved in a short period of time. It is not hard to imagine that rape victims, in a society where no one observes human rights, are treated like cattle.[20] Moreover, when rape victims in a community are known as HIV-positive, they risk a wide range of violence from their family members and neighbours that extends to homicide.[21] Victims of rape would hide the incident of rape in order to maintain their status in their communities.[22] In this context, men take advantage of the situation and commit rape more often than otherwise because the victims-to-be most likely would not reveal the incidents.

Among those perpetrators who were reported, a deputy headmaster in the Eastern Cape province was accused of raping schoolgirls over a period of ten years. The case was not reported until 20 of those girls had become pregnant.[23] The perpetrator was protected by his social status; for a pupil's family to accuse such a man of rape is almost unthinkable. In addition, the prevalence of rape is such that it takes too much effort for schools or local governments to intervene. A report presented by Dr. Rachel Jewkes of the South African Medical Research Council in 1998 shows that roughly one third of child rapists in South Africa were school teachers, followed by relatives (21 per cent).[24]

In showing the prominence of relatives among the child abusers, the social worker Edith Kriel who helps child victims in the Eastern Cape identifies not only the guardians but the fathers.[25] In this case, not only are the victims socially constrained from reporting their cases but it is also financially impossible to accuse the family's earning head and the protector-of-the-house of such a crime. To make matters worse, the recent economic strains in rural South Africa have resulted in widespread unemployment. The fear of losing the breadwinner is, in many cases, greater than the misery of daily assaults. As a result, whenever HIV is brought home, it is easily spread among family members, including children, through domestic sexual violence. UN officials and other researchers attribute the South African HIV epidemic largely to the nation's high rates of child abuse and rape.[26]

---

[18] 'South Africa's rape shock'; Eileen Meier, art.cit.

[19] Helen Epstein, 'AIDS and Africa's hidden war,' *The Virginia Quarterly Review (*Winter 2006): 31-41.

[20] The pamphlet 'Women and Rape', issued by the Federation of Namibian Women et al., includes a five-page section entitled 'How to Be a Friend to a Rape Victim.'

[21] 'Background: HIV/AIDS and Sexual Violence in South Africa', Human Rights Watch Online Publications, http://www.hrw.org, March 2004.

[22] The South African authorities claim that only 2.8 percent of all rape cases are reported. While the methodology of this analysis is in serious question, the authorities have at least an idea that the majority of rape cases are not reported. Binaifer Nowrojee and Bronwen Manby, Violence Against Women in South Africa, 51.

[23] Jane Flanagan, art.cit.

[24] Rachel Jewkes et al. 'Rape of Girls in South Africa', *The Lancet* 359 (26 January 2002): 319-320.

[25] Jane Flanagan, art.cit.

[26] Helen Epstein, art.cit.

So it is that, in a society where women and girls are mistreated, female babies are no exception. As the South African women start to form coalitions against social inequality, South African men who have been enjoying the unquestioned advantage of 'free rape' seek other targets. Within this context, infant rapes become common, for babies cannot by themselves claim their legal rights and equality.

While gender inequality in South Africa is the major cause of rape and the HIV epidemic, financial restrictions also serve to prevent women from accusing their relatives or spouses of rape. Poverty hastens the speed of the HIV transmission. In the case reported by the Teddy Bear Clinic in Johannesburg, the motive of the mother who sold her baby to men had nothing to do with the virgin-cleansing myth; her need was food.[27] President Thabo Mbeki has stated that Africans are vulnerable to AIDS because of poverty and malnutrition.[28] Women and girls in South Africa are vulnerable to rape because of their economic dependence on men.

President Mbeki's views have not gone uncriticized. When Baby Tshepang's case was reported in 2001, President Mbeki doubted the causal relationship between HIV and AIDS, then refused to distribute anti-retroviral drugs to rape victims.[29] While Mbeki found some support in this,[30] his action added to the pessimism. Fortunately, in May 2002, after a massive media campaign against his policy,[31] Mbeki reversed his ban and in 2003 introduced the Sexual Offences Bill, which since 2006 has been under review.[32]

While the incident of Baby Tshepang was certainly exposed in the South African media, the reported numbers of child/infant rapes increased. There were 37,500 cases of rape and sexual assault against children in 1998, rising to 67,000 in 2000.[33] This rapid increase in the number of police reports does not necessarily denote an increase in the violence. It could well mean that the victims of violence have started to trust in South African justice. Thoko Majokweni, South Africa's special director for the prosecution of sexual offences,[34] reports that more and more cases involving infant victims are appearing in court. Barbara Kenyon, director of the Greater Nelspruit Rape Intervention Project (GRIP), has noticed, however, that rape victims at her care center are getting younger and younger.[35]

Tshepang's case in 2001 aroused a new social movement to upgrade the 'under-resourced, under-staffed and low-status sexual offence unit' which had been under a stagnant discussion in the legislature since 1998.[36] Pastor Johannes Stuurman expressed his dismay over the Tshepang incident, in that the entire community had been regarded as a 'community of rapists.' Yet, he did not lose hope because 'enough people spoke up for her when she couldn't speak for herself.'[37]

---

[27] Rachel Jewkes, art.cit.
[28] Helen Epstein, art.cit.
[29] R. W. Johnson, art.cit.
[30] As of 2001, the cost of a 28-day course of double therapy (zidovudine and lamivudine) for a child was 300-500 Rand [about $20-34] which was relatively expensive considering the fact that the efficiency of such treatment is unproven. See: Graeme J. Pitcher and Douglas M. G. Bowley, art.cit.
[31] 'Mbeki makes dramatic turnaround on AIDS', *New York Amsterdam News*, 2 May 2002.
[32] Human Rights Watch, Human Rights Watch World Report 2006 (South Africa), January 2007.
[33] Jane Flanagan, art.cit. Other reports show 20,000-25,000 as the number of child rapes in 2000. Rachel L. Swarns, art.cit. See also: Adele Baleta,art.cit. The number (21,000) is similar in 2001. See Sarah Nuttall, 'Girl Bodies.'.
[34] Rachel L. Swarns, art.cit.
[35] 'Focus on the Virgin Myth and HIV/AIDS', UN Integrated Regional Information Network.
[36] Adele Baleta, art.cit.
[37] Michael Schmidt, art.cit.

In terms of legislature, the government in 1998 passed the Minimum Sentencing Act No. 105[38] focusing on child rapes. Then, in 1999, it introduced more than 20 special courts for sexual offences; it also launched, for child rape survivors, the Thuthuzala Care Centre (located in Manenberg and Mdantsane) and the Simelela Centre in Khayelitsha.[39] In the special courts, as of 2001, the child victims from the Centre no longer need to face the alleged perpetrator, thus sparing the victim a possibly hysterical reaction.[40] Shortly after the report by the South African Medical Research Council (MRC), which pointed out the assaults in schools, the Department of Education passed a ban on student-teacher sexual relationships.[41] However, in light of the prevailing violence and the country's HIV pandemic, Dr Rachel Jewkes of the MRC and other scholars have called for stronger enforcement.[42]

To conclude, whatever the faults of the media in the misreporting of the incidents, infant rape within the virgin-cleansing myth is a social tragedy. To worsen the situation, many South African men living in poverty have no access to medical centres. Thus, despite the country's AIDS pandemic, only a few are able to understand the scientific and medical implications of their HIV infection. The link between infant rape and the virgin-cleansing myth is the result of ignorance. Local society tends to accept infant rape as a matter of course.[43] Gender inequality must similarly be overcome through ethical education. In this education, the national media, local leaders, and traditional healers should exert their influence and assume responsibility. As theatre director Lara Foot Newton says, '[theatre] can heal, bring understanding and insight, and help audiences to catharsis'.[44] Men should not commit rape, not because the law says so, but because rape is wrong.

With or without the virgin-cleansing myth, infant rape should disappear. As for Baby Tshepang, the South African people have showered her with gifts and money to help her on the road to recovery.[45] According to the journalist Sarah Nuttall, 21,000 Rand was handed to the child by the Coalition for Children's Rights.[46] Despite the tragic senselessness of this issue, the example of the people of South Africa in giving hope to Tshepang ('have hope' in local language) can carry a message to the rest of the world.

CONTRIBUTOR'S NOTE

Among the many contributors to this chapter, I should like to thank the following especially: Elise Foreman (social status of women and babies), Rebecca Guthrie (the virgin-

[38] Christopher Stones and Mike Earl-Taylor, art.cit.

[39] Eileen Meier, 'Child rape in South Africa'; also, 'Crime and corruption; Disturbing picture of sexual violence in Khayelitsha,' *Africa News*, 31 March 2006.

[40] In Durban in 2001, a district surgeon was handling a case of an eight-year-old girl. 'The [alleged] rapist was placed in a wheelchair, and wheeled down the same corridor where the girl was lying. When she saw him, she became so hysterical that any examination became impossible,' quoted in Helen Epstein, art.cit.

[41] David McAlary, 'South Africa child rape focuses attention on broad problem', Voice of America, http://www.VOANews.com, 26 January 2002.

[42] Rachel Jewkes, art.cit.

[43] When theatre director Lara Foot Newton sent a researcher on the case of Tshepang, the researcher reported back: 'Nothing ever happens there. Nothing,' Cf. 'This Week's Must-See,' *Sunday Times* (South Africa), 27 February 2005.

[44] Quoted in '"Tshepang' tells a tragic tale', http://joburg.org.za (City of Johannesburg website), 1 March 2005.

[45] Adele Baleta, art.cit.

[46] Sarah Nuttal, art.cit.

cleansing myth), Ashley Hughes (South African legal system and non-governmental organizations, and Bridget Lowey (research and editing).

APPENDIX: SOUTH AFRICAN ANTI-RAPE LAW

*Ashley Hughes**

Year	Document	Impact
1997	Minimum Sentences Act (aka Section 51 of the Criminal Law Amendment Act 105)	Requires the minimum sentence of life imprisonment for: 1. Rape of a person multiple times 2. Multiple rapes at one crime scene 3. Rape with an accomplice with a common purpose 4. Rapist who is convicted of two or more rape offences 5. Rapist knowing he is infected with HIV 6. Rape of a person under 16 years of age 7. Rape of a person who is physically disabled or mentally ill However, a judge still maintains the power to find 'substantial and compelling circumstances' and impose a lesser sentence. As reported by *The Herald* Online Piet Van Niekerk, 'Controversial Act not seen to have reduced serious crimes in SA,' 23 March 2006 http://www,.theherald.co.za
23 October 2002	Compulsory HIV Testing of Alleged Sexual Offenders Bill	• Allows for victims of rape to apply for HIV testing of their alleged perpetrator and to obtain the results of the test. • Establishes legal procedure for access to the government's post-exposure prophylaxis (PEP) program, which provides rape survivors with antiretroviral treatment within 72 hours to prevent HIV infection. • Addresses only those perpetrators who are arrested, thereby leaving many rape cases without court attention. • Establishes a process by which sex offenders can be tested for HIV. From 'South Africa: HIV treatment takes precedence over rape law' CDC News Brief. http://www.thebody.com/index.html
2003	Criminal Law (Sexual Offences) Amendment Bill	• Expands the definition of rape to include: 1. male and female rapists, 2. male and female victims, 3. the role of coercion, 4. the possibility of oral /genital/ sexual violation. • Sets ages and sentences for statutory rape • Requires disclosure of previous sexual offences to employers in any job that involves working with children. Establishes the ability and necessity of people aged 18 years or younger to testify in criminal proceedings against their offender.

* anhughes@bu.edu.

ZIMBABWE

A ragtag government-run paramilitary group known as the National Youth Service, better known as the Green Bombers, had come into existence in 2000. Its purpose was to stifle political dissent among civilians, and more directly, to smother support for the opposition Movement for Democratic Change. Little was known of the group until March 2003, when young Debbie Siyangapi took the pulpit in an Anglican church in Bulawayo and recounted to the congregation how she had been abducted and forcibly enrolled in the group; she was raped almost nightly, and sometimes several times a night, by some of the hundreds of male conscripts there. In April 2003 Amnesty International documented cases of rape within the Youth Service, and in September the Solidarity Peace Trust, a faith-based group of southern African human rights activists, accused the group of sanctioning 'the rape, and multiple rape, of young girls by boys undergoing training with them and by their military instructors. The resulting pregnancies and infections with sexually transmitted diseases, including HIV, not only devastate the lives of the youth concerned but are creating a terrible legacy for the nation.' The group showed no signs of disappearing, and Jenny Williams, head of the organization Women of Zimbabwe Arise (WOZA), later reported that the ranks of women within the youth militia were only increasing.[1]

In addition to everything else that Zimbabweans face, politically and economically, their women now have, as a result of HIV and AIDS, the lowest life expectancy in the world: just 34 years.[2] In an economy that continues to decline, with an inflation rate in 2008 of 11 million percent (sic) and with 80 percent of the population now living below the poverty datum line, dowries have become a means of escaping poverty, and daughters have become a high-priced commodity. The dowry, long known as a cultural practice, has ceased to be merely a social problem and now needs to be seen from an economic point of view, with girl children being used to generate income.[3] Undismayed by the political pressures, the WOZA movement now counts 55,000 members across the country, and finds the courage to accuse the government security forces of descending to the level of taking babies into custody.[4]

---

1 Michael Wines, 'Zimbabwe militia escapees recount routine rape,' *International Herald Tribune*, 29 December 2003.

2 'Zimbabwe: Women bear brunt of violence,' Inter Press Service News Agency, 7 March 2008.

3 'Zimbabwe: Daughters fetch high prices as brides,' IRIN, 17 July 2007.

4 'Zimbabwe police torture women activists,' Reuters Africa, 10 October 2007.

President Robert Mugabe countered on 15 September 2008 with an appeal to outsiders to stay away, urging 'African solutions for African problems.' [5]

D.W.P.

[5] Alan Cowell, 'Africa letter,' *The New York Times*, 20-21 September 2008.

In: Crimes Against Women
Editor: David Wingeate Pike

ISBN 978-1-61470-813-1

Chapter 12

RAPE AMONG THE SHONA IN ZIMBABWE

Tyanai Charamba

INTRODUCTION

This chapter has three goals. Firstly, it proposes that certain traditional Shona marriage procedures, customs and practices are among the major factors that promote illegal sexual encounters of which rape is part. Secondly, it examines the efforts made by different governments in the history of Zimbabwe to curb those customs. Thirdly, it exposes circumstances that continue to sustain those marriage customs that perpetuate unlawful sexual conduct.

According to the law of Zimbabwe, an unlawful sexual conduct means: 'any act the commission of which constitutes the crime of rape, aggravated indecent assault, indecent assault, sexual intercourse or performing an indecent act with a young person, or sodomy.'[1] A young person according to that law means a boy or girl under the age of sixteen.[2] Under the same law, 'If a male person knowingly has sexual intercourse or anal sexual intercourse with a female person who has not consented to it he shall be guilty of rape…'[3] It is on the basis of Zimbabwean law that this chapter proposes that rape is a crime of violence perpetuated by the dominant sex over the dominated one at any given period of history. It is a '…tasteless and violent crime.… [It is not] a crime of sex or a matter of choice but a crime of violence committed against…an unwilling victim.'[4]

In Zimbabwe, rape is rampant. The Young Women's Christian Association (YWCA) established that between 1989 and 1991 there was an upward trend in the number of rape cases, as follows:[5]

---

1 Girl Child Network Manual, No. 2 *Girl Child Network Presents Sexual Offences Act In Zimbabwe*, 1.

2 Sexual Offences Act [Chapter 9:21] (No. 8/2001), 126.

3 Girl Child Network Mannual, No. 1-2.

4 Kevin Howse, et al. *Family Matters: A Guide To Family Life* (Grantham, UK: Stanborough Press, 1989), 73.

5 The Young Women's Christian Association, quoted by Felicia Sakala, *Southern Africa in Transition: A Gendered Perspective*, ed. Patricia McFadden (Harare, Zimbabwe: SAPES Books, 1998), 34.

Year	No. of Cases
1989	2,510
1990	2,643
1991	2,776

The Women's Affairs-ZANU PF Research Wing revealed the following statistics of cases of rape in 1992:[6]

No. of Cases	Sentence
10	Pending judgment
1	1 ½ years in jail
3	3 years in jail
4	4 years in jail
4	5 years in jail
1	4 ½ years in jail
6	6 years in jail
1	Fined
3	Acquitted

The Musasa Project, a voluntary non-governmental organization established in 1988, found that, in 2006, 37 percent of violence within the domestic arena was in the form of sexual abuse including rape.[7]

The large majority of the Zimbabwean people is made up of the Mashona (or simply Shona), constituting 75 percent of the population. The Matebele (or simply Ndebele), make up a further 16.5 percent.[8] Minority groups, which include the Europeans, the Venda, the Kalanga, and the Nambya, make up the rest. Most of the Shona share a common ancestry, history and culture. A certain Professor Clement Doke, by working on the unification of some five mutually intelligible dialects which are spoken in Zimbabwe, came up with a standard orthography for the language.[9] Soon afterwards, Doke recommended that the combination of the dialects be called Shona, and that all those who spoke it be known as Shona. The Shona being the dominant ethnic group, their traditional customs and practices dominate in almost all legal proceedings of customary nature, as well as in some major national agendas. Therefore, for the purpose of the present study, it is the Shona marriage procedures, customs and practices that are selected.

[6] The Women's Affairs–ZANU PF Research Wing, quoted by Felicia Sakala, Ibid., 36.

[7] Musasa Project, *Manual Domestic Violence And Its Magnitude*, 4.

[8] Emmanuel Chabata, *The Nambya Verb With Special Emphasis On The Causative* (Oslo: University Of Oslo Press, 2007), 8.

[9] Clement, M. Doke. *The Unification Of Shona Dialects: A Photographic Reprint*, with an Introduction by Herbert Chimhundu (Oslo: University Of Oslo Press, 2005), 78.

SHONA THOUGHT AND PHILOSOPHY OF MARRIAGE: INTRODUCTION

Traditional Shona marriage customs, practices, philosophies and principles are vibrant and binding when a marriage is initiated and celebrated. It is therefore necessary to examine those customs, practices, philosophies and principles as background for the marriage proceedings that have the potential to cause unlawful sexual conduct amounting to rape.

Central to the Shona people's philosophy of life and thought is the 'idea that every body must marry in the prime of their youth'.[10] The Shona say, *'Hakuna hari inofa isina kubikira'* [no clay-pot breaks before it has cooked]. As such, traditional Shona culture prescribes de jure and de facto marriage customs to make sure that everyone takes part. It also condemns *'wifelessness, husbandlessness, childlessness [and] homelessness...'*[11] In this culture, both motherhood and fatherhood are marked and measured on the basis of procreation and reproduction. *Mukadzi wanhingi* (wife of so and so) remains solely his wife and not a mother (*mai*) as long as she has not given birth to a baby. The same applies to the man. He remains *murume wanhingi* (husband to so and so) and not *baba vanhingi* (father to so and so) as long as a baby is not born to him. A woman who has given birth to a baby becomes both a 'wife to so and so' and 'a mother of children' (*mai vevana*). Once she is both 'wife' and 'mother' she becomes '*mudzimai wanhingi*' (mother of children and wife to so and so).

Marriage, procreation and reproduction are thus important stages in the Shona people's rites of passage. They are cherished and encouraged, while barrenness and sterility are perceived as obstacles to the individual's passage of life. If a couple has been together for a period of a year and has failed to have a child, major steps are taken to correct the problem of sterility, whether it lies on the side of the man or the woman or on both. Firstly, family members recommend the use of herbal medicines to correct the problem of infertility. When the use of herbal medicines proves fruitless, de facto methods of enforcing reproduction are applied. Two of these de facto methods are in popular use among the Shona. These are *kupindira* (getting in), and *chimutsamapfihwa* (setting the fire stones alight).

Since the Shona do not tolerate '*wifelessness*' or '*husbandlessness,*' they uphold both wife and husband inheritance. On the one hand, when a woman dies and is survived by a husband and children, her husband and members of her natal family work together to ensure that the widower marries one of his *varamu*. This is initiated under the traditional Shona custom of *chigadzamapfihwa* (reviving dead firestones). The deceased woman is the 'dead firestone' that needs to be 'revived.' On the other hand, if a man dies and is survived by a wife and children, the widow is to be inherited by one of her de facto husbands (her husband's younger brother or his sister's son). This is done under a custom called *kugara nhaka* (wife inheritance).

It must also be mentioned that the Shona people consider marriage to be a family affair and not merely an affair between bride and bridegroom. A woman is married to a family and not to an individual per se. As such she has de jure and de facto husbands. Once *lobola* (bride wealth) is paid for her, she automatically has a single de jure husband and many de facto ones. The former is the man with whom she has fallen in love. A woman is to enjoy conjugal rights only with her de jure husband. Tradition does not allow her to indulge in a conjugal relationship with her de facto husbands, who include her husband's younger brothers

[10] Okot, p'Bitek. *Artist the Ruler,* 9 (Nairobi: Heinemann, 1986), 16.
[11] Ibid.

(*madzibabamunini*) and his sisters' sons (*vazukuru*). A married man also has de jure and de facto wives. As soon as a man pays *lobola* (bride wealth) for a woman of his choice, he becomes the woman's de jure husband and a de facto husband to the woman's younger sisters (*vanin'ina vemukadzi wake*) and her brothers' daughters (*vana vehanzvadzi dzomukadzi wake*). The two categories of de facto wives constitute the man's *varamu* or *madzimainini.* Pedzisai Mashiri[12] has called the man's de facto wives his 'cultural wives.' That relationship between a woman and her de facto husbands, and between a man and his de facto wives, is what the Shona call *chiramu,* which is both a cross-sex and a jesting relationship. Although tradition proscribes sexual intercourse between a man and his *varamu,* it permits the man to enter into horseplay with them, during which, if he wishes, he can proceed to fondle the woman's private parts. He is also free during the play to resort to verbal teasing, with full use of vulgar sexual innuendo. The varamu, however, are not to consent under any circumstances to the fondling and verbal abuse of the man, but instead are required to resist, using verbal and non-verbal means. The Shona have a saying, *muramu inzungu yakateya gonzo* [a *muramu* is like a peanut that traps a rat in the home]. That means that without proper checks and balances *chiramu* can lead to a sexual encounter between participants.

To the Shona, life and political stability are more precious than the right of the girl child to choose her partner. Diana Auret writes, '*Life conceived of in terms of continuity of the agnatic group is of the highest value among the [Shona] people.'*[13] As a result of their emphasis on life, peace and stability, the Shona approve of *kuzvarira* (child pledging). In times of drought they pledge girls in marriage to those people who can provide them with food, in order to save lives that otherwise would be at stake. They also pledge daughters to rulers for the sake of making peace.

The Shona believe in life after death. They believe, for instance, in the existence of *ngozi* (avenging spirits). *Ngozi* emerge when an individual commits homicide. The spirit of the deceased arrives to take revenge on the culprit's family, causing death or a series of deaths. Be that as it may, the Shona say, "*mushonga wengozi kuripa"* [the solution to *ngozi* is to pay a fine]. That payment is usually in the form of a young girl who is pledged in marriage to one of the members of the deceased person's family. The girl is expected to bear children, who will thus replace the deceased member.

It is a pre-requisite in some chiefdoms for a candidate to chieftaincy to commit incest.[14] Michael Bourdillon mentions that great rulers in Shona history engaged in this practice,[15] committing incest with their blood sisters on the day they were installed as chiefs. Chirisamhuru, for instance, committed incest with his blood sister Ndomboya to become a *rozvi mambo/changamire* (a supreme Rozvi ruler).[16] Although the practice is dying, it is still prevalent among the Rozvi chiefs found in the Gokwe district of Zimbabwe's Midlands Province.

---

[12] Pedzisai, Mashiri, *Interpretations Of The Authors' Visions Of Women In The Shona Novel* (Harare, Zimbabwe: University of Zimbabwe Publishers, 1994), 152.

[13] Diana, Auret, *A Decade of Development: Zimbabwe 1980-1990* (Gweru, Zimbabwe: Mambo Press, 1990), 98.

[14] David N. Beach, *The Shona And Their Neighbours* (London: Blackwell Publishers, 1994), 154.

[15] Michael F. C. Bourdillon, *The Shona Peoples* (Gweru, Zimbabwe: Mambo Press, 1976), 113.

[16] Nobert M. Mutasa, *Nhume YaMambo* (Gweru, Zimbabwe: Mambo Press, 1990), 30.

Shona Marriage Customs and Practices: De Jure and De Facto

In examining de jure and de facto Shona marriage customs, *kukumbira* (asking for a woman's hand in marriage) emerges as the ideal procedure. De facto marriage customs and procedures include: *musengabere* (the act of carrying away a girl in the way a hyena steals a goat), *kuzvarira, chiramu, chigadzamapfihwa, kuripa ngozi* and methods of ensuring reproduction. Most of the de facto marriage customs promote forced marriages and rape, as will now be shown.

De Jure Marriage Procedure

The practice known as *kukumbira* requires the consent of both the girl and the boy who are to marry. After they fall in love, the two need to agree to marry before major marriage procedures commence. *Kukumbira* also requires the consent of both the girl's and the boy's families, after which members of the girl's family demand payment of *lobola* (bride-wealth) for the transfer of the girl. Since *kukumbira* requires the consent of the couple, it provides an exemplary alternative to the nonconsensual sexual encounters that lead to assault, indecent assault and rape. Tradition emphasizes *kukumbira.* It approves of the other forms of marriage only when, for certain reasons, *kukumbira* cannot serve the purpose.

De Facto Marriage Procedure

Musengabere is described as 'the most original, the most adventurous, the most risky (but not illegal) of all the [de facto marriage customs] mentioned here.'[17] *Musengabere* caters to those young men who are either too shy to propose to a girl or whose love proposals are rejected by girls of their age. Since 'no clay pot should break before it has cooked,' the boy who finds himself in either situation embarks on *musengabere*.

The boy in question, possibly with the help of his close associates, would waylay the girl of his choice, manhandle her and run away with her to his own home. Upon entering his sleeping hut (*gota*), the boy would quickly force the girl into a sexual encounter. Once deflowered (*ava mvana*), the girl becomes wife to the boy. A '…fundamental and basic belief of the Shona is that when a couple marry, the wife must be a virgin…'[18] As such, Shona culture does not permit a girl who has been deflowered to visit her people before *lobola* is paid for her. Tradition does not encourage *musengabere*. Everything being equal, the Shona people encourage *kukumbira*, since *musengabere*, although not actually illegal, is risky. A young man who is discovered in the process of 'stealing' a girl is severely punished by members of the girl's natal family.

[17] Kumbirai G. Mkanganwi, 'Indigenous Knowledge And Technology In African And Diasporan Communities: Multi-Disciplinary Approaches,' in Emmanuel M. Chiwome, Zifikele Mguni, and Munashe Furusa, eds (Harare, Zimbabwe: University of Zimbabwe Publishers, 2000), 159.

[18] Michael Gelfand, *The Genuine Shona* (Gweru, Zimbabwe: Mambo Press, 1973), 166.

Musengabere exposes the woman to physical and sexual abuse and rape. Once she is manhandled, the girl struggles to free herself from the death grip of the boy who seeks to marry her. In the process she suffers abuse, from the boy and from his associates that may amount to serious bodily harm. She also suffers from unwelcome touch. The man and his associates grab her without concern for her private parts. Furthermore, she suffers from indecent exposure when the boy and his associates run away with her. Unwelcome touch and indecent exposure amount to psychological abuse and an affront to her dignity and sense of worth. In short, *musengabere* condones nonconsensual sexual encounter that amounts to rape, since the young man, upon entering his bedroom, forces the girl into a sexual encounter that often results in a long-lasting depression. Men who embark on *musengabere* give no thought to the age of the young girls who are their targets. *Musengabere* effectively promotes the rape of minors, by condoning the kidnapping of women by men whose intent is assault.

KUZVARIRA

Although *kuzvarira* is intended to save the lives of starving families and to maintain political stability within a community, in practice it amounts to a crime against women. It represents an important way in which traditional Shona patriarchy takes control of women's sexuality. Those who are pledged are usually young girls, so that *kuzvarira* constitutes sexual harassment and the rape of minors. Instead of proceeding with the girl's consent to marriage, *kuzvarira* represents 'a form of sexual terrorism'[19] in which the victim is forced into sexual intercourse, raped at a tender age.

CHIRAMU

The vertical and asymmetrical relationship known as *chiramu*, consisting of horseplay and verbal teasing, is a further source of crimes against women. The *varamu* has to endure unwelcome touching and indecent exposure as the man advances to fondle her private parts. She also suffers physical abuse, since she is bruised and scratched in her attempts to resist the man's devices. It is the man, and not of course the girl, who initiates the horseplay. The relationship is therefore structured in a way that allows the man (a representative of traditional patriarchy) to have full charge over the woman's body. Unwelcome touch and indecent exposure are avenues to a nonconsensual sexual encounter that amounts to rape. A man can tease the girl with phrases that are pregnant with sexual innuendo and tantamount to sexual harassment. He might say, '*Panei pakati pamakumbo penyu apo zvamunenge murume chaiye?*' [What do you have in between your legs since you seem to be a man?]. Verbal teasing of this nature has the potential to make the girl feel ashamed of her body. *Chiramu* thus widens the gulf between femininity and masculinity to the advantage of the male and subjects the woman to physical, verbal, emotional, and psychological abuse.

---

[19] Carol Sheffield, quoted in Michael S. Kimmel, *Gendered Society*, 2nd ed. (Oxford: Oxford University Press, 2004), 112.

Chigadzamapfihwa

Chigadzamapfihwa is a traditional marriage custom based on force and nonconsensual sexual encounter. Since the custom does not require the consent of the girl child, it allows men an unfair control over women's sexuality and contributes to the prevalence of rape in Zimbabwe.

Kuripa Ngozi

The girl child who is used to settle the problem of an avenging spirit is sexually, emotionally and psychologically abused. She enters marriage before she is prepared for it. Such forced marriage is destabilizing since 'the psychological nature is closely related to the sexual nature.'[20] It amounts to a rape encounter. The girl has to engage in a conjugal union with a stranger and to bear his children as substitutes for the man he murdered.

De Facto Methods of Ensuring Reproduction

To ensure reproduction, two methods are applied: *chimutsamapfihwa* in the case that a woman proves or is assumed to be barren, and *kupindira* if it is the man who proves or is believed to be sterile. However, both of the remedies exert pressure on the woman to consent to indulge in illegal sexual conduct.

Chimutsamapfihwa

Chimutsamapfihwa allows a barren woman to become 'mother of so and so' in addition to her being 'wife to so and so'. If a woman proves or is believed to be barren, tradition expects her to make sure that either her younger sister or brother's daughter marries her husband in order to reproduce on her behalf. Once the young girl gives birth to a baby, the barren woman becomes a de facto mother to the baby, automatically becoming 'mother of so and so.' Traditional Shona culture respects age differences and seniority. It also associates wisdom with age. The Shona say, 'Mukuru mukuru hanga haigari bvunde' [an elder is an elder; he/she should not be challenged by the younger]. Therefore, the barren woman's younger sister and/or brother's daughter is by tradition not allowed to defy the demands of the elder sister.

Since *chimutsamapfihwa* does not require the consent of the woman's younger sister or brother's daughter, it promotes unwelcome sexual encounters that amount to rape. The young girl who is subjected to *chimutsamapfihwa* suffers the traumatic effect of an intimate sexual relationship to which she has not consented. She has to brave an illegal marriage and to take

---

[20] Kevin Howse, Hugh Dunton, and David Marshall, *Family Matters: A Guide To Family Life* (Grantham: Stanborough Press, 1988), 77.

care of illegitimate children, while the barren woman suffers the blow of having to share her husband. The blame for her natural condition is laid on her.

Kupindira

If a man is impotent, Shona culture resorts to *kupindira*. The impotent man's sister exerts pressure on his wife/wives to allow one of her de facto husbands to secretly enter her bedroom and have sex with her. The woman usually gives her consent in order to fulfill the demands of tradition. By forcing a woman to a sexual encounter with a man who is not her de jure husband, *kupindira* similarly robs a woman of power over her sexuality.

Ceremonial Occasions: Installation of a Chief

During the traditional installation of a Shona chief, women again pay a price. A girl child is forced into an incestuous relationship which also amounts to rape, since it 'apparently impairs normal adult development and mechanisms of self-protection.'[21] During the installation exercise, the girl child is indecently exposed and fondled in full view of the majority of the people present. The whole exercise has a negative impact on her self-esteem, and the experience may leave her with sexual dysfunction for the rest of her life.

Governmental Efforts to Curb Rape

In the course of the country's history, various governments have made efforts to overcome the traditional customs that debase the status of women. In 1898, at the beginning of the colonial period that lasted until 1980, the two major provinces of Mashona and Matebele were united to form the British colony of Southern Rhodesia. In 1923, Southern Rhodesia established a settler government and became a self-governing colony. This status came to a halt on 11 November 1965, when Prime Minister Ian Smith signed the Unilateral Declaration of Independence (UDI). The UDI, based on white minority rule, itself came to a halt on 18 April 1980 when the country attained black majority rule and took the name of Zimbabwe.

The colonial administration and the settler government had employed two major means to curb sexual crimes against women. Firstly, they codified specific Acts and Ordinances. Secondly, they presented Christian marriage as a model based on three premises: the consent of both the bride and the bridegroom; monogamy; and marital fidelity.

The Marriage Ordinance of 1901 that was amended in 1912, 1917 and 1929 tried to curb the practice of *kuzvarira* and other forms of nonconsensual sexual encounters, using a three-fold criterion. Firstly, the ordinance required all marriages to be registered with the Native Commissioner. Secondly, it required the woman's consent to marriage before any marriage procedures could take place. Thirdly, it outlawed the marriage of minors, stipulating that

[21] Ibid., 76.

'Any man who enters into a marriage agreement concerning a girl who is not of marriageable age (twelve years old or older) is liable to a fine of up to fifty pounds or to imprisonment with or without hard labour for up to one year.'[22] Four major factors, namely the codification of customary law, the perpetuation of Shona traditional religion, the rise of independent apostolic churches, and economic hardship, joined to push the Shona people to resort to illegal traditional marriage practices.

The customary law of the colonial era recognized traditional marriage practices so long as they did not 'interfere with European concepts of justice and civilized society,'[23] such as the payment of *lobola*. Ironically, those marriage practices perpetuated the illegal sexual encounters that the colonial government sought to curb. As Ngwabi Bhebni writes, 'Colonialism and African patriarchy colluded to debauch African culture and tradition to the disadvantage of women.'[24]

The majority of black Zimbabweans suffered serious economic challenges as a result of the passage of the Land Appointment Act of 1931, the Land Husbandry Act of 1952, the Land Tenure Act of 1969, and from the imposition of economic sanctions on Southern Rhodesia by the international community after Prime Minister Smith had signed the Unilateral Declaration of Independence on 11 November 1965. The three Acts of the colonial parliament gave the colonial government the right to distribute land on racial lines. Blacks were pushed into regions 4 and 5 of the country that have rocky and sandy soils and receive less than sufficient rainfall to support agriculture. The result was the impoverishment of a segment of the black population, and extreme suffering forced some Shona people to resort to traditional marriage customs such as *kuzvarira* to alleviate poverty.

In disregard of Christianity, traditional religious beliefs such as the belief in *ngozi* continue unabated. As such, the Shona continued to appease *ngozi,* making use of minors. Some Zimbabweans, who include Johane Maranke,[25] introduced new churches that approve of child pledging and polygamy. These churches challenged Christian marriage procedures and perpetuated traditional ones that promote illegal sexual unions. At the time that Zimbabwe attained black majority rule in 1980, these regressive factors were back in play.

The incoming Zimbabwean government set out, in the cause of curbing sexual violence, to codify acts of parliament, including the rape of minors and of women in general. In the process, such Acts grapple with traditional marriage customs and practices that promote rape, assault and indecent assault, and include the Legal Age of Majority Act of 1982, the Marriage Act Chapter 5.11, the Sexual Offences Act Chapter 9.21, and the Domestic Violence Act Chapter 5.16.

---

[22] Elizabeth Schmidt, *Peasants, Traders and Wives: Shona Women in the History Of Zimbabwe 1870-1939* (Harare, Zimbabwe: Baobab Books, 1996), 111.

[23] Ibid., 107.

[24] Ngwabi Bhebhe, 'Indigenous Knowledge And Technology In African And Diasporan Communities: Multi-Disciplinary Approaches,' 14.

[25] Johane Maranke, referred to in *The Shona Peoples*, 298.

Legal Age of Majority Act

This Act provides that 'Any one who has reached the age of 18 is now an adult, and can vote, enter a contract, own property, deal with it in any way he or she chooses, and open and operate a bank account.'[26] The Act empowers women to consent or not to consent to any contract or arrangement (including those of marriage) made on their behalf. The Act therefore withholds recognition of traditional Shona marriage customs such as *kuzvarira*, *chigadzamapfihwa* and *chimutsamaphihwa* and on the basis that they fail to respect the right of a woman to give or refuse her consent.

The Marriage Act [Chapter 5.11]

The Act was codified under general law, using different measures to curb marriage practices that promote rape. Firstly, it stipulates that girls under sixteen and boys under eighteen are not permitted to enter into a marriage contract. Secondly, it emphasizes the need to register marriages. Thirdly, it provides that all marriages registered under this Act are to proceed with the consent of both the bride and the bridegroom. Fourthly, it establishes that *lobola* is not a legal requirement for anyone wishing to enter marriage. Hence traditional marriage customs such as *chiramu* that pivot on the payment of *lobola* are rendered inoperative. Fifthly, the act recognizes only monogamous marriages.[27]

There have been setbacks. In addition to the Marriage Act Chapter 5.11, there is the Customary Marriages Act Chapter 5.07 and Unregistered Customary Law Unions. These two tend to reverse the gains of Chapter 5.11, since they: i) do not stipulate the age at which boys and girls can enter marriage; ii) consider *lobola* as a legal requirement for marriage; iii) allow men to marry many wives; and iv) approve of traditional heritance procedures in the case of divorce or death of either spouse.[28]

Sexual Offences Act: No. 8/2001

This Act of 2001 forbids i) 'extra-marital sexual intercourse or immoral or indecent acts committed with young persons',[29] ii) '...rape or certain nonconsensual acts'[30] and iii) 'Detention of persons for sexual purpose.'[31] It provides that a person who indulges in any of these acts 'shall be guilty of an offence liable to...a fine or to imprisonment for a period not exceeding ten years or to both fine and such imprisonment.'[32]

This Act therefore does not recognize traditional Shona marriage practices that condone rape, incest, sodomy, or indecent assault. Since it forbids 'detention of persons for sexual

[26] Ruth Weiss, *The Women Of Zimbabwe* (London: Kesho Publishers, 1986), 113.

[27] Zimbabwe Women's Lawyers Association Manual, Reform Of Marriage Laws in Zimbabwe, 1.

[28] Ibid., 2-3.

[29] Sexual Offences Act [Chapter 9:21] No. 8/2001 Section 3 Subsection (1).

[30] Ibid., Section 8.

[31] Ibid., Section 10.

[32] Ibid., Section 3.

purpose,' the Act effectively outlaws *musengabere*. In the sense that the Act proscribes indecent sexual acts committed against young persons, it militates against *kuripa ngozi* and *kuzvarira*, since in most cases the preferred victims of these customs are young girls below the legal age of marriage, which is sixteen. Furthermore, the Act repudiates every form of nonconsensual sexual encounter, and hence criminalizes all acts of assault and indecent assault suffered by victims of *chiramu.*

THE DOMESTIC VIOLENCE ACT: NO. 14/2006

The Act defines domestic violence as 'any unlawful act, omission or behaviour which results in death or the direct infection of physical, sexual or mental injury to any complainant by the respondent...'[33] Under the Act, sexual abuse covers 'rape, indecent assault, unwanted sexual touching or exposure.'[34] Subsection (1)(l) includes, under domestic violence, 'abuse derived from…cultural or customary rites or practices that discriminate against or degrade women.' These include the 'pledging of women or girls for purposes of appeasing spirits, forced marriages, child marriage, and forced wife inheritance.'[35] The Act strongly condemns all marriage customs that lead to nonconsensual sexual encounters and any forms of unwelcome sexual advances including unwanted sexual touching and exposure[36] which are major occurrences during *chiramu*. In that sense this Act outlaws horseplay during the practice of *chiramu*. Furthermore, the Act stipulates that 'Any person who commits an act of domestic violence…shall be guilty of an offence and liable to a fine…or imprisonment not exceeding ten years or to both fine and such imprisonment.'[37]

Despite these articles of legislation, specific circumstances in Zimbabwe promote illegal sexual encounters. One such circumstance is a call for a cultural revolution, meaning a return to tradition. Another is the high degree of misgovernance under the Mugabe regime that has led to serious economic hardships for the majority of Zimbabweans.

THE CALL FOR A CULTURAL REVOLUTION

Soon after independence, most Zimbabweans believed that the political revolution should be followed immediately by a cultural and indigenous one. In this spirit, some members of Zimbabwean society revived, and continue to revive, traditional Shona marriage customs that promote cases of rape. These customs, suppressed by colonial laws, were then revived at independence by people yearning for cultural bliss. *Kuzvarira, Chiram* and *kuripa ngozi* in periods of drought are among the marriage customs that have been revived.

---

33 Domestic Violence Act [Chapter 5:16] No. 14/2006 Section 3.

34 Ibid., Section 3 (2) (b).

35 Ibid., Section 3 (1) (iii).

36 Ibid., Section 3 (2) (b).

37 Ibid., Section 4 (1).

MISGOVERNANCE AND ECONOMIC CHALLENGES

Natural disasters, such as the droughts that Zimbabweans suffered in 1981, 1982, 1983, 1992, 2002 and 2003, and the effects of the tropical cyclone *Eline* that struck Zimbabwe in 2000, caused famine throughout Zimbabwe. Wanton policies in education and health, corruption especially among the top government officials, the introduction in 1991 of ESAP (Economic Structural Adjustment Programme), the fast-track land grab exercise that the government spearheaded in 2000, and the unprecedented presidential decree in July 2007 for a reduction of prices to below the cost of production are among the factors that devastated the Zimbabwean economy and reduced the majority of Zimbabweans to extreme poverty. The extreme suffering that resulted explains the return to traditional methods of survival, including *kuzvarira*. To fight starvation, some families in the Buhera district of Manicaland province have returned to the pledging of young girls, and at least ten young girls were pledged in marriage between 1991 and 1995.[38]

CONCLUSION

This chapter has put forward the idea that rape, which is a crime of sexual violence, is rampant in Zimbabwe. It has grappled with certain Shona marriage procedures, customs and practices that promote rape, and presented the efforts of government to restrict them. Such efforts may well be effective in an environment that is politically and economically stable, but in a country as politically and economically challenged as Zimbabwe they are ineffective and dysfunctional. A society suffering from extreme poverty and political dehumanization will at times resort to traditional modes of survival, while the Mugabe government that began in 1980 is powerless to resist the return to traditional customs that promote crimes against women in the form of rape. Sadly, a government that maintains itself in power only by smashing democratic proceedings and riding roughshod over the rule of law can contribute nothing to the protection of women's rights.

---

[38] Interview with Assistant District Administrator of Buhera District of Manicaland Province, 8 December 2007.

NIGERIA

The Nigerian government in 2001 reintroduced a strict version of Islamic law which prescribes the death penalty for rape, but Aminuddeen Abubakar, an Islamic scholar in Kano, reports that the penalties have done little to solve the problem and that child rape is on the increase.[1] Equally disturbing was the increase in trafficking. When Isoke Aikpitanyi boarded a plane in Benin City, she dreamed of a new life in Europe. Instead, in Turin, she found a nightmare. In debt and at the mercy of traffickers, Aikpitanyi was forced to work as a prostitute on the Turin streets. It was there that she met Laura Maragnani, a journalist with the newsweekly Panorama, and together they produced a book, The Girls of Benin City, which was published in March 2007.[2] An official Italian study in 2007 of a government program that assists sexually exploited women showed that, over a six-year period starting in 2000, more than 45,000 women, mostly from Nigeria and eastern Europe, had needed and received some sort of social assistance.[3]

D.W.P.

---

1 'Nigeria: child rape in Kano on the increase,' *IRIN Africa,* 3 January 2008.

2 Laura Maragnani, *Le ragazze di Benin City: La tratta delle nuove schiave dalla Nigeria ai marciapiedi d'Italia* (Milan: Melampo, 2007).

3 Elisabetta Povoledo, 'One woman's crusade against modern slavery,' *International Herald Tribune*, 22 September 2007.

In: Crimes Against Women
Editor: David Wingeate Pike

ISBN 978-1-61470-813-1

Chapter 13

DOMESTIC, COMMUNITY AND STATE-SPONSORED VIOLENCE IN NIGERIA

J. Shola Omotola and Saheed Aderinto

INTRODUCTION

As the tenth largest country in the world and the most populous country in Africa (one out of every five Africans is a Nigerian), the population was estimated in mid-2007 at 144 million.[1] Of this population, 49 percent are women and 56% are under 20. HIV prevalence is 5 percent. The fertility rate of the nation is 5.9 percent per woman. The average fertility rate in the North is estimated at above 6.5 children per woman, which explains the size of most families. This situation is encouraged and sustained by some cultural/religious practices such as early child marriage, polygamy, poor girl-child education and the general poverty of families. The average infant mortality rate was calculated in 2003 to be as high as 201 per 1,000 births. Maternal mortality stood at between 1,100 and 3,000 per 100,000 births (exact statistics are hard to determine). In addition to its federal government, Nigeria has 36 state governments; social and health policies are decided and executed at both levels.[2]

Nigeria is composed of more than 250 ethnic groups, of which the most important are the Hausa-Fulani (north), Yoruba (west) and Ibo or Igbo (east). After the Hausa-Fulani (29 percent), Yoruba (21 percent), and Ibo (18 percent), the next most populous and politically influential are the Ijaw (10 percent), Kanuri (4 percent), Ibibio (3.5 percent), and Tiv (2.5 percent). Nigeria is 50 percent Muslim (dominant in the north), 40 percent Christian, and 10 percent indigenous beliefs. The Hausa-Fulani in the north constitute a model of an ethnic group fusion. The Hausa are themselves a fusion, being a collection of West African peoples who were assimilated long ago into the population inhabiting what is now considered Hausaland. The Fulani, for their part, is the name given to the Fulve pastoralists who began to enter the Hausa country in the 13th century, and by the 15th century they were tending cattle, sheep, and goats in Borno as well. The Fulani came from the Senegal River valley, where their

---

1 Population Reference Bureau, 2007 Data Sheet, World's 10 largest Countries in Population.

2 Nigeria Census 2006.

ancestors had developed a method of livestock management and specialization based on transhumance. The movement of cattle along north/south corridors in pursuit of grazing and water followed the climatic pattern of the rainy and dry seasons. Gradually, the pastoralists moved eastward, first into the centres of the Mali and Songhai empires and eventually into Hausaland and Borno. They have intermarried with the Hausa, and have mostly adopted the latter's customs and language, although some Fulani decided to stay 'pure' by retaining a nomadic life.[3]

In Nigeria, as elsewhere, violence against women carries implications for the country's democracy and development. Given the staggering incidence and increasing rate of violence in Nigeria, a solution has to be found.

THE PROBLEM IN HISTORICAL PERSPECTIVE

Violence against women in Nigeria has its roots in antecedents predating the colonial period. The disparate entities that later melded into a single sovereign power had a common denominator: a patriarchal system of gender inequality in which women were socially and politically marginalized. In certain settings, however, women occupied respectable positions and contributed immensely to the development of their communities, to such an extent that women were seen as complementary rather than subordinate to men. Such settings were nevertheless exceptional, and the stature of women never approximated equality with men.[4] Male domination, often repressive, manifested itself in the cultural and socio-economic domains.[5] Across different Nigerian societies—especially Hausa, Igbo and Yorubaa—women were seen as the 'property' of men, to be adapted to roles and conditions that satisfied the interests of their male masters and owners.[6] It was into this skewed system of gender power relations that colonialism arrived.

The colonial interregnum that effectively began in 1900, with Britain creating separate protectorates over Northern and Southern Nigeria, brought further harm to the cause of Nigerian women. The colonial state, by any standard, was patriarchal in nature, since all colonial officers were male. The introduction of indirect rule by Lord Lugard, Britain's first colonial governor in Nigeria, who sought to administer the country through traditional social structures and political institutions, added salt to a festering wound, since it strengthened the existing patriarchal nature of Nigerian society. Colonial policies soon became anti-women both in content and execution. The most notable of these was the introduction, in the Eastern region of the country, of a tax payable by women that was to precipitate the legendary Aba

---

[3] 'The Hausa-Fulani of Nigeria,': http://www.jamtan.com/jamtan/fulani.cfm?chap=3&linksPage=356 .

[4] Eno B. Ikpe, 'The historical legacy of gender equality in Nigeria,' in: Solomon O. Akinboye, ed. *Paradox of Gender Equality in Nigerian Politics* (Lagos: Concept Publications, 2004), p. 21.

[5] Felicia D. Oyekanmi, 'Socio-Economic Dimensions of Gender Equality in Nigeria', in: Solomon O. Akinboye, ed. ibid, pp. 41-61; Iyabo Olojede, 'Public Policy and Gender Politics in Nigeria', in: Solomon O. Akinboye…ibid, pp. 119-135; and Risikat O. Dauda, 'The Economic Context of Gender Equality in Nigeria', in: Solomon O. Akinboye, ed. ibid, pp. 62-90.

[6] Ebenezer E. Lawal and Ronke C. Ojo, 'Politics of Gender Inequality in Nigeria', in: Emmanuel O. Ojo, ed. *Challenges of Sustainable Democracy in Nigeria* (Ibadan, Nigeria: John Archers Publishers, 2006), pp. 330-246.

Women's Riot of 1929. This marked the beginning of the radicalization of female activism in Nigeria.[7]

The post-independence era that began in 1960 has done very little to reverse the trend. Not even the manifold public policies on women's rights that characterized the country's prolonged military rule have brought about any fundamental change. These policies included the Better Life for Rural Women and the Family Support Program, introduced under the Babangida and Abacha regimes, respectively. Equally ineffective was the establishment of the National Commission on Women and the unprecedented upsurge of gender-based NGOs.[8] Their failure represents one of the ironies of Nigeria's successive military regimes. The attendant militarization of state and society, coupled with increasing economic hardship as a consequence of the Structural Adjustment Program, has served to neutralize the positive elements of these developments. Indeed, these measures merely added to the potency of violence against women, such that the transition from marginalization to oppression became almost visible. It is against this background that one now speaks of the feminization of poverty and violence in Nigeria.[9] Owing largely to the unforeseen, unintentional consequences of the Structural Adjustment Program, women now have to shoulder additional responsibilities beyond their traditional roles. This development has made women much more vulnerable to diverse forms of abuse, including domestic violence.[10]

Domestic violence against women, in Nigeria as elsewhere, breaks down into several forms of abuse: psychological, emotional, and physical. Often this takes the form of a vicious cycle that begins when tensions begin to rise. Then comes the 'stand over' phase, when the male becomes threatening, followed by the explosive stage when actual violence occurs, followed by the remorse phase, when the male is apologetic and promises never to do it again. This remorse phase, if successful, is followed by a fourth, the honeymoon phase, when normalcy returns and the man becomes loving and caring again. The collapse of this phase signals a return to the first stage in the cycle.[11]

Among the forms of domestic violence in Nigeria is the situation where one partner, usually a husband or boyfriend, sets out to dominate the other, usually a wife or girlfriend, through violence, the threat of violence, or the control of the couple's finances and social life.[12] A comparative empirical study carried out across selected states in Nigeria found that this kind of violence manifests itself under the form of wife-battering, sexual abuse, marital rape and dowry disputes.[13] Respondents in the study painted the dehumanizing conditions

---

[7] Charles Ukeje, 'From Aba to Ugborodo: Gender Identity and Alternative Discourse of Social Protest Among Women in the Oil Delta of Nigeria', in: *Gender Activism and Studies in Africa* (Dakar, Senegal: CODESRIA, pp. 66-87).

[8] J. Shola Omotola, 'What is this Gender Talk All About After All? Gender, Power and Politics in Contemporary Nigeria,' in: *African Study Monographs,* 28 (1), April 2007, pp. 33-47.

[9] Ibid. p. 39.

[10] Bola Udegbe, 'Female (In)dependence and Male Dominance in Contemporary Nigerian Families', in: Goran Therborn, ed. *African Families in a Global Context,* Research Report No. 131, Nordisika Afrikainstitutet, 2004, pp. 79-97.

[11] World Aid Organization, *Violence against women*, op. cit.

[12] Ibid.

[13] Marietu Tenuche, *The Burden of Marital Vows: A Study of Domestic Violence in Benue and Kogi States of Nigeria.* Reproach Report, Inter-African Committee (IAC) Nigeria on Traditional Practices Affecting the Health of Women and Children in Africa. Funded by IAC with support from the Ford Foundation, April 2003.

under which they had had to live as an inseparable part of the 'burden of marital vows' they had undertaken. Amina, one of the respondents from Kogi State, sums it up:

> Domestic violence is common among all classes of women. In this compound, there are 13 families, and everybody is complaining. Wife battering is very common. There is a woman here whose husband forces her to have sex every night. She often declines, because he goes out with other women, takes drugs and comes home to demand sex. He beats her up when she refuses sex. I know of a woman whose husband would measure some food for her to last for three days. He would travel for a week and, on the occasions when she received a visitor, she could not offer him food. He beats her often and accuses her of infidelity. Most times she gets bruised from the beatings. I know of a woman whose husband is the Chief Executive of a state. He said his father forced him to marry her, so he beats her often and denies her sex. He frustrates her guests and relations by asking the houseboy to watch over their movements, so that they do not take away anything from his house. He instructs his houseboy to spy on the guests to know what they say. Although they have grown-up children, he brings other women to the house and frequently forces the house-girl to sex. Most women who suffer domestic violence do not talk about it. Religion makes them not open up. A lot of women confide in me but would not want to discuss it with other people. I have personally suffered physical abuse, and even now, I suffer from emotional problems.[14]

No less worthy of mention is the barbaric practice, still widespread in Nigeria, of subjecting widows, in the immediate aftermath of the death of their husbands, to traditional, multi-stage mourning rites that include a partial or full shaving of their hair, the wearing of widow beads, and the forfeiture of their claim to any part of their husband's estate, as well as husband succession or widow heritage.[15] As for education, women still lag far behind their male counterparts in every respect, from school attendance to adult literacy. The girl child in family circles remains an object of marginalization.[16]

In the political sphere the situation is worse. It is disappointing that, all official pretences to the contrary, only a slight improvement has been made, as women's voices are yet to be heard in the nation's leadership. In fact, since independence in 1960, no woman has been appointed Chief Executive at the Federal or State levels. Under the Fourth Republic, founded in 1999, there has been only one woman Speaker of a State House of Assembly among the 36 States of the Federation. At the level of the Federal Parliament, women's representation at all levels remains lower than 10 percent, denying women the power to influence national policies.[17]

Other dimensions of violence against women in Nigeria include community-based violence and state-based violence. The former includes issues such as sexual harassment, women trafficking, forced labour and rape. The question of rape encompasses the action and inaction of the state's forces of law and order, especially the police. This takes the form of torture in custody, demand for sex in exchange for cooperation and understanding in custody, and other forms of sexual harassment. This situation becomes worse under war conditions,

---

[14] Quoted in Maeritu Tenuche, *The Burden of Marital Vows*, ibid, pp. 27-28.

[15] Quoted in Iyabo Olojede, *Public Policy and Gender Politics,* op. cit, pp. 132-133.

[16] J. Shola Omotola, 'What is this Gender Talk All About After All? Gender, Power and Politics in Contemporary Nigeria' *African Study Monographs*, 28(1), April 2007, pp. 33-47.

[17] J. Shola Omotola, 'Engendering the Legislature in Nigeria's Democratization: Faltering Prospects, New Hopes.' Paper Presented at the National Conference on: Nigeria Beyond 2007: Issues, Perspectives and Challenges, Faculty of Business and Social Sciences, University of Ilorin, 27-28 February 2007.

when security agents are sent on peace-keeping missions. Under such circumstances, women are converted into instruments of pleasure. This was the fate of Nigerian women during the protracted clashes between the Ife and Modakeke communities in the 1990s and during the Odi and the Zaki-Biam escapades under the fledging democracy, when the army was deployed on a vengeance mission following the assault on military officers.[18]

There is also the religious dimension. For instance, the two imported religions, Christianity and Islam, came and reinforced the existing patriarchal nature of society, elevating male values to a position of divinity, so much so that women's commitment to God is measured in part by the level of their loyalty to their husbands. Informed mainly by this orientation, the Islamic legal and penal codes that derived from Islam and Christianity respectively, as described below, tend to offer more protection to men at the expense of women.[19]

Such actions against women lead to dire consequences, not only for women but also for Nigeria's democratic process. The victims of wife-battering have to contend with miscarriage of pregnancy and diverse forms of injuries that in some cases result in permanent disability and infertility.[20] In the political sphere, violence against women has served to deny Nigerian women their right to participate. Across the length and breadth of the country there is a widespread belief that women in politics belong to the amoral realm; they are often subjected to ridicule. The economic rights of women are also violated; for any income, women are often at the mercy of their husbands, who are often irresponsible. It follows that the meagre resources available to women oblige them to seek and engage in multiple modes of livelihood in order to survive.[21] Cultural practices, especially those connected to widowhood, as already described, serve to limit the rights of the widow in her freedom of movement and association. Gender inequality is thereby perpetuated.

In the long run, it is the democratization and developmental agenda of the state that suffer. As elsewhere, Nigeria's marginalized women constitute about 50 percent of the country's population, thus depriving the state of half its human resources. Women have nevertheless proved their importance, not only as mobilisers but also as agents of positive social change. Indeed, their effective role in the popular protest against oil exploitation and the environmental insecurity in the Niger Delta in the late 1990s led to important concessions by the major oil companies, especially Shell and Texaco.[22]

What is it about Nigeria that makes violence against women so endemic? An explanation can be found in certain cultural, historical and legal factors. Culturally speaking, Nigeria has been, and remains, essentially patriarchal. For this reason, male values not only predominate but have been institutionalized to the point that no appreciation is left to accommodate women's values. Women continue to be considered the property of men and must always succumb to the whims and caprices of their owners. The advent of colonialism served only to add salt to an already festering injury. Not only was the colonial state an exclusively male affair, it was also a law-and-order state based on the use of force. It was here that the culture

---

18 Emmanuel O. Ojo, State Excesses: Military Exploits in Odi and Zaki Biam, Mimeo, Department of Political Science, University of Ilorin, Ilorin, 2007.

19 See, *Innocent Digest*, No. 6, 2000.

20 Marietu Tenuche, *The Burden of Marital Vows*…. op. cit, pp. 30-49.

21 Bola Udegbe, 'Female (In)Dependence ….' art. cit, pp. 84-69.

22 Charles Ukeje, 'From Aba to Ugborodo,' art. cit, pp. 72-81.

of violence, where women were not only quietly repressed but also victimized, began to crystallize. The failure of the post-independent Nigerian state to address this dilemma meant the continuation of the culture of violence. To complicate matters was the entry of the military into the political scene shortly after independence in 1966, an event which represents another paradox. Especially under the second military interregnum in Nigeria (1984-1998), women's issues had blossomed to the extent that the period could be labelled 'the women's era.' Yet, it was the same period that glorified a political culture of violence, in which women and children were the principal victims. It is therefore essential to take into account the legacies both of colonial rule and the prolonged military dictatorship in order to understand fully the phenomenon of violence against women in Nigeria.

It is fundamental, however, to examine Nigeria's system of law. Although the state's social order is founded on ideals of freedom, equality and justice—so that 'every citizen shall have equality of rights, obligations and opportunities before the law' and 'the sanctity of the human person shall be recognized, and human dignity shall be maintained and enhanced'[23]—there are discrepancies in practice. In fact, section 17(3) of the 1999 Nigerian Constitution protects the rights of 'all citizens, without discrimination on account of sex, or any other ground whatsoever.'[24] Nevertheless, gender discriminatory practices in everyday life in Nigeria are clearly noticeable. This is not due to the absence of legal instruments against such practices. Indeed, beyond constitutional provisions, Nigeria is also a signatory to all international legal frameworks against violence against women. These include the United Nations Convention on the Elimination of all Forms of Discrimination Against Women of 1979 (CEDAW), which Nigeria signed on 23 April 1984 and ratified on 13 June 1985, and ratified further in its optional protocol on 8 September 2001; the International Convention on Economic, Social and Cultural Rights, signed on 29 July 1993; the International Covenant on Civil and Political Rights, also signed on 29 July 1993; The International Convention Against Torture and other Cruel, Inhuman Treatment and Punishment, signed on 28 June 2001.[25]

In practice, however, these legal instruments are hardly respected. One explanation is Nigeria's practice of legal dualism. In the Northern part of the country, section 55(id) of the Penal Code of the 19 states of the North and the Federal Capital Territory (Abuja) permits a man to beat his wife for the purpose of 'correcting her', and upholds 'any native law or custom in which such correction is recognized as law,' provided only that the result does not amount to 'the infliction of grievous hurt.'[26] In a related vein, the criminal code that governs the 17 states of Southern Nigeria provides in its section 6 that carnal knowledge between a man and a woman who are married to one another 'is not unlawful,' a provision which has been interpreted to mean that 'a husband cannot be legally charged with raping his wife.'[27] Recently, a Nigerian woman, Amina Lawal, was sentenced to death by stoning in northern Nigeria by an Islamic Shariah Court in northern Nigeria for having had a child out of marriage. This sentence was challenged by human rights activists, and eventually, on 25

---

[23] Section 17 (1a-b) of the 1999 Constitution of the Federal Republic of Nigeria.

[24] Section 17 (3a,e) of the 1999 Constitution of Nigeria.

[25] Mojubaolu Olufunke Okome, 'Domestic, Regional and International Protection of Nigerian Women against Discrimination: Constraints and Possibilities', *African Studies Quarterly*, 6(3), 2004, pp. 1-28. http://web.africa.ufl.edu/asq/v6/v6i3a2.htm .

[26] Section 55 (Id) of the Penal Code of Northern Nigeria. Quoted in Ebenezer E. Lawal and Ronke C. Ojo, *Gender Politics* ... op. cit, p. 336.

[27] Ebenezer E. Lawal and Ronke C. Ojo, *Gender Politics* .... op. cit, p. 336.

September 2002, the sentence was overturned by the Katsina State Shariah Court of Appeal. Earlier, in 2001, Safiya Husaini Tundun had also been freed on a similar charge by a Shariah appeals court.[28] These successes, well celebrated across the country, were nevertheless isolated cases. The Nigerian Constitution itself, and the penal codes, pregnant with inconsistencies, provide little protection for women against societal assault.

CONCLUSION

This article has examined the phenomenon of violence against women in Nigeria, in its diverse forms: political, economic, socio-cultural, educational and domestic. It has also explored its implications, pointing to its negative impact on the health of women, on the family and societal peace and stability; revealing the persistence of gender inequality and the retardation of democracy and development. The pervasive nature of violence against women in Nigeria may very well find its roots in the patriarchal nature of Nigerian society, which was inherited and accentuated by colonialism, then later by the prolonged military rule. Finally, the protection of women, especially in terms of gender equality, has been undermined by the weak institutionalization and implementation of legal provisions.

To put an end to this grave injustice, first and foremost, a constitutional review should be instituted that specifies without ambiguities the equal rights of women vis-à-vis men. Secondly, all legal provisions in the Penal and Criminal codes that give room for the maltreatment of women must be expunged, and a harmonization of the two legal codes undertaken. The process must be open and transparent so that all groups, especially women, can freely participate. Above all, every effort must be made so that, gradually, a democratic political culture can emerge in which, the constitution of the land and the set of principles therein shall protect every Nigerian citizen equally, whether male or female.

[28] Sarah Coleman, 'Nigeria: Stoning Suspended,' *World Press Review*, 50 (12), December 2003.

In: Crimes Against Women
Editor: David Wingeate Pike
ISBN 978-1-61470-813-1

Chapter 14

VESICO-VAGINAL FISTULA IN NIGERIA

Mairo V. Bello Garko

INTRODUCTION

Vesico-vaginal fistula (VVF) has traditionally been regarded mainly as a women's health problem. It is above all associated with war zones (e.g. currently Darfur), where women are often raped or otherwise violently mistreated. Yet Nigeria, whose own civil war ended 40 years ago, still has one of the highest rates of VVF in the world, and VVF often amounts to a crime against women.

What are the causes of VVF, and what are its consequences? VVF and its sister ailment, vesico-rectal fistula (VRF), occur as a result of a prolonged, unrelieved, obstructive labour, in which the baby's head tears through the orifice, creating an opening between the bladder and the vagina or, in the case of VRF, the rectum. In Nigeria, the condition is mainly associated with childbirth by young girls or small-statured women, when the pelvis is small and the baby is large. In other cases, the baby may not be in the correct position when labour begins or other complications arise. Where the women can be taken to hospital quickly and doctors are able to assist the birth, this injury is most often avoided. A few cases of married women of 25 to 45, who have had previously successful vaginal deliveries, have been found to be developing fistula. Of course, in remote communities with limited access to standard medical facilities, women can spend days in fruitless labour. In such cases, the baby is almost always stillborn, and the woman, if she survives, suffers from VVF: she loses control over her bodily functions and suffers from urine and/or faecal matter constantly trickling down her legs.[1]

Perhaps even more damaging than the physical effects of VVF are the social isolation and psychological trauma that in many instances follow. Because of the offensive nature of the sufferers' condition, many find themselves abandoned by their husbands and families and shunned by their friends. Even those families that do try to care for their relatives with VVF often do so from a distance. In many cases, the few sufferers who are able to find their way to a hospital face a long wait before they can receive adequate medical attention, because of the general inadequacy of medical services in Nigeria. So it is hardly surprising that many

[1] The National Task Force of VVF in Nigeria, 1995, *Facts on Vesico-Vaginal Fistula.*

sufferers become destitute and turn to begging to survive. Here is a typical case-history of a VVF victim.[2]

> Jumai is one out of many thousands of girls in Nigeria who have to live with VVF. She was the third of a family of six, born after two boys. She has never seen the inside of a classroom, although her two older brothers and the fifth child, also a boy, were sent to school. Instead, she started hawking in the street to sell different food stuff, from the age of four to help finance the acquisition of her bridal property. Married off at 14, and almost immediately getting pregnant, she did not seek any health care services during pregnancy and attempted to have the baby at home. She was in labour for five days. After a protracted obstructed labour, she was eventually taken to hospital. The baby was delivered by caesarean section. Jumai was discovered to have VVF, and the baby died."[3]

The Nigerian government estimates that there could be as many as 400,000 cases of VVF in the country. According to the Ministry of Health, the number is between 200,000 and 400,000, with up to 10,000 new cases annually and an incidence of 2 per 1,000 deliveries. A UNFPA report, compiled from its visits to 12 sites around the country, produced an even more alarming and complex picture of the frequency, prevention and treatment of fistula in Nigeria. While exact figures are not known, it is estimated that between 100,000 and 1,000,000 Nigerian women live with the condition. Even the training of new fistula surgeons has not reduced the number of cases awaiting repair, as new cases occur faster than existing ones can be treated. The educational, economic, cultural and religious divide that exists between the northern and southern regions of the country applies equally when it applies to fistula: far more women live with the condition and many more are treated in the north than in the south. However, fistula develops in both areas for many of the same reasons: most are obstetric in origin and occur during deliveries that are handled by traditional birth attendants (TBAs), relatives or friends or without any assistance at all.[4]

Not much reliable data is available as to the exact number of sufferers in Nigeria. What is certain, however, is that they can be found across the length and breadth of the country, but appear mostly to be concentrated in the northern, south-eastern, and middle-belt regions of the country. It is obviously more common in the countryside because of the inadequacies of facilities for pre- and post-natal care. In these rural areas, the long distances to health centres, combined with ignorance, poor nutrition and the high cost of care, make women more vulnerable to VVF. [5]

The current figures in use by the health authorities are estimates based on information gathered from those victims who come to seek care in established medical facilities. The reality, however, is that most sufferers, either because of distance or cost, never get to any formal medical establishment to seek specialist health services at all. So the figures probably underestimate the scale of the problem.

Nigeria's National Task Force on Vesico-vaginal Fistula has explained in a booklet how fistulae happen and what can be done to prevent them. It makes clear that early marriage and

[2] K. A. Harrison, *Direct and Indirect Causes of Maternal Mortality*, 1980.
[3] Habiba, 2001, A parent tells her story to AHIP.
[4] 'Nigeria,' UNFPA publication : http://www.unfpa.org/fistula/docs/nigeria.pdf.
[5] Hajia Kindin Yolah, 'Epilogue to childhood encounter,' UNFPA publication, 1 April 2001: http://nigeria.unfpa.org/epilogue.htm.

early pregnancy without seeking health care are major causes of fistulae that lead to the social rejection of many young women.

VVF may have direct or indirect causes. The most common direct causes include simple ignorance coupled with the traditional surgical practice of the 'gishiri cut' (a form of female genital mutilation practised particularly among Hausa communities and executed during prolonged labour to create passage for the baby.[6] Eight out of ten cases are due to prolonged obstructed labour during childbirth.

Indirect causes include poverty, infections that affect the development of the girl-child, and malnutrition that may result in stunted growth. About 80 percent of VVF patients in Nigeria are between the ages of 10 and 14. Compared with their male counterparts, girls receive little education. Often they are married off early, with no life-planning skills or economic power; nor do they get involved in decision-making even when it involves their own lives. Often they have limited or no access whatever to appropriate health or social information and services. Finally, a culture of shame inhibits a girl from admitting that she is pregnant or in pain, even when she is in labour.

Accusing fingers have often been pointed at religion, or sometimes, more accurately, at misinterpreted religious notions and beliefs that encourage early marriage and lead to premature pregnancy. Because the pelvises of the girls are not fully developed, young girls who become pregnant often have obstructed labour, thereby dramatically increasing their chances of developing VVF. Early marriage in Nigeria is prevalent in most northern Muslim communities, where many see the practice as a religious injunction. Some Christian communities in the northern states also practise early marriage, and churches in other parts of Nigeria also discourage women from using medical services, encouraging them instead to believe that faith alone will deliver them safely in times of need, including childbirth.

The UNFPA survey revealed another situation, especially in northern states, in which some women have had successful fistula surgery, but have not returned for delivery in a hospital and have suffered another fistula. More than 5 percent of fistulas at one northern site were reported to be recurrences. Some women have had four or even five repairs after an initial successful one. Although it is tempting to continue to point to poor infrastructures or inadequate access to facilities, most of these women come from a radius of less than 10 km from a hospital. Therefore, one reason may be the need for many of them to obtain the approval of their husbands before seeking care. Another cause is the overwhelming cultural preference for giving birth at home (especially for the first baby), coupled with a strong dislike of delivery by C-section. Some surgeons also report that a C-section may not be necessary after a successful repair.

Nigeria is yet to develop a national strategy for addressing the issues of VVF. The government, both at national and state levels, has put in place legislation and measures aimed at protecting the welfare of women and promoting safe motherhood. Many of those actions, although not specific to VVF, can help to alleviate some of the suffering of the VVF patients.

The National Adolescent Health Policy supports projects that will help young people overcome problems of extreme poverty, stigmatisation and unemployment. So far, however,

---

[6] K. Ampofo, J. Uto, G. Uchebo, 'Epidemology of vesico-vaginal fistula in Northern Nigeria,' *West African Journal of Medecine,* April-June 1990.

these initiatives remain theoretical: the government lacks the leadership to move the programme forward concretely.[7]

The Ministry of Women's Affairs and Youth Development has also spearheaded a multi-pronged effort in this area. This has included the establishment in 1996 of girl-child education units in all state ministries of education as well as at the federal level; the refusal at the state level of legislation to allow girls the right to withdraw from school; the legislation against early pregnancy; the establishment in 1995 of support and cures for VVF sufferers; and the production in 1999 of a video docudrama on the dangers of early marriage. In addition, the Ministry has conducted a survey of harmful traditional practices with the aim of putting in place a policy and legal framework to address the issues involved. The Federal Government has also now adopted a policy on women, encouraging their emancipation. All these fine laws and policies are yet to be widely disseminated and implemented; most public officials do not even know of their existence.

Perhaps reflecting the absence of a national strategy, interest in the plight of VVF patients has been shown mostly by philanthropic organisations (mainly foreign ones), international agencies, and public-spirited individuals. Certain foreign governments have also helped through their aid programmes, and the UNFPA have taken since 2001 a more energetic position in bringing these problems onto the national agenda. A national task force for VVF sufferers worked aggressively from 1991 to 1993, with support from the Ford Foundation, to bring the issue out into the open. Publicity campaigns were also launched to attack the root causes of VVF and to sensitize people to the harm and pain the sufferers have to endure. Also in the past, local non-governmental organisations (NGOs), notably the National Council of Women's Societies (NCWS), were involved in working in the task force on VVF. Recently, centres for VVF treatment have been established by various organisations, notably USAID (through its Access project), Forward United Kingdom, Evangelical Health (Centre Jos), Adolescent Health and Information Projects (AHIP), as well as a few state governments such as Akwa-Ibom, Borno, Calabar, Kaduna, Kano, Katsina, Oyo, Ogun, Sokoto, Zamfara. The eradication of the root causes, namely early marriage, prolonged labour, dire poverty, and gender inequity, still await the necessary political will that can lead to effective legislation.

The circumstances surrounding the development of VVF in girls and women can be perceived as a crime against them. Its victims are usually those young girls and women who have been denied the right to enjoy their childhood, the right to education, the right to health. Married off early, they could choose neither their partners, nor the moment to have a baby, nor the number of children they should desire, nor the frequency of giving birth.

In time of war, women are the first to be targeted, with rape and degrading assaults sometimes the prelude to VVF. Through no fault of her own, the victim becomes a social outcast. The stigma breaks her spirit, the isolation removes her from her peers, her friends, her family, and her lack of education and the skills to earn her living drives her even lower in status within the already low status of women. The Nigerian Government's failure to provide the necessary resources in every community to make motherhood safe and affordable is an offence against womankind.

Certain case-histories serve as testimony to these crimes:

---

[7] Department of Primary Health Care and Disease Control, Nigeria, *National Adolescent Health Policy,* 1995.

An eleven-and-a-half year-old primary school pupil in Ikot Ekpene, Akwa Ibom State (eastern Nigeria), received no prenatal care and suffered a two-week labour. She was transferred back and forth between traditional birth attendants, native doctors, and her church. Thrusting a long stick through her mouth, the 'assistants' eventually forced out a dead, discomposed baby. The girl suffered multiple urethral rupture and underwent twenty repair operations over four years of rehabilitation. Even so, she will probably never again bear a child or have a husband.

In a second case in the same state, a 21-year-old final-year university student in the Arts had attended a prenatal clinic for 38 weeks during her pregnancy. However, she stopped going to the clinic because her church, the Christian Deliverance Centre, prophesised that her labour would be complicated and after caesarean section (CS) lead to her death. Her labour, in fact, lasted three days after which she delivered a dead baby. Profuse bleeding and the inability of the attendants to remove the placenta prompted her return to the hospital, where it was discovered that she had developed VVF. She nevertheless insisted on being discharged before the repair operation, maintaining that her condition would be cured at her church. The expected healing did not happen, so she returned to hospital three months later for the repair. The health personnel found upon examination that she was again pregnant. The second child, delivered by CS, soon died, due to the earlier unskilled interference with her pregnancy.[8]

The third victim, Mary, was gang-raped by nine men for about six hours. Torn everywhere, she was rushed to hospital, but from then on she suffered from severe backache. In the end, she could not control urinary or even faecal functions, a handicap that led to social exclusion.

CONCLUSION

A large part of the responsibility for the complications in child delivery is the result of the negligence shown to young girls by parents, husbands and society in general. Neglect during infancy and childhood usually results in stunted growth. Neglect during pregnancy means a failure to detect a contracted pelvis or foetal mal-presentation. Neglect during labour in the presence of a contracted pelvis leads to obstructed labour, uterine rupture and foetal death.

There are two types of pregnant teenage girls: those who suffer deprivation, and those who do not. Difficult labour is much more frequent in the first group. This explains why teenage girls in affluent societies tend to have easier labour, while their counterparts in most Nigerian communities have such dreadful labour outcomes.

However, this should not happen if:

- the girl-child is educated and allowed to delay marriage until she is fully developed;
- she is allowed to delay the first pregnancy;
- she spaces her births: not too early, not too frequent;
- there is no gender discrimination against the girl;
- she knows what to do during pregnancy;
- she is allowed, or encouraged, to seek proper medical help in time;
- she is allowed to enjoy her full rights as a human being;

---

[8] L. L. Wall, J. A. Karshima, C. Kirschner, S. D. Arrowsmith, *American Journal of Obstetrics and Gynecology*, 2004.

- she is economically empowered;
- she does not suffer violence or discrimination due to her status in society.

The government of Nigeria, at federal, state and local levels, must face up to the problem and take determined action, if the dimensions of this disaster, already grave enough, are not to become worse.

Recommendations for the Way Forward

a. The negative influence of religion, as it affects reproductive health decision-making, needs to be reduced.
b. A girl should not become pregnant (and, of course, no one should force her to that condition) until her body is fully developed and she knows the importance of attending a prenatal clinic in order to prepare for a safe delivery in proper conditions.
c. Through education, information and communication programmes, parents should be led to understand the value of functional literacy for girls. Schoolgirls can be encouraged to find an income for themselves by acquiring certain skills (by making soaps, pomades, arts-and-crafts objects, for sale after school-hours). Girls who would otherwise be married off by their parents at an inappropriately young age could thus remain in the household and contribute to the family income.
d. Although families may receive significant sums of money for their young daughters in bride-price, parents should be made to understand that the long-term financial outlay, if their daughters develop VVF, will be greater.
e. VVF can be prevented by improving the socio-economic condition of the populace, informing them about health facilities and the dangers of teenage pregnancy.
f. Labour should be supervised by trained health personnel who can detect the symptoms of a contracted pelvis and possible difficult labour and refer the young woman in good time to the appropriate health-care facility.[9]
g. Establish fistula treatment sites with counselling centres for both HIV and contraception. All patients should be given the opportunity to be tested for HIV/AIDS.
h. Promote education and vocational training for girls and women. Ensuring that girls continue their education at the end of junior secondary school would help raise their age at marriage, allowing more time for them to reach reproductive maturity.
i. Broaden research at all levels concerning fistula treatment, and create evidence-based protocols. Community-based research should yield more concrete information about patients and the circumstances under which fistula develops.[10]

---

[9] M. A. Ijaiya, P A. Aboyeji, *Obstetric urogenital fistula, the Ilorin experience,* Nigeria. 2001.
[10] UNFPA Country Paper on VVF 2003.

THE AUTHOR WISHES TO THANK THE FOLLOWING:

Mr. Essan Niangoran, Country Representative UNFPA
Dr. Lucy Idoko, National Programme Officer UNFPA
Ministry of Health
Mrs. Eleumaka, Reproductive Health/Public Health Department
Mrs. Beatrice Eluaha, Gender/Women's Health
Development, Reproductive Health Division
Dr. Mope Olanusi, Hospital Services Department
Dr. O. A. Oguntayo, Department of Obstetrics and Gynaecology, Ahmadu Bello University Teaching Hospital, Kaduna
Dr. S. O. Shittu, Ahmadu Bello University Teaching Hospital, Zaria
Dr. Hadiza Galadanci, Department of Obstetrics and Gynaecology, Aminu Kano Teaching Hospital
Dr. Kees Waaldijk, Babbar Ruga Fistula Hospital
Mrs. Rose Peter, Matron-in-charge, Evangel VVF Centre
Dr. Anne Ward, Family Life and Birth Injury Hospital
Dr. Marliyyah Mahmood, Project Development Officer, FOREWORD
Mrs. Hajara Suleiman Umaru, Matron-in-charge, Maryam Abacha Women's and Children's Hospital
Dr. Saduaki, Department of Obstetrics and Gynaecology, Murtala Specialist Hospital
Dr. Nana Tanko, President, National VVF Foundation
Dr. Ekanem, Dr. Mabel I. Ekott, Dr. Etuk, Dr. E.J. Udoma, Department of Obstetrics and Gynaecology, University of Calabar Teaching Hospital
University College Teaching Hospital at Ibadan
Prof. A. O. Ilesanmi, Head of Department of Obstetrics and Gynaecology
Prof. O. A. Ojengbede, Dr. M. A. Okunlola,
Dr. M. Oladokun, Department of Obstetrics and Gynaecology
Prof. B. A. Ekele, Department of Obstetrics and Gynaecology, Usman Dan Fodio University Teaching Hospital

KENYA

In December 1998, as reported in Africa Renewal, a Kenyan police officer, Felix Nthiwa Munayo, came home late and demanded meat for his dinner. There was none in the house. Enraged, he beat his wife, Betty Kavata. Paralyzed and brain-damaged, Ms. Kavata died five months later, on her 28th birthday. But unlike many such cases, Ms. Kavata's death did not pass in silence. The story was covered extensively by the Kenyan media. Images of the fatally injured woman and news of her death generated nationwide debate on domestic violence. Five years of protests finally led the government to pass a family protection bill criminalizing wife-beating and other forms of domestic violence.[1]

It was only in 2006, however, that Kenya, at the insistence of the women rights activist and former MP Njoki Ndungu, introduced the Sexual Offences Act. The general election held on 27 December 2007 put the act to a severe test, since the elections were followed immediately by a spate of violence, especially, against women. In one such episode, a certain Joyce a coiffeuse and her husband were drinking tea in their home in Nairobi on 30 December when two of their neighbours hacked down their door and attacked them with machetes. Joyce recognised the men as the same who had raped her in broad daylight a few days earlier. This time, they grabbed her husband and took him away. After searching the streets, she found him beaten up but still alive hiding on the banks of a filthy river. After two months in Kenyatta National Hospital recovering from his injuries, he found out that his wife had contracted HIV as a result of the rape. He responded by promptly abandoning her and their four children. With her home destroyed and her hair salon burnt down, Joyce moved into a camp for the homeless on the outskirts of Nairobi. There, bereft and bewildered by the brutality meted out by her own people, 'a refugee in [her] own country,' she rallied six months later to testify before the Commission of Inquiry on Post-Election Violence (CIPEV). This international commission, established by the Government of Kenya following the disputed 2007 election, was empowered to investigate crimes of sexual violence committed during the post-election turmoil. Popularly known as the Waki Commission, after its chairman Justice Philip Waki of Kenya's Court of Appeal, it proceeded to collect testimonials and medical records proving that thousands of women were victims of gender-based violence in the months following the disputed presidential elections, and on 15 October 2008 the 529-page the 'Waki Report' was submitted to president Mswai Kibaki and Prime Minister Raila

---

[1] Mary Kimani, "Taking on violence against women in Africa," *Africa Renewal*, Vol. 21, No. 2 (July 2007): p. 4. Electronic version is available on: http://www.un.org/ecosocdev/geninfo/afrec/vol21no2/212-violence-aganist-women.html.

Odinga. Added to the misery of the victims was the indifference shown by the police. 'Four men in police uniforms,' ran one such report by 50-year-old Ellen, 'raped me and my 14-year-old daughter in front of my grandchildren.' Nothing could be more disheartening than the failure of the forces of order to protect the weak.

D.W.P., Irina Massovets and Nicolette Bundy

In: Crimes Against Women
Editor: David Wingeate Pike

ISBN 978-1-61470-813-1

Chapter 15

MULTI-FACETED VIOLENCE AGAINST WOMEN IN KENYA

Lydiah W. Nganga

Kenya is an African country that is home to 42 different tribal groups. These tribes have unique cultural practices, but sexual violence[1] against women is a common trend.[2] Studies in 2003 reported that more than 50 percent of married women had experienced some kind of sexual violence before they were 16, while sexual crimes against children were reported as usually perpetrated by close relatives.[3] The violence takes many forms and is exacerbated by traditional cultural practices. Ideally, marriage is intended to foment strong kinship, but the payment of a dowry[4] by the bride's family is seen as giving the husband the right to own his wife, hence the general perception in Kenya that a married woman is her husband's property. Women are equally customized to accept and tolerate their condition as the property of men. As a result, men rely widely on sexual violence to control women. During the political crisis in Kenya of January-February 2008, sexual assault and gang rapes against women increased by 200-300 percent over the rate in previous years.[5] An earlier report in 2001 by the Federation of Women Lawyers (FIDA)[6] showed that acts of sexual violence against women had been the cause of most deaths (47 percent) within a nine-month period.[7]

---

[1] Sexual violence denotes male domination of females through acts such as the denial of property based on sex. Also included are all forms of abuse perpetrated against women due to cultural and legal practices that condone the degradation of women.

[2] Sitawa R. Kimuna and Yanyi K. Djamba, 'Gender based Violence: Correlates of physical and sexual wife abuse in Kenya,' in *Journal of Family Violence* (Springer, Netherlands), January 2008: 333-342.

[3] Kenya: Sexual and domestic violence prevalent. http://www.irinnews.org/report.aspx .

[4] Traditionally, dowry was a token of appreciation to the bride's family either in the form of goats, cows and/or money. A ceremony intended to celebrate the union of two different families through marriage has now been commercialized. After paying large amounts of money, husbands tend to consider their wives, consciously or unconsciously, a form of property.

[5] United Nations, Geneva, New Film series takes on the culture of silence on violence against women: First global broadcast, Women on the frontline, presented by Annie Lennox on BBC World, 18 April 1930 GMT, 17 April 2008.

[6] FIDA-Kenya. http://data.unaids.org/pub/Report/2006/20060630_GCWA_RE_Violence_Women_Girls_Kenya_en.pdf.

[7] FIDA-K: FIDA Kenya annual report. Nairobi: Federation of Women Lawyers, Kenya (2001).

The report of 2001 further showed that Kenyan women suffered from a deep sense of degradation as human beings.[8] Among the Kisii people, for example, the groom is considered a 'real man' only after he has had a violent sexual encounter with his bride on the night of their wedding, and in general the worth of a man is based on his capacity to inflict pain on a woman during sexual intercourse.[9] The custom of dowry makes the situation worse, since it provides for arranged marriages, usually between teenagers and wealthy old men. Among the Masaai people it is the same: dowry transforms the wedded teenage girls into their husbands' property, susceptible to sexual violence.[10] Equally devastating is the custom of inheriting the widow, which is a common practice in the Luo tribe. In the event of death, any younger brother is entitled to marry the widow. The advent of HIV/AIDS, and the risk for the new wife of contracting the virus, has complicated the issue,[11] and the custom of inheriting the widow may explain why the Luo community has higher cases of the HIV/AIDS virus than other tribes in Kenya. The Kenyan government has passed laws against wife inheritance and other cultural traditions with adverse health ramifications, but Amnesty International is not pleased with the results.

Reporting on the status of sexual violence against women in Kenya, Amnesty International blamed the country's unsupportive legal system for the high levels of crime.[12] Victims of rape, for example, face enormous legal and cultural challenges. To go public is to invite a heavy social stigma and even reprisal, with the result that rape crimes are rarely reported to authorities.[13] In one case where a Kikuyu woman reported the offence, she explained that she had visited her brother-in-law's house and had suffered an assault. The reaction of the family was to scold the girl for having visited the house.

Under Kenya's Penal Code, rape and other forms of nonconsensual sex are punishable by imprisonment. In practice, however, the law is rarely enforced, and society tends to blame rather than support the victim.[14] Equally problematic is a cultural perception that rape is a normal sexual act by males who cannot control their sex drive. Kenya's bi-legal system, blending national and customary laws, further complicates the issue of sexual violence against women. Whereas national laws are formal and informed by the nation's constitution, customary laws are tribal. Customary laws differ from tribe to tribe, but common among them is the support they give to sexual violence against women. Furthermore, customary laws have very deep influence on national law, so that national laws are equally biased against women, and to the extent that sexual crimes against women are tried in a male-dominated judicial system, violence against women thrives.[15] Nonetheless, due to recent legal interventions, national laws are now under review.

---

[8] Human Rights Watch: *Report of the Task Force for Review of Laws Relating to Women*, Nairobi (1998).

[9] December Green, *Gender violence: African women's responses* (New York: St. Martin's Press, 1999): 35.

[10] Caroline Sweetman (ed), *Violence against women* (Oxford, London: Oxfam GB, (1998): 30.

[11] Ajanga Khayesi, A. 'Controversial practices: Luo widow inheritance' (2006). http://www.un-istraw.org.

[12] Amnesty International, Kenya: *Violence against women.* Hadaja Choro, Mary Muragwa, 'Women at risk of domestic abuse.' http://www.amnesty.org/en/library/asset/AFR32/002/2002/en/dom-AFR320022002en.html.

[13] Lydiah Nganga, Personal interview notes, *Gender issues in Kenya*. Personal interview with Jenny Kiaro, 4 July 2006.

[14] Annabel, S. Erulkar, 'Experience of sexual coercion among young people in Kenya,' International Family Planning Perspectives, 2004, 30(4): 182-189.

[15] Amnesty International, *Kenya: Rape—the invisible crime*; This report sets out to answer some of the questions put to Amnesty International by women victims of violence. It looks at violence against women, particularly sexual violence, and focuses on rape committed by both security officials and private individuals. http://www.amnesty.org/en/library/info/AFR32/001/2002, 8 March 2002.

The criminal law amendment bill of 2000 addressed various deficiencies in the Penal Code of Kenya, specifically in combating acts of sexual violence against women. Consequently, the government passed a new Penal Code that outlawed marital rape and provided new guidelines for sexual crimes against women. For example, any person who has sexual relations with a girl under the age of sixteen is now charged with felony, and if convicted faces a maximum of life imprisonment with hard labour.[16] To support this, an act of Parliament in 2003 established the National Commission for Gender and Development.[17] In addition, the constitution of Kenya was modified specifically to guarantee all Kenyans, irrespective of gender, their fundamental human rights and freedoms. The revised constitution, however, fails to give its full support to certain women's issues, as is evident in article 82 (4) that permits gender discrimination with respect to adoption, marriage, divorce, burial, transference of land upon death and/or other matters of personal law. The revised constitution still condones injustice in areas critical to women's rights such as marriage, inheritance, and the application of customary laws. To amend the issue, in 2005 the government initiated a national referendum, but the Kenyan electorate declined to support its initiatives.[18] As a result, and in spite of the government's support of the Convention on the Elimination of Discrimination against Women (CEDAW),[19] sexual violence against women persists. The establishment of a new Ministry of Gender, Sport and Culture is perhaps a sign that the government is still committed to eradicating sexual violence against women. Nonetheless, a male-dominated parliament, by rejecting bills such as the Criminal Law Amendment Bill of 2000 and the Domestic Violence (Family Protection) Bill of 2000, all designed to protect women's rights in Kenya,[20] continues to frustrate the government's efforts.

Despite these frustrations, various non-governmental organizations, such as the United Nations Commission on the Status of Women (UNCSW), the United Nations Development Fund for Women (UNIFEM), [21] and the Convention on the Elimination of Discrimination against Women (CEDAW), throw their support to various women rights' initiatives in Kenya. Because NGOs have the necessary resources and wherewithal to change unjust policies, they have pressured the Kenyan parliament to reconsider its position on issues of sexual violence. For example, due to intense pressure from women rights advocates in Kenya and the support of the United Nations Development Fund for Women (UNIFEM), the Kenyan parliament passed the Sexual Offences Act in July 2006 which criminalized sexual harassment.[22] Further bills are under consideration which, if passed into law, will provide an important foundation

---

[16] Patricia Kameri-Mbote, 'Violence against women in Kenya. An analysis of law, policy and institutions,' International environment law research center, 2000-1.

[17] Gender Donor Roundtable statement to consultative group http://siteresources.worldbank.org/INTKENYA/ Resources/donor_statement_gender.pdf (2005).

[18] *Kenya Gazette* Supplement, The proposed New Constitution, Drafted and published by the Attorney General of Kenya, 2005.

[19] Gender Donor Roundtable statement to consultative group http://siteresources.worldbank.org/INTKENYA/ Resources/donor_statement_gender.pdf (2005).

[20] Mary Kimani, 'Talking on violence against women in Africa: international norms, local activism start to alter laws, attitudes,' *Africa Renewal*, Vol. 21 # 2, p. 4, from http:// www.un.org/ecosocdev/geninfo/afrec/vol 21no212-violence -against -women.html(July 2007).

[21] UNIFEM (the women's fund at the United Nations) provides financial and technical assistance to innovative programmes and strategies to foster women's empowerment and gender equality- Kenya: http://www.unifem-easternafrica.org/kenya_inner.asp?cat=kenya&pcat=countryfocus&pcat1=&sid.

[22] Association for Women Rights in Development: Legislating against Sexual Violence in Kenya: An Interview with the Hon. Njoki Ndungu (2006): 149-154.

for the struggle in Kenya against sexual violence.[23] Apart from changing the laws, much depends on introducing educational curricula that support the development of a national culture that protects all Kenyans irrespective of gender.

[23] United Nations. The Convention on the Elimination of All Forms of Discrimination against Women (CEDAW) http://www.un.org/womenwatch/daw/cedaw/ (1979).

In: Crimes Against Women
Editor: David Wingeate Pike

ISBN 978-1-61470-813-1

Chapter 16

FEMALE GENITAL MUTILATION IN KENYA

Grace B. Nyamongo

The author of this article was born and brought up in the Kisii community of Kenya where female circumcision is prevalent. Her familiarity with this traditional practice and her experiences as an adult have led her to reflect upon the underlying significance of female circumcision and to examine its negative impact on women in other Kenyan communities, notably the Kalenjin, Maasai, Meru, Rendile and the Somalia.[1] Although female circumcision is still practiced in many parts of the country, it is more prevalent among the Kenyan Somalia (97%), the Kisii (96%), and the Maasai (93%).[2]

Circumcision is a rite of passage that has been practised in many parts of Africa for thousands of years. As a cultural practice it gives cohesion to the community. Within some Kenyan communities, circumcision symbolizes the cultural identity of an ethnic group. In a reference to the Kikuyu community, Jomo Kenyatta claimed that circumcision unified the whole community. Hence, abolishing it could destroy the tribal symbol of solidarity, consequently causing the Kikuyu community to disintegrate.[3] People cling to it regardless of its consequences. Any ban, therefore, imposed on the practice is likely to be resisted in the belief that it was part of a strategy to eliminate African culture. In the 1950s, for instance, when the colonial missionaries imposed a ban against female circumcision in Kenya, some girls in the Meru community defied the ban by circumcising one another with razor blades in a daring act that became known as *Ngaitana.*[4] The idea of eradicating the practice could in

---

[1] Female circumcision was and is still practiced by some members of the Kisii, Kalenjin, Maasai, Meru, Rendile, and Somalia communities. The Kisii are located in Nyanza Province in Western Kenya; Kalenjins are found in the Great Rift Valley; Maasai are found in the southern region of the Great Rift Valley in both Southern Kenya and north central Tanzania; the Somalia and Rendile are located in north-eastern Kenya.

[2] Jane Chege, Ian Askew, Susan Igras and Jacinta K Muteshi, 'Testing the effectiveness of integrating community–based approaches for encouraging abandonment of female genital cutting into CARE'S reproductive health programs in Ethiopia and Kenya,' USAID, 2004, 1.

[3] Jomo Kenyatta, *Facing Mount Kenya: the Tribal Life of the Gikuyu* (London: The Hollen Street Press, 1961), 125-127.

[4] Lynn Thomas, '*Ngaitana* (I will circumcise myself): lessons from colonial campaigns to ban excision in Meru, Kenya,' 129-150 in: *Female 'Circumcision' in Africa: Culture, Controversy, and Change*, eds. Bettina Shell-Duncan and Ylva Hernlund (London, Boulder: Lynne Rienner Publishers, 2000), 130.

fact have been received positively, if only it had been presented as part of a search for alternative practices that would not have been harmful. As things stand, since the practice carries severe consequences and is intended to control women's sexuality, it can be considered a crime against womankind and a violation of women's sexual rights.

Female circumcision involves either partial or total removal of the female genitalia. This includes clitoridectomy, excision, infibulation and scarification. The reasons for, and, the extent of, genital cutting varies from one society and culture to another. Despite the method used in the 'cut', however, none of the types of female circumcision is less painful than the others; indeed, whatever the method, women are subjected to intense pain.

Many of the rituals in African communities are marked by celebrations. In the case of circumcision, seen as a symbol of maturity and passage to adulthood, its celebration becomes a social occasion that brings friends and relatives together to recognize and applaud the initiates' bravery. Therefore, to abolish it without providing an alternative social occasion means eradicating a community's symbol of togetherness.

In the Kenyan communities where female circumcision is practiced, it is considered an important aspect of making a young woman 'worthy of marriage'.[5] The institution of marriage gives women the status of respect. Therefore, a woman and her family take eligibility seriously. Furthermore, where female circumcision is a determinant factor for marriage, women have no choice but to accept it. For instance, among the Rendile community, an uncircumcised girl is not allowed to marry or bear children.[6] Similarly, among the Maasai, female circumcision is a 'passport' to womanhood. Therefore, the initiates are free to have sex or get married as soon as they recover from the 'cut'. In *The Daily Nation*, in Nairobi, Stephanie Welsh has argued that, since circumcised Maasai girls are assumed to be mature and can engage in sex, this has jeopardized their lives, since men took advantage of them. As a result, many girls are likely to become pregnant and drop out of school, or get married, but in either case remain uneducated.[7]

The Rendile community further believes that clitoridectomy not only controls women's sexuality and sexual promiscuity but it also protects the girls from malign influences. To discontinue the practice would put their girls in danger.[8] Similar beliefs are held by the Kisii people. Under such circumstances, even those who attempt to join the eradication campaign may be socially ostracized. This forces some people to turn a blind eye to the practice even when they are aware of its after-effects.

In traditional communities that practice female circumcision, the female child is indoctrinated into hating her clitoris. This makes the girl look forward with eagerness to the moment of the 'cut'. Moreover, the cultural importance attached to the practice helps to perpetuate it. Other factors also contribute to the endurance of the ritual. For example, there is

---

[5] Hanny Lightfoot-Klein, *A Woman's Odyssey into Africa: Tracks across a Lfe* (New York: Harrington Park Press, 1992), 50.

[6] Bettina Shell-Duncan, Walter Abungu O. and Leunita A. Muruli, eds., 'The debate over medicalization of female genital cutting and its impacts on a northern Kenyan community,' 109-128 in: *Female 'circumcision' in Africa, culture, controversy, and change*, eds. Bettina Shell-Duncan and Ylva Hernlund (London, Boulder: Lynne Rienner Publishers, 2000).

[7] Stephanie Welsh, 'A dangerous rite of passage,' *The Daily Nation*, 7 May 1995.

[8] Bettina Shell-Duncan, Walter Abungu O. and Leunita A. Muruli, eds., 'The debate over medicalization of female genital cutting and its impacts on a northern Kenyan community,' 109-128 in: *Female 'circumcision' in Africa, culture, controversy, and change*, eds. Bettina Shell-Duncan and Ylva Hernlund (London, Boulder: Lynne Rienner Publishers, 2000).

a widespread assumption that female circumcision controls young women's promiscuity by numbing their sexual urge, thereby preventing them from causing disgrace to the society. In some Kenyan communities, including the Kisii where these beliefs are prevalent although undocumented, those who wish to abandon the practice face pressure from older relatives and friends. This forces them to initiate their daughters. Others continue with the practice because of the fear that their uncircumcised daughters will not be married, and that they will be ridiculed by society for disobeying the cultural norms. This is why, among the Kisii, there have been undocumented incidents where women are circumcised during childbirth as a symbol of identity and assimilation into the community.

Female circumcision has proved to be resistant to change despite its negative effects. The continued practice of female circumcision in Kenya indicates the cultural value attached to it. However, the physical and mental impacts of the practice on the initiate depend on the circumciser's expertise, the nature of the 'cut' and the sanitary conditions under which it is performed.

Traditional circumcisers are women who are believed to be experts in this field. In fact, they have minimal knowledge of female anatomy. The operation is usually performed under unhygienic conditions in which the circumciser does not use gloves, anesthesia or sterilized instruments. Usually these instruments are used on all the initiates in succession without being sterilized. Such conditions are not only cruel but also judged by doctors to favour the transmission of the HIV virus and other infectious diseases. Moreover, incidents have been reported by the media about initiates who, after the 'cut', were hospitalized for hemorrhage or bled to death. Furthermore, among the Somalia where infibulations[9] are commonly performed, a woman has to endure an excessively painful sexual experience. She also suffers extreme pain during first childbirth when her scarified vagina has to be cut open with a knife to permit delivery.[10] Such procedures are not only painful; they also diminish a woman's dignity and her sense of self-worth.

In the 1990s, campaigns against female circumcision in Kenya sought to alert the public about sanitation and the threat of HIV/AIDS. This is not to suggest that female circumcision should be performed under hygienic conditions but to put a permanent end to it. In fact, the intention of this strategy seems to have been misunderstood; that female circumcision could continue only if it was performed under hygienic conditions and with qualified practitioners. This led to the proliferation of the practice in health centres, counteracting the efforts to eradicate it.

The majority of parents prefer the services of the traditional circumcisers mainly because these give the practice a cultural meaning. This method is also less costly. A few parents who can afford more hygienic modern services usually invite medical practitioners to their villages or home yards, or take their daughters to nursing homes where the operation is performed secretly. It is certainly true that reliance on traditional expertise is unwise and outdated.

---

[9] Infibulation is one of the types of female circumcision. It involves the removal of the prepuce of the clitoris, the labia minora and majora and stitching together the two sides of the vulva leaving a very small opening for the passage of urine or menstrual blood. Infibulation is commonly performed in Sudan, Eritrea, Somalia, and by some communities in Mali, Northern Nigeria and the Somalian border of Kenya. For more information on infibulation refer: Bettina Shell-Duncan et al., 2000: 4; Efua, Dorkenoo, 1994: 5; Olayinka, Koso-Thomas, 1987: 17.

[10] Holy Ladislav, *Religion and Custom in a Muslim Society: The Berti of Sudan* (Cambridge, UK: Cambridge University Press, 1991), 170.

Nonetheless, the physical and psychological impact of female circumcision on women is the same, regardless of who performs it, as long as it involves mutilating healthy organs of the body. Studies show that female circumcision leads to health problems both physical and psychological.[11] This has forced the Kenyan government, different religious institutions and non-governmental organizations to seek alternative and more effective strategies to put an end to female circumcision.

Circumcision is not only a cultural practice. It has, for the circumcisers too, both socio-economic and status implications. For circumcisers it is a way of earning a living, while their 'skills' afford them social prestige. To eradicate the practice without providing them with alternative means of income and social recognition would mean depriving them of their economic gains and social status. Consequently, they would fiercely resist any campaign against their work. Traditional circumcisers should be made aware of the effects of their practice, inducing them to abandon it. They should then be engaged in educating girls about the values of the community's culture without the need for them to undergo the 'cut'. In essence, traditional circumcisers should be actively engaged in campaigning against female circumcision.

The Kenyan people are increasingly aware of the negative impact of the practice. Some of them are therefore attempting to enforce the ban through an alternative rite of passage commonly referred to as 'circumcision by words'. Through this strategy, girls undergo a weeklong program of counseling and teaching by elders. During the week of seclusion, initiates learn, through songs, dances and folktales, about the traditions pertaining to the passage. Therefore, they learn the basic traditional values and responsibilities of an adult woman, without experiencing the actual 'cut'. It also allows them to become acquainted with modern ideas relating to their personal health and reproductive life.[12]

Besides educating girls, 'circumcision by words' also sensitizes various communities about the effects of female circumcision and the need to replace the 'actual cut' with the new rite of passage. The 'cut by words' was first celebrated in 1996. Since then it has been performed by various ethnic groups in Kenya where circumcision had been prevalent. This new rite of passage is also practiced in other parts of East Africa, where many girls are still forced to undergo the ritual for cultural and religious reasons,[13] even though the practice is now illegal.

CONCLUSION

Kenya faces a choice. Its government has banned female circumcision, but in some of the more remote parts of the country it continues to be practised. The risks it poses to women's

---

[11] Jamillah Mwanjisi, 'Painless initiation replaces agony of FGM,' *The East African Newspaper,* 9-15 August 2004; Claire C. Robertson, 'Getting beyond the Ew! Factor: rethinking U.S. approaches to African female genital cutting,' 54-86, in: *Genital Cutting and Transnational Sisterhood: Disputing U.S. Polemics*, eds. James M. Stanlie and Claire C. Robertson (Urbana: University of Illinois Press, 2002); Hanny, Lightfoot-Klein, *A Woman's Odyssey into Africa: Tracks across a Life* (New York : Harrington Park Press, 1992); Olayinka, Koso-Thomas, *Circumcision of Women: A Strategy for Eradication* (London: Zed Books, 1987).

[12] Stan Reaves Malik, 'Alternative rite to female circumcision spreading in Kenya,' 1997: http:www.hartford-htwp.com/archives/36/041.html.

[13] Jamillah Mwanjisi, 'Painless Initiation Replaces Agony of FGM,' *The East African Newspaper*, 9-15 August 2004.

health are undisputed, but the force of a long cultural tradition remains. In order for this inhuman custom to be fully eradicated, it is necessary for reformers to move into these areas and explain the dangers of the practice. The reformers have a further task, that of confronting the social stigma and psychological guilt borne by women who defy this tribal custom. This is where the 'circumcision by words' formula offers a solution. This formula, already practiced in several parts of Kenya, must be presented as an alternative rite of passage to elders in the less developed areas. The tribal tradition is thus respected while the actual practice is eradicated. It is therefore a matter of educating Kenyan girls and young women to the need to move away from traditional custom for the sake of their own health and future happiness. As an insider, I point this out not only to women in my community but to my own young daughters.

SENEGAL

Khady Koita, a Senegalese immigrant in France and president of a European network for the prevention of traditional practices harmful to the health of women and children, reports that her fellow immigrants have a tendency to cling tightly to their traditions and customs–sometimes even more so than those who stay at home–for fear of losing them or of being socially rejected.[1]

SOMALIA

The problems of Somalia are special. Superficially, it is one of the most homogeneous countries on earth. Almost all its 8 million people share the same language, religion, culture and ethnicity, but in fact it is one of the most fragmented. Authority tends to be diffuse and clan-based, and for twenty years the country has been without a central government. Islamic local courts have sprouted to fill the power vacuum, and in 2006 they united under an Islamist banner. That led the United States to declare the Islamic courts a terrorist threat, and to support Ethiopia in an invasion of Somalia. America's new ally Ethiopia had become best known for making the abduction and rape of young girls the commonplace way to obtain a bride. In many instances, the parents agreed to the marriage, in the belief that a raped child is no longer fit to marry anyone else.[2]

In Somalia, where millions of its inhabitants were reported to have fled the country or were internally displaced, the Union of Islamic Courts took advantage of its short-lived governance (June-December 2006) to impose strict dress codes and to forbid women to leave their houses without the accompaniment of a male relative. Even after the Union was overthrown, many women, to avoid danger, still comply with the dress code, and this restricts their ability to work in agriculture, fisheries and slaughterhouses, where previously they had been employed in large numbers.[3] While fundamentalism, as well as insecurity, including the ever-present threat of rape, continued to rise, Somalia produced some heroines. The child

[1] 'West Africa: West Africans fight female genital mutilation in France,' IRIN, UN Office for the Coordination of Humanitarian Affairs, 23 June 2008.

[2] Bob Herbert, 'Punished for being female,' *International Herald Tribune*, 3 November 2006.

[3] Kathambi Kinoti, 'The Situation of Refugee Women in the Arab Region,' Association for Women's Rights in Development (AWID), 25 April 2008.

Fadumo Korn had led a near-idyllic childhood, herding goats and travelling with her tribe in Somalia, until the day she turned seven and was subject to the ritual of genital mutilation. Eventually she reached Europe, married a German and became involved in the European campaign against female genital mutilation (FGM), describing her experiences in her published autobiographical account.[4] In another case in June 2006, a Swedish court in Gothenburg sentenced a Somali man with Swedish citizenship to four years in prison for forcing his 13-year-old daughter to undergo female circumcision. Even though the crime had not been committed in Sweden—the father had taken his daughter back to Somalia, where he and his sister held the girl down during the ritual—the conviction was notable as the first since a law banning the procedure went into effect in 1982.[5] Another refugee from Somalia was Ayaan Hirsi Ali, who had fled to the Netherlands in 1992 after refusing to submit to a forced marriage to a man she did not know. After attending the University of Leiden, where she studied political science and philosophy, Hirsi Ali began speaking publicly about the repression of women under Islam, and shortly thereafter started receiving death threats. She fled abroad. Hearing of her fears, Gerrit Zalm, then Deputy Prime Minister of the Netherlands, assured Hirsi that she would be given diplomatic protection wherever and whenever she needed it. With this assurance she returned to the Netherlands, won a seat in Parliament, and continued to champion the rights of women.[6]

D.W.P.

[4] Fadumo Korn, with Sabine Eichhorst, translated from the German and Afterword by Tobe Levin, *Born in the Big Rains: A Memoir of Somalia and Survival* (New York: Feminist Press, 2006).

[5] 'Somali gets 4 years,' AFP, *International Herald Tribune*, 27 June 2006.

[6] Sam Harris and Salman Rushdie, 'A refugee from Western Europe,' *International Herald Tribune*, 10 October 2007.

In: Crimes Against Women
Editor: David Wingeate Pike
ISBN 978-1-61470-813-1

Chapter 17

FEMALE GENITAL MUTILATION IN SENEGAL AND SOMALIA

Tobe Levin

DEFINING FEMALE GENITAL MUTILATION (FGM)

Although some who claim to oppose the amputation of clitoris and labia also insist that cutting is an 'act of love,' a few bold ones who have suffered it call it frankly torture. Eschewing euphemism, Nura Abdi and Fadumo Korn, Somali expatriates in Germany; Maryam Sheikh Abdi, a Somali AID worker in Kenya; and Khady Koita, a Soninké emigrant from Senegal to France, write about female genital mutilation (FGM) in order to condemn and prevent it. Their approaches, though expressing a minority viewpoint, dovetail with the rage of an increasing number of adults excised in childhood.

The purpose here is to broaden the reach of these victims' words and make them available to readers of English. In German and French, their message is strong. Nura Abdi and Leo G. Linder write: 'Nauseous, I wanted to throw up while between my legs someone was busy with a needle in an open wound. It was as if, with all my senses, wholly conscious, I was being slaughtered.'[1] Fadumo Korn describes that life-altering instant as a 'deep blue, ice cold, lightning bolt to the head,' the 'all-consuming, devouring pain'[2] causing a near-death experience as the eight-year-old floats above the scene, watching herself being butchered.

'Carnage' is the concept of choice for Khady Koita as well. Though from Senegal, where the clitoris and labia are excised but, unlike Somalia, the vagina is left unstitched, Khady finds her suffering equally reprehensible. As president of the European Network (EuroNet FGM) in Brussels, Khady (her pen name) wrote *Mutilée*, whose explicit title puts her clearly on the record. Of her travail she notes:

---

[1] Nura Abdi and Leo G. Linder, *Tränen im Sand* (Bergisch Gladbach: Verlagsgruppe Lübbe, 2003). Excerpted as "Watering the Dunes with Tears." Trans. Tobe Levin. In *Feminist Europa. Review of Books*. 3, 1 (2003) & 4, 1 (2004): pp. 28-33, here p. 32, http://www.ddv-verlag.de/issn_1570_0038_jahr2003.4_vol01_nr01.pdf.

[2] Fadumo Korn with Sabine Eichhorst, *Born in the Big Rains. A Memoir of Somalia and Survival*. Trans. and Afterword Tobe Levin. New York: The Feminist Press, 2006, 38.

> On that day [in Senegal], the fourth or fifth in line, I was seated, knees outstretched, frozen with fear, trembling at every howl, my entire body strained by the agony behind the wall. Then two women caught me and dragged me inside. One held my head, her knees crushing my shoulders. The other clasped me firmly by the thighs, spreading my legs. … The wails resound in my ears today.[3]

Since at least the 1960s, activists have been trying to thwart acts of violence such as these, performed each year in 26 African countries and in the African Diaspora on an estimated 3 million females, most of whom are under age 18. The genital assault to which they are exposed is classified by the World Health Organization (WHO) into four categories:

Type I — Partial or total removal of the clitoris and/or the prepuce (clitoridectomy).

Type II — Partial or total removal of the clitoris and the labia minora, with or without excision of the labia majora (excision).

Type III — Narrowing of the vaginal orifice with … a covering seal by cutting and appositioning the labia minora and/or the labia majora, with or without excision of the clitoris (infibulation).

Type IV — All other harmful procedures to the female genitalia for non-medical purposes, for example: pricking, piercing, incising, scraping and cauterization.[4]

Looking at this catalogue of harm, one may wonder what room there is for doubt. Is it not clearly abuse? A violation of human rights? Why is it so difficult to put an end to it? Outside Africa, the discourse is haunted by a history of racism. Inside Africa, practitioners are motivated by a sense of duty and by the fear of exclusion; their refusal to conform invites harm to themselves. Though reports of mutilation[5] are carried by radio, print, and visual media, they do not lead to an effective opposition to the powerful majority. FGM is carried out both in traditional settings and in clinics. Medical personnel perform it, for financial gain of course, but with an argument from reason: if side-effects and pain are the problem, let us simply sterilize and anesthetize. Women's *right* to intact genitalia has not been taken into account. The *right* to sexuality is not discussed.

On the contrary: many campaigns accept traditional gender roles that suppress women's freedom, realized fully only when including the choice of a sexual partner. This idea, however, that of the 'free woman,' means what it means – a loose woman, a whore. To avoid this association, thought to degrade an individual in patriarchal culture, excision's dangers are ignored.

---

[3] Khady, *Mutilée* (Paris: Oh! Éditions, 2005): 18. Author's translation.

[4] World Health Organization, 'Classification of female genital mutilation' (amended 2008), http://www.who.int/reproductive-health/fgm/terminology.htm.

[5] In addition to physical side-effects, a higher rate of posttraumatic stress disorder (PTSD) in excised women was assumed. Studies are only now beginning to emerge that show this to be true. For instance, Behrendt and Moritz assessed the impact of excision on '23 circumcised Senegalese women in Dakar,' with twenty-four intact Senegalese women for comparison. They found that 'the circumcised women showed a significantly higher prevalence of PTSD (30.4 percent) and other psychiatric syndromes (47.9 percent) than the uncircumcised' and concluded that 'Within the circumcised group, a mental health problem [significant memory loss] exists that may furnish the first evidence of … severe psychological consequences of female genital mutilation' (Alice Behrendt and Steffen Moritz, 'Posttraumatic Stress Disorder and Memory Problems After Female Genital Mutilation,' *American Journal of Psychiatry* 162:1000-1002. May 2005 (14 May 2008): http://ajp.psychiatryonline.org/cgi/content/full/162/5/1000.

Courage is therefore demanded of 'positive deviants' bold enough to publish their minority points of view. From Somalia, where an estimated 97 percent of all females are tortured, the desire for infibulation has been carried abroad into emigrant settlements.[6] In Senegal as well, among cutting tribes, the practice remains popular. According to the Health and Demographic Survey (2005), although in Senegal 'only' 28 percent of all women between 15 and 49 admitted they had been excised, in certain areas the proportion was much higher: 94 percent among inhabitants of the Kolda district and 86 percent in Tambacounda[7] despite an allegedly successful interventionist program run by the non-governmental organization Tostan[8] hand-in-hand with UNICEF.[9] The reason most efforts to eradicate FGM fail derives from the reluctance to question the purpose of these operations: to disadvantage women. An explicit feminist approach is rare but remains essential. Both the Inter-African Committee and the European Network FGM regard women's empowerment and increasing gender equality as keys to success.

WRITING PAIN

One morning, a drama, not unlike untold others, unfolds in Nura Abdi's Mogadishu courtyard, where first Nura's elder sister Yurop, then Ifra, Fatma, Muna, Suleiha, and Nasra echo Khady in their desire to escape but, once caught, are hurled 'with fanatical violence' onto an upturned orange crate. Shrieking 'I don't want to!' an already weeping Nura is also grabbed, 'dragged … to the box [and] held … down' – long enough to experience amputation *à vif* of both clitoris and labia minora, creating a 'sound, like knifing burlap … [that] exploded in [her] brain … louder than all the [women's] screams.'[10]

Still worse was to come -- a macabre needlepoint engendering an agony so great that the child faints. But before having her legs bound, the five-year-old revives to feel 'open fire … the *halaleiso* [exciser] rubbing herbs on a fresh wound.' A second return to consciousness

---

[6] Cathy Majtenyi, 'Female Genital Mutilation Still Common in Somaliland,' *Voice of America*, 3 March 2008, http://www.voanews.com/english/2008-03-03-voa26.cfm.

[7] Naffisatou J. Diop, 'Excision.' Chapter 13. Senegal. *Demographic and Health Survey* (2005), http://www.measuredhs.com/pubs/pdf/FR177/13Chapitre13.pdf. The Kolda is a rural district 450 kilometers from the capital, Dakar; Tambacounda, district center of its region, became known as the first village to openly declare, in 1998, an end to FGM, following a well-financed human rights educational initiative run by Tostan.

[8] Tostan, a Senegalese NGO whose name means "Breakthrough" in Wolof, is a 501 © 3 (charity) registered in the U.S. with broad-based funding and a record of success in "Community-Led Development" – the title of founder Molly Melching's speech on 21 February 2008 at a UNICEF Conference on FGM in Bern, Switzerland. Given that its staff is 99 percent African and its approach is to empower insiders through education on 'Democracy and Human Rights,' 'The Problem-solving Process' and 'Hygiene and Health,' and that it has reduced the incidence of FGM by teaching in over 2,500 Senegalese communities in 11 regions since 1991, continuation of the practice suggests limitations to its reach. Melching's UNICEF speech revealed what these might be. At its founding Tostan did not oppose FGM, she was pleased to state, and still does not call it mutilation, preferring the euphemistic 'cutting.' FGM became Tostan's issue only at the behest of women in its classes who saw it as incompatible with what they learned about human rights, certainly a promising development. But lacking a feminist vision and therefore stopping short of challenging sexual oppression and gender roles, the underlying patriarchal powers remain very much intact—as Senegalese Ousmane Sembene's 2004 film *Moolaadé* shows.

[9] For a detailed introduction to Tostan, see chapter 4 in Charlotte Feldman-Jacobs et al., *Abandoning Female Genital Mutilation/Cutting. An In-depth Look at Promising Practices*. Chapter 3 (December 2006), Population Reference Bureau with funding from US AID under Bridge Project (No. GPO-A-00-03-00004-00).

[10] Abdi and Linder, 32.

reveals a blood-soaked floor 'and those parts … [that] had been hacked off all of us…. tossed … in a pile' to be buried later, 'where [they] belong. Under the earth.'[11]

Not idiosyncratic, this devastating picture is emblematic, and Maryam Sheikh Abdi's testimony shares many of Nura Abdi's features. Her narrative poem 'The Cut' captures not only the blade but also the aftermath when 'hot sand' is poured on the gash from which 'blood gushes … and foams.' Drawn by the massacre, 'scavenger birds … circle and perch … on nearby trees' well before a mixture of 'dried donkey waste and many herbs' is applied to the wound. Next 'strong ropes from camel hide' bind the limbs and, with 'long stick[s],' the girls re-learn 'how to walk, sit and stand.' They then 'slide' for three hours in the heat toward home where, for four weeks, they 'heal,' despite lice having infested the bonds and 'scorching urine trickling bit by bit.[12]

Even though she in not stitched, Khady is nonetheless equally enraged. In *Mutilée*[13] she explains what happens in 'mere' clitoridectomy, showing girls made to feel impotent in a way that resembles the prelude to clinical trauma. Longing to flee, overwhelmed by anxiety and therefore unable 'to remember who went first,' she recalls 'hideous shrieks' that bring tears of empathy and angst to her eyes. 'But there was no way out.'[14]

If, then, the subjective experience of FGM is unequivocally violent, how can one explain the constant calls for 'tact and patience'? Why demand a 'non-judgmental terminology [when raising the issue with] practicing communities,' as the *Innocenti Digest*, speaking for UNICEF, does?[15] Regarding how to discuss these 'rites', there is disagreement, with anthropologists and cultural relativists striving to contain the discourse, while many activists are unequivocal -- like the pioneer African campaigners featured in this chapter.[16]

One key document issued by the Inter-African Committee (IAC) at its 6th General Assembly (4-7 April, 2005) is the Bamako Declaration. It condemns euphemisms introduced in the late 1990s to replace the term Female Genital Mutilation used since the late 1970s and explicitly adopted by African women activists. Finding labels such as 'Female Genital Cutting' 'patronizing and belittling,' the IAC charges that 'these changes … trivialize … the suffering of African women and girls. Already regrettably used 'by some UN specialized agencies and bi-lateral donors influenced by specific lobby groups largely based in Western countries,' the new descriptors are deemed counterproductive. They understate excision's effect on the mind.[17]

---

[11] Ibid., 33.

[12] Abdi, Maryam Sheikh, 'The Cut.' *Population Council* (2007), http://www.popcouncil.org/rh/thecut.html.

[13] See also Annor Nimako, *Mutilated* (Tema, Ghana: Ronna Publishers, 2001). An essay on Nimako's forceful anti-FGM work by Anne V. Adams, 'The Novel in Public Education: An Example from Ghana' is forthcoming in *Empathy and Rage: Female Genital Mutilation in Creative Writing,* eds. Tobe Levin and Augustine Asaah. See note 5.

[14] Khady, 29-30.

[15] Innocenti Digest, *Changing a Harmful Social Convention: Female Genital Mutilation/Cutting* (Geneva: UNICEF, 2005), 2.

[16] Those arguing for a milder terminology simply discount United Nations General Assembly Resolution A/RES/53/117 (1 February 1999) and other UN instruments that explicitly condemn 'FGM,' such as the Protocol to the African Union's African Charter on Human and People's Rights on the Rights of Women in Africa (11 July 2003), and the Protocol to the African Charter on Human and Peoples' Rights on the Rights of Women in Africa, adopted by the 2nd Ordinary Session of the Assembly of the Union, Maputo, CAB/LEG/66.6 (13 September 2000). The Maputo Protocol entered into force on 25 November 2005.

[17] 'Declaration on the Terminology FGM; 6th IAC General Assembly, 4 - 7 April 2005, Bamako/Mali'(15 November 2006), http://www.iacciaf.org/index.php?option=com_content&task=view&id=28&Itemid=44&PHPSESSID=ccab7400b78c4c9a3d1c37b99817fa52.

In other words, the Declaration's authors argue, a feminist approach is needed –feminist as Simone de Beauvoir understood it, that women are made, not born, and excision clearly diminishes them. Empowering women therefore entails 'control of ... sexuality and reproductive rights.' Change agents representing NGOS must 'help communities [in Africa and the Diaspora] to go through this painful process; not to confront the issue [of female sexuality] is ... to remain in denial of the gravity of FGM,' an accurate term for the assault on the genitalia of girls and women. Mutilation as the amputation of a healthy organ 'is a cultural reality.'[18]

Nura Abdi, Maryam Abdi, Khady and others agree. A leading NGO, FORWARD UK estimates that 'by the year 2010 nearly 210 million women will bear the scars, traumas and risks resulting from FGM.'[19] Authors from Somalia and Senegal write to protest and hopefully lower those numbers.

LANGUAGE, FORCE AND THE SEX OF HOSTILITY

A Somali myth of origins, uncanny in its gesture toward deep psychological motives, features a matriarch named Arraweelo and illuminates the underlying gender war:

> Arraweelo is a powerful queen of intimidating proportions. To consolidate power, her first act of state is to castrate all men in her domain. But she has a daughter whom she marries to the only man who has escaped the assault. A grandson is born who is destined to kill his unnatural progenitor and re-establish the natural patriarchal order.[20]

Dutch anthropologist Anke van der Kwaak explains: 'After [Arraweelo's] death the men whom she had ruled took revenge on women and began to mutilate by infibulating them.'[21]

This legend, one of many tales about ancient times that purport to account for FGM, places gender violence at the heart of the matter. Khady concurs, contending that 'domination alone is the real reason,' with the cruel addendum that 'men have passed responsibility for execution onto women.'[22]

What then are the real issues? Power and discourse. But these themes are rarely seen as universally present. Instead, the wounding–that is, amputation of an organ–is sometimes reinterpreted in light of traditions that value the conquest of pain as character-building and evidence of courage. Wairimu Ngaruiya Njambi, associate professor of Women's Studies at Florida Atlantic University, is among those who support this belief. In a complicated argument, she contends that if pain itself is constructed, its meaning socially determined, then the psychological comfort of conformity and pride can counteract physical trauma and shock.

Yet she speaks not as a scientist with a researcher's mandate to generalize but from personal experience. Resident in the U.S., Njambi insists that the clitoridectomy she chose to

---

[18] Ibid.

[19] Enshrah Ahmed, e-mail message to author, 19 December 2005.

[20] Charlotte Beck-Karrer, *Löwinnen sind sie. Gespräche mit somalischen Frauen und Männern über Frauenbeschneidung* (Bern: eFeF, 1996), 110. Author's translation.

[21] Anke van der Kwaak quoted in Ibid, 111. Author's translation.

[22] Khady, 30.

undergo in a Kenyan clinic at age 16–called *irua ria atumia* –is not a mutilation.[23] Her academic article, however, never reveals awareness of global figures nor of the Inter-African Committee, who vehemently contest her point of view– a grave omission that suggests the author was insufficiently peer-reviewed.

At the same time, however, Njambi's defense of cutting resembles a strain in Nura Abdi and Fadumo Korn that provides one angle of access to their tales: an emotion telling them their suffering cannot have been for naught, leaving them to fight against internal demons or the entrenched conviction of having been improved by their ordeal. Abdi reveals her shock at discovering herself in Germany among a nation of the unclean. And Korn admits her loathing for genitals neglected and left in the raw.

Passions deeply implicated in retention of FGM, those feelings that favor it subjectively even while an activist openly protests, emerge from a significant passage in *Born in the Big Rains. A Memoir of Somalia and Survival.* Married to a German and wanting sexual relations, Fadumo Korn overcomes a paralyzing reluctance to seek out a gynecologist. Her hesitancy, sadly, proves justified. Upon noticing the bridge between her legs, the physician shrieks, 'My god!!! ... Child, what have they done to you?' Colliding with the lamp, he 'struggles for air' and flees the room. Fadumo writes: 'I cried like I hadn't done since my mother died. I felt dirty, rejected. A doctor, an educated professional whose job it was to examine women, had run screaming from the sight of me. No other woman fled the office sobbing. They had all appeared happy, relieved. What was so monstrous about me? Was there some awful growth between my legs, something I hadn't noticed that made me untouchable?'[24]

Once at home, she creeps into bed, unable to be comforted until her friend Maryan, also from Somalia, gives her insight: " 'You ended up with an old fart who doesn't know his ass from his elbow'," she tells her. Over Fadumo's protest that she will never see a doctor again, Maryan offers to make an appointment with someone younger, better educated and 'more sensitive toward [his] patients' [needs],' in other words, a physician 'who knows about female circumcision.'[25]

> "Do you mean I have a problem because I'm circumcised?"
> Now Maryan was silent. After a while she said, "Yes, Fadumo."
> 'But...' My head spun. ... 'I mean,' I said, 'so ... German women aren't circumcised?'
> 'No, Fadumo.'
> 'But ... But that's disgusting!' I swallowed. Actually, I almost laughed. It sounded so absurd. 'You mean, all the women in this country are dirty?
> 'Well, they're not circumcised.' A spontaneous feeling of superiority overcame me, just a hint at first, then stronger. It filled me up, carried me, and erased my shame, shoving sadness aside. I was clean in a country of the unclean.
> A child chosen by God.[26]

Clearly, FGM is *normal*, indeed, elevating, to those whose ethnicity mandates it as a condition of gender identity and group membership, with beauty and cleanliness thought to ensue. These in turn give the wounded pleasure–if they survive.

---

[23] Wairimu Ngaruiya Njambi, 'Dualisms and female bodies in representations of African female circumcision. A feminist critique,' *Feminist Theory* 5:3 (2004): 281-303.
[24] Korn, 120.
[25] Ibid.
[26] Ibid., 121.

In sum, such emotional anchoring makes it arduous to oppose with rational ethics a custom that many African activists, including those vehemently against it, *feel* to be good. And in the meantime, the carnage goes on. With a gesture chillingly like that of Pulitzer Prize-winner Alice Walker's heroine Tashi in *Possessing the Secret of Joy*[27] and her model, Muthoni in Ngugi wa Thiong'o's *The River Between,*[28] both heroines in novels about FGM who choose to be cut, Pamela Kathambi, forbidden by her mother to undergo clitoridectomy, shocked her Kenyan village by bleeding 'to death after trying to perform female genital mutilation (FGM) on herself.' She had been hazed by her 'age mates and friends,' called " 'mukenye' – the name given to uncircumcised ladies",' her mother Julia Kanuu told BBC News in 2006.[29] Kathambi reminds us how deeply rooted clitoral excision remains, how strong the peer-pressure, and what extraordinary courage the non-conformists bring to bear.

Happily, a specialist in reconstructive surgery and a pioneer in the restoration of the clitoris has emerged in France to serve an avid clientele, proof that significant numbers of African women reject the 'rite'. Pierre Foldès, a urologist formerly with Doctors without Borders, discovered his technique while doing fistula repair. Located at the Clinique Louis XI in St. Germain-en-Laye, Foldès trims the scar from the clitoral surface before rolling back tissue along the root to expose the still-existing organ that extends backward from its tip to the 3rd and 4th vertebrae. It cannot, therefore, be excised in its entirety. The physician excavates and reconstructs, restoring sensitivity in more than 75 percent of patients.[30]

When Fadumo Korn addresses audiences, she also claims her sexual rights, rejoicing in that the gynecologist Maryan recommended 'opened [her] up.' Though she was brought up with considerable disdain for sexuality, her physician offers counseling that enables her to become 'a woman who likes her body and is able to enjoy sex.'[31]

'For women who went through a similar trauma,' Korn says, 'I want to be an example and source of support. And I want to prevent what is happening daily—creation of 6,000 fresh amputees. 'If I can save even one little girl,' Korn insists, 'the effort will have been worthwhile.'[32]

---

[27] Alice Walker, *Possessing the Secret of Joy* (New York: Harcourt, Brace, Jovanovich 1992).

[28] Ngugi wa Thiong'o, *The River Between* (London: Heinemann, 1956).

[29] "Kenya shock at mutilation death," BBC News (26 June 2006), http://news.bbc.co.uk/go/pr/fr/-/hi/world/africa/5109094.stm.

[30] Hubert Prolongeau, 'Victoire sur l'Excision. Pierre Foldès, le chirurigien qui redonne l'espoir aux femmes mutilées,' Preface by Bernard Kouchner (Paris: Éditions Albin Michel, 2006).

[31] Korn, 161.

[32] Ibid.

ETHIOPIA

Across the world, in countries rich and poor, women are being beaten, trafficked, raped and killed.... All of us—men and women, soldiers and peacekeepers, citizens and leaders—have a responsibility to help end violence against women. And each of us must speak out in our families, workplaces and communities, so that acts of violence against women cease.' So said Secretary-General Ban Ki-moon on 25 November 2008, marking International Day for the Elimination of Violence against Women. Although the UN Decade for Women had presented gender-based violence as a prime factor of female subservience, the violence and the violations show no signs of decreasing. This is especially evident in countries such as Ethiopia where patriarchy still governs every facet of society, freezing the very notion of national development.

D.W.P. and Anthoula Parianos

In: Crimes Against Women
Editor: David Wingeate Pike

ISBN 978-1-61470-813-1

Chapter 18

PATRIARCHAL DOMINANCE AND FEMALE SUBSERVIENCE IN ETHIOPIA

Melissa Krall

Girga Anota sits in her windowless home, the room crowded with neighbours gathered there to urge her, as always, to continue what she wants least to perform: her trade as a practitioner of female genital cutting. The debate is heated, but once again Girga bows to their demands. It is for the sake of marriage, they insist: in this community men will not marry an uncut woman.[1]

Like many of her peers, Girga Anota fully understands the problems that result from cutting. A local NGO engaged her to conduct a training programme to educate local practitioners of female genital mutilation (FGM) on the health risks associated with the procedure, such as HIV/AIDS, traumatic shock, haemorrhaging, and even death;[2] she regularly hosts educational seminars in her home. This 22-year veteran of genital cutting can thus succinctly sum up the issue: the lack of impact is not because the information is irrelevant or misplaced, but because the risks involved are more than acceptable, they are coveted.

Customary practices, with or without the status of law, play a significant role in determining women's rights, whatever the sphere of activity, most often failing to provide women with an adequate form of security. The mechanism for better implementation of equitable laws faces a daunting illiteracy rate among women, who work in unregulated sectors of the economy, and the intimidating task of changing long-established behaviour and attitudes.

Sexual and gender-based violence (SGBV) is solidly anchored in gender inequality. In Ethiopia it commonly evolves from the institutions of early marriage, bride inheritance and polygamy. While many cultures may subscribe to a number of socially accepted health risks, from sun-tanning to plastic surgery, such practices become more than calculated risks when

---

[1] Interview: Mrs. Girga Anota, 8 February 2007, Oromiya province, Ethiopia.

[2] 'Community-Based IEC Efforts Bringing a Reduction in the Practice of Female Genital Mutilation: A Case Study in Three Kebeles in Shashemene, Ethiopia', Pathfinder International/Ethiopia, Addis Ababa, 2003.

they target and degrade a particular gender. These practices become gender inequality issues, when the root cause is buried in intentional misinformation and misogyny.

From the moment of birth, a female in Ethiopia is relegated in her community to second-best standing. Females traditionally receive at birth three ululations (congratulatory howling or wailing) at birth while males are given seven. In raising their daughters, women give priority to domestic chores, with the understanding that their daughters' lives will inevitably be devoted to running their husband's home. For the majority of women in Ethiopia, education, traditionally, is not at all a priority, given that, upon their day of marriage, they are generally expected to stop their schooling to attend to their husband.[3] In this context, early marriage is a widespread problem, especially in rural Ethiopia, with 84 percent of rural girls and 73 percent of urban girls married before the legal age of 18. These customs can be considered harmful traditional practices (HTPs).

On the other hand, Ethiopian women enjoy rights that are greater than those of most other African countries.[4] The Civil Code of the Empire of Ethiopia (known as the Code of 1960) called for uniform legal provisions to govern all personal matters, and the invalidation of all customary laws. As a result, the married Ethiopian woman has a *de jure* right to an equal portion of common household property; upon divorce, she is entitled to her own property and to half of the common property. And in matters of inheritance, she must not be discriminated against.

At another level, however, the Code merely restates certain customary practices, designating the husband as the head of the family, thus giving him authority to administer household property. He has the right to control and manage common property and to make all decisions regarding such property. While the Code requires that the husband act judiciously and not alienate property without the consent of his wife, strong traditional and cultural beliefs discourage women from enforcing this requirement.

The Code notwithstanding, over the last 48 years ethnic groups have for the most part continued their own practices and customs. The Constitution, which reiterated the concept of gender equality and non-discrimination on the basis of sex, was reexamined in 1995 where it concerned the validity of customary law. It was stipulated that if parties to a dispute of personal status agree to the applicability of customary law, then that law should apply. Legislation has yet to clarify whether such agreements include gender-discriminating customary laws.

The 1995 Constitution also clearly specifies that all land belongs to the state. The former principle, that land belonged to whomsoever should cultivate it, was abrogated, thus allowing female heads of households to have greater access to land. However, land is allotted to married women only through their husbands. On the positive side, several laws do exist within the Ethiopian Constitution to protect women against early marriage, FGM, rape and abduction.[5] The issue, however, is not the government's role in lawmaking but rather the insignificance of these laws in rural communities.

In general, women and children make up the striking majority of the poverty-stricken. The likelihood of a woman experiencing some form of violence in her lifetime far surpasses

[3] 'Report on Causes and Consequences of Early Marriage in Amhara Region', Pathfinder/USAID, Ethiopia, 2006.

[4] 'Gender and Law: East Africa Speaks', 1997 Conference, The World Bank and UNECA.

[5] Articles 34-37, The Constitution of the Democratic Republic of Ethiopia.

that of a man. Abduction and rape in Ethiopia are quite common,[6] especially in areas afflicted by poverty and the lack of opportunity, such as access to education, employment or health care. Basic needs such as water, food and shelter must be constantly sought out, leaving young children to fend for themselves. This lack of supervision makes young girls easy targets for rape within their own communities. Given the remoteness of many locations, the lack of means of communication, and the lack of information on laws and legal protections, an overwhelming majority of rapes and sexual abuses go unreported, dismissed and unpunished.[7]

As a whole, the abuse of a wife is seen not only as a private issue but, legally, as a non-gender-specific practice. It could be argued, however, that the debased status of women in rural Ethiopia is the main cause of customary wife-battering; the acceptability and banality of wife-beating suggest that its cause is based more on the inequality of the sexes than on internal domestic strife.[8]

Patriarchal dominance, with its attachment to cultural and religious teachings and its ignorance of Ethiopia's laws, keep women subservient and deny them a basic education and health services. Physical and sexual violence against women is more common or severe in settings where traditional gender norms support male superiority and entitlement, where social norms tolerate or even justify violence against women, and where weak community sanctions against perpetrators seem not only to tolerate gender inequality but encourage its persistence.[9] In brief, higher levels of SGBV tend to occur in settings where communities fail to punish men who use physical and sexual violence against women, and where violence against women is considered normal or justified.

There are serious and potentially life threatening health sequels with all types of SGBV, such as suicide, death in childbirth and AIDS-related death. There are also acute and unremitting physical consequences, such as infection, chronic pain and gastrointestinal problems that cannot be treated as medical resources and health clinics are often too far from remote communities to be of any help to the victim.[10] In addition, SGBV victims are at high risk for severe psycho-social problems that go untreated, due to a scarcity of trained psycho-social counsellors; the potential for debilitating long-term effects of emotional trauma should never be underestimated.

Acts of SGBV violate a number of principles enshrined in international and regional human rights conventions, including the right to life, equality, security, equal protection under the law, and freedom from torture and other cruel, inhumane, or degrading treatment.[11]

---

[6] National Committee on Traditional Practices of Ethiopia, 'Harmful Traditional Practices in Relation to Reproductive Health', NCTPE, Ethiopia, 2000.

[7] Interview: Ms. Faantaayee Zawudee, Chair, *Woreda* Women's Committee, 7 February 2007, Shashemene, Ethiopia.

[8] 'Ethiopia in Gospel: Gender & Law – East Africa Speaks', Report Proceeding a World Bank/ECA Conference, World Bank, Ethiopia, 1998.

[9] 'Glossary of Violence Against Women – To Share Understanding of Terminology', The Working Group on Violence Against Women, Ethiopia, 2007.

[10] 'Addressing Gender-Based Violence through USAID's Health Programs', USAID, Washington D.C., 2006.

[11] The numerous international instruments related to the prevention of SGBV include, but are not limited to, the *Universal Declaration on Human Rights*, 1948; *Convention on the Suppression of Trafficking of Persons and Exploitation of Others*, 1949; *The Geneva Conventions* and their Additional Protocols, 1949 & 1977; *Convention on Consent to Marriage, Minimum Age for Marriage and Registration of Marriage*, 1964; *International Covenant on Civil & Political Rights*, 1966; *International Covenant on Economic, Social & Cultural Rights*, 1966; *Convention on the Elimination of Discrimination Against Women (CEDAW)*, 1981; *Convention Against Torture & other Cruel, Inhuman or Degrading Treatment/Punishment*, 1987; *Convention*

Impunity for SGBV perpetrators is one of the main obstacles in combating gender violence. Ethiopian law-enforcement authorities are often helpless in preventing or responding to SGBV, due to a lack of information on legal issues and the community's preference for keeping such matters within closed circles. When cases are simply not reported, there is little that police officers–or the international community–can do. This, again, demonstrates the need for communities themselves to be the strongest advocates for gender equality.

Taking into account the blatant gender inequality in Ethiopian traditional law, the effective implementation of cultural and behavioural change should not be considered a short-term project but one that requires enormous commitment, resources and opportunity. Commitment has to come not only through financial and legal means but from the community itself. A society has to choose its own destiny; it must elect to change from within. Those who hold power in the community, such as law and government officials, teachers and religious leaders, have a special responsibility.

The community itself is the *raison d'être* of aid work, a point made blatantly clear by the cluster of curious neighbours and friends congregating in Girga Anota's home, learning thereby about the risks of genital cutting despite their intention to pursue it. Anxious to know about the health issues that affect their daughters, these mothers and fathers are seeking information to understand how they can improve the lives and health of their families, yet they remain burdened by the customary practices of their community. These are the women, men and children who will be the initiators of change in every facet of society, and will themselves determine the outcome. For this they need a reliable flow of information, access to basic resources, and the opportunity to be responsible for their own future.[12]

on the Rights of the Child, 1989; *Recommendation 19 of the Committee on CEDAW*, 1992; *UN Declaration on the Elimination of Violence Against Women*, 1993; *Vienna Declaration & Plan of Action* (VDPA), 1993; *Global Platform for Action*, Beijing 4th World Conference on Women, 1995; *The Rome Statute of the International Criminal Court*, 1998; The *African Charter on the Rights and Welfare of the Child*, 1999; *United Nations Security Council Resolution 1325* (2000); and *The African Union's Protocol to the African Charter on Human and People's Rights on the Rights of Women in Africa*, 2003.

[12] 'Sexual & Gender-Based Violence against Refugees, Returnees, and Internally Displaced Persons: Guidelines for Prevention & Response,' UNHCR, Geneva, 2003.

TURKEY

In Turkey, as elsewhere in similar societies, the family typically rules that, once news of the family's shame has spread to the community, it is only through death that its honour, or namus, can be restored. In its hopes of entering the European Union, Turkey has revamped its penal code in respect to 'honour crimes' by imposing life sentences for murder, regardless of whether the murder is committed by a minor. This has resulted, not in an end to honour-killing, but in a change in its practice. In order to spare their sons from the harsh punishment imposed on them for killing their sisters, some families resort to pressing their daughters into taking their own lives instead, or to killing them and disguising the murder as an act of suicide. The crime committed by a 17-year-old girl named Derya was to fall in love with a boy she had met at school. When the news of the love affair spread to her family, her mother warned her that her father would kill her. Then came the threatening messages, sometimes 15 a day, sent by her brothers and uncles, every messsage the equivalent of a death sentence. 'I felt I had no right to dishonour my family,' Derya wrote in a note, 'no right to be alive. So I decided to respect my family's desire and to die.'[1]

D.W.P.

---

[1] Dan Bilefsky, ' "Virgin suicides" save Turks' "honor",' *International Herald Tribune*, 13 July 2006.

In: Crimes Against Women
Editor: David Wingeate Pike
ISBN 978-1-61470-813-1

Chapter 19

HONOUR KILLINGS AND THE LAW IN TURKEY

Ece Göztepe

INTRODUCTION

Since the beginning of the 1980s, violence against women in Turkey has become a focal point of the organized women's movement. Over the past ten years, the women's movement has succeeded in mobilizing broad public support to counteract this form of violence. The media has meanwhile engaged in critical reporting on this topic, and feminist-political activities are receiving more attention and support than ever before. Violence against women in Turkey, as in other parts of the world, takes various forms that defy simple classification. The definition given by *Watts/Zimmerman*[1] covers the pre-birth phase (e.g., gender-selective abortion), the early childhood phase (e.g., female infanticide), and all the later occurring forms of physical and psychological violence committed by the victim's current or previous partners or family members of either gender, notably:

- Coerced sex,
- Rape,
- Sexual abuse including harassment,
- Deprivation of medical treatment or education,
- Murder, especially by poison,
- Murder in the name of family honour (the so-called "honour killings").

This chapter limits itself to the last in the list, namely "honour killings".

In 1993, the General Assembly of the United Nations passed its Declaration on the Elimination of Violence against Women, defining gender-specific violence as '… any act of gender-based violence that results in, or is likely to result in, physical, sexual or psychological

[1] Charlotte Watts and Cathy Zimmerman, 'Violence against Women: global scope and magnitude,' *The Lancet,* 359 (2002): 1233.

harm or suffering to women, including threats of such acts, coercion or arbitrary deprivation of liberty, whether occurring in public or in private life'[2].

In Turkey, honour killings, which constitute concrete acts of violence against women, respond to a wide variety of motives, notably: an out-of-wedlock pregnancy, a marriage unaccepted by the family, a love affair outside of marriage, a visit to a cinema in the company of friends, a love message to a current or potential lover, rumours of dishonourable conduct, the wish to divorce, the forfeiture of a woman's honour after rape. The distinguishing feature of honour killings is the concept of family honour–irrespective of whether the woman is married or single. Within the concept, not only closely related family members, including half-brothers and half-sisters, but also distant relatives can become honour 'safeguards'. It is important furthermore to understand that honour killings are not limited to fundamentalist Islam and feudal society structures to be found in the south-eastern regions of Turkey. The fact that honour killings are committed among many Turkish migrant families in Europe and that family honour is now the primary motive for violent acts against women in large Turkish cities, despite modern economic living standards, shows why a simple socio-economic or religious explanation for honour killings is not sufficient.[3]

This chapter, while not attempting a sociological analysis of the causes of these acts[4] or of the counter-measures employed,[5] examines the laws regarding murder committed in the name of honour and the exculpatory clauses that remain in the Turkish Penal Code after the 2005 reform. A comparison will be made with the norms of the former Penal Code, while public opinion and decisions of the Court of Appeal will also be examined.

CONFLICTING INTERPRETATIONS OF THE PREVIOUS PENAL CODE (1926-2005)

The previous Penal Code placed crimes against the sexual integrity of women and children (rape, sexual coercion, sexual abuse, kidnapping for sexual motives, etc.) under the title 'Crimes against public morality and the family.' As such, the concept of honour was made out to be a public good that sought to protect not only the interests of the individual but also the interests of all members of the family affected by the action. This interpretation held sway from the time of the enactment of the previous law in 1926 until the new penal code went into effect on 1 June 2005.

Article 462, which was finally removed in July 2003 in order to satisfy the EU legal adaptation, served as the standard norm relating to honour killings. The norm carried the

---

[2] 'Article 1 of the Declaration on the Elimination of Violence against Women,' UN General Assembly Resolution 48/104 of 20 December 1993.

[3] See also Purna Sen et al., 'Violence against Women in the UK (CEDAW Thematic Shadow Report 2003),' Womankind Worldwide, http://www.womankind.org.uk/upload/CEDAW-report.pdf, p. 23.

[4] See for such analysis: Ayhan Sev'er and Gökçe Yurdakul, 'Culture of Honour, Culture of Change. A Feminist Analysis of Honour Killings in Rural Turkey,' *Violence Against Women Journal* 7 (2001): 966-1000; Radhika Coomaraswamy, 'Integration of the Human Rights of Women and the Gender Perspective,' UN Economic and Social Council, E/CN.4/2002/83, 31 January 2002; Ayhan Sev'er, 'In the name of fathers: Honour Killings and some examples from south-eastern Turkey,' *Atlantis* 30 (2005):129-145; Yakin Ertürk, 'Implementation of General Assembly Resolution 60/251 of 15 March 2006 entitled "Human Rights Council",' UN General Assembly, A/HRC/4/34/Add.2, 5 January 2007.

[5] See among others, Filiz Kardam, 'The Dynamics of Honor Killings in Turkey. Prospects for Action,' UNDP/UNFPA, November 2005.

subtitle '*in flagranti* situation: exceptional, severe provocation' (a special norm of *unjust provocation* in §51 of the Penal Code) and allowed for sentence reduction for homicide and assault and battery crimes in *in flagranti* situations. These crimes could be committed against wives or husbands, sisters (but not brothers), or descendants of the assailant or partners of the above. Only wives or husbands, parents and sibling–independent of their gender – could benefit from the sentence reduction. An additional element of that crime was the direct *in flagranti* situation, in which the timeframe might be extended from the moment before or after sexual intercourse, as long as there was no doubt about the deed. It did not matter whether the victims of the crime were married or single. According to this rule, the sentence would be reduced to 1/8 the normal penalty, since the law considered the *in flagranti* situation as an exceptional, severe provocation for the offender.

Some authors claim that extramarital sexual intercourse on the part of adult unmarried daughters or sisters did not in that period constitute an unlawful act and should not, therefore, be considered as unjust provocation. In the case of adultery, laws concerning unjust provocation should have applied, which in reality invalidated a special rule such as §462.[6] Of particular interest is the creation of a direct link between §462 and unjust provocation, which were understood as interlinked norms, as a general rationale for mitigating guilt (§51).[7] Thus, a crime 'committed out of rage and pain over an unjust provocation' (§51) is linked with the honour concept relating to the family as well as the sexual autonomy of individuals.[8]

This perspective was also adopted by the Court of Cassation. Instead of applying the special rule of §462, the general sentence reduction rule (§51) was applied in principle, and in crimes in the name of honour an automatic sentence reduction was carried out. This is connected not least with the widely held understanding of provocation and the closely linked concept of honour in judicial opinion. The facts that most victims are female and most offenders are male suggests that female sexuality both within and outside marriage are understood to be a family good, a guiding societal principle of morally permissible behaviour. The decisions of the Court of Cassation (Yargitay) between 1975 and 2003, which were chosen because of the application of (as well as reference to) §51 and §462, point clearly to this connection. In the resulting jurisdiction, the concept of honour is not viewed in connection with religion, but rather indicates culturally specific forms of gender roles in which women are assigned moral behavioural models.

A broad definition of honour killing has been used for this analysis of jurisdiction of the Court of Cassation. Briefly summarized, the criteria can be presented as follows:

- The victims were killed by family members, understood in a very broad sense. Here the perspective of the perpetrator is especially noteworthy. In one case, the General

---

[6] Sahir Erman and Çetin Özek, *Ceza Hukuku Özel Bölüm. Kişilere Karşı İşlenen Suçlar (Penal Code Special Part. Crimes Against Persons)* (İstanbul: Alfa, 1994), 154.

[7] §51 of the former Turkish Penal Code: 'If someone perpetrates a crime under the influence of rage or severe suffering produced by an unjust provocation and such crime is found to require punishment of death, he or she is sentenced to the grave punishment of life imprisonment, ...' (even though the authors used the term 'unlawful provocation' it seems more proper to use the term 'unjust' regarding the jurisdiction of the Court of Cassation. See for the English translation of the Penal Code regulations 'The Success of the Campaign for the Reform of the Turkish Penal Code From a Gender Perspective' (Summary Outcome Report), p. 7. (http://www.wwhr.org) (last accessed 11 February 2007). (Emphasis added by author).

[8] See Faruk Erem, *Türk Ceza Kanunu Şerhi. Özel Hükümler Cilt. 3 (Comment on Turkish Penal Code. Special Part, Vol. 3)* (Ankara: Seçkin, 1993), 2132.

Criminal Division of the Court of Cassation granted sentence reduction to a man who lived on the same street and came from the same small town as the girls who were molested, since he – as a 'countryman' (in this sense, 'part of the larger family') – had suffered significant pain and rage resulting from the dead man's assault on the girl.[9]

- Although the majority of victims of honour killings are women, their partners or, in the above-mentioned case, their molesters can also be victims. Since the 'honour of the woman' as the subject of protection is the focus of all these cases,[10] such crimes against male victims should also be considered as honour killings.
- The perpetrators were not restricted by age or gender since, although most of them are male and generally minors, there are also cases in which women committed the crime. Particularly in the case of honour killings determined by the tribal council or family assembly, minors are often contracted since they receive reduced sentences due to their age. However, neither a formal decision by a tribal council or family assembly nor the young age of the offender is a decisive criterion.

The established jurisdiction of the Criminal Division of the Court of Cassation defined unjust provocation (§51) as a crime of the perpetrator, which he/she committed under the influence of rage and pain, without premeditation.[11] However, despite an attempt to restrict unjust provocation, the Court of Cassation interpreted this norm quite broadly in connection with the concept of honour and applied honour as a general, almost arbitrary justification. The Court assumed a fundamental societal consensus on the meaning of honour. Accordingly, this (fictional) consensus regarding the perpetrator-victim relationship was always applied in favour of the perpetrator and taken as justification for sentence reduction. Bearing this in mind, one cannot speak of the Court of Cassation having a forward-thinking societal function.

THE LEGAL FRAMEWORK FOR THE PROTECTION OF WOMEN

The most important UN-level convention designed to level the field for men and women, namely the Convention on the Elimination of All Forms of Discrimination against Women (CEDAW) of 1979, was ratified by Turkey on 14 October 1985; the Optional Protocol of 2000 was subsequently ratified on 18 September 2002. Turkey's only reservations concerned CEDAW's Article 29, paragraph 1 and Article 9, paragraph 1.[12] The original reservations of 20 December 1985 relating to the regulations of the Turkish Civil Code were lifted following the major legal reform in 2001, when the domestic laws were modernised.

In 1995 Turkey took part in the Fourth World Conference on Women held in Beijing and continues to participate actively in the resulting Action Plan 'Beijing+5 Process and

[9] Yargıtay Ceza Genel Kurulu (General Criminal Division of the Court of Cassation), E. 1989/1-133, K. 1989/192, T. 22.05.1989, *Yargıtay Kararları Dergisi*, Cilt: XV, Sayı: 10, Ekim 1989, p. 1468-69.

[10] Exceptionally, women set a measure in this case, but one cannot argue that means an equalization with men! See for discrimination in law Sandra Fredman, 'Discrimination,'' in *The Oxford Handbook of Legal Studies*, ed. Peter Cane and Mark Tushnet (Oxford: Oxford University Press, 2005), 202-225.

[11] General Criminal Division of the Court of Cassation, E. 2003/1-173, K. 2003/198, T. 24.06.2003; E. 1990/1-176, K. 1990/194, T. 25.06.1990; E. 1989/1-99, K. 1989/159, T. 24.04.1989; E. 1989/1-55, K. 1989/113, T. 20.03.1989; Y4.CD E. 1993/5283, K. 1993/6515, T. 05.10.1993.

[12] See http://www.un.org/womenwatch/daw/cedaw/reservations-country.htm (accessed on 11 February 2007).

Beyond.'[13] Within this framework, Turkey presented a report to the UN in 1997; a follow-up report promised for 2005 has not yet been delivered. The Beijing Action Plan explicitly covers violence against women in the name of tradition and clearly states that the abuse of women's rights is equivalent to the abuse of human rights.[14] In the UN General Assembly's Resolution of 30 January 2003, the member states were again called upon to address honour killings, to take appropriate measures, and to refuse to allow religious and cultural values as justification for such acts.[15]

The campaign between 2002 and 2004 of the Turkish network Women for Women's Human Rights (WWHR) for a gender-equal Penal Code reform should be considered within this framework.[16] The network, which included NGO representatives, lawyers, and researchers from various universities, submitted to Parliament a model bill for a penal code with full gender equality. The new version of the penal code owes much to the network's activities. However, the new regulations concerning honour killings and unjust provocation cannot yet be considered a triumph for the women's organisations.

THE NEW PENAL CODE (AS OF 1 JUNE 2005): §29 UND §82

With the help of the above-mentioned campaign of the WWHR, the active efforts of some members of the Parliament, as well as public debate, the regulations on unjust provocation were changed (§29)[17], and murderous crimes in the name of 'custom' (in Turkish: *töre*) were entered into the catalogue of major-sentence crimes (§82/k).[18] Thus, manslaughter for custom reasons as well as killings for 'blood revenge' were classified as murder and given tougher sentences. However, the wording, the method and the lawmaker justification for the changed regulations call for caution in the application of these norms through the courts. Up to now it cannot be shown that tougher sanctions have had any impact in reducing honour killings. As such, scepticism regarding current jurisdiction is called for.

The reservation has to focus on the wording of the new norm. With help of the differentiation between 'honour killings' and 'murder in the name of "custom",' the lawmakers attempted to restrict the extent of tougher sanctions in the case of murder in the name of honour. As such, violent acts committed in the name of honour should not be completely banished from the legal system since, as shown above, the jurisdiction of the

[13] At the 23rd special session of the General Assembly on 'Women 2000: gender equality, development and peace for the twenty-first century' which took place on 5-9 June 2000, a Political Declaration and outcome document entitled 'further actions and initiatives to implement the Beijing Declaration and Platform for Action' was adopted. See for the assessment of the implications of the Political Declaration and 'further actions and initiatives to implement the Beijing Declaration and Platform for Action' the Report of the Secretary-General (A/55/341).

[14] 'Actions to be taken by Governments: (g) Take urgent action to combat and eliminate violence against women, which is a human rights violation, resulting from harmful *traditional or customary practices, cultural prejudices and extremism*' (Emphasis added by author).

[15] UN *General Assembly Resolution No. A/RES/57/179 (30.01.2003).*

[16] 'The Success of the Campaign for the Reform of the Turkish Penal Code From a Gender Perspective' (Summary Outcome Report). See http://www.wwhr.org (last accessed 11 February 2007).

[17] §29 of the new Penal Code: 'A person perpetrating a crime while under the influence of emotional or physical suffering caused by an unlawful act is given punishment…' (Emphasis added by the author).

[18] §82 of the new Penal Code with the subtitle 'aggravated homicide': 'In cases where murder with intent is perpetrated, k) by motivation of custom, the perpetrator is punished with the aggravated punishment of life imprisonment.' (Emphasis added by author).

Court of Cassation as well as the lawmakers consider the current honour codices of society as facts to be accepted. The explanatory statement of the lawmakers covering §29 and §82 confirm this conclusion.

According to §82/k, manslaughter in the name of 'custom' now counts as murder. Although the representatives of women's organisations called for a more comprehensive formulation such as 'in the name of honour,' the challenge found no ear among the lawmakers. The lawmakers' justification text for the norm-which for the application of the law is not binding, but as part of its historical interpretation will be taken into account-admits that the application of this norm is only possible 'in the absence of an unjust provocation.' This means then that the provocation clause, contrary to hopes, will continue to be applied for murder in the name of 'custom' (as well as honour killings). This justification is supplemented through §29 and the whole connection becomes clearer.

Still unclear is what is to be understood as murder in the name of 'custom' and which elements of crime are required to determine that an act as such constitutes a murder. According to public and parliamentary discussions, a murder in the name of 'custom' requires a decision by a so-called tribal council or family assembly, which names the victim and contracts the person to carry out the killing. It remains unclear who belongs to this council or assembly and whether the gender of the victim as well as the killer is meaningful in evaluating the elements of the crime. The concept of 'custom' suggests for Turkish circumstances a feudal background, which for many judges might mean a geographic limit (mainly the south eastern part of Turkey) for murder in the name of 'custom'. Although both types of murder are characterized by a sexuality and lifestyle imposed on rather than self-selected by women, the sexual integrity of women will not be protected fully through the rules of the new Penal Code.[19]

Since the new Penal Code has come into effect, new 'forms' of honour as well as 'custom' murders have emerged. Instead of contracting a family member to commit a murder, the victims are forced into suicide, and in most cases, the circumstances surrounding the suicide are not even investigated. Although such criminal circumstances are foreseen in §84 of the Penal Code, they do not constitute aggravated murder.

According to the new rules of §29, a perpetrator can benefit from sentence reduction if the motive for the crime was of rage or pain resulting from an unlawful act. The definition of 'unlawful act' is decisive for the application of the law. In the justification given by the lawmakers, it was revealed that honour as well as 'custom' murders (in this, both terms were used synonymously) played a major role in the reformulated rule. Thus the clause allowing sentence reduction in the case of interfamily killings was stricken. It has been further clarified that the factual circumstances surrounding a potential victim may not be deemed an unlawful act. Still, the example provided by the lawmakers makes it clear that they still hold a very specific idea of honour and that the Penal Code reform was able to offset only a small part of the abuse. According to the example presented, the perpetrator may not claim an unlawful act and provocation if the victim were no longer considered 'pure' because of rape and the family

---

[19] According to one newspaper report, many perpetrators recognize the loophole in the law and use this improper differentiation to their benefit. In an actual case, 20-year-old Gülistan Gümüş fled from her husband and sought shelter at her parents' home. When her husband came to her parents' house with seven of his relatives, Gülistan hid in a chest in which she was shot numerous times. In his defence, the husband claimed he had committed the murder in the name of 'honour', in which 'custom' had played no role. Therefore, his crime could not, according to §82, be considered as aggravated murder (*Radikal*, 21.12.2006).

felt itself under attack because of these circumstances, since the rape itself was not an act targeted *directly against the perpetrator*. The killing of a female family member who is rendered 'dishonourable' after being raped is therefore not covered by §29. However, if an unlawful act (by which is meant an *unjust act* as in the former Penal Code) has been directed against the perpetrator, the possibility is presented to apply this norm. The logical conclusion of this justification would be that adultery, out-of-wedlock sexual relationship or a women's request for divorce could be understood as *unlawful* behaviour having a direct impact upon the perpetrator. The above-mentioned Court of Cassation decisions support such an assumption.

Given that the norms have been applied only in the first instances of jurisprudence since the new Penal Code took effect on 1 June 2005, and no Court of Cassation decision has been reached, it remains to be seen whether the Court will develop a more progressive opinion on the question of the concept of honour.

CONCLUSION

That murder in the name of 'custom' has been classified as an aggravated crime in the new Penal Code is a welcome development. Still, in light of the fact that the main focus of penal regulations should lie in the prevention of all violence against women, the more general concept of 'honour killings' must also be considered in the law.

In order to guarantee the effective application of such a norm, a clear provision about the connection with unjust provocation should be foreseen (§29). A clear prohibition of the application of the sentence reduction norm in all cases making reference to the concept of honour would ensure sufficient clarity, because, up to now, even actions that are not crimes or unlawful civil actions have been deemed unlawful behaviour. But legal norms alone cannot effect a change in societal attitudes. Only through interdisciplinary collaboration on various levels (from politics to social work to the courts) can the societal honour code as an excuse for violence against women be combated.

REFERENCES

Coomaraswamy, Radhika. "Integration of the Human Rights of Women and the Gender Perspective. Violence Against Women, Report of the Special Rapporteur on violence against women, its causes and consequences." *UN Economic and Social Council, E/CN.4/2002/83, 31 January 2002.*

Dönmezer, Sulhi. *Kişilere ve Mala Karşı Cürümler (Crimes against Persons and Objects)*. İstanbul: İÜ Hukuk Fakültesi, 1990.

Erem, Faruk. *Türk Ceza Kanunu Şerhi. Özel Hükümler (Comment on Turkish Penal Code. Special Part)*, Vol. 3. Ankara: Seçkin, 1993.

Erman, Sahir, and Çetin Özek. *Ceza Hukuku Özel Bölüm. Kişilere Karşı İşlenen Suçlar (Penal Code Special Part. Crimes Against Persons)*. İstanbul: Alfa, 1994.

Ertürk, Yakın. "Implementation of General Assembly Resolution 60/251 of 15 March 2006 Entitled "Human Rights Council". Report of the Special Rapporteur on violence against women, its causes and consequences, Mission to Turkey." *UN General Assembly, A/HRC/4/34/Add.2, 5 January 2007.*

Fredman, Sandra. "Discrimination." In *The Oxford Handbook of Legal Studies*, edited by Peter Cane and Mark Tushnet, 202-225. Oxford: Oxford University Press, 2005.

Göztepe, Ece. "'Namus Cinayetleri'nin Hukuki Boyutu: Yeni Türk Ceza Kanunu'nun Bir Değerlendirmesi (Legal Aspects of 'Honour Killings': An Assesment of the new Turkish Penal Code)." *Türkiye Barolar Birliği Dergisi* 59 (2005): 29-48.

Kardam, Filiz. "The Dynamics of Honor Killings in Turkey. Prospects for Action." *UNDP/UNFPA, November 2005.* http://europeandcis.undp.org/?menu=p_cms/showandcontent_id=3E9DF3A2-F203-1EE9-B57B90A9C97A1717 (accessed 14 August 2007).

Kogacioglu, Dicle. "The Tradition Effect: Framing Honor Crimes in Turkey." *Differences* 15 (2004): 118-151.

Lloyd, Moya. "(Women's) human rights: paradoxes and possibilities," *Review of International Studies* 33 (2007): 91-103.

Savaş, Vural, and Sadık Mollamahmutoğlu. *Türk Ceza Kanunu Yorumu (Comment on Turkish Penal Code)*, Vol. 4. Ankara: Seçkin, 1995.

Sen, Purna et. al., "Violence against Women in the UK (CEDAW Thematic Shadow Report 2003)," http://www.womankind.org.uk/upload/CEDAW-report.pdf (accessed 14 August 2007).

Sen, Purna. "Development practice and violence against women." *Gender and Development* 6 (1998): 7-16.

Sev'er, Ayhan, and Gökçe Yurdakul. "Culture of Honour, Culture of Change. A Feminist Analysis of Honour Killings in Rural Turkey." *Violence Against Women Journal* 7 (2001): 966-1000.

Sev'er, Ayhan. "In the name of fathers: Honour Killings and some examples from south-eastern Turkey," *Atlantis* 30 (2005): 129-145.

Tellenbach, Sylvia. "Zum neuen türkischen Strafgesezbuch (About the new Turkish Penal Code)." *KAS-Auslandsinformationen* 4 (2005): 76-93.

The Success of the Campaign for the Reform of the Turkish Penal Code From a Gender Perspective (2002-2004) (Summary Outcome Report) (http://www.wwhr.org) (accessed 14 August 2007).

Türkiye Büyük Millet Meclisi. "Töre ve Namus ile Kadınlara ve Çocuklara Yönelik Şiddetin Sebeplerinin Araştırılarak Alınması Gereken Önlemlerin Belirlenmesi Amacıyla Kurulan Meclis Araştırması Komisyonu Raporu." 2006. (Grand National Assembly of Turkey, Report of the Parliamentary Inquiry Commission on Searching for Honour Crimes, Reasons of and Submitting Provisions to Prevent Violence Against Women and Children, 2006).

UN Division for the Development of Women. "Violence against women: a statistical overview, challenges and gaps in data collection and methodology and approaches for overcoming them." Expert Group Meeting (11-14 April 2005), http://www.un.org/womenwatch/daw/egm/vaw-stat-2005/index.html (accessed August 14, 2007).

UN General Assembly. "Declaration on the Elimination of Violence against Women." A/RES/48/104 (23 February 1994).

UN General Assembly. "In-depth study on all forms of violence against women. Report of the Secretary-General." A/61/122/Add.1 (6 July 2006).

Watts, Charlotte, and Cathy Zimmerman. "Violence against Women: global scope and magnitude." *The Lancet,* 359 (2002): 1232-1237.

AFGHANISTAN

In war-torn Afghanistan, the first political party dedicated to women's rights had its birth on 19 February 2008, when its driving force, the parliamentarian Fatima Nazari, launched National Need. At the inauguration ceremony in Kabul, Nazari expressed her hopes that the new party would put women's rights at the forefront of the national political debates.[1]

Another champion of Afghan democracy and women's rights is Malalai Joya, who was only 25 in 2003 when she sprang to fame for speaking out against the ex-Mujahideen leaders dominating the country's constitutional assembly. For having the courage to speak her mind she was called a 'prostitute' and an 'infidel', but she succeeded in 2005 in winning election to Afghanistan's national parliament, where she has continued to press her case, despite physical attacks upon her and threats of rape. The BBC had already, in 2003, proclaimed her 'the bravest woman in Afghanistan.'

D.W.P.

---

[1] 'New party to focus on women's rights,' Radio Free Europe/Radio Liberty, 20 February 2008.

In: Crimes Against Women
Editor: David Wingeate Pike

ISBN 978-1-61470-813-1

Chapter 20

FEMALE SUICIDE IN AFGHANISTAN

In memory of Saeed

Carol Mann

Since the fall of the Taliban and the mass return of refugees from early 2002, a wave of suicides of women and girls by fire has swept through Afghanistan, starting from the western part of the country, near the Iranian border, and spreading throughout the country. This escalating trend, which has baffled humanitarian agencies, has warranted only one investigation, the report published in December 2006 by Medica Mondiale.[1] This enquiry, like the media generally, has put the blame on arranged marriages and domestic violence. The verdict begs the question as to why such traditional treatment of women, typical of rigid patriarchal and tribal societies,[2] has become unbearable for the younger generation.

The case of Afghanistan needs to be analyzed in context and may well reveal itself to be an indicator of regional trends. Suicide has been rising amongst women in parts of the ex-Soviet Union and elsewhere in Central and East Asia. The countries with the highest rate of female suicide today, China, Republic of Korea, Lithuania, and Sri Lanka[3] despite their obvious differences, share points in common: faster social mobility and a recent access to global media and consumption. Indeed China, especially in its rural areas, is the only place in the world where female suicide exceeds that of men.

This process is going global, with comparable results. An increase in suicide amongst young women has been observed in countries where this was a relatively rare occurrence, namely Iran, Bangladesh and Turkey, especially eastern Anatolia; this is the subject of Nobel laureate Orhan Pamuk's novel *Snow*. These countries are socially and structurally close to Afghanistan, in that they are Muslim societies where pre-Islamic, strictly patriarchal tribal codes prevail, governing honour, revenge and the extremely restricted place of women. These societies have been exposed to brutal change through mass capitalism, global technology and the media, initially imported by their own migrant communities.

---

[1] Medica mondiale: http://www.medicamondiale.org/_en/presse/pm/aktuelles/mm-pm06-11-17b.html.

[2] Charles Lindholm (*Generosity and Jealousy*, 1982) provides comparable information for Swat Pathans at the Afghan border, as Germaine Tillion (*Le Harem et les cousins*, 1966) did nearly fifty years ago for Kabyl populations in North Africa.

[3] WHO statistics for 2007: http://www.who.int/mental_health/prevention/suicide_rates/en/index.html.

In all these countries, one encounters similar configurations: rural surroundings for women while men work in cities or abroad; traditionally minimal female rights and recognition; the recent arrival of technology (especially TV), closer contacts with migrant communities abroad, and the disintegration of family structures. Hitherto secluded women are becoming increasingly aware of alternatives to their restricted life-styles. It seems that many of the suicide victims, aware of their potential rights, had become fatally depressed by the disparity between their lives and what was displayed by the media. The latter have also led the men in their community to change their expectations regarding marital relationships.

Even if suicide is forbidden in Islam, Afghanistan, Iran and the neighbouring countries remain strongly influenced by Zoroastrianism and Buddhism where self-immolation is considered as religious sacrifice and life on earth generally perceived to be tragic, characterized by pious suffering.[4] Afghan, Iranian or Kurdish women who pour petrol on themselves follow this unspoken tradition and are perceived as martyrs.[5] Their action, in fact, elicits admiration from young girls elsewhere who feel empowered to do likewise whenever conditions are perceived as truly impossible. Female suicide, however painful it may be, suddenly appears as the only dignified alternative to a life of despair.

* * * * * * *

Between 1980 and 1990, following the Soviet intervention to aid the pro-Communist government in Kabul, some six million Afghan citizens fled their homeland mainly in the direction of Iran and Pakistan, thereby constituting the world's largest refugee community. Since March 2002, over 4.7 million refugees have returned, the figures steadily dwindling over the years as the situation in Afghanistan continues to be socially and economically unstable.

Since the fall of the Taliban and the allied intervention, living conditions in Afghanistan, especially regarding women, have not improved in a significant and enduring manner.[6] Safety, education and adequate living standards, which had been promised to them by the Karzai government and international aid, have revealed themselves so abysmal that most returnees regret their decision to leave refugee camps or Iranian shanty towns, however difficult the conditions might have been for them in exile. As if by reaction, a wave of suicides has swept Western Afghanistan[7] affecting female rural returnees, especially those coming back from Iran. Both in Iran and in Pakistan, the simultaneous presence of traditional and modern institutions had been instrumental in effecting a real measure of change. The highly religious government in Iran gave an Islamic stamp on education and vocational training for girls[8] that made such innovations acceptable even to the most traditionalist refugee Afghan patriarchs, whereas they would have been reticent in more secular Pakistan.

[4] B. J. Good, M J. Del Vecchio, E. Good, R. Moradi, 'Interpretations of Iranian Depressive Illness and Dysphoric Affect,' 1985.

[5] Another aspect of this feature is demonstrated in present-day Shiite Iran where extreme self-flagellation with chains is part of the Shura religious rituals.

[6] Nancy Hatch Dupree, 'Afghan women under the Taliban,' 1996.

[7] C. Mann: 'Le suicide des femmes en Afghanistan depuis la chute des Talibans,' in: Jane Freedman, Jérôme Valluy (dir.), *Persécutions des femmes - Savoirs, mobilisations et protections* (Paris: Éditions du Croquant, 2007).

[8] Chahla Chafiq. *Femmes sous le voile, face à la loi islamique*, 1995.

Furthermore, the rural illiterate women have been the ones to take advantage of the offers of modernity. Health programmes, by addressing women, have challenged the inevitability of pain and suffering and introduced a notion of personal well-being, which entails the even more novel concept of self-worth. In different ways, the humanitarian agencies in Pakistan and Iranian social structures have made women aware of their responsibility as educators as well as nurturers, which is why they have been increasingly involved with their children's schooling, including their daughters.'[9] They thus acquired a sense of empowerment, and expectation was bolstered through literacy programmes which gave women a measure of control of their environment and the possibility for independent thought and even employment.

This made the return to Afghanistan all the more difficult for young women born in exile, as few of these innovations were available to them outside Kabul. In this 85 percent rural ultra-patriarchal country, the lack of the most basic facilities such as running water, electricity and health care has been made even worse by the increasing lack of schooling and work opportunities for girls. Despite the Afghan Ministry of Education's claim in 2005 that up to 5.2 million children are now registered in primary school,[10] the figures do not take into account the drop-out rate which is escalating for girls. Girls are often forbidden to attend because of safety problems and paternal preference towards sons, which means that girls are less likely to be encouraged to get an education.[11]

As the Taliban continue to torch schools and fundamentalist politics rule Kabul, the prospects are getting steadily bleaker. This situation has been compounded by a return to the pattern of highly unequal marriages, where the girls' feelings are totally ignored. Marriages have always been arranged on the basis that women submit totally to their mother-in-law and their new families. Nevertheless, personal arrangements were at least possible and the girls' well-being was at least an aim, if not a priority.[12] Today, for economic reasons, marriages are increasingly enforced between pubescent girls and much older men; alternatively, girls are given in payment of debt, or practically sold, as the settlement received by the parents may well be the only source of income for the whole family. Considering that families used to live near one another, the present situation frequently involves the young wife being sent far away from her home with no one to turn to in case of trouble. As an overall result, domestic relations continue to be characterised by an escalating violence. Whereas male brutality was considered as part and parcel of traditional marriage in a generally violent society, as this researcher has observed directly, it is now considered unacceptable.

According to the Ministry of Women's Affairs in Kabul, more than half of all Afghan brides are under sixteen at the moment of marriage, and the UN puts this figure at over 65 percent.[13] Another problem is that educated female returnees who have benefited from education abroad are hostile to being forced to marry an illiterate spouse. This is also difficult for the families of the men, who usually marry women beneath their social station, which is why the wives of many educated men in Afghanistan are illiterate. The resentment felt by uneducated men towards women that they cannot impress or dominate, except by brute force,

[9] Micheline Centlivres-Demont: 'Hommes armés, femmes aguerries,' 2001.
[10] World Bank, 'GenderStats: Database of Gender Statistics,' http://devdata.worldbank.org.
[11] See C. Mann: 'La scolarité des filles en Afghanistan aujourd'hui,' *Pro-Choix*, Paris, March 2007.
[12] Louis Dupree: *Afghanistan*, 1973.
[13] U.S. Department of State, Bureau of Democracy, Human Rights, and Labor: 'Afghanistan: Country Reports on Human Rights Practice,' 2006, http://www.state.gov/g/drl/rls/hrrpt/2005/61704.htm.

destroys any pride in acquiring a wife of higher status: this is the painful reverse of the traditional configuration. This problem was already present in Iran, where Afghan men worked mainly as labourers, and girls went to school. In fact, a number of teachers and nurses trained in Iran were among the victims of the first wave of suicides.

For the past year, the suicide wave has spread to girls who never went into exile. The exposure to alternatives through the media has made life even more intolerable for women; they are now fully aware of other lifestyle possibilities, even within devout Islam. As one informer, an elderly woman in a remote village in the Farah region, said: '*In the olden days, we were beaten by husbands and mothers-in-law who made us work like slaves, even as we gave birth to one child after the next. We were unhappy, we suffered, but we didn't know it; life was just like that for women. Now girls are learning through TV, school and travel that it is not normal, and it has made matters worse for them. They cannot put up with traditional hardship, so they set themselves on fire.*' Forced marriages and domestic violence are certainly contributing factors, but the timing of this spate of suicides reflects the inability of young women of the post-war generation to resume life according to rigid patriarchal traditions.

The escalating suicide situation is dramatic. The victims' ages range from 9 to 40, the average being between 14 and 18.. While no accurate statistics are possible, unofficial estimates report hundreds of victims. Only a minority of these make it to hospitals, and even then are not listed as suicide victims. The lack of roads, transport, health and social services make this option unavailable to inhabitants of remote villages, which also helps to explain why Afghanistan has one of the world's highest maternal and infant mortality rates. Furthermore, suicide is perceived as extremely shameful for the families concerned, and sometimes they are revealed to have been cold-blooded murders committed by spouses or mothers-in-law, who are rarely punished.

Suicide as a last resort was not unknown under the Taliban regime, as reports by the independent Afghan feminist organisation RAWA[14] have shown. But these used to concern desperate women, especially widows abandoned by their families. The situation today is completely different, as these suicides take place within families. The girls are indeed surrounded by their immediate social group as they try to reconstruct their lives according to traditional parameters. The situation in Afghanistan, extraordinarily contradictory, contributes to this trend.

Afghanistan has signed the CEDAW convention, but its hybrid constitution, a mixture of orthodox Sharia and conventional democratic forms, does not embody the principle of equal rights. The major political formations depend on former warlords who remain close to fundamentalism. Malalai Joya, a woman of the new generation, stands alone. A 28 year-old elected representative of the Farah province, her outspoken manner and systematic opposition to the warlords in power have made her popular with a large segment of the public. Nevertheless, her life has been threatened, and she was arbitrarily expelled from office in May 2007. Her main opponent, until he was ousted in 2007, the Chief Justice Fazul Hadi Shinwari, whose office was said to be decorated solely with a Quran and a whip, is exclusively versed in Islamic law. He attempted to enforce systematic repression of women, banning female singers, opposing co-education and publicly condoning the stoning of 'adulterous' women (i.e. women convicted of having had any extramarital, even non-sexual,

[14] Revolutionary Association of the Women of Afghanistan, founded in Kabul in 1977 by Mina Keshwar Kamal.

relationship). Shinwari has been responsible for appointing judges who, like himself, have no training in secular law. No human rights effort attempted by foreign NGOs working on short- to mid-term projects from their offices in Kabul could equal Shinwari in influence.

The general outlook is dim indeed. Women's lives are threatened if they attempt any kind of public career, and the spate of suicides must be seen in conjunction with an equal rise in the number of murders of young women. Murder and suicide are sometimes closely linked. Perhaps the most recent and tragic example was the fate of the 25-year-old poet Nadia Anjuman from Herat, whose first volume of poetry, *Dark Flower,* had been highly successful, especially as it described the tragic situation of women. This, however, displeased her husband who, in November 2005, was ultimately jailed for murdering her, despite his claim that her career had brought dishonour to his family. The refusal to recognize women as professionals and public figures has contributed to the recent assassination of young female journalists and TV announcers. In June 2007, in the space of five days, Sanga Amach and Zakia Zaki were slain, and among the suspects were males of the respective families who feared for family honour, as in the case of Anjuman. Zaki, a seasoned journalist and women's rights activist, had furthermore been increasingly threatened for having attempted to represent the plight of women in the media. This case was not unprecedented. In 2005, Shaima Rezayee, an announcer on the youth channel Tolo TV, was murdered, and many of her colleagues were officially rebuked for showing their faces on TV. Female singers who in the 1970s led successful careers under communist rule have all fled abroad out of fear for their safety if they continue to perform in their home country. For all these reasons, women in fact are becoming increasingly aware politically, and the radio plays an important part in this. Because they sense that change will be of special benefit to them, women turned out massively for the last elections, voting where necessary with a thumb-print.

Maria Bashir, Afghanistan's first woman attorney, who managed to have Anjuman's husband convicted for murder until he bribed himself out of jail, seeks to defend the victims of marital violence.[15] Working from the court of Herat, she attests to the problems she faces: "*Whenever I manage to put one of these brutal husbands away, he generally finds the way to buy himself out of prison. Judges are never on the side of women, and it is getting worse.*" She has refused job offers from foreign NGOs, and prefers her badly paid job in her miserable, unequipped premises. "*Otherwise, there would be no one to defend these women,*" she explains. Likewise, in investigating the predicament of those who attempt suicide or escape murder and manage to reach Herat's hospital, she has found that their lives are often so brutal that self-immolation is seen as the only way out.

Despite purported foreign aid, the conditions in Herat's hospital are dreadful: the sheets are filthy, while proper analgesics, bandages and even food need to be brought in from outside and remain scarce. Almost all casualties are listed as 'accidents'. Those who survive suicide attempts are generally rejected by their husbands when they emerge from hospital, and there are no social structures to look after them. These victims are simply left to their fate. It would seem that the registry is consulted by the police at best once a day, which leaves plenty of time to modify any incriminating information. As the director Dr Niazi states: *'We are here to look after them, nothing else.'* This, in the furious response of Maria Bashir, is the hospital's policy, potentially aiding and abetting criminal families that continue to elude any

[15] Two interviews held in the law-courts in Herat in June 2006.

kind of prosecution. This mentality thwarts her attempts to aid victimized women in Afghanistan

It would seem that suicide represents the only individual act of defiance to which women can resort. It is interesting to note that this trend has coincided with the increase in female kamikaze in other tribal Muslim societies, such as the Palestinian or Chechen. Whereas superficially opposed in their intent, these forms of suicide have much in common. The rise of Islamic fundamentalism in these regions has meant an increase in the repression of women, even by traditional patriarchal standards. Resorting to such desperate measures has become a public, visible way of reacting that has focused attention on crimes against women. By choosing to die in excruciating pain in the name of Islam, or in protest against their families' domination, these women are claiming the right to an expression of desperate personal decision and refuting the life-style imposed upon them.

The field research[16] *for this paper, carried out in Afghanistan in 2005 and 2006, consisted of meetings with patients, doctors and families in hospitals in Kabul, Herat and Farah, with the women's rights attorney Maria Bashir, and with the unaffiliated parliamentarian Malalai Joya.*[17]

References

Centlivres-Demont, Micheline, 'Hommes armés, femmes aguerries,' *in* F. Reeysoo (ed.): *Hommes armés, femmes aguerries, rapports de genre en situations de conflit armé.* Berne: UNESCO, 2001.

Chafiq, Chahla; and Khrosrokhavar, Farhad, *Femmes sous le voile, face à la loi islamique.* Paris: Felin, 1995.

Dupree, Louis, *Afghanistan.* Princeton: Princeton University Press, 1973.

Dupree, Nancy Hatch, 'Afghan Women under the Taliban' *in* William Maley (ed.), *Fundamentalism Reborn, Afghanistan and the Taliban.* Lahore: Vanguard, 1996.

Edwards, David B., *Before Taliban.* Berkeley: University of California Press, 2002.

Good, B. J.; Del Vecchio, M. J.; Good, E.; Moradi, R., 'Interpretations of Iranian Depressive Illness and Dysphoric Affect', *in:* A. Kleinman and B. Good, *Culture and Depression.,* Berkeley: University of California Press, 1985.

Lindholm, Charles, *Generosity and Jealousy: the Swat Pukhtun of Northern Pakistan.* New York: Columbia University Press, 1982.

Mann, Carol, 'Les shahidé du monde traditionnel : le suicide des jeunes filles afghanes,' TERRA-Ed., Coll. *'Esquisses'*, February 2006 : http://terra.rezo.net/article439.html.

Mann, Carol. 'La scolarisation des filles en Afghanistan,' *Pro-Choix* (Paris), no 39, February 2007.

Mann, Carol. 'From camps to capital: How fundamentalist politics of the Afghan refugee camps influenced Kabul and women's lives today,' in *Images of Muslim Women*, Faegheh Shirazi, ed. Austin: University of Texas Press, 2010.

[16] This combines academic research with practical research carried out within the framework of my own NGO FemAid, based in Paris (www.femaid.org).

[17] Interviews in Kabul and Farah were arranged with the help of Alia N. to whom this author remains eternally grateful, as also to Ibrahim Farozesh and to the ever-patient Saeed.

Study of suicides among Afghans. Medica Mondiale, 2006.
http://www.medicamondiale.org/_en/presse/pm/aktuelles/mm-pm06-11-17b.html
Tillion, Germaine. *Le Harem et les cousins*. Paris: Seuil, 1966.

PAKISTAN

In Pakistan, domestic violence has reached such a level that Human Rights Watch, based in New York, devoted a special study to it. In a highly detailed account published in 1999, it found that up to 90 percent of Pakistani women were subject to verbal, sexual, emotional or physical abuse within their own homes. As a result of the increased awareness, a draft Protection against Domestic Violence of Women and Children Act was drawn up in early 2007 by the Federal Law Ministry, but it still awaits enactment. In January of that year, when the Karachi police arrested Mohammad Moin Khan, the former captain of Pakistan's cricket team, after his wife complained of being beaten by him, it seemed that a page had been turned, but the action did nothing to stop the upward trend. The Human Rights Commission of Pakistan (HRCP) reported in April 2008 that violence against women in Pakistan had more than doubled, rising from 1,821 cases in 2006—itself an increase over 2005—to 4,276 cases in 2007. In launching the report, the HRCP Secretary Iqbal Haider called 2007 'a brutal year for women,' with 736 kidnapped, 731 raped, and 636 victims of honour killing.

A case in Pakistan, however, of a young woman falling victim to both rape and honour killing caught the attention of the world. In the little village of Meerwala, southeast of Islamabad in Punjab province, Mukhtaran Bibi (known in the Pakistani press as Mukhtar Mai) was an illiterate and devout Muslim who found herself in June 2002 at the centre of a village dispute. A tribal council decided to punish a family for the alleged crime of their son by sentencing his sister to gang-rape. Four of her neighbours carried out the sentence and then made her walk home naked. It was then supposed that her shame would drive her to suicide. Instead, she found the courage to prosecute her attackers, and six were sentenced to death. With her compensation money of $8,300, she founded two elementary schools, one for boys, one for girls, and enrolled in her own school. In March 2005, however, a Pakistani court freed five of the six attackers, understandably so. In Pakistan, if a woman reports a rape, four Muslim men must normally act as witnesses before she can prove her case. Otherwise, she risks being charged with fornication or adultery, and punished with a public whipping and long imprisonment. In November, however, Muktaran was invited to Washington, where she was greeted by senior officials in the White House, the State Department and Congress. At a banquet given to her, Laura Bush expressed her admiration: 'Don't assume that it's only a tale of heartbreak. Mukhtaran proves that one woman can really change the world.' The First Lady's sentiment was not shared by everyone in Pakistan. As Mukhtaran put it, 'the traditional landowners want me dead and the government doesn't want me around either.' The authorities continued to confiscate her mail and feed vicious propaganda to supportive journalists, portraying her as a liar, a cheat, and an unpatriotic dupe of India. The woman who was presented at the United Nations television studios on 19 January 2006 as 'the bravest woman on earth' was—as a result of intervention by the Pakistani authorities—denied the right to speak.[1]

D.W.P.

[1] Nicolas D. Kristof, 'Sentenced to rape,' *International Herald Tribune*, 30 September 2004; 'When rapists walk free,' *IHT*, 7 March 2005; 'A woman of courage,' *IHT*, 9 November 2005. A crime still to be fully investigated took place on 13 July 2008 in Jafferabad, in the province of Baluchistan. Three women in the village of Baba Kot who were members of the Umrani tribe planned to get married before a civil court in the town of Usta Mohammad, thus going against the decision of members of the tribe. The three women, together with two other women who were family members, were abducted and driven into the desert in a car with provincial government plates. There all five (two of them minors) were buried alive. Souhayr Belhassen, president of the International Federation for Human Rights (FIDH), called it 'intolerable that heinous crimes like this continue to be perpetrated with impunity in Pakistan.'

In: Crimes Against Women
Editor: David Wingeate Pike

ISBN 978-1-61470-813-1

Chapter 21

AN NGO'S LONG-TERM STRATEGY IN PAKISTAN

Naeem Sarfraz

EXTREMISM AND INTOLERANCE IN THE REGION

On New Year's Day 1979 Shah Raza Pahlavi fled Iran. On 31 January, exiled Ayatollah Ruhollah Khomeini returned in triumph to Tehran, ushering in the first fundamentalist Islamic state of the 20th Century. Women were its first victims. Later the same year Soviet troops marched into Kabul, unleashing strong reactions from the Western and Islamic worlds.

US and Saudi money poured in to train and equip thousands of Muslim volunteers who flooded in from across the Muslim world to evict the Soviets. Hundreds of camps were set up in madrasas (religious schools) in the tribal areas of Pakistan bordering Afghanistan. From there they launched a war of attrition which totally sapped the might of the Soviets and led to their humiliating defeat and exit from Afghanistan. While pandering to the religious fighters, Pakistan's military dictator General Zia-ul Haq introduced the Hudood Ordinances, a set of laws ostensibly intended to implement Islamic Shariah. Women become the main victims of this so-called Islamisation of Pakistan, as these laws stripped them of their basic rights as equal citizens and exposed them to injustice and violence.

Following the Soviet defeat, former war comrades fought each other to grab power in Kabul. This led eventually to the rise of the Taliban—the Pakistan-based, Saudi/American-funded students who emerged victorious and formed a repressive, theocratic fundamentalist state in Afghanistan. They provided sanctuary and safe haven to other Muslim 'freedom fighters': Chechens, Uzbeks, Tajiks, Arabs and others, the most prominent being Osama bin Laden and his Al-Qaeda organization. Their mantra was to establish abrasive, Taliban-style regimes throughout the Muslim world.

The strict code of Taliban was harsh on women, who were no longer allowed to work or even to go to school. Denied all rights they become no more than domestic slaves to an arrogant, misogynistic society. The world failed to recognize the danger posed by the Taliban until the fateful September 11th attack, when it was jarred awake by the collapsing World Trade Center. America's response was swift and harsh. In a lightning military operation the

Taliban regime was destroyed. But not the Taliban or Al Qaeda, who simply melted away into the local population and into the rugged mountains along the Afghan-Pakistan border. Here they have regrouped, expanding their influence and militancy, particularly into Pakistan.

A Very Rough Neighbourhood

A resurrected Taliban Sunni fundamentalist theocracy in Afghanistan to the north is undoubtedly the biggest threat to Pakistani society, particularly to its women. The other three neighbours of Pakistan do not inspire much confidence in championing human rights either. To the east lies atheist communist China, a growing economic powerhouse but with a dismal human rights record. To the south is secular India, with its powerful and growing anti-Muslim, anti-Pakistan fundamentalist Hindu Shiv Sena and BJP groups. To the west lies the Ayatollas-dominated Shia fundamentalist theocracy of Iran, where women have been ruthlessly suppressed for the last thirty years. Over the decades the pressure of extremist movements of all four neighbours has obviously had its impact on Pakistan in different ways, particularly in each border area.

Women's Protection and Violation of Rights

Despite a troubled neighbourhood, the vast majority of the people of Pakistan continue to be liberal and tolerant. Some basic points need to be kept in mind. 97% of Pakistanis are Muslims whose religion is one of peace and tolerance and which grants full fundamental rights to women. The Constitution of Pakistan, based on Islamic principles, protects women's rights, especially through the following Articles:

a. Article 25: All citizens are equal before law and are entitled to equal protection of law. There shall be no discrimination on the basis of sex alone.
b. Article 34: Steps shall be taken to ensure full participation of women in all spheres of national life.
c. Article 35: The state shall protect the marriage, the family, the mother and the child.
d. Article 37: The state shall make provisions for securing just and human conditions of work, ensuring that children and women are not employed in vocations not suited to their age and sex and for maternity benefits for women in employment.
e. Article 21: The total seats in National Assembly are 332, of which 60 are reserved for women.

The misfortune of women lies in the violation of the Constitution, to the extent that even some legislation has been passed which is contrary to Islamic principles and to the Constitution itself. The worst examples of such aberrations are the following aforementioned Hadood Ordinances:

1. Offence of Zina (enforcement of Hadood) Ordinance 1979.
2. Offence of Qazf (enforcement of Hadd) Ordinance 1979.

3. Offence against Property (enforcement of Hadood) Ordinance 1979.
4. The prohibition (enforcement of Hadd) Order 1979.

These draconian laws enabled the zealous dictator and his supporters amongst the radical male population to further terrorize women. But violence against women is rooted in culture and tradition, not in religion or the law. Today violence against women is present in many forms, the most prominent being the following:

1. *Honor Killings:* A warped sense of honor exists amongst elements of the male population which arrogates authority to itself through the historic tribal culture and traditions of the country. For example, tribal customs deny a woman the right to marry a man of her choice. Shamelessly disregarding the Quran, the Constitution and the laws of the land, women are killed for marrying men of their choice; for getting out of a bad marriage; or for not marrying a spouse chosen by the family. These are considered acts of disobedience. The parents feel that they have been put to shame, which they feel permits them to kill the young women. In 2006 approximately 1,000 cases of honor killings were reported. It is believed that twice as many go unreported. Under the Hadood Ordinances there is a loophole which enables murderers to get away Scot free by paying blood money as compensation to the girl's family.
2. *Wani*: This is a terrible custom where a woman is given in marriage to settle a dispute between families. It is common in Sindh and the Frontier provinces of Pakistan. While being completely barred under Pakistani law, illegal gatherings of tribal elders called *jirgas* arrogate to themselves the authority to punish anyone they feel has committed a crime. They then order the family of the accused to hand over a female, tragically even a girl-child as young as five or six years old, in marriage to any one of the aggrieved party. This reprehensible custom even deteriorates to such disgraceful levels as gang rapes, as in the Mukhtara Mai case.
3. *Forced Marriages:* The custom of forced marriages, again in conflict with both Islam and the Pakistan Constitution, continues to be widely prevalent, particularly in the backward rural areas of the country. Once forced into an unpleasant marriage, the woman is destined to spend the rest of her life in total servitude.
4. *Domestic Violence:* Statistics are hard to come by, but domestic violence is more the norm rather than the exception in the male dominated Pakistani society. It is estimated that 70 percent of women are victims of regular domestic violence in almost every household in the country, at the hands of all male members: fathers, brothers, husbands and even sons.
5. *Acid Attacks*: This is a very strange phenomenon which was common in the past but is gradually dying out. Husbands, upset by the perceived infidelity of their wives, disfigure them permanently by throwing acid on their faces.
6. *Stove Bursts:* Primitive gas stoves are used for cooking. Numerous cases are reported of housewives being burnt to death by the bursting of stoves. While some accidents may be genuine, it is widely acknowledged that others are intentional cases of husbands murdering their wives. In such cases murder is very difficult to prove. More awareness as well as better quality stoves has reduced these occurrences.

Bold Initiatives to Counter Intolerance

With the growth of education, communications, road networks, tele-communications and general awareness, civil society has become more and more concerned about of all forms of violence against women. A growing body of civil society representatives is coming out strongly in support of victims of violence against women. Prominent organizations working in this field include the All Pakistan Women Association, the Women's Action Forum, the Human Rights Commission of Pakistan, the Women's Crises Centres, the Aurat Foundation and the All Pakistan Women Lawyers Association. Their activities include taking to the streets and petitioning government departments to seek relief for victims and punishment for perpetrators of these heinous crimes. The judiciary of Pakistan, particularly the Supreme Court led by the courageous Justice Iftikhar Chaudhary, has taken strong corrective action on cases brought to its notice.

The government has taken some initiatives, including setting up of Crises Centres to assist victims of violence. Parliament has also attempted to repeal the hated Hadood Ordinances, but a powerful Mullah lobby succeeded in stopping the initiative. A watered-down Women's Empowerment Law was eventually passed in 2007. Though not sufficient, it has succeeded in removing some of the more punitive components of the Hadood Ordinances. It is an excellent first step. Immediately after the Bill was passed, about 1,200 women awaiting trial were released on bail.

All these measures are reactive. They come into play after an incident takes place. While they are undoubtedly important for countering violence, very little attention has been paid to the more critical issue of preventing such incidents in the first place.

The Fazaldad Institute is an NGO founded in the memory of the late Dr. Fazaldad Wahla, a committed young professional, who gave his life while attempting to save a young girl from becoming an honour-killing victim. The Institute's programme is unique. It concentrates exclusively on 'changing the mindset' in society through a long- term sustained program of mass education so that such abuse and victimization do not happen in the first place. It is 'preventive' rather than 'reactive.'

The Institute worked with the government over three years to help incorporate human rights education in the curriculum taught in schools from Class 1 to High School level. This has now been made a formal part of study for the 20 million students in the country. Over 800 Master Trainers and 32,000 teachers in 66 cities have been trained by the Institute and they, in turn, are teaching millions of students. Literature has been developed and translated into five regional languages and over 100,000 copies distributed. Additional interactive programs have been held for over 35,000 students. Hundreds of judges, police officers and bureaucrats have also been trained by the Institute who, as a consequence, are more aware of their obligations towards the rights of citizens.

The Sufi Tradition: Mazar of the Sufi saint, Bari Imam, at Islamabad

The Fazaldad Institute's initiatives of mass awareness and education have a very sound foundation. Pakistan is not, and never has been, a land of extremism or so-called fundamentalism. Only the *madrassas*, funded heavily by Saudi Wahabis, propagate Taliban bigotry. The rest of the nation (mostly converts from Hinduism) has been brought up in a Sufi culture. Islam was introduced into this region by a series of great Sufi saints, all of whom preached peace, love, care and tolerance. Through their own example and their teachings they won the hearts of the people who then converted to Islam. Tens of millions visit their shrines (or *mazars*) every year where men and women learn, worship, sing, dance and interact freely together — a far cry from the obscurantist intolerance and violence of the Wahabi Taliban.

The Fazaldad Institute's training programs are very much in keeping with the historic and traditional Islamic values of the people of Pakistan. Undoubtedly such programmes will contribute towards creating an environment where the oppressed women of Pakistan will resume their high status in society, free from discrimination, violence and terror. The experience of the last eight years has been very successful. In the years ahead the dream of 'changing the mindset' will surely become reality.

INDIA AND ITS DOWRIES

A UN report on India in 2006 estimated that, over the last two decades, infanticide and prenatal sex selection accounted for an annual loss of half a million girls. Each year thousands of wives were murdered or maimed—many of them doused with kerosene and set ablaze—by husbands angry about their wives' behaviour or dissatisfied by the size of their dowries. Dowry demands, reported the Delhi Commission for Women, account for approximately 85 percent of cases of wife-abuse, and the National Crime Records Bureau estimated that on average one dowry death was reported in India every 77 minutes. Kiran Walia, chairwoman of the Delhi Commission, took note of the increase over the past five years in violent dowry harassment and attributed it to the rise across India of an increasingly materialistic way of life: 'It is one thing to give and take dowry. But what is really obnoxious is the torture women undergo because the dowry is less than expected.'[1]

D.W.P.

[1] Amelia Gentleman, 'Brides pay the price for Indian dowry fever,' *International Herald Tribune*, 23 October 2006.

In: Crimes Against Women
Editor: David Wingeate Pike

ISBN 978-1-61470-813-1

Chapter 22

DOWRIES IN INDIA

Ruchi Anand

> There are many recordings of the ambivalence associated with the woman—as daughter, wife, mother, widow and so on—in Indian culture.... The Indian woman's identity is defined by her relationship to others in these phases of her life.[1]
>
> Feminism does not see its view as subjective, partial, or undetermined but as a critique of the purported generality, disinterestedness, and universality of prior accounts. These have not been half right but have invoked the wrong whole...; men create the world from their own point of view, which then becomes reality to be described.[2]

INTRODUCTION

There is a self-evident disparity in the roles and position of men and women in society, which are sociological and ideological constructs fabricated worldwide since time immemorial. Sociologists explain this pattern by tying these constructs with social statuses that both men and women acquire either by the roles that they play, the biological considerations attached to sex differences and the nature of rights and obligations that these pressures impose on the two sexes.[3] Such a process of socialization is reciprocal, since the targets usually learn to respond to the stimuli that society expects from them. Starting from the day one is born through the stages of childhood, youth, adulthood and old age, socialization is a continuous process.[4]

The family structure plays a crucial role in this phenomenon, which is one of the primary groups in the process of socialization. However, families and family systems invariably

[1] Stanley J. Tambiah, , 'Bridewealth and Dowry Revisited: The Position of Women in Sub-Saharan Africa and North India,' *Current Anthropology*, vol. 30, no. 4, August-October 1989, p. 417.

[2] Catherine MacKinnon, 'Feminism, Marxism, Method, and the State,' in *Feminist Theory*, ed. Nannererl O. Keohane, Michelle Z. Rosaldo, and Barbara C. Gelpi (Chicago: University of Chicago Press, 1982), p. 23.

[3] See Lucile Duberman (ed.), *Gender and Sex in Society* (New York: Praeger, 1975).

[4] The concept of `gender' which determines the socially and culturally determined differences between men and women was introduced to avoid any confusion about the difference between sex and gender. So, while sex is biologically determined, gender is a sociological construct. See Maria Mies, *Patriarchy and the Accumulation on a World Scale* (New Jersey and London: Zed Books, 1986), p. 22.

depend on the pulls and pressures that are superimposed, knowingly or unknowingly, on each individual in the family, the roles they assume and the social, economic, psychological and political effects of their role-taking. The problem arises because social life appears to be fabricated 'within the social experiences that are characteristic of men.'[5] The challenge of feminism is to disrupt the continuation of an oppressive, patriarchal, male-dominated and unequal man-woman relationship.[6]

> What is needed is an understanding of the divisions that arise along lines of race, class and gender, between men and women and within women themselves. As Kishwar and Vanita put it,
>
> Vast differences distinguish the life of women in different parts of the country and within different caste, class, religious and ethnic groups. It is therefore very difficult to make generalizations and to put together a comprehensive description of the life and struggles of Indian women.[7]

The differences in question concern the following: the rights of inheritance of men and women to acquire or give away their wealth or properties; the economic and occupational activities of men and women and their corresponding remuneration; the liberty of marital partners to seek and get a divorce; social interaction of people of different ages and stages; the right to property; participation in the religious, economic and political arena, separate rather than mixed participation for men and women in societies, associations and groups; and lastly, the linguistic forms that represent gender differences.[8]

This chapter is divided into four sections. The first section summarizes the definitions, interpretations and complications surrounding 'dowry' in India. The second section explores the origins of the custom and how its practice has changed and escalated over a period of time. The third section draws the linkages between patriarchy, capitalism and dowry as a form of violence that aids in the patriarchal primitive accumulation of capital; the fourth and final section concludes with some preliminary results of the author's hypothesis.

It is interesting to note that, in the past, there has been a wealth of literature concerning the accumulation of capital on a world scale, leading to a system that perpetuates certain patriarchal trends; and there is ample literature on the theory and practice of 'dowry' as practiced in India. However there has been no material to link dowry as a direct source of violence contributing to this global accumulation of capital. The closest reference is Maria Mies, who attributes violence to means such as dowry, sati, rape, infanticide, colonization and housewifization to show how the common feature of production and labour relations uses structural or direct violence.[9] Economists such as Andre Gunder Frank support this argument:

---

[5] Sandra Harding, 'Introduction: Is there a Feminist Methodology?' in Harding (ed.), *Feminism and Methodology* (Milton Keynes: Open University Press, 1987), p. 6.

[6] Steven Goldberg, *The Inevitability of Patriarchy* (New York: William Morrow, 1974, 1975).

[7] Madhu Kishwar and Ruth Vanita (eds.), *In Search For Answers*: *Indian Women's Voices from Manushi* (London: Zed Books), 1979, 1983, p.1. Also see Jeanne Bisilliat and Michele Fieloux, *Women and the Third World*: *Work and Daily Life* (London and Toronto: Fairleigh Dickinson University Press, 1987).

[8] Stanley J. Tambiah, 'The Position of Women in Sub-Saharan Africa and North India,' *Current Anthropology,* vol. 30, no.4, August-October 1989, pp. 413-414.

[9] See Alice W. Clark (ed.), *Gender and Political Economy*: *Explorations of South Asian Systems* (Delhi: Oxford University Press, 1993).

Within the capitalist market economies, violence against women can be explained by the necessity for 'ongoing capital accumulation,' which constitutes the precondition for the so-called capital accumulation process.[10]

What is Dowry? The Indian Context

Dowry (*dahez*) has been defined in a number of ways, giving either positive or negative connotations to the custom. In *legal terms*, the Dowry Prohibition Act of 1961[11] defines 'dowry' as 'any valuable or property given "as a consideration for the marriage" or as inducement for marriage.'[12] In *economic terms*, dowry can be defined as 'value of the cost of supporting a woman over a lifetime if female earnings drop to zero and something less if female earnings drop below the cost of subsistence but not all the way to zero.'[13] In *customary terms*, dowry is simply 'a kind of tribute from the bride-giving family to the bride-receiving family.'[14] And in purely *human terms,* dowry 'is a clear manifestation of a structurally hypergamous, non-reciprocal, asymmetric and extractive relationship between a) bride-giving and bride-receiving families, and b) between men and women.'[15] One author defines dowry as 'a passport to a good match, a high status husband and the favour of one's in-laws.'[16]

Dowry is 'the net transfer at the time of marriage from the bride's family to the groom's; the reverse transaction is a "bride-price."'[17] More specifically, dowry is really 'groom-price' that has spread at an outrageous pace despite the laws that prohibit it. This has been attributable to `family' being viewed as a `private' sphere, in which law enforcement agencies are reluctant to interfere, until and unless there is a registered complaint filed against a dowry-related incident. Societal consent to this custom is another reason for the lucid legal response that such heinous incidents deserve.[18]

---

[10] Maria Mies, p. 170.

[11] *Joint Sitting of Houses of Parliament [in India] Debates*, vol. 1, no. 6, May 1961.

[12] The Dowry Prohibition Act was passed in 1961 and amended three times in the 1980s. It forbids 'dowry' but allows 'gifts.' Among the flaws in this law are issues regarding the nature of a 'voluntary' gift and that of a 'dowry' on demand? The law lays out the rule of proportionality, i.e. gifts should not be excessive in relation to the financial status of the person donating, or the person on behalf of whom the donation is given. How are we to decide what is excessive when incomes are not always declared? Many such flaws exist. Many cultural arguments that justify dowry were also presented in this report and were defeated, i.e. Since inheritance is male-oriented, dowry is the only way daughters can receive their share of the inheritance; Dowry allows the man and woman in a relationship to be equal partners; dowry is a return for 'gifts' the husband and his family give the bride. See Madhu Purnima Kishwar, Manushi India, 'Strategies for Combating the Culture of Dowry and Domestic Violence in India,' Division for the Advancement of Women, Expert Group Meeting, UN Division for the Advancement of Women, 17-20 May 2005, Vienna, Austria.

[13] Indira Rajaraman, `Economics of Bride-Price and Dowry', *Economic and Political Weekly*, vol. XVIII, no 23, 4 June 1983, p. 276.

[14] Maria Mies, p. 160.

[15] Maria Mies, p. 161.

[16] Ursula Sharma, *Women, Work and Property in North West India*, London/New York: Tavistock, 1980, p. 53.

[17] Vijayendra Rao, 'The Rising Price Of Husbands: A Hedonic Analysis of Dowry Increases in Rural India,' *Journal of Political Economy*, vol. 101, no 4, p. 666.

[18] There are at present 28 million women from the Indian population who are missing, due either to abortion, infanticide, overwork, under-nourishment or the overall subordinate status of women in society. Despite being a secular parliamentary democracy, highly considerate and respectful of other religions, social customs and family law, some of the most excessive forms of brutality toward women that are so much in evidence have proven resistant to all legal and educational pressures. Conversely, there has been a growth in such outlawed

A typical dowry can be seen as a marriage transaction and the role of gender.[19] Dowry is said to comprise three sub-parts.

> One part, not insubstantial, that the bride may keep as her personal property, the second part, the most substantial, being controlled by the groom's joint family (especially his parents) and susceptible to use as 'circulating goods' in the marriage of its daughters, and the third part meant as gifts to the women of the groom's joint family and his married sisters and father's sisters. The third portion, especially that given to the groom's married sisters and his father's sisters, is in alliance terminology given to the groom's superior 'wife-takers,' the groom's family in turn being superior wife-takers to the bride's family.[20]

This description of the *dahez* shows quite clearly that, in the dowry transactions, a very large number of people are involved in carrying out the custom.

These transactions are not merely divided along gender lines as a gift of wealth from the bride's father to the bridegroom, but the women of the bridegroom's family are equally a part of the demand structure. Feminists view this as the male way to socialize a system in such a way that even the women are made to become agents in the process of give-and-take, and resort to violent means for this purpose. This manifests itself in the typical mother-in-law, daughter-in-law animosities when the 'dowry' from the bride-giver is not `adequate' in the eyes of the groom's family. And these interactions differ along class, caste, religious and societal lines.

Besides the exchange of money and other wealth, dowry has the potential and manifests itself in various other societal ills that perpetuate an inequality and unfairness deeply embedded in the patriarchal society that India represents. Such related incidents include dowry-related murders, suicides, female infanticide (due to the pressure on the bride's family to muster up a dowry), early marriages because of the race for a suitable and economical `deal' in the marriage market,[21] second-rate treatment for single women, rituals such as sati, pressure on women to `produce' sons, differing treatment for the girl child, the psychological feeling of subordination and the 'housewifization' of women's labour.

> Dowry is one of the means to maintain the existing structure of male dominance. As Stanley J. Tambiah puts it,
>
> Seen in its wildest social, political and economic framework, we can say that the Indian valuation of a woman as 'the gift of a virgin,' as auspicious Lakshmi,[22] as a carrier of dowry, and so on, organically fits into the strategies and processes by which, in a multi-caste context suffused with hierarchical concerns and status competition, groups of

practices such as domestic violence in the form of dowry or sati or other discrimination. See Dorothy Stein, 'Burning Widows, Burning Brides' in: 'The Perils of Daughterhood in India,' *Pacific Affairs,* vol. 61, 1988, p. 465.

19 V. T. Oldenburg, *Dowry Murder: The Imperial Origins of a Cultural Crime* (London: Oxford University Press, 2002).

20 Tambiah, pp. 425-26.

21 This implies that the families of older nubile brides are willing to give a larger amount as dowry to outbid the offers made by families of younger brides. The pressure that accompanies this is the preference given to the `virgin bride', which was considered to be the father-of-the-bride's gift (Kanyadan) to the groom. In Brahmanical scriptures, this would ensure spiritual gains to the bride-giver. The essence of this patriarchal schema is the objectification of the bride as being 'property' rather than person. See Maria Mies, pp. 160-161.

22 Lakshmi is the Indian goddess of wealth.

'dominant caste' males dispersed in villages over a region strive to maintain (and increase) their regional dominance through the lateral links of hypergamous marriage and of affinity.[23]

Due to its complex and contradictory nature, a complete study of dowry is possible only by studying the intensity of the problem in the context of the 'Indian patriarchal system, caste system and capitalism.'[24]

A relatively new democracy, with a population of 1.12 billion, a GDP of $805.5 billion and per capita income of US $3,800, India is a rising force in the rapidly globalizing world. Despite its rising status in world politics, education in India continues to be gendered, with literacy rates 73 percent male but only 48 percent female.[25] The flip side of the coin shows a rather dark patriarchal reality of dowry murders and crimes against women in the 'private' realm of the family.[26] Crime statistics are so grossly inaccurate, due to 'silences' at social and cultural levels, that it is meaningless to present them.

While overall crime rates in India are dropping, crimes against women, such as rape, molestation, sexual harassment, dowry harassment, dowry deaths and abduction) are on a steep rise.[27] In India, dowry death rates alone have risen drastically from five per million population, to seven per million population while overall cruelty rates have risen from 31 per million to 45 per million in the last ten years or so. Small differences exist between various States and Union territories, but the overall rise of violence substantiated by official figures is staggering. Despite efforts to reform the status of women in India,[28] deaths due to violence against women are on a steady increase. According to official statistics, over 7,000 women's deaths can be linked to dowry murders.[29] Of course, these official statistics may reveal only the tip of the iceberg, with the iceberg hidden under the fog of an Indian patriarchal system in the heat of capitalism and progress.[30]

---

[23] Tambiah, p. 426.

[24] Maria Mies, p. 160.

[25] The World Bank Group: Gender Stats (2007). Summary gender profile. http://devdata.worldbank.org/genderstats/genderRpt.asp?rpt=profile&cty=IND,India&hm=home (last visited 16 January 2008).

[26] Prasad, B.D. 1994. Dowry-related violence: A content analysis of news in selected newspapers. *Journal of Comparative Family Studies*, 25(1), 71-89. UNIFEM. *Not a Minute More: Ending Violence Against Women* (New York: 2003). UNIFEM. Women's Movement in India. New Delhi: 2003. UNIFEM. Report of the 4th South Asia Regional Meeting. New Delhi: 2004. UNIFEM. ICRW (International Centre for Research on Women). 2004a. *Panchayat Involvement on Violence Against Women*. New Delhi: ICRW. ICRW (International Centre for Research on Women, 2004b. *Violence Against Women in India: A Review of Trends, Patterns and Responses* (New Delhi: UNFPA). ICRW (International Center for Research on Women). 2002. *Domestic Violence in India: Exploring Strategies, Promoting Dialogue*. Washington DC: ICRW.

[27] Singh, K. 2004a. 'Violence against women and the Indian Laws,' pp. 77-147 in: Savitri Goonesekere (ed.). *Violence, Law and Women's Rights in South Asia* (New Delhi: Sage, Centre for Women's Development Studies, 2002). *Crimes Against Women: Bondage and Beyond* (New Delhi: CWDS).

[28] See Mangala Subramaniam, 'A Symposium: Bridging Scholarship: The Indian Women's Movement,' *Contemporary Sociology*, Vol. 33, No. 6, November 2004, pp. 635-639.

[29] CWDS (Centre for Women's Development Studies). 2002. *Crimes against Women: Bondage and Beyond*. New Delhi: CWDS.

[30] Bandana Purkayastha, Mangala Subramaniam, Manisha Desai, Sunita Bose, 'The Study of Gender in India: A Partial Review,' *Gender and Society*, Vol. 17, No. 4, August 2003, pp. 503-524.

DOWRY: ITS ORIGINS

The custom of dowry was associated with the Sanskritic Brahmanical caste, the highest caste in the Hindu hierarchy.[31] One of the explanations for the spread and increase of dowry is that it can be attributed to the process of `sanskritization,' which implies the adoption, by means of imitative behaviour of upper-caste social patterns, of behaviour, values, norms and institutions by lower castes in order to acquire a higher social status.[32] The vital interest that the Brahamins had in this whole system was that being the learned priests, uninvolved in any other work of their hands in which the Kshtriyas, Vaishyas and Shudras were involved, they lived off gifts given to them by the rich as well as the poor who would be spiritually enlightened by these gestures.[33]

The man-woman relationship in the Brahaman caste was that of the gift giver and gift receiver, where the woman gave 'her body, her work, her children, on top of that money and other goods, to her husband, and she receives the "honour" of being a wife.'[34] This makes the woman's worth get weighed up in terms of monetary or materialistic terms, be it the bride price or dowry. The phenomenon is related to the upward mobility, socialization, westernization and sanskritization of classes, dominated by patriarchal attributes.

The male element of society seemingly uses the females in society to transfer as `wealth' or `possession,' in order to further the dynamics of male aspirations. Women and their bodies became more and more `occupied territories', alienated from them to become a part of men's control.[35] This was the divulgence of the patriarchal system of India which subjected a woman to being a daughter first, a sister next, a wife, a mother and lastly, if ever, herself. All these roles demanded from her a certain stereotyped role-playing which sustained the patriarchal patterns of society.[36]

In such a system, then, quite obviously, as Maria Mies points out, 'The relationship between the bride-giving and bride-receiving families is never an egalitarian one. The bride-

---

[31] Dorothy Stein, 'Burning Widows, Burning Brides: The Perils of Daughterhood in India,' *Pacific Affairs*, vol. 61, 1988, p. 475.

[32] Vijayendra Rao, 'Dowry "inflation" in Rural India: A Statistical Investigation,' *Population Studies,* vol. 47, 1993, p. 283.

[33] The Indian caste structure, as chalked out by Manu, was as follows: At the top of the hierarchical lineage were the *Brahamans*, who were the learned people or priests; the next in the line were the *Kshatriyas*, who were the warrior tribe; to follow was the *Vaishya* community who were the businessmen; and at the bottom were the *Shudras* who were mineal workers. See M.N Srinivas, `A Note on Sanskritization and Westernization', *The Far Eastern Quarterly*, vol. XV, November 1955-August 1956, pp. 492-536.

[34] Maria Mies, p. 161.

[35] Maria Mies, p. 25.

[36] Tambiah Stanley, p. 417. See also, Maria Mies, p. 51. Mies criticizes the Freudian statement that 'anatomy is destiny,' and rejects biological determinism. Mies explains that this approach does not take into account the fact that 'unequal, hierarchical and exploitative' relationships are caused by social and historical factors. This approach not only affects the analysis but the tools of analysis such as concepts of nature, labour, sexual division of labour, family and productivity, thereby evading reality. By this approach, women's nature is defined as 'nature' and all the roles and functions that she performs, i.e. child bearing, rearing children, domestic work etc, are considered as extensions of her nature rather than an active interaction of human beings with nature. Such a conception creates a relationship of dominance and exploitation between men and women, with the men dominating nature. Similarly, the work that women perform is not considered a work of labour, which is a concept exclusively used for the productive work by men under capitalist conditions for the production of 'surplus value.'

receiving groom's family has, per definition, a higher status. The relationship between the two families is always an asymmetric, non-reciprocal one.'[37]

An important issue in the entrenchment of the institution of dowry came from the imposition of British rule in India. Despite the general influence of Western ideas and religious pluralism, the British colonialists preferred the legal, textual and Brahmanical discourse which was most sensitive to the incentive system the British laid out for them by making them participate in the governance of colonial India. In doing so, they ignored the diversity that existed in society, constituting a large part of the population who were not Brahamans. This link added to the social status that went with imitating the customs of the higher caste structure, that of the Brahmins.[38] The clash of cultures ushered in Britain's difficulties with India. These difficulties seem to have been a tendentious response to some inherent native problems and preoccupations. According to Stanley J. Tambiah, 'It is possible that both sides dialectically constructed and negotiated a colonial reality shot through with different emphasis, interpretations and misinterpretations.'[39] On the one hand, the paradox of combining modernity and capitalism, which was imposed on pre-capitalist structures of the Indian economy leading to the concentration of wealth in fewer hands, and, on the other hand, the need to hold on to traditions and the Indian identity, led to a sharp rise in dowry transactions. The colonial era also questioned the allegiance of feminists who were, on the one hand, torn between support for their men, country, patriarchal tradition, and families albeit oppressive, and, on the other hand, a fight for liberation, equality and human rights.[40]

The questions that arise are: 'In all the transactions between bride-giver and bride-taker families, the caste system, the patriarchal system, the colonial rule, the religious texts and the societal context, where is the status of the bride, the groom and their individual relationship?' Have changed circumstances changed the status of dowry practices? What is the status of women in India today? Can we really generalize about their status or are they treated differently according to their race, class, status etc? Interestingly, there is an intrinsic risk in appraising the position of women based on any one set of explanations, customs, influences or circumstances. The danger lies in the fact that, depending on the case that one wants to make, women can be construed as being held in either the highest esteem or in the lowest, depending on what gets highlighted. Such explanations can be very misleading and flawed, contributing to the slowing down of the women's movement to make known their oppression and subordination.

---

[37] See Maria Mies, p. 160.

[38] Dorothy Stein, p. 466. What is interesting is that in Bengal, the centre of British rule in India, *sati* (self-immolation by a bride after the death of her husband) was one of the issues which were politicized by the dualistic responses of the 'liberals' (who believed in outlawing *sati*, dowry, discrimination against women, etc.) and the 'conservatives' (who did not want to interfere in native religious practices that lay outside their vital interests) in their struggle for power and status. Yet, at that stage, what provided 'spiritual justification' was the association of such customs with the *Brahaman* tradition.

[39] Tambiah, p. 414.

[40] V. T. Oldenburg, 2002. *Dowry Murder: The Imperial Origins of a Cultural Crime* (London: Oxford University Press). S. Mandal, 'Modernization and Women's Status in India: A Gender in Developmental Perspective on Dowry Deaths, Sex Ratios and Sex-selective Abortion,' Ph.D. dissertation, University of Texas at Austin., 2001.

As Sunder Rajan explains,

> Culture appears as the chief matter and consequence of dominant ideological investment, powerfully coercive in shaping the subject; but since it is also heterogeneous, changing to open interpretation, it can become a site of contestation and consequently of the re-inscription of subjectivities. Therefore cultural analysis both calls forth the critique of ideology, and—given the crucial function of representation in the dialectic of social process—enables political intervention, scenarios of change, theoretical innovation and strategic reinterpretations.[41]

It is thus important to understand the custom of dowry not only from a cultural, societal context but also from a more holistic dimension, taking into account the social, political, economic, psychological, cultural and ever-changing dimensions of the phenomenon.[42]

From a matrilineal society in the remote past to the present-day patriarchal pattern, the position of women has increasingly deteriorated through different periods of history. The reasons that are attributed to the downfall of the status of women in society are 'the imposition of brahmanical austerities on society, foreign invasions of India affecting women's status adversely, the introduction of the non-Aryan wife into the Aryan household ... lack of educational facilities for women, and the role of the caste system and joint family system.'[43]

There has been a steady increase in the cases of dowry in India and South Asia. Since this is not a positive sign, many authors have attempted to explain its causes and effects. One of the causes, as mentioned earlier, is the continuous process of sanskritization, westernization and socialization, adding to the desire of certain castes low in the hierarchy to rise upwards, either by imitating customs, values and practices or by marrying someone from a richer, more well-to-do social background.

Another reason for the steady rise in dowry is even more interesting. Some authors explain that women in India tend to marry older men for reasons of having been brought up to believe that the man you marry is your protector, your guide, your strength, almost substituting for the role that the father played in his daughter's life before her marriage. This signifies the transition of the sphere of control of `woman' from father to husband. When more and more younger women marry more and more older men, there arises a surplus of women over men in the marriage market. This phenomenon is referred to as the `marriage squeeze.' [44] The 'marriage squeeze explains why households with marriageable daughters are willing to endure monetary hardship to find scarce husbands. The degree of `marriage squeeze' depends on 'the rate of population growth, the average age difference between spouses, and the difference in sex-specific mortality schedules.'[45] Conscious reductions in the age differences of the bride and groom may result in a more equivalent status of males and females in the marriage market. The `woman question' in India is very urgent and crucial, because even though India has been politically independent for many years, social and

---

[41] Rajeshwari Sunder Rajan, *Real and Imagined Women: Gender, Culture and Postcolonialism* (London/New York: Routledge, 1993), p. 10.

[42] See Maristella Botticini and Aloysius Siow, 'Why Dowries?' *The American Economic Review*, Vol. 93, No. 4, November 2003, pp. 1385-1398.

[43] Prabhati Mukherjee, *Hindu Women - Normative Models* (New Delhi: Orient Longman, 1978), p .5.

[44] See Lena Edmund, 'The Marriage Squeeze Interpretation of Dowry Inflation: A Comment,' *The Journal of Political Economy*, Vol. 108, No. 6, December 2000, pp. 1327-1333.

[45] Vijayendra Rao, 'Dowry Inflation in Rural India,' *Population Studies*, vol. 47, 1993, p. 285.

economic independence for women is still to catch up with the status of men in this `patriarchal' society.

However, as Maris Mies puts it, 'Women's problems today cannot be explained by merely referring to the old forms of patriarchal dominance.'[46] Therefore, it is important to see that patriarchy and capitalism operate simultaneously and create the latest developments and manifestations of man-woman discriminations[47] by an accumulation of capital on a world scale.

CAPITALIST-PATRIARCHY AND DOWRY

The hypothesis here is that dowry serves as a social phenomenon or custom that culminates in forms of violence against women through personal relations and *housewifization* of their labour, eventually contributing in whatever little way to the system of primitive accumulation of capital.

When one looks at the dynamics of dowry and at the question `Who competes for what?' there are three broad responses. One is that dowry originally led to competition between female-female in order to gain the best mates. This thesis argues that 'males are competitors when bride wealth is given, and females are competitors when they bring dowry into the marriage.'[48] The other explanation is that dowry does lead to female competitiveness but only because it is a competitive tactic to secure a husband with more economic and reproductively relevant resources.[49] A third explanation is that 'Dowry is not a tactic that women use in the competition for reproductive success but one that men use in the competition for social alliances of various kinds.'[50] This is assuming that girls with larger dowries and men with larger bride prices usually marry wealthier spouses.

This hypothesis uses Maria Mies's model of `Patriarchy and accumulation of capital on a world scale: Women in the international division of labour.' A concept central to the understanding of the subordination of the women's movement trans-historically and cross culturally, patriarchy has often been used to explain various phenomena of concern to women

[46] Maria Mies, p. 38.

[47] In the last forty years, there has been a drastic increase in South Asia in the real value of transfers from brides and their families to grooms and their families. The reverse transaction is called 'bride-price' which has seen today a sudden and sweeping switch to dowry. Bride-price usually takes place for a couple of reasons; one, when there is a woman from a matriarchal lineage getting married, she is the sole inheritor of her family property and it is she who then is in the privileged place of superiority, despite her biological role and characteristics; secondly, this is practiced when the groom is from a lower social class, caste or economic stratum and is getting an opportunity to marry into a higher social bracket. He is then paying the price for sanskritization and upward mobility, using the bride as the agent in this transformation. Unfortunately, the system sees a role reversal when the couple gets married, because that re-ignites and re-establishes the patriarchal lineage that society practices, accepts and almost advocates. Other reasons for bride price could be the imbalance in the male-female population ratio, and the situation that obtains when, instead of the marriage squeeze that results from fewer eligible grooms than prospective brides, there are more prospective grooms than brides. A third reason is the practice of female infanticide on a large scale. See Vijayendra Rao, 'Dowry "Inflation" in Rural India: A Statistical Investigation,' *Population Studies*, vol. 47, 1993, p. 283.

[48] Alice Schlegel, 'Dowry: Who Competes for What?' *American Anthropologist*, vol. 95, 1993, p. 155.

[49] Steven J.C. Gaulin and James S. Boster, 'Testing Explanatory Models of Dowry: A Reply to Schlegel,' *American Anthropologist*, vol. 95, 1993, p. 154.

[50] Alice Schlegel, p. 156.

and the women's movement.[51] Mies analyzes the system that she refers to as `capitalist patriarchy,' a system that transcends national and class boundaries and draws a significant relationship between capitalism and patriarchy. She argues that capitalism invariably requires patriarchal appropriation of women's labour for the accumulation of capital, perpetuating a certain status quo. In this context, `dowry' and its related phenomena are examined here as a means of coercion and violence, which are monopolized by men to establish relationships of dominance and exploitation.

Violence against women can neither be explained by pure economic arguments inherent in capitalist supply-demand calculations, nor by biological arguments, but is actually a historically produced phenomenon integrated deeply into the system of accumulation. Dowry as an institution can be considered as a source of wealth that is accumulated by 'extraction, blackmail or violence' rather than by the man's own hard work.[52]

Thus, violence against women is the main common denominator that epitomizes women's exploitation and oppression, irrespective of class, nation, caste, race, capitalist or socialist systems, third world or first world. Violence against women can be explained neither by purely economic arguments inherent in capitalist supply-demand calculations, nor by biological arguments about 'male' nature, but is instead a historically produced phenomenon integrated into the system of accumulation. Despite many ideological differences, the accumulation of capital is based on the expropriation of subsistence producers from their means of production.

Men take on the role of those who own property, which in this case includes the womenfolk who symbolize wealth getters. These men enter into contractual relationships with each other on the basis of the principle of exchange of value equivalents. Women are seen as historical subjects who were once property and thus, could not be themselves owners of property.[53] Thus, the contract of exchange is between the property owners i.e., the bride's father and the bridegroom. Men are considered to hold the means of production, whereas women's first and last means of production is their own body.[54]

For the Indian woman, dowry comes into existence when the economic or productive combination of woman, namely her housework, her child-bearing capacity and her participation in income earning work, is outweighed by the consumptive costs of her husband having to feed and clothe her. Dowry is then just a means to compensate, in part or fully, for a lifetime of subsistence of women in their husband's homes. This attitude stems from the 'housewifization' of women's work.

The central focus of this justification or explanation is that women are assumed to be non-productive dependent housewives, despite the possibility that these women may be working women employed in regular jobs that pay enough, if not more, towards contributing towards subsistence when married in a patriarchal system.

It should also be noted that dowry is a clear example that the capitalist law of exchange of equivalents does not operate when the women's contribution is housework or child bearing or wage work or some sort of gainful employment. What is required to disprove this exchange

---

[51] Roisin McDonough and Rachel Harrison, 'Patriarchy and Relations of Production,' in Annette Kuhn and AnnMarie Wolpe (eds.), *Feminism and Materialism: Women and Modes of Production* (London/Henley/Boston: Routledge and Kegan Paul, 1978), p. 11.

[52] Maria Mies, p. 162.

[53] This is part of the reason attributable to women's not holding the rights to inheritance or voting rights.

[54] Maria Mies, p. 169.

of equivalents is to disregard any distinctions that are drawn between productive and non-productive work. If we were to accept `work' as work, without classifying or categorizing or 'housewifizing'[55] women's work as different and less productive, it would be more than apparent that men depend on women's work much more than men contribute to their wives' subsistence as the breadwinner in the family. Conversely, an increased value attributable to women's labour is largely responsible for the decline in dowry cases. Under the umbrella framework of capitalist patriarchy, the causes of dowry are a consequence of pressures caused by economic transformation, the low economic value of women, the loss of effective social control of abuse through delocalization,[56] and the sexual division of labour, 'housewifization' and violence. However, as Mies explains,

> Whatever the difference between the various production relations through which women are integrated into development, or rather subordinated under the global process of capital accumulation, one thing is clear: this integration does not mean that they become free wage labourers or proletarians. They also do not become free entrepreneurs, in spite of all the rhetoric used by developmental agencies. Nor do they become real housewives. On the contrary, the common feature of all the production and labour relations described above is the use of structural or direct violence and coercion by which women are exploited and super-exploited.[57]

The violence inherent in the patriarchal men-women and class relations led to the extraction of female labour while the housewife producer was faced with the super-exploitation. Dowry lends to both these levels.

Violent techniques against women, it should also be noted were not a class phenomenon restricted to the rural and poor areas but were prevalent even among the educated middle class. Dowry, for instance, as mentioned earlier, pervades the entire social fabric in ways that vary very considerably in terms of violence, its impact and its implications.

Most marriage negotiations require a certain amount of dowry, which for reasons socially constructed by society at large, are followed through in the form of monetary assets, luxury items, or in some rare cases, a regular income. The degree and kind of this dowry almost determine the treatment the bride would receive in her new home. Dissatisfaction leads to a resort to crimes, such as bride-burning or bride-abuse or at least maltreatment, sometimes resulting in the bride/prospective bride committing suicide due to the loss of a sense of `self' and to her attention to ancient societal patterns. Such atrocities are part of India's feudal past.[58] Thus, 'the command over dowry gives all men the chance to get hold of money which

---

[55] See Mies, p. 115. The exclusion of invisible work of women (and men) who are not recognized as engaged in 'productive labor,' or possessing any productive power. Mies refers to this phenomenon as the 'housewifization' of labour which is present not only in the Third World but also in the first two worlds. The international capital uses this strategy of 'housewifization' to integrate women into the worldwide process that splits up the economy into the 'formal' and 'informal sector' and has a patriarchal logic of exploitation to it. This is because of the underlying assumption that women are in the work force temporarily, are thus paid less than their male counterparts, and belong to 'peripheral activities.'

[56] Delocalization implies a situation in which the son leaves home for a bigger city or another country in order to enter higher education. The parents begin to see dowry as the amount to be spent on their son's education so that he can provide subsistence to his wife. This obviously undermines the status of the job for which the women are hired, and from which she earns her income.

[57] Mies, p. 145.

[58] Advances in science, technology and know-how in the field of agriculture bereft the female rural labour force of its status. See Mies, p. 157.

they have not earned and to have access to modern consumer items which they might not otherwise buy. The dowry creates a market for such goods, even among people who have to take up consumption loans in order to secure their survival. It paves the way for the spread of market values and market commodities, even among the poor.'[59]

Conclusion

Incongruence in dowry relationships leads to violence, and violence serves as the common denominator representing some sort of oppression and exploitation transcending barriers of race, class, or nation. The relationships that ensue from dowry affect the production relationships in which women are involved, and are closely knitted to the web of economic arguments, biological debates, social constructs and capitalist demand-supply curves.

Even on a small-scale, grassroots level, dowry contributes indeed to the patriarchal capitalistic system that thrives on violence and subjugation, in various stratifications of social, national and international life. The gender overtones are more than obvious, while the class aspects are all-pervasive, differing only in the nature of dowry transactions that take place. The caste element offers possible changes, in terms of upward (or downward) mobility, while the international network picks up on the thread of `violence' as the common factor, linking the causes of the feminist movements worldwide.

In conclusion, Maria Mies has this to offer:

> ...Violence against women is a historically produced phenomenon that is closely related to exploitative men-women, class and international relations. All these relations are today more or less integrated into the systems of accumulation.[60] These systems of accumulation are either capitalist or market oriented, or they are centrally planned or socialist. Irrespective of the ideological differences, the accumulation of capital in both the systems is based on the expropriation of subsistence producers from their means of production.[61]

The subsistence producers in this case are women, who despite the various means of production that they manage, are nevertheless dispossessed by brutal patriarchs.

Often considered deeply rooted in the society, culture and tradition of Indian marriage systems, the dowry system is not universally unchangeable but rather a custom which has the potential to be changed, remedied and made obsolete. It serves as a constant reminder of how women are oppressed in a socially constructed male-dominated world, offering a vision of a different world consecrated to the general good, to the universal, the just, the fair and the equal.[62]

---

[59] Mies, p. 162.

[60] See Jane Jenson, Elisabeth Hagen and Ceallaigh Reddy (eds.), *Feminization of the Labour Force: Paradoxes and Promises* (New York: Oxford University Press, 1988).

[61] Mies, p. 169.

[62] Nancy J. Holland, *Is Women's Philosophy Possible?* (USA: Rowman and Littlefield, 1990).

INDIA AND ITS UNTOUCHABLES

'Untouchability' was abolished in 1950 under the Indian Constitution, but the concept has not disappeared. The concept refers to the demeaning traditional work that includes manual scavenging of trash and the sweeping and cleaning of human excrement from India's roads and dry latrines. All that has changed is the name: 'Untouchables' are now known as 'Dalits', or 'scheduled castes. The group, however, still falls outside the traditional four-fold caste system. If the Dalits can no longer be legally forced to perform any 'impure' occupation, and if migration and the anonymity of the urban environment have allowed some Dalits some upward mobility, the fact remains that they are still considered by the upper castes as impure and polluting, and the majority of Dalits still find themselves performing their traditional functions.

The reality of the current status of the Dalits was exposed in 2007 in a report, drawn up by Human Rights Watch and the Centre for Human Rights and Global Justice, and submitted to the UN Committee on the Elimination of Racial Discrimination. India's National Human Rights Commission countered that the greatest violator of the human rights of Dalits was India's own law-enforcement machinery.

Another report on Untouchability, submitted in 2007 by India's NHRC to the UN, found that, in almost 80 percent of the villages surveyed, the police had systematically failed to protect Dalit homes and Dalit individuals from acts of looting, arson, sexual assault, torture, and other inhumane acts such as tonsuring (shaving a person's head), stripping and parading of Dalit women, and forcing Dalits to drink urine and eat faeces. Social interaction between Dalits and upper castes was strictly prohibited, and the rights of Dalits to choose their spouses were routinely violated. Dalits who have married 'above' their caste are reportedly forced to break all ties with their families. The report reminded the Indian government that it is bound by its obligations under Article 1 of the UN Convention on the Elimination of all Forms of Racial Discrimination. Article 1 defines 'racial discrimination' as 'any discrimination, exclusion, restriction or preference based on race, colour, descent, or national or ethnic origin which has the purpose or effect of nullifying or impairing the recognition, enjoyment or exercise, on an equal footing, of human rights and fundamental freedom in the political, economic, social, cultural or any other field of public life.' The Indian government responded with the claim that discrimination based on caste falls outside the scope of Article 1 of the Convention. As a result, added the Indian government in its response, the reports submitted to the UN failed to show any instances of failure by the government to address caste-based discrimination. Meanwhile, non-government organizations such as the National Campaign on

Dalit Human Rights and the National Federation of Dalit Women remain very active in campaigning and raising awareness of the human rights of Dalits.[1]

D.W.P.

[1] Rochelle Jones, 'The intersection of caste and women's rights in India,' AWID, 26 October 2007.

In: Crimes Against Women
Editor: David Wingeate Pike
ISBN 978-1-61470-813-1

Chapter 23

THE DALIT WOMEN OF INDIA

Rajeni Chagar

It is a great irony that we try to implement the act through an agency that is perceived as an agency of oppression.

Christodas Gandhi, then Tamil Nadu implementation officer for the Atrocities Act.[1]

On 29 September 2006, in the Bhandara district in Maharashtra, 45-year-old Surekha and her 17-year-old daughter Priyanka, were gang-raped by upper-caste villagers. They were then paraded naked and, with Surekha's two sons, 23-year-old Sudhir and 21-year-old Rahul, all four were lynched. The men accused of these attacks have not yet been charged with any crime. Throughout the region tensions exploded, with Dalits, or Untouchables, angry at the Maharashtra government's laxity in protecting their rights, while upper-caste villagers continued to commit acts of violence against them. In response to the government's failure to protect them, Dalit groups reacted by burning tires, blocking the busy Mumbai-Howrah national highway, pelting stones at state transport buses and engaging in other large-scale disorders across the state.

Such incidences of violence against Dalits in India, far from uncommon, have forced the Indian state to address this complex problem of inequality through legal measures. Yet, even with protection policies in place, the state is still plagued by a rigid social hierarchy that types Dalits as outcasts of society. Currently, there are approximately 250 million Dalits living in India and, unfortunately for the majority of them, their 'untouchable' status defines their social position and quality of life. Caste violence in the Indian context has generally been understood as violence by upper-caste members against the Dalit community. Violence against Dalit women continues to escalate in India despite commitments to equality and legislative measures by the central government. The number of murders and rapes committed against Dalit women has increased since the early 1990s, being no doubt an attempt by upper-caste community members to quash the growing Dalit rights movement.

Socio-economic vulnerability, especially for a Dalit, exposes Dalit women to extra violence and exploitation. The interaction of caste and gender has a significant impact on the

---

[1] Human Rights Watch, '*Broken People: Caste Violence Against India's "Untouchables"*' New York: Human Rights Watch, 1999.

quality of life of Dalit women as they remain politically invisible, economically deprived, and socially excluded. The essential dilemma of this chapter concerns the inadequate enforcement of the 1989 Prevention of Atrocities Act, supposedly a demand for accountability in governance while in fact it leaves Dalit women even more vulnerable to acts of violence. Indeed, Dalit women have come to recognize that the state, far from protecting them, exposes them by its failure to hold the perpetrators to account. In these circumstances, Dalit women are driven to seeking their own protection.

The Caste System and 'Untouchability'

The Hindu caste system, made up of a rigid hierarchy, maintains that a person is born into one of four castes, predetermined before birth on the basis of purity and karma, in other words, how one lived in her or his past life. The first of these castes is the *Brahmins* (priests and teachers), the second is the *Ksyatriyas* (rulers and soldiers), the third is the *Vaisyas* (merchants and traders), and the fourth is the *Shudras* (artisans and labourers). Within the four castes, there are many sub-castes that are defined by one's place of birth, by dialect and by profession. A certain category, the Dalits or 'untouchables,' falls outside of the caste structure. Caste identities begin from birth and cannot be changed in one's lifetime. The Dalits (now officially known as the Scheduled Caste) are outcasts and deemed unworthy to be part of the caste system; they are considered too 'impure' and 'polluted' to qualify as a caste. According to the 2001 Census of India, Scheduled Castes represent 16.2 percent and Scheduled Tribes 8.2 percent of the population.[2] These groups, alongside the *Shudras* (now known as Other Backward Class), account for more than 52 percent of India's Hindu population, while Brahmins constitute only between 3 and 5 percent of the same.

The Invisible Women

Dalit women are faced with a triple oppression: their status as women serves to marginalize them, but their class status and their social position as Dalit women further intensify the brutal nature of exploitation, abuse and trauma. Dalit women are beaten and raped should their family members disobey or challenge higher authorities, namely police, shopkeepers or the local Brahmins. Again, the state fails to hold accountable those who are responsible for these acts of violence. Cases reported of Dalit women being raped because of actions that their husbands took against upper-caste villagers are common, but accountability and justice for those women remain to be seen. There are daily reports of beatings, bondage, burnings, rapes, torture, and everywhere denial of their basic rights. There are also numerous reports of police abuses against Dalits, and up to now the state has failed to provide any form of substantive justice for up to a quarter of its population. Lityati,[3] a Dalit woman who migrated from Bihar to Punjab, recalls her experience of abuse:

---

[2] Government of India, *Census of India: Area Profile*. 2001. http://www.censusindia.gov.in/Census_Data_2001/Census_Data_Online/Area_Profile/India_Profile.aspx.

[3] Her name has been changed to protect her identity.

> One time I was so sick, I couldn't work. I had a bad fever. I had chills and could not work for a few days. When I went to work, they [the employer] came and started screaming at me, calling me a *pan choth*, an 'untouchable,' these sorts of names. This is the sort of stuff I grew accustomed to. I told my husband of this, and he was very angry, so he went to the police to file a complaint of abuse. The police did not take his statement, and they turned him away and said he should go back to work. The police came to my employer's house and told him my husband had been there to see them. My employer came and grabbed me and started to beat me. He beat me so much, he broke my leg. That was two years ago, I have switched employers now, but my leg is still broken. See, I cannot walk the same.[4]

It is evident that the state is plagued by a social hierarchy that designates Dalits to be socially inferior, making their rights as Indian citizens irrelevant. As a community they are ostracized, and as a result they are refused permission to attend the same temples, to use the same glassware in the outdoor tea stalls, or to drink from the same water wells as upper-caste members. Furthermore, since 'untouchables' are placed at the lowest end of the social hierarchy, they are offered employment only in the most menial and 'unclean' of tasks: such work as clearing away dead animals, cleaning latrines by hand, farming at the lowest level, and even scavenging. Without a doubt, the Hindu caste structure has created an inescapable cycle of poverty, marginalization, and oppression.

Caste, gender and class all condition the way that Dalit women are treated by local community members and the state. Many young Dalit women are forced to become 'female servants of god' through the religious practice of *devadasis*, which forces them to have sexual relations with upper-caste members. As they get older, they are eventually sold to urban brothels. Dalit women are constantly subjected to sexual assault by local upper-caste villagers and by employers, landlords, and police officers. With little hope of justice, these women are fearful of reprisal if they should report the crimes. Most reports of violence and sexual assault are either dismissed or are classified as false by the police.

'Anti-Discrimination' Practices by the Indian State

The framers of the Indian Constitution (1950) afforded all Indians a single citizenship in which every citizen has the same legal rights and enjoys the same privileges. These formal, constitutionally protected rights need, however, to be examined, as it is evident through India's social hierarchy that all citizens are not considered equal as long as caste status, gender, religion and place of birth determine a citizen's rights to protection by the State. A number of Articles in the Indian Constitution are designed to protect and ensure the safety and security of India's most marginalized group. Article 14 ensures that the State shall not deny any person equality before the law or the equal protections of the laws. Article 15 of the Indian Constitution ensures that the State shall not discriminate against any citizen on grounds of religion, race, caste, sex, or place of birth. In addition, Article 17 states that 'untouchability' is abolished and that its practice in any form is forbidden. It is nevertheless evident that these articles are dismissed as irrelevant, not only by local community members but also at the levels of the central and state governments; the cultural norms and practices of

[4] Interview conducted with Lityati Kumar in Punjab, India on 23 December 2005.

adherence to the caste-class-gender hierarchy hold greater authority than does constitutional law.

Two main formal laws have been enacted to protect Dalit persons from their 'untouchable' status. The first is the Scheduled Castes and Scheduled Tribes (Prevention of Atrocities) Act, 1989. The Act is focused primarily on the exploitative and oppressive social hierarchy that denies members of the Dalit community fair and equal access to their state-protected rights. On behest of the central government, the state-level government is required to take measures as may be necessary for the effective implementation of the Act. The second is the Employment of Manual Scavengers and Construction of Dry Latrines (Prohibition) Act of 1993, which contends that all states must eliminate the dehumanizing practice of employing persons as manual scavengers of human excreta as well as builders of dry latrines, mainly considered a Dalit occupation. The central government has determined such work to be dehumanizing, not because of the labour intensive nature of the occupations, but rather, because of the hierarchal structure in which occupations are distributed, wherein this work is considered to be beneath the other castes.

While these Articles and Acts are formally recognized by all of the state-level governments, as well as the central government, it is evident that the Indian Government has shown no will, no driving determination to put an end to the discrimination and violence that are daily concerns for Dalit women. The state-level government, through an appointed authority, is to ensure that the provisions of these Acts are carried out. The terms of equality for all and for all equal treatment are given mere lip-service.[5] There is not as yet the moral resolution to enforce the strict application of the law.

Notions of high caste and low caste, masculinity and femininity, wealth and poverty have a monumental impact on the quality of a Dalit woman's life. Since the central and state-level governments have failed to respond to the exploitation and violence that pervades the lives of Dalit women, many Dalits have redefined the law for themselves in order to provide security to their community. Dalits have begun to retaliate, as shown in the train bombings in Mumbai in 2006, to demonstrate that violence will be met with violence until they are recognized as equal citizens.

Corruption occupies a great place in the Indian state. State corruption has led to a lack of governmental transparency, accountability and implementation of policies afforded to Dalit women. Probity in public life and good governance are mere slogans espoused by political parties in order to maintain their image status as the 'least corrupt.' In the Indian context today, corruption is linked with power; many politicians and law enforcement officials have therefore adopted a cynical attitude towards political morality.[6] Once more, Dalit women must turn towards their own community for support and the redressing of injustice.

---

[5] Ratna Kapur and Brenda Cossman, 'On Women, Equality and the Constitution: Through the Looking Glass of Feminism,' in *Gender and Politics in India*, ed. Nivedita Menon (New Delhi: Oxford University Press, 1999), 199.

[6] R. Upadhyay, 'Political Corruption in India: An Analysis,' *South Asia Analysis Group*. Paper 219, (March 2001).

Conclusion

In May 2007, The United Nations Committee on the Elimination of Racial Discrimination (CERD) concluded, on the basis of reports submitted by India under Article 9 of the convention, that despite the formal abolition of 'untouchability' *de facto* segregation of Dalits persists, particularly in places of worship, housing, hospitals, education, water sources, markets and other public places. In particular, the Committee noted the ongoing atrocities committed against Dalit women and the 'culture of impunity for perpetrators of such atrocities.' There are still an alarming number of allegations of acts of sexual violence against Dalit women, committed by men from dominant castes; many Dalit women are victims of sexual exploitation and are repeatedly raped, trafficked and eventually forced into prostitution. A large number of Dalit women, forced to work as manual scavengers, are subject to extremely unhealthy working conditions and exploitative labour arrangements. Despite existing provisions in the central government's legislation to protect Dalit women from acts of violence, the police still fail to register and investigate complaints about acts of violence and discrimination. Reports registered under the Scheduled Castes and Scheduled Tribes (Prevention of Atrocities) Act of 1989[7] show low rates of conviction and a high percentage of acquittals.

The elimination of caste discrimination in India is now the focus of a wide variety of NGOs. One such organization is the National Campaign on Dalit Human Rights that works to bring attention to the plight of the Dalit people and the practices of the Indian state that deny them their basic human rights.[8] The organization recently reported that more than 99 percent of crimes against Dalits are committed with impunity. In 39 percent of cases of violence, the victims do not seek legal redress out of fear for their family, lack of support and lack of faith in the judicial process. They also note that in 18 percent of the cases reported, the police have been found to threaten the victim, with the result that the victim refuses to file the complaint.

In recent years, many Dalit women have mobilized in their local villages, with the assistance of NGOs, to bring the plight of Dalit people to the attention of the international community and to document the atrocities they continue to endure. The ultimate goal is to abolish this caste social hierarchy and eliminate caste-gender-class based discrimination. It is only when the government begins to hold accountable those accused of caste violence that Dalit women can finally become visible members of the Indian state.

---

[7] Committee on the Elimination of Racial Discrimination, *International Convention on the Elimination of all forms of Racial Discrimination*. May 2007. http://www2.ohchr.org/english/bodies/cerd/docs/CERD.C.IND.CO.19.doc.

[8] The National Campaign on Dalit Human Rights, *Women's Rights Overview*. 2007. http://www.ncdhr.org.in/ncdhr/campaigns/womensrights/.

BANGLADESH

Despite its signature in 1984 to the Convention on the Elimination of All Forms of Discrimination against Women, and despite the laws it subsequently introduced (the Acid Crimes Control Act of 2002 and the Suppression of Violence Against Women and Children Act of 2003), Bangladesh remains among the countries with the highest levels of physical and sexual violence. In 2005, according to the World Health Organization, 57.5 percent of women fell victim to such violence.[1] Although Bangladesh's Constitution recognizes gender equality in all spheres of public life, it also recognizes religious personal laws[2] (governing marriage, divorce, child custody and inheritance) that deny the very concept of equality.[3]

In a society with a strong patriarchal tradition such as Bangladesh, not many women can summon up the courage to fight against their oppressors. They prefer to remain silent, softly crying in lonely places, allowing a callous system to continue. Taslima Nasrin is one of those whose story is shared by millions but one of the few courageous enough to stand up against oppressive custom and tradition. As a Bangladeshi journalist, she became known in the late 1980s for her articles denouncing the discrimination against women in certain Asian countries. In 1994 Muslim fundamentalists called for her execution by hanging, and the government itself charged her with insulting the religious feelings of the people. As a result, she was forced to flee from Bangladesh. Despite continued death threats from the fundamentalists, she continues to fight for a new civil code in her country, a code based on gender equality and secular education. While most of her books, including her memoirs, have been banned by the Bangladeshi government, in 2004 she was awarded the prestigious Unesco-Madanjeet Singh Prize for the Promotion of Tolerance and Non-violence. In her acceptance speech at the ceremony held at Unesco in Paris on 16 November 2004, she cried out for change: 'For centuries, women have been taught that they are slaves of men, that they are not supposed to protest against the patriarchal system, that they must remain silent against their abusers…. Through my writing, I tried to encourage women to fight for their rights and

---

[1] 'MDGF-1706: Joint UN Programme to Address Violence against Women in Bangladesh,' MDG Achievement Fund (8 June 2007): http://sdnhq.undp.org/opas/en/proposals/suitable/203.

[2] Personal laws are those laws that govern a particular religious community and apply to the regulation of that community and its adherents.

[3] Sharmeen A. Farouk, Bangladesh National Women Lawyers Association, 'Violence against women: a statistical overview, challenges and gaps in data collection and methodology and approaches for overcoming them,' experts meeting organized by UN Division for the Advancement of Women in collaboration with the Economic Commission for Europe and the World Health Organization on 11-14 April 2005, Geneva Switzerland: http://www.un.org/womenwatch/daw/egm/vaw-stat-2005/docs/expert-papers/Farouk.pdf.

freedom…. I have cried loudly for equality and justice, justice for all people whatever their religion and gender.' Up to the present Nasrin has had to live in exile, an outcast from her home, but her voice, calling for rational, logical thinking against blind, irrational faith, has become a symbol of courage for many women around the world. In the words of Nasrin, the diversity of our world's many religions, languages, cultures and ethnicities is not a pretext for conflict but is a treasure that enriches us all.

D.W.P. and Irina Massovets

In: Crimes Against Women
Editor: David Wingeate Pike
ISBN 978-1-61470-813-1

Chapter 24

ACID ATTACKS IN BANGLADESH

Mahera Khaleque

INTRODUCTION

Although violence against women is universal, the degree and form of violence varies from society to society. The phenomenon of acid attack is a form that occurs particularly in South Asian countries such as Pakistan, Bangladesh, and India, with some sporadic cases in Afghanistan and Iran. In focusing this chapter on Bangladesh, the author draws from her experiences in that country in 1999, when she had the opportunity to meet and speak with some victims of acid attack, together with their family members, doctors, and members of a women's rights organization in Dhaka that works closely with the survivors. The author is also an artist whose paintings (reproduced here) reflect on the horror of this form of gender violence. For the past decade, acid attack has been a popular way of expressing the anger or frustration of men in Bangladesh. Although it occurs mostly outside the capital and the big cities, the number of attacks points to an epidemic of gender violence.

ACID THROWING AND ITS RESULTS IN PHYSICAL AND PSYCHOLOGICAL TRAUMA

Acid attack is one of the most dreadful of all crimes perpetrated against women, since it disfigures the victim for life. The acids chosen are of concentrated sulfuric, nitric or hydrochloric substance that causes the skin tissue to melt, often exposing the bones below the flesh, sometimes even dissolving the bone. A single drop of these concentrated acids, thrown in the eyes, is enough to damage the victim permanently. The effect is to debilitate and handicap the victim in every conceivable way.

Most of the victims are young, between the ages of 13 and 30. Recovery from the physical trauma alone consumes most of their remaining lives, but the victims are traumatized also both socially and psychologically. Veils, gloves and socks are powerless to conceal the severity of their injuries. Their physical appearance damages their self-esteem while it seriously undermines their professional and personal future. Most survivors are forced to abandon their education or occupation or any other important activity in their lives. Even if the victims should think of starting on a career, very rarely can they think of a social or married life, as they are themselves scared to look at their faces in the mirror. They have little chance of meeting new people, making new friends, and, if unmarried, they have no chance of ever entering into a romantic or matrimonial relationship.

In the case of Bangladesh, the first documented case of acid violence was reported in 1967,[1] and the current wave of attacks against women began in 1992. In 1999 the Dhaka office of UNICEF reported 200 cases of such attacks, adding that many cases go unreported. Figures since then show some improvement, from 485 in 2002, to 410 in 2003, to 332 in 2004, to 267 in 2005,[2] and this downward trend has continued since.[3] In 2004, some 5,000 people, including hundreds of Bangladeshi men, took part in a rally in Dhaka to denounce acid attacks and other violence against women. The rally drew not only the survivors but many well-known cricketers, film-stars, educators, writers, civil leaders and human rights organizations.

The Perpetrators

The most trivial reason can be proffered to justify the crime of throwing acid. Refusal of a marriage proposal, rejection of a suitor, dispute over property, giving birth to a baby girl, tardiness in the preparation of the evening meal are among the justifications thrown out alongside the acid. In a few cases the victim is male. The use of acid to obtain revenge, according to Shakespeare Shil,[4] has become increasingly more acceptable in society.

The Victims

The author of this chapter has interviewed survivors in the Burn Unit of Dhaka Medical College Hospital. Parveen, just 14 years of age, was attacked by a neighbour with concentrated sulfuric acid. Her crime was to have refused a romantic relationship with a man who declared: “If I can’t have her, no one can!” Sitting beside her bed, Parveen’s mother showed the author a photograph, taken only a few months earlier, of her daughter posing like an appealing movie star. At the same moment a nurse came to check on the breathing tube in Parveen’s burnt throat. Her right eye had been melted by acid. While the distressed mother did what she could to comfort her suffering daughter, a silent tear dropped from the girl’s remaining eye.

On the author’s third visit to the Dhaka Burn Unit, she saw Sabera, aged 23, already struggling with her own intense physical pain, mourning the death of her six-month-old daughter. Her husband had poured acid both on her and on their daughter, who died a few hours later. The husband and his family declared their desire for a baby boy, not a baby girl.

[1] Bangladesh International Community News, 1999.
[2] Acid Survivors Foundation.
[3] ‘Au Bangladesh, le difficile combat contre les attaques à l’acide,’ 24 November 2008: http://www.la-croix.com/article/index.jsp?docId=2356979&rubId=786.
[4] Ibid.

A relative mentioned to the author that Sabera's elder sister had gone through a similar tragedy when she was attacked by her husband for her father's failure to comply with his constant demand for a dowry.

The Availability of Acids

Acid is easily and widely available on the open market; a medium-sized bottle is sold for about 60 cents. The acids are needed for various reasons in jewelry factories, hardware stores and many other small businesses. The government refers to regulations on the import, sale, use, storage, and export of acids, but even if all the trades were regulated, the amount of acid that can be found in an old car-battery is more than enough to disfigure a person. When acid is used for so many purposes, how is it possible to check on the buyers' intentions?

The Treatment of the Victims

The suffering of acid victims is compounded by the expensive, albeit mediocre, treatment facilities in the developing countries. The only treatment for burnt skin is the excruciatingly painful process of skin grafting, which aims at reassembling the natural skin surface through numerous surgical operations. Although grafting helps to reconstruct the mutilated skin, it is virtually impossible to return the skin surface to its original state.

Bangladesh is one of the world's poorest countries and it lacks specialized burn units. Even if there were more, the cost of treatment would be beyond the reach of most victims. At Dhaka Medical College, even seriously burnt patients have to wait for years to get admission and treatment.[5] The College's Burn Unit has only eight beds for all its female patients. It has no modern equipment. The patients are bathed in the same bathtub; their dressings are often changed by the maids who clean the floor. Doctors can perform only the most basic reconstructive surgery, in a one-hour operation costing several hundred dollars in a country where the average income is $25 a month. Most acid-attack victims need several surgical operations, with each lasting four to five hours.[6]

The Laws, their Application and Non-application

The Bangladesh Women's Directorate, which prosecutes on behalf of the victims, also runs a center to provide shelters for the survivors. The survivors and their family members are constantly under threat of death from the violators if they refuse to withdraw their lawsuits.

In 2002, when the number of victims of acid-throwing for the previous year had risen to nearly 500, the crime became punishable by death. But in 2004 no fewer than 267 people fell victim to the crime, and campaigners attributed it to the failure to enforce the law. Salma Ali, a lawyer with the Bangladesh National Women Lawyers' Association, describes the law as

[5] Shil, 1999.
[6] Chung, 1999.

'just like a dead law.'[7] Lawyers in Bangladesh continue to call for better implementation of the existing laws.

The prevalence of violence against women in Bangladesh can be easily attributed to the weakness of a society in which a large part of the population is uneducated and accepts these practices without questioning them. Using ignorance as the chief religious weapon, barely educated priests empower men over women through their dubious religious teachings. Their teachings are taken seriously, and they work to the clear advantage of the men. The law enforcement groups, deep in corruption, fail to act against the wealthy and the powerful, who, for their own advantage, often shelter the violators and demand their release from prison.

Bangladesh, one of the poorest of nations, is an example of a male-dominating society with a high level of illiteracy and an even higher level of male indifference to the suffering of women. By failing to take appropriate action, the Bangladesh government encourages such crimes. The violators are often sheltered by 'higher connections,' and roam free without fear of punishment. A responsibility thus rests on the donor nations on whom Bangladesh depends for its international funding to exert more pressure on the government in Dhaka to act against this hideous crime. Meanwhile, many of the survivors of acid-attacks now serve heroically as counselors to the new victims, teaching them how they themselves survived. As such, they represent the spirit of hope and moral strength.

PAINTINGS

Symbols in the Author's Paintings

Symbols such as masks and raised hands serve as ambiguous signs. Masks may be used as metaphors for hiding events, issues, or people (painting entitled *Claustrophobia*). They are the voice of those who are silenced, of those who want the violence to stop; in some cases, of those who want the silence and the violence to continue, so that the violators and the corrupt authorities can hide their faces and pass freely under the mask of hypocrisy. Women in masks represent the acid survivors who cannot denounce the powerful violators. The hands are a metaphor for protection, for a demand that the oppression stop. The animal-like mask image is a reminder of the animal instinct in human beings (painting entitled *Grafting*).

The use of symbols containing assorted meanings is similar to the use of layers of paints denoting complex human emotions. The concept of layering is also reminiscent of the layers of skin that cover flesh and bone, as well as the excruciatingly painful process of skin grafting. The sewing of human skin is similar to the craft of quilting, a favorite pastime of women in many parts of the world. The sewing of quilts expresses creative ideas and human stories, while a grafted body hides scars and pain. The stitches across the surface of the paintings symbolize the physical reality. The sewing of the bodies becomes the sewing of the quilts (painting entitled *Pomegranate*). The artist writes: 'My emotions found a spontaneous expression through the process of creating art. The subject matter itself, the application of paints, the rugged textured surfaces—all of which are my conscious aesthetic choices—became a catharsis for my emotions.'

[7] BBC Dhaka, 28 July 2006.

Painting entitled *Claustrophobia.*

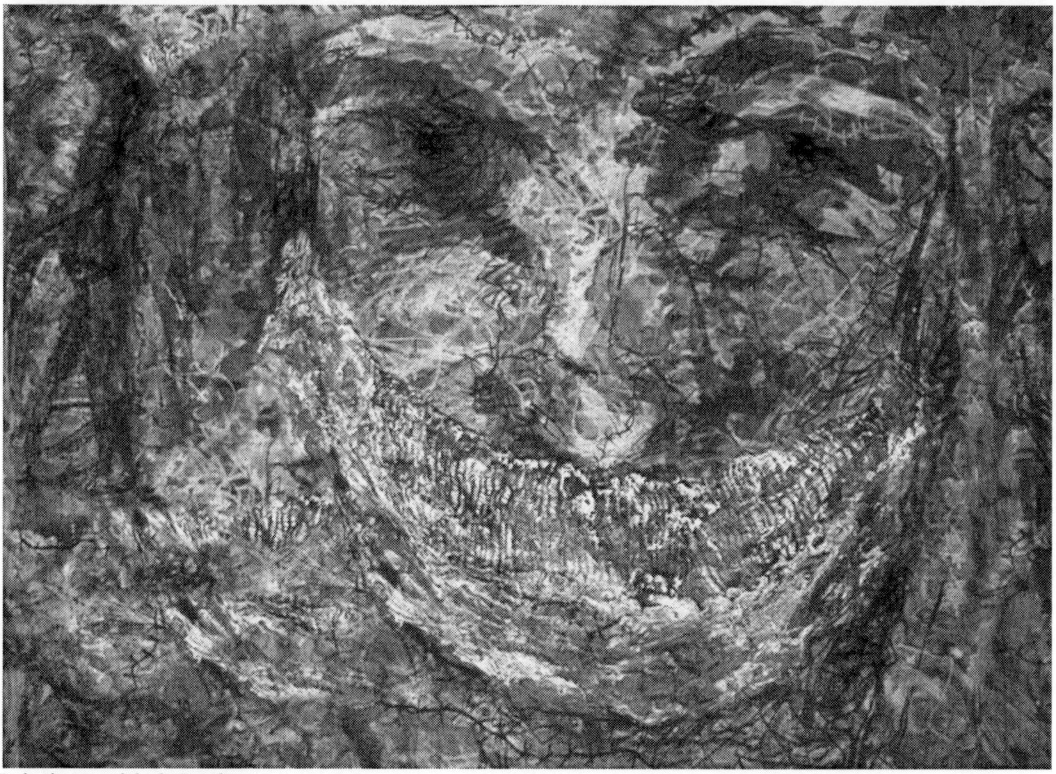

Painting entitled *Grafting.*

Painting entitled *Pomegranate.*

REFERENCES

BBC Dhaka. 'Bangladesh's acid attack problem,' 28 July 2006. Available at: http://news.bbc.co.uk/2/hi/south_asia/5133410.stm.

BBC News (World: South Asia). 'Joyous homecoming for acid attack victims,' 22 July 1999. Available at: http://news.bbc.co.uk/2/hi/south_asia/401093.stm.

BICN (Bangladesh International Community News) Available at: http://www.bicn.com/ezine/features/lifeinbgd/acidsurvivors.htm.

Chung, Connie. 20/20 ABC news, 1999. Available at: http://www.acidsurvivors.org/html/PressLinks/acidvictims_faces%20of%20Hope.htm.

Feminist News, 8 May1998. 'Men burn women with acid in Bangladesh.' Available at: http://www.feminist.org/news/newsbyte/uswirestory.asp?id=3593. This article is based on an original in *The Economist,* 16 February 1998.

Schmetzer, Uli (*Chicago Tribune* Foreign Correspondent, 31 January 1999). News from Bangladesh: 'Acid ruins women's faces and their dreams.' Available at: http://www.acidsurvivors.org/html/PressLinks/Women%20and%20Global%20Human%20Rights.htm.

Shil, Shakespeare. (1999). 'Men use acid to scar Bangladeshi women who say No.' Available at: http://www.geocities.com/HotSprings/Bath/5900/menuseac.htm.

V-Day: Acid Attacks as Defined by UNICEF. Available at: http://www.vday.org/contents/violence/glossary/acidattacks.

In: Crimes Against Women
Editor: David Wingeate Pike

ISBN 978-1-61470-813-1

Chapter 25

THE JHUMMA WOMEN IN BANGLADESH

Anonymous

In a little known region of Bangladesh called the Chittagong Hill Tracts (CHT), human rights abuses have been perpetrated for several decades.[1] The CHT is a lush landscape of bamboo jungles and banana groves, comprising seven valleys and several rivers. Peopled historically by tribal communities that subsist on local *jhumming* (slash and burn) agriculture, it is a culturally and religiously heterodox region composed of approximately twelve tribal communities who practise the Buddhist, Hindu, Christian and animist faiths.[2] Until the 1940s, the CHT was part of colonial India, governed by semiautonomous local chieftains or minor 'princes' as British administrators dubbed them.

Among these *jhumma* communities, the Buddhist Chakmas make up the largest ethnic and religious group. They have lived in the region for several hundred years, through medieval Muslim imperialism and British colonialism, and claim descent from the Shakya Buddhist line of Gautama Buddha.[3] At the time of Partition in 1947, the peoples of the Hill Tracts voluntarily opted through plebiscite to join secular India. Instead, due to the conflicts of geographic contiguity, the region was placed within the political boundaries of a largely Islamic nation, known then as East Pakistan.

With the creation of Pakistan and later the birth of Bangladesh in 1971, the Chakma Buddhists suffered ethnocide and genocide. During the Bangladesh war for independence, the *jhumma* people's alleged 'indifference' and support of West Pakistan made them a target, and with the subsequent arrival in 1975 of a far more fundamentalist Islamic centre, the region became fully militarized.[4] In addition, due to the 1960 development scheme of the Kaptai hydroelectric dam project, funded by American multinational companies and international aid institutions, some 100,000 indigenous people were forced off their lands and fled as refugees to India and Burma/Myanmar. Forty percent of the region's arable land was inundated and

---

1 Amena Mohsin, *The Politics of Nationalism: The Case of the Chittagong Hill Tracts, Bangladesh* (Dhaka: The United Press Limited, 1997), 11.

2 Philip Gain, 'Life and Nature at Risk' in: *The Chittagong Hill Tracks: Life and Nature at Risk* (Dhaka: Society for Environment and Human Development, 2000), 4-8.

3 Raja Tridiv Roy, *The Departed Melody* (Islamabad: PPA Publications, 2003), 28.

4 Mohsin, 164-167.

countless flora, fauna and wildlife, including the Bengal tiger, leopard, panther, bison, sambur, and barking deer, have disappeared.[5]

In addition, as part of a nationalist purification process, the Bangladesh government has encouraged the migration to the CHT of plains-dwelling Bengali Muslims. This policy of resettlement is quickly changing the demography of the region, with more and more Bengali Muslims presenting themselves as candidates for seats in local and national assemblies.

The crimes against tribal women, including murder, massacre, gang rape, coerced marriage and forced conversion to Islam, are particularly egregious. Since 1980, there have been eleven major massacres of the *jhumma* people (the last being noted in 1995). The chart below provides an illustration of the tactics used by the Bangladeshi army and the nature of these armed encounters. These incidents include the Kaukhali-Kalampati massacre on 25 March 1980, when fifty Hill people were gunned down. The military had assembled the villagers, supposedly to discuss the building of a Buddhist temple, when the gunfire erupted. The Barkal massacre on 31 May 1984, which involved a brigade and battalion of the Bangladesh army as well as Bengali settlers, killed 110 villagers, including women and children. During the Panchari massacre on 1 January 1986, army officers and Bengali settlers killed hundreds more; their homes were burnt down and thousands fled to neighbouring Tripura in India. In the Matiranga massacre in May 1986, seventy Hill men were killed by the Bangladesh army. Another two hundred tribal people were gunned down in the Comillatilla-Taindog massacre in August 1986 while they were crossing over to India. During the Hirachar, Sarbotali, Khagrachari and Pablakhali massacres in August 1988, hundreds more Hill people were killed and many women gang raped. In the Longdu massacre in April 1989, the army, a paramilitary group and Bengali settlers killed thirty more people, burnt homes and destroyed Buddhist temples in the area.[6] The Logang massacre of 1992 marked the largest massacre in a single day, with the military killing well over 400 people, hacking the men to death and forcing the remaining women, old people and children into their homes to be burnt alive. This resulted in the flight of more than 2,000 people across the border to Tripura in India.[7]

Once the military began searching for the indigenous guerrilla resistance in the form of Shanti Bahini rebels, the rape of young women and girls became commonplace. Forced conversions and marriages were also common.[8] In 1990, a survey carried out at an Indian refugee camp noted that one in every ten of the women who had fled the Hill Tracts had been raped, and that the military were responsible for 94 percent of these cases. Of the victims, over 40 percent were girls under 18 years of age.[9] By sexually assaulting a tribal woman, the army was committing, in the eyes of the *jhumma* community, a violation against both the individual and the entire community.[10]

That the Bangladesh army has been responsible for the detention and torture of the *jhumma* people has been reported by Amnesty International. Women in particular have been the targets, especially in retribution if they are related to men opposed to the regime. In 1996,

[5] Gain, 37.
[6] Mohsin, 182-183.
[7] Ibid.
[8] Gain, 40.
[9] Hill Women's Federation. Leaflet distributed on the occasion of the NGO Forum on Women, 4th UN Conference on Women, Beijing, 30 August–10 September 1995.
[10] Mohsin, 178.

the case of Kalpana Chakma resulted in a particularly loud outcry. Chakma was only 23 years old and a first-year graduate student at Baghaicchari College; she was also the organizing secretary of the Hill Women's Federation, which was fighting for the rights of indigenous women. On 19 March of that year, her village was targeted in an operation conducted by a local unit commanded by Lieutenant Ferdous; in their search for men belonging to the Shanti Bahini they set fire to seven houses. Incensed by the scene, she protested to the lieutenant, who afterwards routinely patrolled her house. Despite the threats, she soldiered on, until, on the following 12 June, she disappeared, apparently kidnapped by military personnel. She was never seen again, and although no clear evidence has been obtained it is commonly believed she died in the hands of the military. Her abductors still remain at large.[11] Her family and friends believe her abduction was a form of revenge by the lieutenant for her resistance.[12] In her diary, which was found after her disappearance, she had written these words of courage:

> When a caged bird wants to be free, does it mean that she wants freedom for herself alone? Does it also mean one must necessarily imprison those who are already free? I think it is natural to expect the caged bird to be angry with those who imprisoned her. But if she understands that she has been imprisoned in a cage and that cage is not her rightful place, then she has every right to claim the freedom of the skies![13]

Other abuses against women were related not to sexual violence but to psychological coercion. The writer Meghna Guhathakurta describes the predicament of a tribal girl who was harassed by a Bengali officer into a forced marriage. A captain in the division that was posted in the vicinity of the village frequently visited the school with some of his friends. His orders were that two or three girls of class eight and nine should parade in front of him each day so that he could pick one of them as his bride. He took a liking to a girl called Shikha and bothered her continuously by going to her house. Shikha had no desire to marry the captain, but he with some friends would disturb her and threaten her parents and neighbours to the point that they were coerced to make Shikha consent to marry him. When the wedding took place, the army forced the villagers to attend. They gave a big feast and deliberately cooked two different types of menu: *biryani* and beef for the Muslims and pork for the Chakmas. After their marriage it was reported that the captain would make Shikha wear traditional Chakma attire, thus showing everybody that he was respectful to her tradition.[14]

Chakma women have also suffered as a result of the deterioration in religious tolerance throughout the region. Army personnel have offended local communities by entering Buddhist temples wearing shoes, requiring military approval of religious ceremonies, and making it difficult for the faithful to travel on pilgrimage to distant temples.[15] This particularly affects Chakma women who customarily attend Buddhist rituals and temple ceremonies on behalf of their families. The restrictions on religious freedom and the forced assimilation of non-Muslims has become a state-endorsed policy. Equally resented is the Muslim interference in standards of dress. The tribal women of the CHT dress and behave very differently from their Muslim Bengali counterparts. In certain regions, the *jhumma*

---

[11] Gain, 39.

[12] Meghna Guhathakurta, 'Women's Survival and Resistance' in: *The Chittagong Hill Tracts: Life and Nature at Risk*, 90.

[13] Ibid., 91.

[14] Ibid., 81.

[15] Mohsin, 180.

women walk outdoors bare-breasted and do not cover their heads or legs; they are expressive, and their relationships with their brothers and husbands are more egalitarian. For Muslim men, who see virtue in their womenfolk being fully clothed and veiled, this mode of dress and behaviour appears to be an open invitation by hill women for coercion and sexual violation.

The majority of these crimes and violations against *jhumma* women have gone unpunished, as in the case of the abduction of Kalpana Chakma, where nothing has been achieved despite the pressure of national and international organizations.[16] Actions taken by the authorities appear more symbolic in nature than motivated by a real desire to find and punish the transgressors. Meanwhile in 1997, the Jana Samhati Samiti (JSS), the political wing of the *jhumma* people, signed peace accord with the Bangladesh government. The treaty did nothing to protect the *jhumma* people, and it was largely used by the Bangladesh government as a superficial policy to please donor aid countries. Instead of reining in the Bengali Muslim settlers and curbing the militarization of the CHT, it served to legalize the presence of the new settlers.[17]

Few indeed among the crimes described above, from rape to coerced marriage and outright massacre, have resulted in legal action against the perpetrators or in any kind of human rights tribunal. No one responsible for a human rights violation has ever been tried in a court. The crimes themselves would have remained unknown outside the CHT were it not for those who were forced to migrate to metropolitan cities in Bangladesh or India and thus were free to recount their tales of horror.

REFERENCES

Primary Sources

Anti-Slavery Society, *The Chittagong Hill Tracts: Militarization, Oppression and the Tribes*. London: Indigenous Peoples and Development, Series 2, 1984.

Dewan, Kamini Mohan. *Parbattya Chattagramer Eik Deen Shevoker Jiban Kahini* [The autobiography of a humble servant of the CHT.] Rangamati: Dewan Bros., 1970.

Hill Watch Human Rights Forum, Chittagong Hill Tracts: 'A Land of Blood and Tears.' An account of human rights violations in the Chittagong Hill Tracts, Bangladesh, 1992.

Hill Women's Federation. Leaflet distributed on the occasion of the NGO Forum on Women, Fourth UN Conference on Women, Beijing, 30 August –10 September 1995.

Religious Persecution and Islamization of the Chittagong Hill Tracts,' in *Jumma Sangbad Bulletin*, No 14, JSS Publications, 1993.

Roy, Raja Tridiv. *The Departed Melody (Memoirs)*. Islamabad: PPA Publications, 2003.

Secondary Sources

Aftab, Ahmed, 'Insurgency in the Chittagong Hill Tracts: Modalities for a Solution.' Paper presented at the International Conference on Insurgency and Counterinsurgency: South

[16] 'Abduction of Kalpana Chakma': http://www.angelfire.com/ab/jumma/rape/kalpana.html.

[17] 'Background of Jummas and CHT': http://www.angelfire.com/ab/jumma/bground.html.

Asian Experiences. Organized by the Bangladesh Defence Services Command and Staff College, Dhaka, 5-6 December 1994.

Gain, Philip, 'Life and Nature at Risk,' in *The Chittagong Hill Tracks: Life and Nature at Risk.* Dhaka: Society for Environment and Human Development, 2000.

Guhathakurta, Meghna, 'Women's Survival and Resistance' in *The Chittagong Hill Tracts: Life and Nature at Risk.* Dhaka: Society for Environment and Human Development, 2000.

Islam, Safiqal, 'Failure in State-Building: The Case of Pakistan,' in *Asian Profile*. Vol. 2, No. 6, 1984.

Mohsin, Amena, *The Politics of Nationalism: The Case of the Chittagong Hill Tracts, Bangladesh.* Dhaka: United Press, 1997.

Internet Sources

'Background of Jummas and CHT': http://www.angelfire.com/ab/jumma/bground.html

'An analysis of the Bangladesh Government Report on the Logang Massacre of 10 April 1992': http://www.angelfire.com/ab/jumma/massacre/logangrp.html

'Abduction of Kalpana Chakma': http://www.angelfire.com/ab/jumma/rape/kalpana.html

Russia

'A man who beats is a man who loves.' So runs an ancient Russian proverb. Theoretically, Russian women are protected against the practice. Article 19 of the Constitution of the Russian Federation guarantees equal rights to women and men, and women's equality is further upheld under the Family Code and the Criminal Code. The Criminal Code's Article 113 criminalizes action that causes 'physical or mental suffering by means of systematic beating or other violent actions,' and its Article 115 criminalizes any 'deliberate infliction [even] of light harm.' As for domestic rape, Article 313 makes it punishable by imprisonment for three to six years, which can be increased by four to ten years for aggravating factors.

Russia is also bound by certain international agreements. In 1993 it signed the United Nations Declaration on the Elimination of Violence against Women, followed in 1995 by the Beijing Declaration Platform for Action to raise the status of women. In 1996 the Kremlin set up an inter-governmental commission to promote gender equality and women's rights. The Kremlin then stepped back, and in 2004 it abolished the commission. As a result, in 2005 there were fewer than 200 centres and shelters for victims in operation across the Federation, and the number continues to dwindle as state funds are slashed and shelters are forced to close. Moscow itself, despite the efforts of the crisis centre for women known as ANNA (directed by Marina Pisklakova) and the women's NGO known as Siostry (directed by Maria Mokhova), lacks a shelter to its name.[1]

Meanwhile, violence is reported in all 89 regions of the country and in families of every socio-economic and ethnic background. If a perpetrator is arrested, he is often released quickly and sometimes returns home even more violent than before, so that the first step in redressing these crimes is to sensitize the authorities. Counter-measures at the local level are now being taken by a few police departments: in Moscow, St Petersburg, Yekaterinburg, Kazan, Saratov and Barnaul. It was in Barnaul that the Association of Crisis Centers, under the direction of Natalya Abubikirova, held a landmark conference with the city's police inspectors to discuss ways of treating women victims of domestic abuse. Nevertheless, Yelena Makkey, the centre's legal consultant, warned that 'the number of police inspectors

---

[1] Claire Bigg, 'Russia: domestic violence continues to take heavy toll,' Radio Free Europe / Radio Liberty (15 December 2005): http://209.85.229.132/search?q=cache:ZmqVr__vSKIJ:www.rferl.org/content/Article/1063891.html+amnesty+international+domestic+violence+the+biggest+human+scandal+of+our+times&cd=1&hl=fr&ct=clnk&gl=fr.

willing to work with us is still small.'[2] Again in Barnaul, an NGO set up a Women's Alliance under the direction of Yelena Schitova, who toured the United States in March 2003 to report on violence against women in the Altai and other Siberian regions. She reported that in the Altai region women seeking to prosecute their husbands face severe legal and bureaucratic hurdles. Victims are not entitled to the free services of a lawyer, and in the Altai region hiring a lawyer (in 2005) cost some 3,000 roubles ($ 100), the average monthly salary.[3]

It was only when a celebrity became involved that public attention to the problem significantly increased. Valeria, a well known Russian pop-singer whose real name is Alla Yurievna Perfilova, went public on the abuse she had suffered from her ex-husband Alexandr Shulgin. Throughout their marriage he was her producer and held full control of her finances, her professional activities and her lifestyle. For years he beat her severely until she summoned up the courage to divorce him.[4] In another case, reported by the crisis centre ANNA, the husband of a young female pianist broke all her fingers in a jealous rage. The court found him guilty of causing 'slight physical damage' and gave him a suspended sentence. As for his wife, her career was ruined.[5] Clearly, no easy solution was in sight in cutting through the crust of Russia's deep-rooted disdain for the rights of women.[6]

D.W.P. and Irina Massovets

[2] 'Violence against women in the Russian Federation,' Amnesty International: http://www.amnesty.org/russia/womens_day.html.

[3] art. cit.

[4] ibid.

[5] Mariya Rasner, 'Russian women struggle to survive domestic violence,' Women's ENews (3 October 2005): http://www.womensenews.org/article.cfm?aid=2215.

[6] Gail Lapidus, a Sovietologist and Russianist at the Hoover Institution at Stanford, recounted in Paris on 30 June 2009 her predicament while preparing her work *Women in Soviet Society* (Berkeley: University of California Press, 1980): she found that there was no Russian equivalent of the term 'sexual harassment.' It seems that since that time a term (сексуальное домогательство) has indeed entered the language and won an important currency. Beyond that, article 131 of the Federal Criminal Code now makes such acts punishable by law.

In: Crimes Against Women
Editor: David Wingeate Pike ISBN 978-1-61470-813-1

Chapter 26

TRAFFICKING IN WOMEN IN RUSSIA

Anonymous

INTRODUCTION

Despite attempts over the years to address the problem of human trafficking in the Russian Federation, this issue has developed into a cause for serious concern. According to police statistics, between 30,000 and 60,000 women are transported annually out of Russia for purposes of sexual exploitation. In most cases, people are taken in and out of Russia under the pretext of employment abroad.[1] Furthermore, some seventy thousand individuals, most of whom are young women, are listed annually as missing without trace.[2] It is highly probable that the women were abducted to be used for slave labour or in prostitution in Russia or abroad. According to police information, criminal groups conduct regular abductions of young and underage women, especially in economically depressed areas. Abducted women are usually brought to criminal bases, where they are prepared for transportation to other cities or abroad.[3]

There are no reliable statistics on crimes committed in this sphere, due to the latent nature of this phenomenon. According to the Ministry of Internal Affairs (police), since 2004, when human trafficking was declared a crime in Russia, 66 crimes involving trade in humans were registered in Russia; however, only 26 criminal investigations were initiated, and only 12 people were sentenced by courts.[4] Russian officials attribute their inability to curb trafficking to the lack of legislation, complaining that prostitution and prostitution-related activities are not subject to prosecution. Furthermore, Russian police cite problems in investigating such violations, as these crimes that begin in Russia are usually consummated abroad, and accordingly they seek to introduce a precise definition of the term ‘slave trade’ into domestic

---

[1] Nabi Abdulaev, ‘Lack of laws helping sex trade to flourish,’ *The St. Petersburg Times*, 30 August 2002.
[2] Alexasnder Kolesnichenko, ‘Exportnyi potok’ [Export stream], *Novye Izvestia*, No. 74, 27 April 2006, p. 2.
[3] State Duma of the Russian Federation. Report on fight against human trafficking, Moscow, 2006, p. 74.
[4] Report of the Russian Ministry of Internal Affairs, published on 16 May 2006, available at www.mvd.ru/press/release/4165.

legislation. Presently, Russian authorities are focusing on strengthening control over commercial agencies that could be used as a cover for slave trading.

In 2002, Russia recognized the fact that people in various regions were being traded, and it began to work on adopting the essential law in this sphere. In April 2002, the investigation of trafficking-related crimes was transferred to the jurisdiction of police departments charged with combating organized crime,[5] and on 30 October 2002 a working group was created to draft the Law on the Fight Against Trafficking in Humans. The group included representatives from the office of the President of the Russian Federation, the Parliamentary Committee on Legislation, and from interested non-government organizations. The U.S. Department of Justice was to provide operational, technical, and financial support to the working group;[6] however, all these efforts resulted merely in changing the wording of the Criminal Code without affecting the power of law enforcement.

TRAFFICKING-RELATED LEGISLATION

Even though Russia has a unique responsibility in international human trafficking, being as it is both a resource of victims and a recipient of trafficked persons from one or other of the former Soviet republics, Russia remained for many years the only part of the former USSR that did not have anti-trafficking legislation.

In Russia, there are at least three reasons why this problem has not been in the centre of public and legislative interest:

- Trafficking is a relatively new phenomenon, and legal and criminological studies have not kept up with its development;
- Trafficking is a latent phenomenon with a very low level of reporting and limited statistics, possibly because of police corruption;
- Public opinion is not yet sufficiently aroused to give the problem priority attention.

Before 2004, all Russian anti-trafficking legislation was covered under two articles of the Russian Criminal Code: article 152, which dealt with trafficking in minors, and article 240, which prosecuted the engagement in prostitution. The first was now abrogated, and the second completely rewritten. By concentrating on the trafficking in minors and prosecuting the pimps rather than tackling the problem of human trafficking in general, the Russian police authorities seemed to focus on age and gender issues rather than on a resolution of the problem as a whole.[7]

At least seven articles of the Criminal Code had some relationship to this type of crime, making it a criminal offence to force anyone to perform a sexual act (art. 133), to trade in minors (art. 152), to swap babies (art. 153), to engage in illegal adoption (art. 154), to engage in the illegal (sic) deprivation of a person's freedom (art. 127), and enticement into prostitution (art. 240). However, no single article was addressed to the trade in humans.

---

[5] *Rossiiskaia Gazeta* [Government-owned daily newspaper], 29 April 2002.

[6] G. Ilyichev, 'Bortsy s aisbergom' [Fighters against the iceberg], *Izvestia*, 30 October 2002.

[7] O. Yablokova, 'Slavery in Russia,' *Moscow Times,* 2 July 2005.

Because the commitment of these crimes requires usually a group of people, they were primarily covered by article 210 of the Criminal Code, under the heading: Organizing a Criminal Community or a Criminal Organization. This relatively large number of provisions was not matched by the measures taken to combat these crimes, and the shortcomings in criminal legislation were not eliminated by the amendments to the Code adopted in 2003. For instance, article 126, Abduction of People, still required proof of an act of forceful transfer and violent detention in order to convict a person. Trafficked people, moreover, are not always held by force. Fearing that they are violating the domestic laws of the country where they are held captive, and led to believe that they have committed a crime under the laws of their home country, the victims eschew the chance of recourse to law enforcement or consular agencies. That is why, in prosecuting criminals who prevent victims of trafficking from leaving their hiding places, it is the provisions of article 127 (illegal deprivation of freedom) that are more often effective.

Amendments to the Criminal Code, adopted in December 2003, did not establish a comprehensive definition of human trafficking. The Code was supplemented with two new sections criminalizing trade in humans and usage of slave labor. The present version of Russian law follows the UN definition, which from a legal point of view is very complicated. As stated in the UN Protocol on Trade in Humans, trading in people is defined as hiring, transporting, transferring, concealing or receiving people either by threat, fraud, deception or coercion, or by making or receiving illegal payments or by otherwise benefiting from the consent of the person controlling another person for the purpose of sexual exploitation or forced labor. Despite the fact that most of these qualifying features were included in Russia's legislation, Russian laws do not provide immunity to victims of trafficking from possible further prosecution (for instance, for illegal border crossing), nor do they provide a mechanism to prosecute recruitment, nor do they specifically protect those in a dependent position. Proposals pushed by interested Russian non-government organizations to accept the definition adopted under U.S. law in its Victims of Trafficking and Violence Protection Act of 2000, which goes beyond the policy definitions used in the UN documents, were not accepted.

An interesting example of ineffective Russian legislation is article 241 of the Criminal Code, which provides punishment for 'organizing and keeping brothels for prostitution [sic].'[8] The disposition of this article states that this crime consists of organizing and 'maintaining premises used permanently and exclusively for prostitution.' The word 'brothels' is used in this provision in the plural, and law enforcers interpret this article literally. If there are several brothels, the owner/manager may face criminal responsibility. If there is only one brothel, then, based on a literal interpretation of this article, the owner/manager is exempt from criminal responsibility. According to current court practice, this interpretation is the only one in use. The 2003 amendments to the Criminal Code renamed this article the 'organization of the business of prostitution' but retained the

[8] "Brothels for prostitution" is the exact wording of a Russian legal document and reflects Russian specifics of providing sex services and prosecuting those who are involved in this business. Because there is no term for brothel in the Russian Criminal Code, only a place where prostitution is conducted on a regular basis can be recognized as a brothel. While sexual services can be offered in a variety of places (residential premises, clubs, sporting facilities, cars, and other locations), substantive proof is required before any of these places can be legally named a brothel. The law, however, also states that a brothel is any place used for engagement in prostitution, so that a call centre where telephone requests for prostitutes are received, or a place where prostitutes report before being sent to a client, are considered as brothels too.

qualification of this activity as 'systematically conducted.' This would entail criminal responsibility only if the premises used for conducting prostitution were offered (even though repeatedly) by the same person over a short period of time, usually no longer than one year. It is not specified whether a brothel, to be a brothel, has to be in the same place, which makes prosecution more discretionary. Nor is it clear whether these requirements apply, for example, if a manager provides the services of the same women in various locations. Following existing interpretation, 'systematic involvement' means that if someone uses one place today, another tomorrow, and the following day yet another place, this is not construed as a 'systematic' activity. Similarly, a one-time offer of premises for a brothel does not constitute a crime punishable by this article. Recent changes to this article have not made the article more enforceable, since the authorities still do not prosecute engagement in prostitution as prescribed by the International Convention, requiring the prosecution of anyone who forces another person to commit prostitution, even if that person's involvement in the activity arrived after the initial induction. Other articles have similar weaknesses.

As a result of the gaps in Russian legislation, the Code is not clear about the prosecution of recruitment of potential victims of trafficking.[9] Article 127-1 recognizes recruitment of a person as a preparatory step to the commission of sale or purchase of a human individual. Recruitment is not considered a separate crime, even if an agreement between a mercenary and an individual has been concluded, because, according to the Code, an individual act of recruitment can be prosecuted only if it results in the sale/purchase of an individual for purposes of his/her exploitation. The issue of group recruitment is not regulated at all. Russian law does not provide punishment for the seizure of women's identification documents, an action taken in order to isolate the woman-victim and prevent her from contacting the police. The seizure of the victim's documents is an aggravating factor that makes the punishment of another crime (e.g., exploitation of slave labour) more severe, in the event that such a seizure occurred while another crime was being committed. Another imperfect feature of Russian criminal legislation contends that a criminal who violently threatens or harms another person can be prosecuted for trafficking only if the victim of the act is the trafficked woman in person. If violence is used toward relatives of the trafficked person, this action is considered as a regular crime not related to trafficking. Relatives still cannot bring charges against the traffickers on behalf of the victim and have no rights in court except for some coverage under the witness protection program.

On 20 August 2004, the Federal Law on State Protection of Crime Victims, Witnesses, and Other Parties to the Criminal Process was adopted. The law provides for some protective measures, including the right of victims, witnesses, and relatives or representatives of the victims to conceal their identity, including their residence and place of work. This law requires implementation, together with other security measures such as providing the persons under protection to a change of appearance, a temporary sojourn in a safe house, a new residence and place of work, and to personal bodyguards. If such measures have not yet been implemented it is the result of inadequate financing.

---

[9] According to the Commentaries on the Russian Criminal Code published by the Supreme Court of the Russian Federation (Moscow, 2006 at 621), recruitment into prostitution and fraudulent employment in prostitution-related spheres of business (art. 240) are punishable only as a component of a bigger crime defined as 'involvement in engaging in prostitution' and is associated with the application of force.

LEGAL MEASURES PROPOSED TO FIGHT TRAFFICKING

Recognition of human trafficking as a crime should entail the introduction of administrative and criminal measures to hold to account all individuals and legal entities engaged in, assisting in, and/or benefiting from human trafficking. This requires that trafficking be considered a form of organized transnational criminal activity. Consequently, the legislative approach should be changed, in order to prosecute crimes which may be committed in one country while the *corpus delicti* is in another. Today, gaps in legislation create often paradoxical situations, when the investigation of trafficking cannot be conducted because foreign women in Russia who are found sexually exploited are deported to their homelands, even though foreigners are under the jurisdiction of the Witness Protection Law.

At present, the approach of the Russian authorities is to focus on political issues rather than on the building of a legal mechanism to fight trafficking. For example, the program covering protection of children against sexual exploitation was included in the federal Youth Policy Program developed by the administration of the President and prescribes social and administrative activities aimed at improving situations in this field. Proposals related to changes in legislation fall within the framework of old concepts and definitions. They provide for the extension of the list of activities considered as crimes; the specifics of organized crime, however, are not taken into account. Laws on immigration, labor-force migration, and study-abroad programs should also be amended. No trafficking-related amendments to these laws have yet been discussed in Russia.

Strong enforcement of the existing legislation could lessen the risk of trafficking, but tough laws alone do not solve all the problems. Quite the contrary, they can escalate, with all the ensuing consequences: rising crime, corruption, and spreading violence.[10] Proposed measures can be effective if they establish provisions aimed not only at punishing the wrongdoers but also at helping the victims, by allowing them to bring a personal cause of action against their abusers and to be fully protected by the state. Adoption of a comprehensive legislative act encompassing all the issues of human trafficking, rather than a piecemeal solution, is advocated by certain parliamentarians as well as Russian and foreign NGOs. This act, if adopted, would create conditions for close cooperation between the state and civil society, give priority to the services providing help and refuge to the victims of this crime, and establish a central authority that would galvanize government and private efforts against the heinous crime of human trafficking.

CONCLUSION

It is of course unlikely that the adoption in Russia of legislation criminalizing the buying and selling of women, increasing the penalties for pimping, and ordering the confiscation of the assets of traffickers and pimps will solve the problem and end this shameful practice. However, together with many other related measures, such as developing policies to ensure the safety of women during the criminal prosecution of pimps, adopting social legislation, increasing the funding of social services, and assisting the victims of trafficking regardless of

[10] L.D. Erohina, M. Yu. Buriak, *Torgovlia zhenschinami v tseliah seksualnoi ekspluatatsii* [Trade in women with the purpose of sexual exploitation] (Vladivostok, 2004), p. 54.

their nationality, the situation could be changed. That would indeed indicate that Russia has risen to a higher level of legal and political thinking.

Despite the efforts of the international community and Russia's non-governmental organizations, there is no mechanism yet for making Russia a country with a viable legal system, able to come to terms with the crime of trafficking. The responsibility lies with the Russian leadership to act in concert and with resolution, in order to weigh the gravity of the problem, to eradicate any existing links between criminals and the authorities, to adopt international standards and, finally, to create a comprehensive plan to put an end to the crime of human trafficking.

SPAIN

In Andalusia and other parts of Spain, the seven centuries of Moorish occupation obviously left their cultural mark, so that the emphasis on chastity and the concept of woman as male property lingered on, through Medieval and Early Modern times into the present. According to a UN report issued in 2003, some 2.5 million Spanish women are terrorized in their homes. This dramatic rise in domestic violence induced Rosa Aguilar, the mayor of Cordoba, to begin in September 2001 monthly meetings of the city council to discuss gender violence. 'It's a way of raising awareness, of committing to militant action,' said Aguilar, of the United Left coalition.[1]

In January 2005, Spain's newly elected Socialist government followed in this path by introducing the Law for Comprehensive Protection against Domestic Violence. Two years later, Ana María Pérez del Campo, president of the Foundation for Separated and Divorced Women, had to admit that Spaniards were still loath to taking domestic violence seriously. 'The law was a big step forward,' added Eva Suárez, head of Amnesty International's domestic-violence project in Spain, 'but a lot remains to be done before the rights that women hold on paper become a reality.'[2]

The chapter on Spain included in this work refers to a Spain in the Early Modern Age in which 'society was more suspicious of women and more lenient with rapists.' The subject points to a similar account of rape in France in that period, presented in the classic work of Roland Barthes.[3]

D.W.P.

---

[1] María Hernández Martí, 'Saying "stop" to murder,' *International Herald Tribune,* 17 February 2003.

[2] Geoff Pingree and Lisa Abend, 'Spanish lesson on fighting spousal abuse,' ABC News/*Christian Science Monitor*, 11 January 2007.

[3] Roland Barthes, Anne-Marie Sauzeau-Boetti, Eva Menzio, Artemisia Gentileschi, *Actes d'un procès de viol en 1612* (Paris: Éditions des Femmes, 1984).

In: Crimes Against Women
Editor: David Wingeate Pike

ISBN 978-1-61470-813-1

Chapter 27

Abuse of Women in Medieval and Early Modern Spain

Isabel Pérez Molina

During the Medieval and Early Modern ages, honour and dignity were closely linked to the human body, so that a woman was called chaste or unchaste, pure or impure according to her sexual behaviour, whether this was free or forced. Codes of honour were usually supported by the law, as part of the social patriarchal order. In this order, rape was viewed more as the pollution of a man's property, vested in a woman's virtue, than as a criminal offence against the woman. For this reason, the attitude of jurists towards the crime of rape is characterised by its ambiguity, an attitude shared both by moralists and by a society suspicious of women. Blaming the victim is a commonplace that modern societies have inherited from the past, and it is still sometimes the practice to exonerate the rapist by finding excuses for him and raising doubts regarding the honesty and role of the victim. Nevertheless, together with this tradition, there is, in Spain and elsewhere in Europe, another opposing tradition, taking a different approach, more sympathetic to women. Both traditions are found in Europe and in Spain during the Middle Ages, the Early Modern age, and later.

Punishment of the crime of rape differs according to cultures and periods. The various peoples that entered Europe with the fall of the Roman Empire brought different traditions to the territories that they occupied.[1] Legal punishment against rape followed two different traditions: either the death penalty for the rapist or his forced marriage to his victim.

It was common in some Germanic kingdoms for a man to pay a dowry as a price for the bride. Marriage through abduction or violence was not unusual. It was known as 'marriage through rape,' even though the law disapproved of such acts and heavy fines were imposed. In Frankish kingdoms, punishments were rescinded and penalties reduced if the rapist married

---

[1] The example of Spanish law would support works by Peggy R. Sanday. According to her studies on a broad spectrum of band and tribal societies, historical and current, the incidence of rape differs greatly, and makes the distinction between rape-free and rape-prone societies, see: Peggy R. Sanday, 'Rape-free versus rape-prone: How culture makes a difference,' in Cheryl B. Travis (ed.) *Evolution, Gender and Rape* (Cambridge, MA: Massachusetts Institute of Technology Press, 2003). This book refutes the idea of rape as a natural act in evolution defended by sociobiologists R. Thornhill and C. Palmer in *A Natural History of Rape* (Cambridge, MA: MIT Press, 2000).

his victim. However, in the Visigothic kingdom, the *Liber Iudiciorum* established tougher penalties. If a free man raped a free woman, the man was given two hundred lashings in public. Whatever the case, he became a servant of the victim, if she was not married, or a servant of the victim's husband, if she was married. The perpetrator could also forfeit his estate into the same hands unless he had children of his own. If he abducted or kidnapped a free woman, she would receive half the abductor's estate. In any case, marriage between perpetrator and victim under Visigothic law was prohibited. [2]

In Spain, the unification of Castile and Aragon in the Spanish crown did not mean the abolition of the local customs and laws that pertained to the two separate territories. There were clear differences between the customs and laws in Castile and those in Aragon's Catalonia. In Catalonia, the *Usages* of Barcelona, written between 1149 and 1151, were the basis of the legislation later adopted by the *Corts* (parliament), the *Constitucions i altres drets de Catalunya* (Constitutions and Other Rights of Catalonia), while in Castile the *Fuero Real* and *Las Partidas*, together with the local *fueros* (municipal charters), were equally important.[3]

Although Castilian and Catalan legal texts contain some significant differences, one of the first perceptions gained from reading these texts is the ambiguity in the use of language, where boundaries are blurred between rape, described also as forced sex, clandestine marriage (elopement), abduction and consensual sex. Some scholars, such as Kathryn Gravdal, have studied the use of language regarding rape in French medieval texts.[4] In Catalonia, there is evidence of a similar use of language and a similar pattern of confusion and ambiguity. The *Constitucions* 'Jacme per la gratia' (by James's grace), and 'Com fer, o contraure' (How to proceed or contract)[*] which regulate paternal consent to marriage, are proof of this terminological ambiguity in which elopement, abduction and rape are converged. The first law allows for the disinheritance of a daughter who 'allows herself to be raped or elopes.' The second law disinherits a girl who consents to abduction or rape, and punishes the man who 'has carnal knowledge of a virgin or rapes her with or without her consent.'[5]

The *Usage Si Quis Virginem*, included in the *Constitucions*, is the most specific Catalan regulation on rape. It uses the terms 'corrupt' (corrompra) and 'adulterate': 'violently corrupt a maiden,' that is, a virgin, and 'violently adulterate a female who is not a maiden.' Both terms have clearly negative connotations and are applied to the victim, not the rapist. When reading juridical texts, one also has the impression at times that the rapist is treated as the victim, not the criminal. Many times, jurists tried to see a gap through which the rapist or

---

[2] This legislation was kept alive in Castilian territory under the term *Fuero Juzgo* until replaced by Castilian law. See M. Rivera, "Dret i conflictivitat social de les dones a la Catalunya feudal i pre-feudal", in M. Nash (ed.), *Més enllà del silenci*, Barcelona, Generalitat de Catalunya, 1988, p. 69.

[3] The Usages of Barcelona were one of the first legal codes written in medieval Europe. Countess Almodis of Barcelona was a co-author. It was the base code for the *Constitucions i altres drets de Catalunya*, the main source of law in Catalonia until the 18th and 19th centuries. I have studied the juridical literature of the Catalan and Spanish Early Modern Ages, the body of law and the works of the most important Catalan jurists of the 17th century Joan-Pere Fontanella and Jaume Cáncer. In Castile, *Las Partidas or Las Siete Partidas* (the Seven-Part Code) were a compilation of laws made by Alfonso X of Castile that remained in force not only in Castilian territories but also in the Spanish colonies until the 19th century.

[4] K. Gravdal, *Ravishing Maidens. Writing Rape in Medieval French Literature and Law* (Philadelphia: University of Pennsylvania Press, 1991).

* 'Contraure' means "contract," although here it refers to "contraure matrimoni", that is, getting married.

[5] *Constitucions i altres drets de Catalunya*, Barcelona, 1704. Book V, tit. I, II, III. On the use of language: K. Gravdal, *Ravishing Maidens. Writing Rape in Medieval French Literature and Law* (Philadelphia: University of Pennsylvania Press, 1991), pp. 1-7, 25-30, 92-107, 123-131.

criminal perpetrator would be exonerated, for instance, by casting doubt about the woman's morality. Likewise, in the case of women who are not virgins, and particularly married women, rape is intertwined with adultery.[6]

Castilian juridical texts use similarly ambiguous language but seem to be, in general, more sympathetic to the victim than is found in Catalan law. Both the *Fuero Real* and *Las Partidas* mix abduction and rape. While in *Las Partidas* the woman involved could be considered 'accomplice' and both actions are left indistinct, in the *Fuero Real* both cases imply the use of violence against the woman's will, resulting in a slight difference between the two legal codes, since abduction could be followed or not by rape. In this case the law defines both abduction and rape as actions carried out without the woman's consent.[7]

Legislation against rape had as its aim to protect the honour of the family represented in the body of the woman. As expressed above, rape was not considered a crime against women but rather an attack against the masculine control over the family's womenfolk. Nevertheless, there are remarkable differences in the materialisation of this principle. In Catalonia, rape was seen as an act of theft of a young girl's virginity, perpetrated against her father since it resulted in her depreciation in the marriage market. It could lead even to her family rejecting her, or to her inability to find a husband. Subsequently, the law also covered widows, though punishment was rare in cases where the victim was not a virgin, leaving married women unprotected. Conversely, in Castile it was more important to protect the institution of marriage and the concept of husbands' honour-property, and for this reason married women were the first to be protected by the law against rape. Municipal charters—such as the so-called *Fuero de Soria*—protected in particular married women against rape, providing for much heavier punishments. Later on, the *Fuero Real* and *Las Partidas* introduced punishment for crimes against maidens, widows and nuns. Rape perpetrated against nuns was considered a serious crime in both Catalan and Castilian legislation.[8]

Again, tendencies differ between Castile and Catalonia during and after the Middle Ages. During the Late Middle Ages in Catalonia, the *Usage Si Quis Virginem* stipulated marriage to the victim or the mandatory payment of a dowry—that is, give her a husband—if she happened to be a virgin. Where the victim was not a virgin but fell pregnant as a result of the crime, the same regulation might apply. The *Usage* reads: 'If somebody violently corrupts a maiden, he shall take her as his wife, if she and her parents consent and give her a dowry, or shall give her a husband of her social status. Likewise, if somebody violently adulterates a female who is not a maiden, and makes her pregnant.'[9]

This *Usage*, included in the *Constitucions*, was largely modified in subsequent legislation. The *Constitució Jacme per la gratia*, as noted above, did not make a clear difference between marriage without consent, abduction and rape. The law, with the aim of preventing unapproved marriages between daughters of the wealthy class and lowborn men, punished with disinheritance the woman who 'consents to be abducted/raped,' while the

[6] Constitucions i altres drets, Book IX, tit. VIII, I. Texts by 17th century Catalan jurists such as Joan-Pere Fontanella, Jaume Càncer and others are full of negative assumptions towards the victim. See note no. 10.

[7] Partidas, no. 7, tit. XX, 1-2. *Fuero Real*, Book IV, tit. X, 1, tit. III, 2.

[8] For a more extensive perspective on honour, women and law, see my book: *Honour and Disgrace: Women and the Law in Early Modern Catalonia*, Florida, Dissertation.com, 2001. A descriptive work regarding rape, the *Fuero de Soria*, and other Castilian legislation can be seen in V. Rodríguez Ortiz, *Mujeres forzadas. El delito de violación en el derecho castellano (Siglos XVI-XVIII)*, Almería: Servicio de Publicaciones de la Universidad de Almería, 2003, pp. 44-57.

[9] *Constitucions i altres drets*, Book IX, tit. VIII, I.

perpetrator was sentenced to lifelong banishment. In the same line, the *Constitució Com fer, o contraure* ratified the penalty of lifelong banishment, 'and even the death penalty, should there be abduction or any other violent deed.' The penalty would depend on the social status of the rapist and his victim. The law afforded the possibility of acquittal for the abductor. In accordance with the *Usage Si Quis Virginem*, if the young woman's parents insisted on it the transgressor had to marry the victim, who would be disinherited, unless she was over twenty-four years of age and unmarried.[10]

During the Early Modern period, numerous juridical texts on the rapist's obligation to pay a dowry to the raped virgin indicate that this practice continued to be in force. According to Joan-Pere Fontanella, for the crime to be considered there had to be evidence of violence, which could seldom be provided if the woman was not a virgin. This evidence would be compelling only if the rapist were caught in the act, given the deceit normally displayed in this type of evidence. Blaming the victim, as well as demanding specific evidence, allowed the Courts easily to avoid sentencing. Fontanella also refers to the matter of incestuous rape, particularly in cases between parents and children, this crime being punishable by the death penalty; the most common cases cited are those committed by a father on his daughter. Where the crime was perpetrated by collateral relatives, such as a brother on his sister, the penalties imposed were less severe, but they nevertheless included corporal punishment.[11]

As noted above, in Castile the rape of a married woman was considered a greater offence than the rape of a non-married woman, since it constituted a threat to the husband's honour that was valued higher than that of the father or other male relatives. Municipal charters considered revenge by the victim's relatives a duty. The *Fuero de Soria* imposed the death penalty for the rapist if the woman was married, and a cash fine if she was not. It seems that these fines were not very significant, because later the *Fuero Real* claims that legislation had hitherto left virgins and widows unprotected; it therefore increased the fines for the rape of non-married women, although those fines were lower than those paid to married women for a similar offence. The *Fuero Real* also contemplates the death penalty for the crime of rape, as does *Las Partidas*. This important code of law decreed the death penalty and loss of estate for rapists if the victim was considered honest, regardless of whether she was married, widow, single or nun. If the woman was not considered honest, the punishment, at the judge's discretion, would depend on the status of the parties. The law contemplates the possibility of marriage between rapist and victim, 'she willingly' and 'there being no other husband,' but then his estate would belong to her parents, 'if they did not consent to the rape and marriage.' Otherwise, the estate would go to the Royal Chamber. However, and particularly during the Early Modern age, rapists could escape harsh penalties if they were from noble families. From the mid-16th century, the death penalty for rape was commuted to enslavement in the galleys.[12]

---

10 Ibid., Book V, tit. I, II, III.

11 Jurists Jaume Cáncer and Tomás Mieres assert the *Usage* was totally in force. Jurist Lluís de Peguera also referred to this *Usage* and abduction, naming widows and young maidens. J. P. Fontanella, *De Pactis Nuptialis sive capitulis matrimonialis tractatus*, Barcelona, 1612-1622, cl. 5, gl. 5, part II, 3-8, 73, 75-76, 80-82. J. Cancer, *Variorum Resolutionum Juris Cesarei Pontifici et municipalis tractatus*, 1594-1608, Part III, ch. II, 46. L. De Peguera, *Decisiones aureae in actu practica frequentes ex varii Sacri Regii Cathaloniae conclusionibus collectae*, Barcelona, 1605-1611, ch. 43, 1-15.

12 *Partidas*, no. 7, tit. XX, 1-3; tit. 33, 6. *Fuero Real*, Book IV, tit. X, 1, tit. III, 2. Rodríguez, pp. 99-102.

The Medieval and Early Modern Church never regarded rape as a canonical issue. Rape was not considered a crime under ecclesiastical law, except where it involved a betrothed maiden. The Church was deliberately indulgent in this sense when compared to civil law. The 12th century canonist and jurist Gratian, in his *Decretals*, believed that the right penalty for rape was excommunication. From then on, excommunication and isolation for a specific period of time, between one and two years, became in canon law the punishment for rape in the case of laymen. If a rapist took refuge in a church, he was guaranteed immunity. If the rapist was a clergyman, he easily avoided punishment.13

In conclusion, the treatment of the crime of rape in Spain differed according to the area and the period. Medieval society was, particularly in Castile, more sympathetic to women than it would be later. During the Early Modern Ages, society was more suspicious of women and more lenient with rapists, casting doubts on the true nature of violence involved in the act of rape. If the woman was married, the suspicion of adultery was always present. In Catalonia, the harsh penalties for feminine crimes, such as adultery, are at odds with the treatment of crimes against women, and particularly rape, which were punished less severely. Castile followed a different tradition, viewing rape as a serious crime to be punished by harsh penalties, including death, and although later changes still did not confer on women the presumption of innocence, punishments remained severe.

[13] In his study of Medieval England, John M. Carter indicates that 39 percent of rapists were clergymen. See: J. A. Brundage, *Law, Sex and Christian Society in Medieval Europe* (Chicago: University of Chicago Press, 1987), p. 313.

UNITED KINGDOM

Female genital mutilation (FGM) is outlawed in the United Kingdom under the Prohibition of Female Circumcision Act of 1985 and the Female Genital Mutilation Act of 2003. Practitioners and those sanctioning the abuse could be jailed for up to 14 years, but no one has yet been prosecuted. Immigrants, whether parents or guardians, from FGM-practising countries are thought to be taking their children abroad to undergo the operation that consists of cutting off and stitching up their genitalia, without anaesthetic. However, so-called 'excisors' are also said to be operating in Britain, especially in London, Birmingham, Manchester and Leicester. The campaigning group Forward, in association with the Department of Health, released their estimate on 9 October 2007 that as many as 66,000 women and girls in England and Wales may have undergone the operation.[1]

D.W.P.

---

* The author, an Assistant Professor at AGSIRD, is a former British High Commissioner to Pakistan.

[1] Roger Cohen, 'Down time from murder,' *International Herald Tribune*, 24 September 2007.

In: Crimes Against Women
Editor: David Wingeate Pike

ISBN 978-1-61470-813-1

Chapter 28

FORCED MARRIAGE AS A FOREIGN POLICY ISSUE IN THE UNITED KINGDOM

Sir Christopher MacRae

Forced marriage has been practised across the world for many centuries. However, it was not until 1948 that the element of consent was codified in international law by the UN Universal Declaration of Human Rights whose Article 16 states that 'Marriage shall be entered into only with the free and full consent of the intending spouses.'' Later UN conventions strengthened this important initial stand. Thus, 'A woman's right to choose a spouse and enter freely into marriage is central to her life and her dignity and equality as a human being,'[1] and 'No marriage shall be legally entered into without the full and free consent of both parties.'[2] Other texts, especially within the 1989 UN Convention on the Rights of the Child,[3] showed the desire of the international community to establish norms of behaviour pertaining to marriage which would transcend national boundaries.

Diplomats, specifically consular officials, soon found themselves having to deal with individual cases. But it is only now, half a century later, that foreign ministries and embassies in the field have begun at last to adapt their structures and working practices in order to tackle the problem systematically. Britain's response is instructive: but even the UK's proactive and innovative approach is still only ten years old.

Some preliminary clarifications are necessary. First, a *forced* marriage must never be confused with an *arranged* marriage. 'A forced marriage,' reads an official report produced in 2006, 'is conducted without the valid consent of one or both parties and is a marriage in which duress—either physical or emotional—is a factor.... It is an abuse of human rights, and a form of domestic violence and child abuse when it involves young people.... [On the other hand] an arranged marriage is entered into freely by both people, although their families take

[1] UN Convention on the Elimination of All Forms of Discrimination Against Women, of 1979, General Recommendation no. 21.

[2] UN Convention of Consent to Marriage, Minimum Age for Marriage and Registration of Marriage, of 1962, Article 1.

[3] See Articles 19 and 35.

a leading role in the choice of partner.'[4] Secondly, forced marriage is not a concern for women only. Some men are also forced to marry, but they are a relatively small minority (although the statistics do not take into account the number of males who accept forced marriage in the knowledge that they can abandon their partners later). Thirdly, almost all cases of forced marriage in the United Kingdom concern families who have migrated to Britain and still retain strong links to their country of origin—where one of the two young people involved usually resides. That means that most forced marriages usually take place abroad. The primary reason for this is that it allows the parents to retain (or regain) control over their children, being aware that in Britain women have opportunities to seek help and are likely to do so. Even when both parties are British nationals, the prospective bride is likely to be taken out of the country first, and her passport, airline tickets and mobile phone removed. As the number of dual nationals living in Britain has hugely increased, along with expanded international mobility encouraged by cheap air travel, so the number of cases involving cross-border forced marriages has multiplied. Finally, the problem does not exclusively concern any single community living in Britain. Nevertheless, it is fact that about 65 percent of the cases currently being dealt with by the British authorities involve forced marriages to nationals, or dual nationals, from Pakistan,[5] and 25 percent from Bangladesh.

The British government has in recent years moved incrementally, but quite effectively, to tackle this problem. A working party was set up in 1999 to consider the whole issue of forced marriages in the general context of Human Rights. The co-chairmen were Lord Ahmed of Rotherham and Baroness Uddin of Bethnal Green, both establishment figures of South Asian origin. Their report, *A Choice by Right*, was published by the Home Office in June 2000. This emphasized the need for the issue to be addressed on a multi-agency basis, and it recognised that 'forced marriage raises many issues that cannot be dealt with solely in ... domestic forums, for example when a person is taken against [her or his] will overseas to be married.' This led, *inter alia*, to the setting up of a 'Community Liaison Unit,' with the Foreign and Commonwealth Office (FCO) as lead department, and including the Home Office (HO) in close liaison with the Social Services Inspectorate. It dealt with several quite disparate issues, including assistance to British Muslims undertaking the *Hajj.*

In 2005, the Forced Marriage Unit (FMU) was created as a separate joint FCO/HO team, physically located in the FCO. At present it consists of six officers, three from the FCO, two from the Home Office, and one recruited from the voluntary sector to act as an independent case-worker. The team has three functions:

- to develop government policy in this area;
- to deal with case-work (so far about 300 cases a year, but likely to increase);
- to do outreach work, including awareness-raising.

[4] From *Forced Marriage: A Wrong not a Right*, a summary of responses to the consultation on the criminalisation of forced marriage, published jointly in June 2006 by the Foreign and Commonwealth Office, the Home Office, and the Scottish Executive.

[5] Strictly speaking, from Pakistan and Kashmir. Of the roughly 850,000 people living in Britain who are of 'Pakistani' origin, probably over 60 percent originate from two small districts of Azad Kashmir (as Pakistan describes that part of the former Princely State of Jammu and Kashmir which it controls), near Mirpur. Their families' land was flooded during the construction of the Mangla Dam in the early 1960s, when many agricultural workers emigrated to textile-manufacturing towns in the north of England in search of temporary jobs—never to return. But strong family links remain.

The last task has led to the publication of useful and well-written booklets, offering guidance and advice to bring the problem to the attention of health and education professionals, social workers and police officers.[6] The team is also beginning to work with schools, in order to change attitudes among the young, and explain how and where help is available.[7]

It is, however, the FMU's case-work that is the most gripping. In about 85 percent of reported cases of forced marriage, it is the women who are forced. On the male side, the number is increasing as a larger number of homosexual men, who in the past were unwilling to identify themselves, are increasingly coming forward. Although the majority of all cases involve families originating in South Asia—notably Pakistan, Bangladesh and India—the FMU has also had to deal with cases from other places in the world. Other human rights issues are sometimes involved; the Unit occasionally deals with child victims or has to operate under potentially dangerous circumstances. Embassies in the field must often rely on the co-operation of the local police.

The dry facts presented above give no impression whatever of how heart-rending, sometimes dramatic, some of these cases actually are. One such case, graphically described last year in the London daily *The Guardian,*[8] concerned Yasmin, a 21-year-old girl from Bradford in the north of England. She was rescued from a village in the Punjab by a special team, formed for this purpose, by the British High Commission in Islamabad. Its members regularly have to carry out such operations, thereby saving over a hundred young people a year from forced marriages. 'Caught between cultures and pressured by their families,' wrote *The Guardian*, 'hundreds of young British-Pakistani women are trapped in forced marriages in Pakistan every year. The ordeal results in tears, trauma, and sometimes brutal domestic violence. Parents prod the young women to fly back to Pakistan for a short holiday to visit an ailing granny or celebrate a cousin's wedding. Then it all goes wrong. The weeks stretch into months. Passports go missing and return flights are cancelled. Mysterious suitors appear on the doorstep. A sour truth dawns on the woman: the wedding being planned is her own.... Running away is rarely an option." In this instance, for the first time, the journalist was allowed to witness what happened. After a wrenching interview with the parents, the girl rushed away to join the British diplomat and his armed Pakistani bodyguard aboard a Land Rover which raced back to Islamabad. The High Commission then issued an emergency passport, and put Yasmin on a plane home—although sometimes victims have to be hidden under a shawl, or flown from a regional airport. Many even more harrowing stories were supplied in *The Guardian*'s coverage. The youngest victim helped in 2005 was a 15-year-old British boy with a 13-year old Pakistani bride.

The way in which the British government is tackling this problem illustrates several aspects of how modern foreign policy formulation and diplomacy are changing. First, globalisation has pushed many new issues onto the foreign policy agenda, including some that would formerly have been considered 'domestic.' Until fairly recently, forced marriage would not have been considered an issue to be dealt with by foreign ministries and diplomats.

[6] *Dealing with Cases of Forced Marriages—Guidance for Education Professionals: 2nd ed.*, 2006; and ibid. *...for Police Officers, 2nd ed., 2005* (Joint FCO/Home Office publications.)

[7] See www.fco.gov.uk and navigate via quick search box to 'Forced Marriage.'

[8] See www.guardian.co.uk/pakistan/Story/0,,1663387,00.html.

Secondly, as several recent studies have pointed out,[9] foreign ministries are now having to abandon their pretensions to being 'gatekeepers' of foreign policy. Instead, they are obliged to adopt the role of main co-ordinator, though other ministries may contest this. In the case of forced marriage, the FCO will have found it easier to collaborate with the Home Office simply because, for decades, the teams in British embassies abroad which deal with migration and nationality issues (e.g. issuing visas) have contained roughly equal numbers of FCO and HO officials, which is not the pattern for most other countries; so they are used to working side by side. Like the walls of Jericho, bureaucratic fences are a'tumblin' down.

Thirdly, foreign policy formulators and diplomats alike must now take much more notice of the role of non-government actors. The change in British government policy over forced marriages was not simply a response to public demand. However, once the problem was identified, the government took care to include in its original working party seven people who represented neither the political class nor officialdom.[10] There was an equal number of officials, but they were merely advisors and had no vote. Similarly, the willingness of the FCO and British High Commission in Islamabad, noted above, to allow a journalist to observe a secret operation to resolve a forced marriage situation, shows how much less defensive towards the media diplomats have become. That is not all. A formidable coalition of British NGOs concerned with women's rights has formed the 'End Violence towards Women Campaign.' It continues to monitor, on an annual basis, the actions taken by different government departments in this area, and to publish its findings, including detailed 'score-cards.'[11] In its latest report, the FCO was rated only 3 out of 10! But then, only the Ministry of Health fared any better, at 3.5. Most were worse; and the FCO was at least said to 'set an example to other departments.'

Finally, dealing with the problem of forced marriage has served to highlight what diplomats have always known: that in most cases effective action can succeed only in close collaboration with the host government. For example, the Pakistani police service has often been actively and constructively involved in resolving cases of forced marriage with their British colleagues. In 2004, the Metropolitan Police in London signed a ground-breaking agreement with their Pakistani counterparts to encourage across-the-board co-operation. Pakistani NGOs, too, have often played a valuable and active role.[12]

---

[9] See, for instance, Hocking, Brian (ed.): *Foreign Ministries: Change and Adaptation* (Basingstoke: Macmillan, 1999); and Hocking, Brian and Spence, David (eds.): *Foreign Ministries in the European Union: integrating diplomats* (Basingstoke: Palgrave, 2nd edition, 2005).

[10] Lord Dholakia, chairman of the National Association for the Care and Resettlement of Offenders, and member of the Home Secretary's Race Relations Forum (HSRRF); Yasmin Alibhai-Brown, author and journalist and member of the HSRRF; Surinder Singh Attariwala, education and language consultant; Thomas Chan, Member of the Metropolitan Police Committee, member of the HSRRF, and Deputy Chairman of the Chinese in Britain Forum; Humera Khan, consultant to the Muslim Women's Organisation, the Al-Nisa Society; Rita Patel, Chairman of the 1990 Trust, Director of the Belgrave Baheno women's organisation; and Hannana Siddiqui, member of the Southall Black Sisters organisation (resigned 24 May 2000).

[11] See www.endviolenceagainstwomen.org.uk, and navigate to 'Making the Grade.'

[12] e.g. Struggle for Change (SACH), Pakistan (www.sachonline.org).

This may not be the stuff of 'High Diplomacy' as described by writers of the classic works of fifty or more years ago.[13] Nevertheless, 'delivering high quality consular services to British nationals' is now one of the FCO's strategic priorities. Indeed, in the 21st century, issues surrounding violence towards women, including forced marriages, are increasingly on the world's foreign policy agenda. Foreign ministries and diplomats are having to adapt in order to cope with this fact.

[13] e.g. Harold Nicolson, *Diplomacy* (Oxford: Oxford University Press, 3rd ed., 1963).

THE UNITED STATES

'If slavery is America's original sin,' writes Richard Lingeman, 'lynching is its capital crime.' Ida Bell Wells-Barnett, born to slave parents in 1862 in Holly Springs, Mississippi, dedicated her life to bringing this outrage to the attention of the American people and the world. Her campaign started in 1892 after the murder by a Memphis mob of her friend Tommy Moss and two others. Defenders of the New South claimed that lynching was a necessary response to an alleged epidemic of attacks on white women by predatory black men. Defying Victorian gentility, and at the risk of her life, Wells debunked this propaganda with evidence that accusations of rape were a factor in less than one-third of lynchings. 'She was among the first to grasp,' adds Lingeman, 'that the battle against lynching was the moral cutting edge of African-Americans' struggle for equality. In fighting words and brave personal witness, she exposed lynching as a crime against a people.'[1]

D.W.P.

---

[1] Richard Lingeman, review of Paula J. Gidding, *Ida: A Sword Among Lions* (New York: Amistad/HarperCollins, 2008), *International Herald Tribune*, 23 May 2008.

In: Crimes Against Women
Editor: David Wingeate Pike
ISBN 978-1-61470-813-1

Chapter 29

A CELEBRATED LYNCHING IN THE UNITED STATES

Carol Bowers

Ellen Liddy Watson gazed placidly at the photographer with a faint smile as she posed beside her husband, Bill Pickell, for her wedding portrait in the late fall of 1879.[1] Her prospects for wedded bliss would quickly fade as she soon discovered that her new husband was a violent, philandering alcoholic, who battered her whenever he was so inclined. During the second year of their marriage, Pickell flew into a drunken rage and beat Ellen viciously with a horsewhip. No longer willing to endure his abuse, Ellen fled to her parents' Kansas homestead. When she had recovered from her injuries, she set out on her own, working as a cook and domestic in Red Cloud, Nebraska. Ellen filed for divorce from Pickell in 1884 and headed west to Wyoming, the first territory in the United States to give women the vote, to search for new and better opportunities.[2]

Ellen arrived in Rawlins, Wyoming in 1884, and quickly found work as a cook and domestic at the Rawlins House, reportedly the best hotel in town, where she worked until 1886. During this time, Ellen met James Averell, the man believed to be her second husband. Though little is known of the circumstances of their meeting and courtship, on 17 May 1886, Ellen and James Averell were issued a marriage license in Lander, Wyoming.[3] Although evidence strongly suggests that the marriage occurred, there is no existing documentation of the event.

In 1886, Ellen moved to Sweetwater valley to join Averell in a homesteading venture. Three years later, twenty-eight year old Ellen Liddy Watson was dead. A sheriff's posse would find her lifeless body gently twisting in the breeze at the end of a hangman's noose. Ellen's senseless murder at the hands of her neighbor, wealthy cattleman Albert John

---

[1] George Huffsmith, *The Wyoming Lynching of Cattle Kate, 1889* (Glendo: High Plains Press, 1993), p. 41.

[2] Ellen filed for divorce on the grounds of extreme cruelty and infidelity,. The divorce, however, was not granted until March 1886 on Pickell's grounds of desertion. Petition and Order of Divorce on file at Webster County Court, Red Cloud, Nebraska.

[3] Application for a Marriage License and Marriage License, 17 May 1889, Fremont County, Territory of Wyoming, Records of Fremont County Clerk of Court, Lander, Wyoming.

Bothwell and five of his cronies, earned her the dubious distinction of being the only woman ever lynched in Wyoming.

Attempts were made in the *Cheyenne Daily Leader,* a newspaper sympathetic to the interests of Wyoming's wealthy cattlemen, to justify the actions of Ellen's executioners by alleging that Ellen was a prostitute and cattle rustler, known as 'Cattle Kate,' who took unbranded calves in payment for her sexual services.[4] The truth is that Ellen Liddy Watson was guilty of nothing more than being an independent, industrious woman homesteader and defying her avaricious neighbor, Bothwell, who demanded that she sell him her homestead and leave the county.

Letters written in the late 1800s by Wyoming cattlemen, many of whom were members of the Wyoming Stock Growers' Association, frequently contain discussions about the 'rustler' element in Wyoming and sometimes allude to plots to kill suspected rustlers or drive them out of the region. This culture of violence was defended by many of the wealthy cattlemen who felt they could not obtain convictions against suspected cattle thieves in the courts and regarded vigilantism as their moral right, despite constitutional guarantees of an individual's right to due process.[5] The high-handed tactics of Wyoming's cattle barons, who went to great lengths to control the range, access to water and the annual round-ups, were resented by the less affluent ranchers, often unjustly accused of being rustlers, who protested against the abuses they suffered under the hated Maverick Law and other legislative measures which favoured the wealthy cattlemen.[6]

To encourage settlement of its western territories, the United States Government passed a series of land laws during the 1800s, which opened vast tracts of the public domain to private

---

[4] 'A Double Lynching: two notorious characters hanged for cattle stealing: Jim Averill and his partner Ella Watson meet their Fate at the hands of the outraged stock growers,' *Cheyenne Daily Leader*, 23 July 1889, Cheyenne, Wyoming.

[5] Letter, James L. Smith to Thomas B. Adams, Wyoming Stock Growers Association Papers, Accession Number 14, Box 25, Folder 7, American Heritage Center, University of Wyoming, Laramie, Wyoming. In an excerpt from the letter, Smith, a freelance detective and former Union Pacific Rail Road detective, comments: 'The country for 50 miles up the Sweetwater from this ranch is in the complete possession of rustlers and … the longer they are allowed to run the worse it will be for cattlemen. There is [sic] enough good men in this and Carbon County to forever put a quietus on this class … such men as Tom Sun … and many others … need have no fear about any after claps. Their past reputations is [sic] a guarantee against the clamor of a few who would no doubt deprecate [sic] or pretend to do so the extermination of these pests of society.'

[6] The Wyoming Stock Growers Association met in Cheyenne on 9 November 1883, and resolved to create a black list of suspected stock thieves, who would be discharged from the ranches on which they worked and not hired by any association members. In most cases, the men designated as rustlers had no formal charges filed against them and had not been found guilty of the crime of rustling in a court of law. The 1884 Wyoming legislature passed the Maverick Law, which gave the Wyoming Stock Growers Association full control of roundups in the territory and set up procedures for dealing with mavericks. 'Maverick' is a term referring to unbranded cattle whose ownership is uncertain. Prior to the passage of the Maverick Law of 1884, anyone finding such unbranded cattle on the range could brand that animal with his own brand and claim ownership. The Maverick Law of 1884 declared all mavericks the property of the Wyoming Stock Growers Association and directed that the cattle be auctioned to the members of the association and the proceeds used to employ stock detectives to protect the cattle of the Association's members. In 1886 the law was amended so that any person wishing to bid on mavericks at auction had a chance to purchase at least one maverick. In practice, however, the small cattlemen were always outbid, but regardless of what was bid, the cattle barons never paid more than ten dollars per maverick when settling their bill. The 1886 legislature also passed legislation making it unlawful for any person at any time to brand any maverick except on the official roundup under the supervision of the round-up foremen (T. A. Larson, *History of Wyoming* (Lincoln: University of Nebraska Press, 1978), pp. 184-185.

settlement.[7] However, in arid Wyoming approximately forty acres of land are required to support one cow, so, in addition to privately owned land, cattlemen relied on the use of the public domain to obtain sufficient range on which to graze their herds of cattle. The arrival of homesteaders led inevitably to conflicts with cattlemen, who resented the intrusions of the newcomers on their traditional range. Nevertheless, the opportunity to obtain land at little or no cost under these land acts enticed James Averell and Ellen Watson to take up homestead claims in Wyoming's beautiful Sweetwater Valley.

In 1885, James Averell filed claims under the Homestead and Desert Lands Acts in a prime, well-watered location along the Ft. McKinney-Rawlins military road between Horse Creek and the Sweetwater River.[8] In addition to his agricultural pursuits, Averell operated a general store and small saloon and served meals to passers-by.

On 30 August 1886, Ellen filed papers under the Pre-emptive Act on land adjacent to Averell's that she intended to homestead.[9] She immediately began making improvements on the land and had a small one-room log cabin built, so she could live on her land and comply with the residency requirement for proving title to the claim. Because final ownership of homesteads could be granted only to U.S. citizens, Ellen, a native of Canada, completed an application on 25 May 1887 to become a naturalized citizen of the United States.[10]

Ellen and Averell's lands lay in the middle of public domain used and illegally fenced by Albert John Bothwell, who had been running cattle on the open range in the Sweetwater Valley along Horse Creek since 1883. Bothwell was determined to drive Ellen and Averell off their homesteads and reclaim control of the range. When attempts to buy them out failed, the couple began to find skulls and crossbones tacked to their doors. Both ignored the ominous warnings and continued with the work of homesteading and running the store and saloon at Averell's place.

Anxious to begin ranching on her own, Ellen purchased a herd of twenty-eight foot-sore cattle for one dollar a head from an emigrant, who was headed west to Washington State. She also purchased her registered "LU" brand from John Crowder on 16 March 1889.[11] Heifers in Ellen's herd calved later that spring and by the time of her death Ellen is reported to have owned a herd of forty-one cattle, which she branded in mid-July 1889 with her "LU" brand. Albert Bothwell, incensed by Ellen and Averell's homesteading success and infuriated by the failure of his attempts to drive them off their land, felt the situation had become intolerable and decided to take more decisive action.

On 20 July 1889, Ellen was abducted from her homestead by a lynching party of six men led by Bothwell, who threatened to rope her and drag her to death if she did not get into the wagon they were driving and go with them. The group then traveled a short distance to Averell's homestead, where Averell was forced at gunpoint to accompany them. The group then proceeded on toward Sweetwater River. Gene Crowder, Ellen's eleven year old foster

[7] These acts included the Pre-emption Act of 1841 and its later amendments, the Homestead Act of 1862, the Timber Culture Act of 1873, and the Desert Land Act of 1877. By obtaining land under each of these acts, it was possible for an individual to obtain 1,120 acres of land.

[8] Bureau of Land Management Records, U.S. Bureau of Land Management, Cheyenne, Wyoming.

[9] Pre-emption Entry, 30 August 1886, Carbon County Court House, Rawlins, Wyoming.

[10] Application for Naturalization, 25 May 1887, Carbon County, Territory of Wyoming, Wyoming State Archives, Cheyenne, Wyoming.

[11] Registry of Brands, Record Book B, p. 169, Carbon County, Territory of Wyoming in Crime and Criminals: Cattle Kate Court Records File, Wyoming State Archives, Cheyenne, Wyoming.

son, hurried to Averell's saloon, where he told Averell's nephew Ralph Cole of his uncle's abduction. Hearing the news, Frank Buchanan, a local cowboy and a friend of the couple, raced to overtake the group hoping to get an opportunity to free Ellen and Averell from their abductors. Concealing himself behind some rocks, Buchanan saw the men order Ellen and Averell out of the wagon and force them to stand on rocks near the embankment of the river, while nooses fashioned from common lariats were placed around their necks. Buchanan opened fire on the lynch mob with his pistol but was driven back by withering rifle fire. During the gun battle, Ellen and Averell were shoved off the rocks on which they were standing and after a drop of less than two feet, were left to struggle and slowly strangle to death over the course of several minutes.[12] Unable to save the lives of his friends, Buchanan raced off to alert the authorities to the murder. Satisfied with the results of their grisly, sadistic act, Bothwell and his companions returned to Ellen's homestead, where they tore down her corrals and drove off most of her small herd of cattle.[13]

At approximately 3 a.m. on 22 July 1889, members of a sheriff's posse arrived at the scene of the execution and discovered the two corpses still dangling from the limb of a scrub pine extending over the embankment of the Sweetwater River. After more than thirty-six hours of exposure to the hot July sun and the elements, the bodies had begun the putrefaction process and the bulging eyes, engorged, blackened faces and protruding tongues made them nearly unrecognizable.[14] The bodies were taken to Averell's homestead where a coroner's jury was empanelled to conduct an inquest. The jury heard eyewitness testimony from Frank Buchanan, Ralph Cole, Ellen's foster child Gene Crowder, and John DeCorey, a young teenage boy employed by Ellen. Both boys had been with Ellen at the time of her abduction. The determination of the coroner's inquest was that Ellen Liddy Watson and James Averell came to their deaths by hanging carried out by cattlemen Albert John Bothwell, Tom Sun, John Henry Durbin, Robert M. Galbraith, Robert B. Conner, and M. Ernest McLean. Following the inquest, Ellen and Averell were buried in a common grave on Averell's homestead.[15]

Word of the lynching quickly reached Rawlins, where someone sent a terse telegraph to George Henderson in Cheyenne, advising him of the deaths of Ellen and Averell. Henderson, a friend of Bothwell and the other perpetrators, went directly to the offices of the *Cheyenne Daily Leader,* where he spoke confidentially with reporter Ed Towse.[16] Towse wasted no time in concocting a story to besmirch Ellen and Averell's reputations and turn public opinion in favor of their executioners. During the late 1800s, little was more devastating to a woman's reputation or more thoroughly destructive to her credibility than to be considered a prostitute. Using the press for this type of character assassination was a tactic successfully employed by cattlemen and their sympathizers in other Wyoming cases in which respectable women were

---

[12] Coroner's Inquest on the bodies of James Averell and Ellen Watson, 23 July 1889, Carbon County, Territory of Wyoming, in Crime and Criminals, Cattle Kate Court Records File, Wyoming State Archives, Cheyenne, Wyoming.

[13] Petition, George W. Durant, Administrator of the Estate of Ella Watson, Plaintiff v. Andrew [sic] J. Bothwell and John Durbin, Defendants, 12 September 1889, Territory of Wyoming, County of Carbon, District Court, Third Judicial District, Wyoming State Archives, Cheyenne, Wyoming.

[14] 'Lynching Rustlers,' 27 July 1889, *Laramie Weekly Sentinel*, Laramie, Wyoming.

[15] Testimony of Charles Buck, Coroner's Inquest on the bodies of James Averell and Ellen Watson, 23 July 1889, Crime and Criminals, Cattle Kate Court Records File, Wyoming State Archives, Cheyenne, Wyoming.

[16] Helena Huntington Smith, *The War on Powder River* (Lincoln: University of Nebraska Press, 1966) pp. 126-127.

deemed troublesome and their credibility destroyed.[17] None of these cases, however, resulted in the murder of the offending woman.

On 22 July 1889, Towse printed a lurid account of the lynching, which referred to Ellen as 'Cattle Kate,' a name never before associated with Ellen Liddy Watson, but a name commonly associated with Kate Maxwell, a notorious prostitute in Bessemer, Wyoming. The article alleged that Ellen was a thief and cattle rustler and that Averell was the operator of a 'hog ranch,' where Ellen and several other women engaged in prostitution. Towse presented a fictionalized, titillating version of the lynching to his readers, alleging that Ellen 'exhausted a blasphemous vocabulary upon the visitors" and then "when preparations for the short trip to the scaffold were made she called for her own horse and vaulted to its back from the ground.' Towse commented that when a noose was placed around her neck and her horse led from under her, 'she died with curses on her foul lips.' Towse reassured his readers that the lynchers had 'acted in self-protection.'[18]

Following suit, the *Laramie Weekly Sentinel* referred to Ellen as a 'fearless maverick' who was the 'equal of any man on the range' and 'a daredevil in the saddle, handy with a six-shooter and an adept with the lariat and branding iron.'[19] In truth, Ellen owned only a side saddle.[20] There is no evidence that she had experience with a pistol or a lariat, although many women assisted in the branding of cattle on the Wyoming ranches. Sadly, nearly one hundred and eighteen years later, Ellen Liddy Watson is more commonly known as 'Cattle Kate' and is still believed to have been a prostitute who took unbranded cattle in payment for her services despite overwhelming evidence to the contrary.

When apprehended, Tom Sun and Albert Bothwell freely admitted their role in the lynching and provided the names of the other perpetrators.[21] Once the remainder of the accused had been arrested, they were taken to Rawlins and placed in the custody of Carbon County Sheriff Frank Hadsell. Quite likely the wealth and political influence of the accused and their supporters were brought to bear to insure that the accused, despite their arrest, would never be brought to justice. During the pre-dawn hours of 23 July, Justice of the Peace B. F. Emery convened an extralegal court in a Rawlins horse stable and held a preliminary hearing for the accused, allowing the prisoners to post bail for one another in the amount of $5,000.00 each.[22] Once bail had been posted, the men were freed and returned to their ranches.

---

[17] Another example of this type of character assassination used to discredit the testimony of Glendolene Myrtle Kimmell, a witness in the high profile murder case against Wyoming stock detective Tom Horn, can be found in an article in the *Cheyenne Leader* on 13 October 1902, which alleges that Miss Kimmell, a rather prim young school teacher, 'was located in the Pennington Saloon on Curtis Street in Denver.' Only prostitutes and women of low character would frequent saloons in the early 20th century American West. Consequently, the implication is that Miss Kimmell is a woman of questionable moral character. The tactic was sufficiently effective to result in her being required to present affidavits attesting to her reputation for chastity prior to her being allowed to provide testimony. Following her deposition, she was charged with perjury, arrested and imprisoned until the execution of Horn, at which time all charges against her were dropped when the prosecuting attorney said that he had made a 'mistake' in charging her with perjury.

[18] 'A Double Lynching,' *Cheyenne Daily Leader* (Cheyenne, Wyoming), 23 July 1889.

[19] 'Lynching Rustlers,' *Laramie Weekly Sentinel* (Laramie, Wyoming), 27 July 1889.

[20] Inventory of Chattel Property of Ellen Watson, Crime and Criminals: Cattle Kate Court Records File, Wyoming State Archives, Cheyenne, Wyoming.

[21] 'The Lynchers', *The Cheyenne Daily Leader* (Cheyenne, Wyoming), 26 July 1889.

[22] Ibid. Justice Emery's actions were in direct violation of Chapter 5, Sections 947 and 966, Revised Statutes of Wyoming, Territory of Wyoming, 1887.

Other irregularities occurred when the acting Carbon County attorney declared the original coroner's inquest over Ellen and Averell's bodies to be illegal and ordered a new inquest with a new jury, none of whom had been present at the scene of the crime nor had the opportunity to view the bodies. However, despite Albert Bothwell and Tom Sun's earlier confessions of guilt, the determination of the second inquest was that Ellen and Averell 'came to their death by violence by persons unknown to the jury.'[23]

As additional information about the lynching streamed out of Sweetwater Valley, concerned citizens became increasingly uncomfortable about what had happened. An editorial in the *Salt Lake Tribune* on 27 July 1889, stated, 'The men of Wyoming will not be proud of the fact that a woman—albeit unsexed[24] and totally depraved—has been hanged within their territory. That is about the poorest purpose a woman can be put to.... We do not believe the men who strangled her are just the class of men that decent people would like to make their homes among.'[25] *The Fremont Clipper* of Lander, Wyoming editorialized, 'some people, and we regret to say, some papers, condone the hanging of this helpless woman and her paramour on the grounds that the laws cannot be enforced. All such know that they are giving utterance to false statements and do it simply to give a coloring of legality to a most hideous crime, simply because the guilty parties are men of "standing" in the communities where they live.'[26]

By the time the grand jury convened in October 1889, the prosecution's case was in shambles, due to the loss of the four original eyewitnesses. Averell's nephew, Ralph Cole, died under suspicious circumstances in August 1889. Ellen's foster child Gene Crowder, together with Frank Buchanan (the cowboy who had tried to rescue Ellen and Averell) and Ellen's hired boy John DeCorey, simply vanished. Many believed that they were killed to prevent them from testifying against the accused, but there is no conclusive proof. It took the grand jury only a short time to issue a finding of no true bill.[27] All charges against Bothwell, Sun and the other assassins were dropped and their bonds were returned. Bothwell and his companions had murdered two innocent people with impunity. They would receive no punishment for their actions.

Wyoming Territory was governed under the Constitution of the United States of America and the Territorial Statutes. These provided many protections which should have shielded Ellen from the actions of her executioners.[28] These included protections against unreasonable

---

23 'Lynching Bee,' *Laramie Daily Boomerang* (Laramie, Wyoming), 27 July 1889.

24 The term 'unsexed,' as it is used here, implies that Ellen Watson was so utterly depraved and immoral as to be devoid of any of the socially accepted attributes of a respectable 'true woman,' which included piety, purity, domesticity and submissiveness.

25 Editorial, *Salt Lake Tribune* (Salt Lake City, Utah), 27 July 1889.

26 Editorial, *Fremont Clipper* (Lander, Wyoming). 15 August 1889.

27 Indictment for Murder, No. 258, Territory of Wyoming v. Albert J. Bothwell, Ernest McLean, Robert B. Connors, Tom Sun, Robert M. Galbraith and John Durbin, 24 October 1889, Crime and Criminals: Cattle Kate Court Records File, Wyoming State Archives, Cheyenne, Wyoming. The phrase 'no true bill,' endorsed by a grand jury on the indictment, is a legal term equivalent in meaning to 'not found,' 'no indictment' or 'not a true bill.' It means that in the opinion of the jury the evidence presented was insufficient to warrant the return of a formal charge. An indictment is an accusation in writing found and presented by a grand jury, legally convoked and sworn, to the court in which it is impaneled, charging that a person therein named has done some act or been guilty of some omission which by law is a public offence punishable on indictment.

28 The Territory of Wyoming was governed by the United States Constitution and the Session Laws of the Territory of Wyoming. Ellen Watson was guaranteed protections under the Bill of Rights, the first ten amendments to the Constitution of the United Sates of America. Under the Bill of Rights, Article I guarantees the inherent right to life, liberty and the pursuit of happiness. Article IV guarantees that the right of the people to be secure in their persons, houses, papers and effects against unreasonable searches and seizures shall not be violated.

search and seizure, the right of due process, and the right to life, liberty and the pursuit of happiness. Despite these constitutional guarantees, Ellen's life was cut short by men who believed that their wealth and political influence placed them above the law. Ellen's murder was motivated by Boswell's insatiable greed and his determination to prevail in what was nothing more than a transparent land grab. To shield themselves from public censure, Ellen's executioners successfully slandered her reputation so thoroughly that their base allegations have become widely accepted as historical fact by the general public for more than a century. The hanging of Ellen Watson remains one of the most infamous acts ever perpetrated in Wyoming.

Article V guarantees that no person shall be deprived of life, liberty or property without due process of law. Article VI provides recourse through the courts to every person for an injury sustained to their person, property or reputation and provides for the right of a defendant to a trial by jury in criminal cases and the right of the accused to know the nature of the charges against him, to be confronted by the witnesses against him, to have the right to a speedy trial and to offer a defence, personally or through an attorney to the charges against him. Article VIII prohibits the imposition of cruel or unusual punishment.

Biographical Notes on Contributors

Saheed Aderinto, born in Nigeria, is a PhD candidate in the Department of History, The University of Texas at Austin. His research interests include gender and sexuality in Africa, African Diaspora history, and peace and conflict studies. He is the author of 'Prostitution and urban social relations' and 'Policing urban prostitution: Prostitutes, crime, law and reformers,' in Hakeem Ibikunle Tijani (ed.), *Nigeria's Urban History: Past and Present* (2006); 'Discrimination in an urban setting: The experience of Ijebu settlers in Colonial Ibadan, 1893-1960,' in Olayemi Akinwumi, Okpeh O. Okpeh Jr and Gwamna D. Je'adayibe (eds.), *Inter-group relations in Nigeria during the 19th and 20th centuries* (2006); 'European invasion and African resistance,' in Hakeem Ibikunle Tijani, Tiffany Jones and Raphael Njoku (eds.), *Africa and the Wider World* (forthcoming); 'Blacks in Britain,' in Hakeem Tijani, Tiffany Jones and Raphael Njoku (eds.), *Africa and the Wider World* (forthcoming).

Ruchi Anand, born in India, was educated at Lady Shri Ram College in New Delhi and the Jawaharlal Nehru University in Delhi before receiving her doctorate from Purdue University in International Studies. An Associate Professor at the American Graduate School of International Relations and Diplomacy (Paris), she also teaches at the Centre d'Étude Franco-Américain de Management (CEFAM) in Lyon and at Princeton University in its Junior Statesmen of America summer program. Her research interests include international relations, international law, international organizations, foreign policy, environmental policy, politics of developing countries and women's studies. She is the author of 'International environmental justice: A North-South dimension,' in *Debating Environmental Regimes: Looking Forward, Looking Back* (2002); *International Environmental Justice: a North-South Dimension* (2004); and *Self-Defense in International Law* (at press).

Carol Bowers, born in the United States, is the Reference Manager at the American Heritage Center at the University of Wyoming and a Lecturer in the University of Wyoming's Department of History. She holds a BA in Education from the University of Florida and a MA in American Studies from the University of Wyoming, where she is currently pursuing a PhD She is the author of 'School bells and Winchesters: The sad saga of Glendolene Myrtle Kimmel,' in *Annals of Wyoming* (Winter, 2001); 'The secret scrapbook of a soiled dove,' in Susan Tucker et al, eds., *The Scrapbook in American Life* (2006). The book received the Pioneer American Society's 2006 Allan G. Noble Award for best edited book on American material culture and was named one of the top ten books on crafts and hobbies by *Booklist* (December 2006).

Cenap Çakmak, born in Turkey, holds a PhD in Global Affairs from Rutgers University. He currently teaches international law and global politics at Mugla University, Turkey, and conducts research on regional and global issues at a strategic research institute. He is the author of 'The International Criminal Court in world politics,' *International Journal on World Peace*, Vol. 27, Issue 1, 2006; 'Pitfalls of the enlargement: Withering human rights protection in the Council of Europe?' *Insight Turkey*, Vol. 8, Issue 3, 2006; 'The problem relating to the Margin of Appreciation doctrine under the European Convention on Human Rights,' *Review of International Law and Politics*, Vol. 2, No. 3, 2006; 'Turkey's foreign policy, the EU and the International Criminal Court,' *Insight Turkey*, Vol. 7, No. 4, 2005; 'Turkey in the Second World War: 'Evasive' or 'active' neutral?' *Journal of Academic Studies,* Vol. 7, No. 26, 2005; 'The NGOs, norm creation and human rights,' *Alternatives: Turkish Journal of International Relations,* Vol. 3, No. 1, Spring 2004; 'Human rights, the European Union and Turkey,' *Alternatives: Turkish Journal of International Relations*, Vol. 2, No. 3-4, Fall-Winter 2003; 'American foreign policy and September 11,' *Perceptions: Journal of International Affairs,* Vol. VIII, No. 1, March-May 2003. He contributed to *Encyclopedia of Social Justice and Activism* (entries: 'Muslim brotherhood,' 'Jihad,' 'Genital integrity activists, 'International Criminal Court,' 'Shirin Ebadi,' 'Jodi Williams,' 'Genocide Watch,' 'Red Cross') and *Encyclopedia of Love in World Religions* (entries: 'Compassion in Islam,' 'Charity in Islam,' 'Modesty in Islam').

Rajeni Chagar, born in Canada, currently resides in Toronto. As a doctoral candidate (ABD) at Carleton University, her research interests are in the areas of gender and migration, citizenship, and sustainable and equitable development in South Asia. Her current research examines the relationships among the feminization of labour migration, development and citizenship in India. She is the author of 'Feminist internationalism: Is this an acceptable approach for the International Woman?' in *Annual Meeting of the Feminist Research Group* (May 2004); 'Women, labour and the State: Discrimination in the workplace,' in C. P. Nandini, *Discrimination in the Workplace* (2007).

Tyanai Charamba was born in Zimbabwe and usually resides there. He holds an MA in African Languages and Literature, with a special honours degree in Shona. He is currently a Lecturer at the Midlands State University in Zimbabwe, where he is engaged in language planning and policy issues in Africa. He has presented the following papers: 'Culture and cultural studies at higher institutions of learning;' 'Cases of romance and sex in selected English and Shona war novels;' 'Is Pfambi prostitute and prostitute Pfambi? Is Hure whore and whore Hure? A review of Gaidzanwa's *Understanding of a prostitute in Images of Women in Zimbabwean Literature*;' 'The interface of family and nation in the war novel in Zimbabwe;' "Managing a crisis: Women's poetic response to the plight of women in Zimbabwe;' 'Economic movement and migration in Post-colonial Zimbabwe; A socio-historical approach;' 'Rape in Zimbabwe;' 'Mutswairo's poetic message to the new Zimbabwean nation;' 'Towards abrogating foreign languages and promoting indigenous languages in academic discourse' and 'Mhuri Pachivanhu.'

Robynn Collins was born in Canada where she continues to live. She holds a MA in Peace and Conflict studies at Saint Paul University in Ottawa. She has worked as a consultant on gender, peace-building, and security issues, and has worked with various governmental and non-governmental organizations in community development and crime prevention initiatives. She is a doctoral candidate in Criminology at the University of Ottawa, where her research is in the field of the former 'lost' boys and girls of Sudan and revolves around the conflictual gender experiences of unaccompanied minors in refugee camps immigrating to, and resettling in, Canada.

Mairo V. Bello Garko was born and resides in Nigeria. As the founder-director of Adolescent Health and Information Projects (AHIP) based in Kano, she is a pioneer in adolescent reproductive health and has been active in the labour movement and in the national and international women's movement. She has presented various papers on youth and women's issues, and published some educational books for young people. She is co-author with Annabel S. Erulkar of *The Experience of Married Adolescent Girls in Northern Nigeria* (2007).

Ece Göztepe, born in Düsseldorf, now resides in Ankara where she received her BA and LL.M degrees at the University of Ankara. A postgraduate fellow at the Friedrich Ebert Foundation, she obtained her PhD in European public law from the University of Münster. Since September 2005 she is assistant professor of constitutional law at Bilkent University in Ankara. Her research and teaching interests focuses especially on citizenship, democracy and legitimation, political rights, gender equality, European public law with special emphasis on sovereignty, integration theories and European identity as well as the juridical and political system of Turkey.

Mag.a Dr.in *Brigitte Halbmayr* received her PhD in political science from the University of Vienna. Since 1992 she has served as social scientist at the Institute of Conflict Research in Vienna. Her research interests include racism, right-wing extremism, National Socialism, the Holocaust, and gender studies. She is the author of 'Sexzwangsarbeit in NS-Konzentrationslagern in Dokumentationsarchiv des österreichischen Widerstandes' (ed.) *Jahrbuch 2005 zum Schwerpunkt: Frauen in Widerstand und Verfolgung*; 'Kommunikation – Macht – Geschlecht. Die Thematisierung von sexualisierter Gewalt in Interviews mit weiblichen und männlichen KZ-Überlebenden,' *Sechster Österreichischer Zeitgeschichtetag* 2003, 2004); co-author 'Sexualisierte Gewalt im Kontext nationalsozialistischer Verfolgung,' in: *Zeitschrift für Genozidforschung,* 1/2004; 'Mauthausen im Gedächtnis der Überlebenden,' in: BM für Inneres (Hg.): *Das Gedächtnis von Mauthausen* (2004).

Tomoyuki (Tom) Hashimoto was born in Hamamatsu, Japan, and resides in London. He is currently Lecturer in Political Science and International Relations at the University of New York in Tirana (UNYT), Senior Associate Researcher at the Albanian Institute for International Studies (AIIS), as well as Contributing Editor to *Tirana Times.* His research interests include development and security in the post-Cold War era. He has been a Fellow of the World Association of International Studies (WAIS) at Stanford since 2005. He presented a paper at the 2006 WAIS Conference entitled 'Modernization of the post-war Japanese imperial system.' His recent articles can be found in *Trend News* (Azerbaijan), *BCS Express*

(Russia), and *Libre Magazine* (UK). He translated *Pride* (a novel by Mary A. Turzillo) into Japanese (2007).

Mahera Khaleque was born in Dhaka, Bangladesh, and currently resides in Georgia, USA. She received an MA in Painting and an MA in Visual Communications Design from Purdue University and now works as a free-lance artist. Her work addresses issues in human rights, environmental pollution, and educational environment in developing countries. In 2008 she was invited by the McCord Museum at McGill University to present 'Exploring the perceptions of veil through Shirin Neshat's *Women of Allah*,' which joins her most recent painting series on veil and the perceptions surrounding costume.

Stefan Kirchner was born in Marburg an der Lahn and normally resides in Frankfurt am Main. He studied law at Giessen, Utrecht, The Hague, Cambridge, Helsinki and Izmir, with a focus on public international law and human rights. He was admitted to the bar in Germany, received a Magister Juris Internationalis, and is a member of the German Red Cross Expert Pool on International Humanitarian Law. After working in the Legal Department of the German Foreign Ministry, he founded his own law firm, Rechtsanwaltskanzlei Kirchner, which deals primarily with civil rights cases, in particular before the European Court of Human Rights. While director of the PEOI Fund in New York, he is also in charge of the Public Law Department of the law firm Pawellek and Partner in Frankfurt am Main. Currently a researcher-lecturer at the universities of Giessen and Göttingen, in 2010 he will be Visiting Professor at the Faculty of Law of Vytautas Magnus University in Kaunas. His publications include *Wartime Rape: Sexual Terrorism in the Eastern Provinces of the Democratic Republic of Congo—International Law and Human Rights* (2008); *Human Rights and International Security* (2008); *Freiheit und Revolution* (2008) and *Public Private Partnerships* (2008); 'Rape under International Law: Human Rights, International Humanitarian Law and International Criminal Law,' in: C. P. Nandini (ed.), *Rape Law and Reform—Comparative Perspectives* (2009); 'Target Area Bombing,' in: Natalino Ronzitti / Gabrielle Venturini (eds.), *Current Issues in the International Humanitarian Law of Air Warfare* (2006); 'Hell on Earth – Systematic Rape in Eastern Congo,' in: 13 *Journal of Humanitarian Assistance* (6 August 2007).

Melissa Krall was born in Houston, Texas, and travels throughout the world. She received a BS in Public Relations from The University of Texas at Austin and an MA in International Relations from Webster University in Geneva. She has worked for the UN, international organizations and NGOs in the US, Switzerland, Sri Lanka, Ethiopia, Pakistan and Liberia.

Angèle Kremer-Marietti was born in Paris where she lives and directs two collections by L'Harmattan. She has taught at Hollins College (Virginia), at the Sorbonne and at Jules Verne University in Amiens, and has also worked as associate researcher at the University of California at Berkeley. She directs with Thierry Simonelli the electronic review *Dogma: http://dogma.free.fr*. A specialist of Comte and Nietzsche, and also of Jaspers, Dilthey and Husserl, she has published essays on general philosophy, on history of philosophy, and also on epistemology, centering on the Husserlian question: 'What is our epistemological origin?' She is the author of *L'Homme et ses Labyrinthes. Essai sur Friedrich Nietzsche* (1972, 1999);

Michel Foucault et l'archéologie du savoir (1974) ; *Lacan ou la rhétorique de l'inconscient* (1978) ; *Le Projet anthropologique d'Auguste Comte* (1980, 1999) ; *L'Anthropologie positiviste d'Auguste Comte* (1980) ; *Entre le signe et l'Histoire : L'Anthropologie positiviste d'Auguste Comte* (1982, 1999) ; *La Morale* (1982, 2007) ; *Le Positivisme* (1982, 2006) ; *La Symbolicité ou le problème de la symbolisation* (1982, 2000) ; *Le Concept de science positive : ses tenants et ses aboutissants dans les structures anthropologiques du Positivisme* (1983, 2007) ; *Michel Foucault : archéologie et généalogie* (1985); *Les Racines philosophiques de la Science moderne* (1987) ; *Éthique* (1987, 2001) ; *Nietzsche et la rhétorique* (1992) ; *Les Apories de l'action : essai d'une epistémologie de l'action morale et politique* (1993) ; *La Philosophie cognitive* (1994, 2002) ; *Morale et politique : court traité de l'action morale et politique* (1995) ; *La Raison créatrice moderne ou postmoderne* (1996) ; *Parcours philosophiques* (1997) ; *Sociologie de la Science* (1998) ; *Philosophie des Sciences de la Nature* (1999, 2007) ; *Éthique et épistémologie autour des impostures intellectuelles de Sokal et Bricmont* (2001) ; *Carnets philosophiques* (2002) ; *Cours sur la première recherche logique de Husserl* (2003) ; *Épistémologiques philosophiques anthropologiques* (2005) ; *Jean-Paul Sartre et le désir d'être* (2005) ; *L'épistémologie : État des lieux et positions* (2006) ; *Seven Epistemological Essays from Hobbes to Popper* (2007) ; *Auguste Comte et la science politique* (2007) ; *Le kaléidoscope épistémologique d'Auguste Comte : Sentiments, Images, Signes* (2007) ; *Trois études sur la loi constructale d'Adrian Bejan* (2008) ; *Michel Meyer et la problématologie* (2008) ; *Réflexions sur les temps actuels* (2009).

Tobe Levin was born in New Jersey and resides in Germany, where she is Professor at the University of Maryland University College in Europe. She also teaches at the University of Frankfurt and is an Associate at the W.E.B. Du Bois Institute, Harvard University. With a PhD in comparative literature from Cornell University, she was the first in the world to write a dissertation on Nobel laureate Elfriede Jelinek, and, in 1985, she pioneered the literary essay on FGM in creative writing. An activist since 1977, she is founder and president of FORWARD-Germany and editor-in-chief of *Feminist Europa: Review of Books*. She has translated Fadumo Korn and Sabine Eichhorst, *Born in the Big Rains: A Memoir of Somalia and Survival* (2006), and while a scholar-in-residence at Brandeis University and research associate at Mt. Holyoke College, she edited *Violence: 'Mercurial Gestalt'* (2008). With Augustine H. Asaah of University of Ghana, she is co-editor of *Empathy and Rage. Female Genital Mutilation in African Literature* (2009).

Sir Christopher MacRae, KCMG, was educated at Rugby School, England; and at the universities of Oxford and Harvard (Henry Fellow in International Relations). After two years in the Royal Navy, he entered the British Diplomatic Service and served as a career diplomat for 35 years. His ten posts included spells in Africa (Tanzania, Gabon, Nigeria), the Middle East (Lebanon, Iraq, Iran), Western Europe (Brussels, Paris, European Commission) and Pakistan. He was head of mission in Tehran; and Ambassador/High Commissioner in Libreville (Gabon), Lagos/Abuja (Nigeria), and Islamabad (also responsible for Afghanistan). After retiring he served as Secretary General of the Order of St John. He taught at AGSIRD 2006-8; and currently lives in Provence, France. He is co-author of *The Dar Mutiny of 1964* (2007).

Elissa Mailänder Koslov was born in Italy and resides in Paris. She earned her PhD in historical anthropology and cultural history at the École des Hautes Études en Sciences Sociales (Paris) and the University of Erfurt (Germany). She is currently a research fellow at the Centre of Interdisciplinary Memory Research at the Institute of Advanced Study in the Humanities in Essen. Her research interests include the history of perpetrators, bystanders and helpers; the study of everyday existence in Nazi concentration camps; gender history; and the history and theory of violence. Her research project 'Workaday Violence: Female Guards at Lublin-Majdanek (1942-1944)' examines the structures, mechanisms and dynamics of violence in this concentration- and extermination camp.

Farhad Malekian, born in Zanjan (Iran), is the founder and director of the Institute of International Criminal Law in Uppsala and travels widely as Distinguished Visiting Professor. He is the author of *The Interrnational Criminal Responsibility of States* (1985), *The System of International Law* (1987), *International Criminal Law: the Legal and Critical Analysis of International Crimes* (1991), *Condemning the Use of Force in the Gulf Crisis* (1992, 1994), *The Monopolization of International Criminal Law in the United Nations* (1993, 1995), *Islamic International Criminal Law: A Comparative Study* (1994), 'International criminal responsibility of individuals and states' in M. Cherif Bassiouni, *International Criminal Law* (1999), and *Documents on the Principles of International Human Rights* (2007). In 2005 he introduced the Principle of International Tribunality of Jurisdiction at Cornell Law School, embodying it in his article 'Emasculating the philosophy of international criminal justice in the Iraqi Special Tribunal' (*Cornell International Law Journal*, 2005), and in the same year contributed to 'Sixty years after the Nuremberg Tribunal,' a conference held at the Robert Jackson Center, Chautauqua (New York), 2005.

Carol Mann was born in London and resides in Paris. With a PhD from the École des Hautes Études in Paris, she is social anthropologist, historian, novelist, activist and researcher on the role of women in armed conflict, especially the Second World War, Bosnia and Afghanistan. She holds the post of Research Associate at the School of Oriental and African Studies, University of London, and leads the only seminar in France on Gender and Armed Conflict, at the Sorbonne. She is also director of FEMAID (www.femaid.org), a grass-roots aid organization specializing in education and health programmes, mainly in Afghanistan. Her publications on Afghanistan, women and war include: 'Women in war,' presented at the AAUW Education Foundation Symposium. 'International Perspectives: Global Voices for Gender Equity,' Washington DC (2002); 'Models and Realities of Afghan Womanhood,' Unesco (2006); 'Les shahidé du monde traditionnel : le suicide des jeunes filles afghanes,' TERRA Travaux, *Études: Recherches sur les Réfugiés et l'Asile* 2006 ; 'The influence of British imperial politics in Northern India on present day Afghan self-representation,' presented at the ASEN conference at the London School of Economics (2006); *Kucne Amazonke* [Amazons of the home, the resistance of women during the siege of Sarajevo] (2006) ; 'Stratégies de résistance des femmes en Afghanistan,' *Tumultes* n° 27 (December 2006) ; 'La scolarisation des filles en Afghanistan,' *Pro-Choix*, March 2007; 'Malalai Joya, la pasionaria de l'Afghanistan,' *Pro-Choix,* 2007; 'Gender and Culture in Afghanistan,' in Unesco, *Museum International: Gender Perspectives on Cultural Heritage and Museums* (December 2007) ; *Les Femmes face à deux guerres mondiales* (2010).

Lydiah (Nana) Nganga was born in Central Kenya and now resides in Casper, Wyoming. She is an assistant professor of Elementary and Early Childhood Education at the University of Wyoming, where she received a PhD. Her research interests include human rights, social justice, multicultural curriculum issues, and global, international and transformative education. In 2009 she received from the University of Wyoming College of Education the Outstanding Faculty Research and Scholarship Award and the Mary Garland Early Career Fellowship. She is the author of *My Sister Kairitu is Sick* (2007); *Multicultural Curriculum Issues in Early Childhood Programs: Are We Creating Culturally Relevant Early Childhood Programs for the 21st Century?* (2009); 'Global and cultural education prepares pre-service teachers to work in rural public schools: teaching for social change in the 21st century,' in: *Journal of Education Research* (2009); 'Early childhood education programs in Kenya: challenges and solutions in early years,' in *International Journal of Research and Development* (2009); 'Collaborative student-centered interdisciplinary pedagogy: reducing resistance to social justice and knowledge compartmentalization', in *Journal of Education Research* (2009); 'Teaching for democracy and social justice in isolated rural settings: challenges and pedagogical opportunities,' in Susan Greonke and Amos Hatch (eds.), *Critical Pedagogy and Teacher Education in the Neoliberal Era: Small Openings, K-12 Preservice Teacheer Education (*2009); 'Moving from a stand-alone/teach-alone model to integrated pedagogical practices in a teacher education program,' in Anthony Selkirk and Maria Tichenor (eds.), *Teacher Education: Policy, Practice and Research* (2009); 'Teaching for social change in the 21st century: Global education prepares educators to work in rural public schools,' in Frank Columbus, ed. *Rural Education in the 21st Century* (2009); 'Social change and public education in the USA,' in Brooke H. Stroude and Scott E. Corbin (eds.), *Handbook for Social Change* (2009); 'Education in Kenya: primary and secondary schools curriculum development since independence,' in J. Kirylo and A. Nauman (eds.), *Curriculum Development: Perspectives from around the World* (at press).

Grace Bosibori Nyamongo was born in Western Kenya and is currently Visiting Assistant Professor at Dartmouth College. She attended Kenyatta University and University of Nairobi before receiving her PhD from York University, Toronto. A specialist in the fields of Kiswahili (the Bantu vernacular) and of gender and colonialism in Sub-Saharan Africa, she is the author of 'Gendered silence: sexual violence against women during ethnic conflicts in Kenya,' in *Asian Women Journal*, Vol. 23. No 4 (2007). Her conference papers (at Southern Connecticut State University, Missouri State University, York University, and Southern Illinois University at Edwardsville) include: 'Media and violence against women: a case of ethnic conflicts;' 'Globalization and invisible labourers in Kenya;' 'Female genital mutilation/female circumcision: a strategy for controlling women's sexuality,' 'Globalization and women tea farmers in Kenya;' and 'Ethnicity and resources control: a study of border conflicts in Kenya.'

J. Shola Omotola, born in Nigeria, is currently a PhD candidate in Political Science at the University of Ibadan and teaches at Redeemer's University. His research interests include comparative African democratisation, oil and environmental politics, peace and conflict studies, and identity issues, including gender and ethnic minorities. His articles can be found in *Africa Insight, Africa: Journal of International African Institute, Africa Today, African and Asian Studies, African Study Monographs, Conflict Trends, Contemporary Security Policy,*

International Journal of Regional and Local Studies, Journal of African Law, Journal of Conflict Studies, Journal of Security Sector Management, Nigerian Journal of International Affairs, Philippine Journal of Third World Studies, Representation, South African Journal of International Affairs and *Unilag Journal of Politics*.. He is the author of *The Next Gulf? Oil Politics, Environmental Apocalypse and Rising Tension in the Niger Delta* (2006).

Isabel Pérez Molina holds a MA in women's history and a PhD in Early Modern history at the University of Barcelona. She has served as Lecturer in Spanish and European Studies at the University of Technology, Sydney, and is currently a researcher at the Women's Studies Centre *Duoda* at the University of Barcelona. She is the author of: *Isabel de Villena: La Corona d'Aragó i els Reis Catòlics* (1992), *Dones en el temps* (1992), *La dona davant la llei a la Catalunya del segle XVIII* (1995); *Las mujeres ante la ley en la Cataluña moderna* (1997); *Honour and Disgrace: Women and Law in Early Modern Catalonia* (2001); 'Catholic Coalition in Spain' and 'Popular Front in Spain,' in: *World Encyclopedia of Protest and Revolution*, directed by Eric Martone and Immanuel Ness (2007). She is also contributor to *La diferència de ser dona. Recerca i ensenyament de la història* (2005).

David Wingeate Pike was born in England and resides in Paris. He attended Blundell's School, McGill University, and Universidad Interamericana before receiving doctorates from the Université de Toulouse (contemporary history) and Stanford University (Latin American studies), where he served as Assistant Director at the Institute of Hispanic American and Luso-Brazilian Studies. He is Distinguished Professor Emeritus of Contemporary History and Politics at the American University of Paris, Director of Research at the American Graduate School of International Relations and Diplomacy, Sociétaire des Gens de Lettres de France, and Fellow of the Royal Historical Society. He is the author of *Vae Victis!* (1968); *Les Français la guerre d'Espagne* (1975); *Latin America in Nixon's Second Term*, ed. (1982); *Jours de gloire, jours de honte* (1984); *The Opening of the Second World War*, ed. (1991); *In the Service of Stalin* (1993); *Spaniards in the Holocaust* (2000); *The Closing of the Second World War*, ed. (2001); *Españoles en el holocausto* (2003, 2004, 2006); *L'Enfer nazi en Autriche* (2004); *Betrifft: KZ Mauthausen: Was die Archive erzählen* (2005); *Franco and the Axis Stigma* (2008); *Franco y el Eje Berlín-Roma-Tokio: La alianza sin firma* (2010); *France Divided: The French Press and the Spanish Civil War* (at press); La Galia dividida (in preparation); Called to Account: The Killers of Mauthausen on Trial (in preparation); *The Eyes of Mauthausen*: full-feature screenplay under contract to KanZaman Film Company (Madrid).

Captain *Naeem Sarfraz,* born in Gujranwala (Punjab), was educated at Lawrence College in Ghora Gali (North West Frontier Province) and at the Royal Naval College Dartmouth, where his training included Operation *Aid to the Civil Power* in Georgetown, British Guyana (1960-1961). He then spent 15 years in the Pakistan Navy, partly as a trainer on HMS *Dryad,* the RN School of Navigation. He saw service during the Indo-Pakistani wars of 1965 and 1971 and reached the rank of captain before retiring. He then became a private ship-owner, based in New York, with offices in London, Jeddah, Piraeus and Karachi, engaging in container-liners and tramping. After 15 years he returned to Islamabad, still with some limited shipping interests but working mainly in the oil, gas, and minerals sectors in Pakistan. After experiencing a personal tragedy—his highly promising young son-in-law was pointlessly murdered while attempting to defuse an 'honour-killing' dispute—he founded the Fazaldad Human Rights Institute (FHRI), a Pakistani NGO charity dedicated to countering religious extremism and intolerance by changing the mindset, particularly of the young. His op-ed articles on human rights and other political issues appear frequently in the Pakistani English-language press.

Eileen Servidio, born in the United States and resident in Paris, is president and Chair in International Law at the American Graduate School of International Relations and Diplomacy, in Paris. She also heads the department of Anglo-American Law at the Université de Cergy-Pontoise. She received her PhD in International Criminal Law from the Université de Paris II–Assas. She is the author of *Le Rôle de la Chambre d'accusation et la nature de son avis en matière d'extradition passive* (1993) and *Common Law—Introduction to the English and American legal systems* (2004).

INDEX

A

B

H

I

J

K

L

M

N

T

U

V